THE PLACE-NAMES

OF

DORSET

THE PLACE-NAMES

OF

DORSET

INAUGURAL DISSERTATION

BY

ANTON FÄGERSTEN

EP Publishing Limited
1978

First published by Uppsala University, Sweden, 1933

Republished 1978 by
EP Publishing Limited
East Ardsley, Wakefield
West Yorkshire, England

Copyright © 1978 EP Publishing Limited

ISBN 0 7158 1237 8

British Library Cataloguing in Publication Data
Fägersten, Anton
The place-names of Dorset.
1. Names, Geographical – England – Dorset
I. Title
914.22'3'0014   DA670.D7
ISBN 0–7158–1237–8

Please address all enquiries to EP Publishing Limited
(address as above)

Printed in Great Britain by
Redwood Burn Limited
Trowbridge & Esher

CONTENTS

Corrigenda

p. 79, l. 11. Read: 131 G 3
p. 79, l. 18. Read: There is another Leigh

Preface

The place-names of Dorset as a whole have not previously been dealt with, and I have therefore thought it best to include the names of the whole county, provided they are recorded in medieval documents. Another method would have been to deal with only those names which are of particular interest, and to exclude the bulk of commonplace names; that might have enabled me to treat difficult names more in detail and to use more comparative material. But my own experience as a place-name student has taught me the value of having the whole name-material of a county collected, and I have therefore, chiefly for practical reasons, adopted the former line of work.

When completing this monograph on the place-names of Dorset, I feel it a pleasant duty to offer my thanks to those who have assisted me in carrying out my work. In the first place my thanks are due to Professor R. E. Zachrisson. The subject of the present monograph was suggested to me some ten years ago by him, and throughout my investigation he has generously put his great experience and erudition at my service. Professor Zachrisson also subjected the first version of my manuscript to systematic criticism and gave me valuable hints on the interpretation of several difficult names. For all this, as well as for the great personal interest Professor Zachrisson has always shown me, I beg him to accept my sincere gratitude.

Thanks to the kindness of the English Place-Name Society it has been possible for me to work at this monograph during all these years without fear of being forestalled by any of the Society's own publications, and the Society has added to my sense of obligation by sending me — via Professor Zachrisson — several identifications of OE charter forms, and by allowing Mr J. E. B. Gover to send me a great number of early forms from unprinted Dorset Subsidy Rolls, for which I beg to offer

Mr Gover my sincere thanks. I am also indebted to Professor A. Mawer, to Professor and Mrs F. M. Stenton, and to Mr Gover for much personal interest.

Through the kindness of the British and Swedish Foreign Offices and the Ordnance Survey I was enabled to have the use of a great number of 6″ maps for the county. My thanks are also due to the officials of the University Library of Uppsala, the British Museum and the Public Record Office in London, the University Library at Reading, and the County Library at Dorchester.

To my old friend and former fellow-student Dr Mats Redin, to Dr J. K. Wallenberg, Dr S. Karlström, Dr B. Blomé, Mr E. Tengstrand, and Mr O. von Feilitzen I wish to acknowledge my indebtedness for many stimulating discussions on English place-and personal names. The present monograph owes much to the proof-reading of Mr von Feilitzen and to his kind assistance in compiling my bibliography, and I beg to thank him most heartily for this evidence of friendship.

Finally, I wish to thank those Dorset people — known and unknown — who during my rambles in their beautiful country gave me so much valuable information on the modern pronunciation of Dorset place-names.

ANTON FÄGERSTEN.

Uppsala, Sweden, *October* 1933.

BIBLIOGRAPHY

I. SOURCES.[1]

Abbr   Placitorum abbreviatio, Richard I-Edward II. London 1811.

AC   Ancient charters, royal and private, prior to A.D. 1200, ed. J. H. Round. Pipe Roll Society 10. London 1888.

AD   A descriptive catalogue of ancient deeds. London 1890-1915.

Adam de Domerham   Adami de Domerham Historia de rebus gestis Glastoniensibus, ed. Th. Hearne. Oxford 1727.

ASC   Two of the Saxon chronicles parallel, ed. J. Earle and Ch. Plummer. Oxford 1892-99.

Ass   *Assize Rolls for Dorset, nos. 200 and 201, 28 Hy III [PRO].*

Asser   Asser's life of King Alfred, ed. W. H. Stevenson. Oxford 1904.

Athelney   Two cartularies of the Benedictine abbeys of Muchelney and Athelney, ed. E. H. Bates. So Rec Soc 14. London 1899.

Bayly   J. Bayly. Map of Dorset 1773.

BCS   Cartularium Saxonicum, ed. W. de Gray Birch. London 1885-93.

BM   Index to the charters and rolls in the British Museum, ed. H. J. Ellis and F. B. Bickley. London 1900-12.

Bruton   Two cartularies of the Augustinian priory of Bruton and the Cluniac priory of Montacute, ed. C. H. Maxwell Lyte and T. S. Holmes. So Rec Soc 8. London 1894.

Burghal Hidage   In Maitland, F., Domesday Book and Beyond p. 502-3.

Cerne   The cartulary of Cerne Abbey. Do Field Club 28 and 29. 1907-8.

Ch   Calendar of the charter rolls 1226-1341. London 1903-16.

ChancR   Variant readings from the chancellor's copy of Pipe Rolls, as noted in Pipe Roll Society's editions.

ChR   Calendarium rotulorum chartarum et inquisitionum ad quod damnum. London 1803.

Cl   Calendar of the close rolls 1227 ff. London 1892 ff.

ClR   Rotuli litterarum clausarum 1204-27. London 1833-44.

Crawford Ch   The Crawford collection of early charters and documents,

[1] Abbreviations for unpublished records are printed in italics.

	ed. A. S. Napier and W. H. Stevenson. Anecdota Oxoniensia. Medieval and modern series 7. Oxford 1895.
Cur	Curia regis rolls of the reigns of Richard I. and John. London 1922 ff.
Cur (P XIV)	Three rolls of the king's court, 1194-95, ed. F. W. Maitland in P vol. 14. London 1891.
CurR	Rotuli curiæ regis, ed. F. Palgrave. London 1835.
DB	Domesday-Book, ed. A. Farley and H. Ellis. 4 vols. London 1783-1816.
Do Field Club	Dorset Natural History and Antiquarian Field Club. Proceedings. Sherborne 1877 ff.
DoIpm	Abstracts of Dorset inquisitiones post mortem, Charles I; ed. E. A. Fry and G. S. Fry. Dorset Records. London 1894.
Dorchester R	The municipal records of the borough of Dorchester, ed. C. H. Mayo. Exeter 1908.
Dugdale	Dugdale, W., Monasticon Anglicanum. New ed. 8 vols. London 1846.
Earle	Earle, J., A hand-book to the land-charters and other Saxonic documents. Oxford 1888.
Exon	The Exon Domesday in DB vol. 4.
FA	Feudal aids 1284-1431. London 1889-1920.
Fees	The book of fees commonly called Testa de Nevill 1198-1293. London 1920-1931.
FF	Full abstracts of the feet of fines relating to Dorset [1195-1485], ed. E. A. Fry and G. S. Fry. Dorset Records 5 and 10. London 1896 & 1910.
Fine	Calendar of the fine rolls 1272 ff. London 1911 ff.
FineR	Excerpta e rotulis finium A.D. 1216-72. London 1835-36. — Rotuli de oblatis et finibus tempore regis Johannis. London 1835.
Flor Worc	Florentii Wigorniensis monachi chronicon ex chronicis, ed. B. Thorpe. London 1848-49.
France	Calendar of documents preserved in France, ed. J. H. Round. London 1899.
Geld Roll	In DB vol. 4, fol. 17-24.
Geoffr Mon	Geoffrey of Monmouth. Historia Britonum, ed. J. A. Giles. London 1844.
Glaston C	Rentalia et custumaria Michaelis de Ambresbury, 1235-52, et Rogeri de Ford, 1252-61, abbatum monasterii beatæ Mariæ Glastoniæ, ed. C. I. Elton. So Rec Soc 5. London 1891.
Glaston F	Feodary of Glastonbury Abbey (to 1342), ed. F. W. Weaver. So Rec Soc 26. London 1910.
Greenwood	Greenwood, C. and J. Map of Dorset 1826.
Harl. 61	British Museum MS Harley 61: The Shaftesbury register (cf. Dugdale II p. 474-76).

Higden	Higden, Ranulph. Polychronicon, ed. C. Babington and J. R. Lumby. London 1865-86.
Hutchins	Hutchins, J., The history and antiquities of the county of Dorset. 3rd ed. by W. Shipp and J. W. Hodson. 4 vols. Westminster 1861-70.
Inq aqd	Inquisitiones ad quod damnum, see ChR.
Ipm	Calendar of inquisitions post mortem, Henry III-Edward III; Henry VII. London 1904 ff.
IpmR	Calendarium inquisitionum post mortem. London 1806-28.
KCD	Codex diplomaticus ævi saxonici, ed. J. M. Kemble. London 1839-48.
Layamon	Layamon's Brut, ed. F. Madden. London 1847.
Leland	The itinerary of John Leland in or about the years 1535-43, ed. L. Toulmin Smith. London 1907-10.
Lib	Calendar of the liberate rolls 1226-40. London 1916.
LibHyda	Liber Monasterii de Hyda, ed. E. Edwards. London 1866.
LibR	Rotuli de liberate ac de misis et præstitis. London 1844.
LN	Liber niger scaccarii, ed. Th. Hearne. Oxford 1728. (quoted from RBE)
Misc	Calendar of inquisitions miscellaneous. London 1916.
Montacute	See Bruton.
NI	Nonarum inquisitiones temp. regis Edwardi III. London 1807.
OM 1811	The earliest ed. of the Ordnance Survey maps for Dorset.
Orig	Rotulorum originalium in curia scaccarii abbreviatio. London 1805-10.
Osmund	Vetus registrum Sarisberiense: the register of S. Osmund, ed. W. H. R. Jones. London 1883-84.
P	The great roll of the pipe. The Pipe Roll Society, London 1884 ff.
Pap	Calendar of entries in the papal registers relating to Great Britain. London 1893 ff.
Pat	Patent rolls of the reign of Henry III. London 1901-3. — Calendar of patent rolls 1232 ff. London 1891 ff.
PatR	Rotuli litterarum patentium 1201-16. London 1835.
PR	Magnus rotulus scaccarii 31 Hen. I., ed. J. Hunter. London 1833. — The great roll of the pipe, 2, 3, 4 Hen. II., ed. J. Hunter. London 1844.
QW	Placita de quo warranto temporibus Edw. I., II. & III. London 1818.
RBE	The red book of the exchequer, ed. H. Hall. London 1896.
RC	Rotuli chartarum 1199-1216. London 1837.
RH	Rotuli hundredorum temp. Hen. III. et Edw. I. London 1812-18.
Rob Gl	The metrical chronicle of Robert of Gloucester, ed. W. A. Wright. London 1887.

Saints	Die Heiligen Englands, hrsg. von F. Liebermann. Hannover 1889.
Sarum	Sarum charters and documents, ed. W. D. Macray. London 1891.
Sim Durh	Symeonis monachi opera omnia, ed. Th. Arnold. London 1882-85.
SoDoNQ	Notes and Queries for Somerset and Dorset. Sherborne 1890 ff.
SoRecSoc	Somerset Record Society. Publications. London 1887 ff.
Speed	Speed, J. Map of Dorset 1610.
SR	Subsidy rolls for 1327 and 1333 [PRO].
Tax	Taxatio ecclesiastica Angliæ et Walliæ circa A.D. 1291. London 1802.
Taylor	Taylor, I. Map of Dorset 1765. 2nd ed. 1795.
Thorpe	Diplomatarium Anglicum ævi Saxonici, ed. B. Thorpe. London 1865.
TN	Testa de Nevill. See Fees.
Treswell	Treswell, R. Map of Dorset 1585-86. (Facing p. 462 in Hutchins vol. 1).
VE	Valor ecclesiasticus temp. Hen. VIII. London 1810-14.
Wace	Wace. Roman de Brut, ed. A. J. V. Le Roux de Lincy. Rouen 1836-38.
Wm Malm	Willelmi Malmesbiriensis monachi de gestis regum Anglorum libri V, ed. W. Stubbs. London 1887-89.
Wm Malm P	Willelmi Malmesbiriensis gesta pontificorum, ed. N. E. S. A. Hamilton. London 1870.

II. OTHER WORKS CITED.

Articles in periodicals have as a rule not been included.

Alexander, H., The place-names of Oxfordshire. Oxford 1912.
The Ancestor. A quarterly review of county and family history, etc.
Anglia.
Anglia Beiblatt.
Antiquity. A quarterly review of archæology.
Archiv für das Studium der neueren Sprachen.
The Archæological Journal.
Baddeley, W. St Clair, Place-names of Gloucestershire. Gloucester 1913.
Bannister, A. T., The place-names of Herefordshire. Cambridge 1916.
Bardsley, Ch. W., A dictionary of English and Welsh surnames. London 1901.
Bartholomew, J. G., The Survey gazetteer of the British Isles. Edinburgh 1914.
BBC: Broadcast English II by A. Lloyd James.

Björkman, E., Nordische Personennamen in England. Halle 1910.
——, Zur englischen Namenkunde. Halle 1912.
——, Studien über die Eigennamen im Beowulf. Halle 1920.
Blomé, B., The place-names of North Devonshire. Uppsala 1929.
Bowcock, E. W., Shropshire place-names. Shrewsbury 1923.
Bradley, H., English place-names. In Essays and Studies I. Oxford 1910.
Brandl, A., Zur Geographie der altenglischen Dialekte. Berlin 1915.
B.T.: Bosworth, J., and Toller, T. N., Anglo-Saxon dictionary. Oxford 1882-1921.
Bülbring, K. D., Altenglisches Elementarbuch. Heidelberg 1902.
Camden's Britannia, ed. E. Gibson. London 1695.
Chadwick, H. M., The origin of the English nation. Cambridge 1907.
Coker, J., Survey of Dorset. London 1732.
Cortelyou, J. van Zandt, Die altenglischen Namen der Insekten, Spinnen und Krustentiere. Heidelberg 1906.
Danske Studier.
Dictionary of National Biography, ed. L. Stephen and S. Lee. London 1885-1900.
Dijkstra, W. Friesch Woordenboek. Leeuwarden 1896-1911.
Duignan, W. H., Notes on Staffordshire place-names. London 1902. [Duignan, PN St].
——, Worcestershire place-names. London 1905. [Duignan, PN Wo].
——, Warwickshire place-names. Oxford 1912. [Duignan, PN Wa].
EDD: Wright, J., The English Dialect Dictionary. Oxford 1896-1905.
EHR: The English Historical Review.
Ekblom, E., The place-names of Wiltshire. Uppsala 1917.
Ekwall, E., Contributions to the history of Old English dialects. LUÅ 1916.
——, Scandinavians and Celts in the North-West of England. LUÅ 1918.
——, The place-names of Lancashire. Manchester 1922. [Ekwall, PN La].
——, English place-names in -ing. Lund 1923. [Ekwall, PN in -ing].
——, English river-names. Oxford 1928. [Ekwall. ERN].
——, Loss of a nasal before a labial consonant. [In Klæber Celebr. Vol. p. 21-27].
——, Studies on English place- and personal names. Lund 1931. [Ekwall, Studies on PN].
Ellis, H., A general introduction to Domesday-Book. London 1833.
English Studies.
EPN: Mawer, A., The chief elements used in English place-names. EPNS I: 2. Cambridge 1924.
EPNS: The English Place-Name Society, Publications.
Essays and Studies.
ESt: Englische Studien.
Ewen, C. L'Estrange, A history of surnames of the British Isles. London 1931.

Eyton, R. W., A key to Domesday, exemplified by an analysis and digest of the Dorset survey. London 1878. [Eyton].

——, Domesday Studies: an analysis and digest of the Somerset survey. London 1880. [Eyton, DB Studies: So].

Fabricius, A., Danske minder i Normandiet. København 1897.

Forssner, T., Continental-Germanic personal names in England. Uppsala 1916.

Freeman, E. A., History of the Norman conquest. Oxford 1867-79.

Förstemann, E., Altdeutsches Namenbuch. I. Personennamen. 2. Aufl. Bonn 1900. II. Ortsnamen. 3. Aufl. Bonn 1913-16.

Förster, M., Keltisches Wortgut im Englischen. F. Liebermann Celebration Volume. Halle 1921.

Gevenich, O., Die englische Palatalisierung von k > č im Lichte der englischen Ortsnamen. Halle 1918.

Godefroy, F., Dictionnaire de l'ancienne langue française. Paris 1880-1902.

Goodall, A., Place-names of South-West Yorkshire. Cambridge 1914.

Gover, J. E. B., The place-names of Middlesex. London 1922.

Gross, C., The sources and literature of English history. 2nd ed. London 1915.

Guest, E., Origines celticæ. London 1883.

Hall, J. R. Clark, A concise Anglo-Saxon dictionary. 3rd ed. Cambridge 1931.

Hellquist, E., Svensk etymologisk ordbok. Lund 1920-22.

Holder, A., Alt-celtischer Sprachschatz. Leipzig 1891-1913.

Hopwood, D., The place-names of the county of Surrey including London in Surrey. Annals of the University of Stellenbosch. Capetown 1926.

Hutchins, see under Sources.

IPN: Introduction to the survey of English place-names. EPNS I: 1. Cambridge 1924.

Jellinghaus, H., Die westfälischen Ortsnamen, 3. Aufl. Osnabrück 1923.

Johnston, J. B., The place-names of England and Wales. London 1914.

Jordan, R., Handbuch der mittelenglischen Grammatik I. Heidelberg 1925.

The Journal of English and Germanic Philology.

Karlström, S., Old English compound place-names in -ing. UUÅ 1927.

Kelly's Directory of Dorsetshire. London 1923.

Klæber Celebr. Vol.: Studies in English philology. A miscellany in honor of Frederick Klæber. Minneapolis 1929.

Kluge, F., Etymologisches Wörterbuch der deutschen Sprache. 10. Aufl. Berlin und Leipzig 1924.

Langenfelt, G., Toponymics or derivations from local names in English. Uppsala 1920.

Lindqvist, N., Bjärka-Säby ortnamn. Uppsala 1926.

Luick, K., Historische Grammatik der englischen Sprache. Leipzig 1914 ff.

LUÅ: Lunds universitets årsskrift.
Mc Clure, E., British place-names in their historical setting. London 1910.
Maitland, F., Domesday Book and Beyond. Cambridge 1907.
Mawer, A., Animal and personal names in Old English place-names. MLR 14. Cambridge 1919.
——, The place-names of Northumberland and Durham. Cambridge 1920. [Mawer, PN NbDu].
——, English place-name study. London 1921. (From the Proceedings of the British Academy, Vol. X).
——, Place-names and history. Liverpool 1922.
——, Problems of place-name study. Cambridge 1929.
Mayo, C. H., Bibliotheca Dorsetiensis. London 1885.
Middendorff, H., Altenglisches Flurnamenbuch. Halle 1902.
MLR: The Modern Language Review.
Moorman, F. W., The place-names of the West Riding of Yorkshire. Thoresby Soc. Publ. 18. Leeds 1910.
Moule, H. J., Old Dorset. London 1893.
Mutschmann, H., The place-names of Nottinghamshire. Cambridge 1913.
Namn och Bygd.
NED: A New English Dictionary, ed. J. A. H. Murray, etc. Oxford 1888-1928.
Olson, E., De appellativa substantivens bildning i fornsvenskan. Lund 1916.
OM: Ordnance Survey Maps. 1″ and 6″.
Oman, C., England before the Norman conquest. 2nd ed. London 1910.
PBr Beiträge: Beiträge zur Geschichte der deutschen Sprache und Literatur, hrsg. von H. Paul und W. Braune.
Peerage, The Complete, ed. G. E. Cokayne and V. Gibbs. London 1910 ff.
Philips' Atlas of the counties of England. New ed. London 1875.
PN BedsHu: The place-names of Bedfordshire and Huntingdonshire, ed. A. Mawer and F. M. Stenton. EPNS 3. Cambridge 1926.
PN Bk: The place-names of Buckinghamshire, ed. A. Mawer and F. M. Stenton. EPNS 2. Cambridge 1925.
PN D: The place-names of Devon, ed. J. E. B. Gover, A. Mawer and F. M. Stenton. EPNS 8 and 9. Cambridge 1931-32.
PN Nth: The place-names of Northamptonshire, ed. J. E. B. Gover, A. Mawer and F. M. Stenton. EPNS 10. Cambridge 1933.
PN NRY: The place-names of the North Riding of Yorkshire, by A. H. Smith. EPNS 5. Cambridge 1928.
PN Sx: The place-names of Sussex, ed. A. Mawer and F. M. Stenton. EPNS 6 and 7. Cambridge 1929-30.
PN Wo: The place-names of Worcestershire, ed. A. Mawer and F. M. Stenton. EPNS 4. Cambridge 1927.
Redin, M., Studies on uncompounded personal names in Old English. UUÅ 1919.
Reynolds, J. J., The ancient history of Shaftesbury. Shaftesbury (n. d.).

Ritter, O., Vermischte Beiträge zur englischen Sprachgeschichte. Halle 1922.

Searle, W. G., Onomasticon Anglo-Saxonicum. Cambridge 1897.

Sedgefield, W. J., The place-names of Cumberland and Westmorland. Manchester 1915.

Skeat, W. W., The place-names of Bedfordshire. Cambridge 1906. [Skeat, PN Beds].

——, The place-names of Berkshire. Oxford 1911. [Skeat, PN Berks].

——, The place-names of Cambridgeshire. Cambridge 1911. [Skeat, PN C].

——, The place-names of Suffolk. Cambridge 1913. [Skeat, PN Sf].

Smith, A. H. See PN NRY.

Stenton, F. M., The place-names of Berkshire. Reading 1911.

StMSpv: Studier i modern språkvetenskap utgivna av Nyfilologiska Sällskapet i Stockholm.

StNPh: Studia Neophilologica.

Stratmann, F. H., A Middle-English dictionary. New ed. by H. Bradley. Oxford 1891.

Tait, J., The feudal element. (In IPN).

UUÅ: Uppsala universitets årsskrift.

VCH: The Victoria history of the counties of England. — Dorset vol. II, ed. W. Page. London 1908.

Vising Celebr. Vol.: Mélanges de philologie offerts à J. Vising. Göteborg 1925.

Walker, B., The place-names of Derbyshire. Journal of the Derbyshire Archæol. Soc. 36-37. Derby 1914-15.

Wallenberg, J. K., Kentish place-names. UUÅ 1931.

Watson, W. J., The history of the Celtic place-names of Scotland. Edinburgh 1926.

Weekley, E., Surnames. London 1917.

——, The romance of names. 3rd ed. London 1922.

Wright, J., The English dialect grammar. Oxford 1905. [Wright, EDG].

——, Old English grammar. 3rd ed. Oxford 1925.

Zachrisson, R. E., A contribution to the study of Anglo-Norman influence on English place-names. LUÅ 1909. [Zachrisson, AN Infl.].

——, Some instances of Latin influence on English place-nomenclature. LUÅ 1910.

——, The French definite article in English place-names. Anglia 34. 1911.

——, Some English place-name etymologies. StMSpv. IX. 1924.

——, English place-names and river-names containing the primitive Germanic roots *vis, *vask. UUÅ 1926. [Zachrisson, PN and RN].

——, Romans, Kelts and Saxons in ancient Britain. Uppsala 1927. [Zachrisson, Romans].

——, Five years of English place-name study. ESt 62. 1927.

——, English place-name puzzles. StNPh V. 1932.

ZONF: Zeitschrift für Ortsnamenforschung.

ABBREVIATIONS
(not given in the Bibliography)

AFr	Anglo-French	Mx	Middlesex
al.	alias	N	north
AN	Anglo-Norman	n.	note
Beds	Bedfordshire	Nb	Northumberland
Berks	Berkshire	n. d.	no date
Bk	Buckinghamshire	NE	New English
Brit	British	Nf	Norfolk
C	Cambridgeshire	Nt	Nottinghamshire
cent.	century	Nth	Northamptonshire
Ch	Cheshire	O	Oxfordshire
Co	Cornwall	OE	Old English
Cu	Cumberland	OFr	Old French
D	Devonshire	OHG	Old High German
Db	Derbyshire	OS	Ordnance Survey
Do	Dorset	(p)	place-name form derived
Du	Durham		from personal name
E	east	pers. name	personal name
el.	element	pl--n.	place-name
Ess	Essex	S	south
Fm	Farm	Sa	Shropshire
Fr	French	s. a.	sub anno
G	German	Scand.	Scandinavian
Gl	Gloucestershire	Sf	Suffolk
Ha	Hampshire	s. n.	sub nomine
He	Herefordshire	So	Somerset
Herts	Hertfordshire	Sr	Surrey
Ho	House	St	Staffordshire
Hu	Huntingdonshire	s. v.	sub vocabulo
K	Kent	Sx	Sussex
L	Lincolnshire	TRE	tempore regis' Edwardi
La	Lancashire	W	Wiltshire, west, Welsh
Lat	Latin	Wa	Warwickshire
Lei	Leicestershire	We	Westmorland
m.	mile(s)	Wo	Worcestershire
ME	Middle English	Wt	Isle of Wight
MLG	Middle Low German	Y	Yorkshire

Introduction

Great caution is certainly needed in drawing conclusions from place-name material with regard to the early history of a district. The nomenclature of the western parts of Dorset has many points in common with that of South-east Devon, the occupation of which probably did not begin until after the year 658.[1] To what extent the other parts of Dorset were at that time in the hands of the Saxons, is a question which must be left to experts in early English history to decide. It may, however, be safely assumed that the West Saxon occupation of these parts, too, took place at a comparatively late date.

It seems now to be generally acknowledged that uncompounded -*ing* names belong to the earliest stratum of English place-nomenclature.[2] There is only one safe instance of this type in the county, viz. Uddens (*infra* 83), and it will probably not be without significance to note that this place is situated in the extreme east. It should also be noted that Gillingham, the only example of an -*ingaham* name in Dorset, is in the northern extremity of the county.

On the whole the local nomenclature of Dorset is of a decidedly English character. It is true there are a few Celtic names, but their number seems to be far smaller than has hitherto been assumed.[3] Allowance must, of course, be made for wrong interpretations on the part of the present author, but even so, the result of the investigation will show that, out of the thousand names included, only about a dozen are of Celtic origin.[4] Of

---

[1] Cf. PN D Introd. p. xviii.   [2] Cf. Zachrisson, StNPh V, 6.

[3] Cf. PN D Introd. p. xix. The Celtic river-names may here be left out of the discussion; they are about twenty in number, cf. Ekwall, ERN Introd. p. LVI.

[4] It is of course possible that, among the names left uninterpreted *infra*, a few, such as Caundle, Kimmeridge and Owermoigne, may be Celtic in origin, but this cannot materially affect the general conclusion that the number of

these Chideock is in the south-west, Mayne is in the south, Creech and Lytchett in the south-east, and practically all the others, of which several are of a hybrid type, are in the north-eastern corner of the county.[1]

The different English elements (including a few of Celtic origin) which enter into Dorset place-names will be found in the list printed *infra* 305 ff. A few remarks on the distribution of these elements, chiefly for the purpose of comparison with the Devon elements, may be offered here. *cot(e)* is extremely rare, and, in contrast to Devon, it was not a living suffix after the Norman Conquest. With the exception of two lost *Chaldecot(e)s* on the Channel (and a dropped *cote* in Coryates), there is only one clear instance of this element, viz. Woodcutts in the extreme north-eastern corner of the county. The typical Devon element *worðig* is practically unknown in Dorset (see *infra* 319), *hlæw*, *hōh* and *stow* are totally absent, *healh* is unknown in its un-compounded form (cf. the many Devon names *Hele, Heale*) and has been noted only once as a second element (Wraxall), *stede* is also found only once (Ringstead), and the only name going back to *hāmstede* is lost. As a contribution to the discussion of *hām* and *hamm*[2] it may be mentioned that we seem to have three or four clear examples in Dorset of the use of *hamm* in the sense of 'river-meadow'. There are two instances of the Devon element *gierd*, both in the west of the county.

Dorset is a country of hills, valleys and moors, and elements denoting these topographical features (*dūn, hyll, cumb*[3], *mōr*, etc.) are well represented. The frequency of *wudu, lēah, bearu*, and (to a smaller extent) *hyrst* tells us that the county must once have been well wooded.

The most common of all place-name terminals in Dorset is *tūn*, and it should be noted that this element also enters into a

---

Celtic names is surprisingly small. Some names which were previously con-sidered to be Celtic have afterwards been interpreted as English; Worgret (*infra* 131) is a case in point. The *Mel*-names (cf. *infra* 27) would seem to be another case.

[1] For conclusions as to the survival of a Celtic speaking population in this part of Dorset, see Zachrisson, Romans p. 55.

[2] Cf. PN D p. 677 f.

[3] For this element cf. e. g. PN D Introd. p. xxiii f. The element *torr* is unknown in Dorset.

great number of post-Conquest place-names (of which more below), the first part of which is the name of an early ME owner. In this connexion attention should also be drawn to the use of *(ge)hæg*, ME *hay*, in Dorset. With one exception (Gummershay in Stalbridge) this element is confined to the west of the county, where it is of equally frequent occurrence as in the adjacent parts of Devon; cf. the *note* to Bilshay Fm *infra* 254.

The list of elements at the end of this book also includes those used in the first part of place-names. Thus we get *inter alia* a convenient survey of the names of plants and animals used in the place-names of the county. In the former category we find represented wheat, rye, barley, bean and flax, oak, ash, alder, elder, hazel, maple, holly, pear and plum, rush, reed, willow, withy, thorn, woad, broom, fern, cress and nettle; in the latter group cattle (*neat*), cow, calf, horse, hog, swine, sheep, dog, cat, boar, hart, hind, roe-buck, goat and buck, cock, hen, duck, crane, hawk, lark, owl, raven, rook and crow, eel and frog, as well as louse, and an insect of unknown description (OE *pie*).

Some elements and names are of interest from various points of view. Note for instance Arne (*infra* 129), Belchalwell (46), Blashenwell (118), Branksea Island (124), Cann (20), Cheddington (269), Cobb (286), Combs Ditch (63), the *corf*-names (Corfe Castle 116, Corscombe 269, etc.), Dowerfield (239), Duntish (203), Ebb (292), Eype (293), Gussage (91), Hewstock (263), Hile (46), Picket (280), Pilsdon (290), Pipsford (271), Plush (205), Quarr (128), Sixpenny (19), Sleight (111), Spettisbury (76), (Broad)windsor (265), Wraxall (243). A few of these contain words not hitherto evidenced in English, others are calculated to throw fresh light on rare place-name elements or to carry the history of certain English words considerably back in time, others again, such as Pilsdon and Windsor, may afford some contribution to the discussion of genitival compounds in English place-names.

In this connexion a few words may be said about the question as to what extent we are entitled to interpret the first element of a place-name as a personal name. The problem is of fundamental importance, and has recently been brought to the fore by Zachrisson in a paper in StNPh V. The chief conclusions arrived at by Zachrisson may be briefly summed up as follows.

(1) Personal names enter into English place-names to a much smaller extent than has hitherto been supposed; (2) we are not entitled to assume a greater frequency of monothematic personal names (short-names, type *Lulla*) than of dithematic ones (full-names, type *Wulfgār*) in place-name compounds, recorded short-names being in reality much less numerous than full-names; (3) with very few exceptions, personal names enter only into place-name compounds in which the second element is a habitative terminal (*tūn, hām, cot, hiwisc,* etc.), whereas terminals which merely denote natural features (*dūn, brōc, wudu,* etc.), are seldom if ever compounded with a personal name. The list of personal names assumed to enter into Dorset place-names of presumably OE origin (see *infra* 319 f.) seems on the whole to confirm Zachrisson's theories. This list includes only about 75 names. It is true that the number of short-names is somewhat larger than that of full-names, but the etymologies of many, if not the majority, of the place-names supposed to contain short-names are marked as very doubtful and do not claim to be final. As was to be expected, these personal names enter mostly into habitative compounds, chiefly into names in *-ton,* but a few other terminals are also represented. Among these we find one certain and one somewhat uncertain case of a *full-name* compounded with *lēah* (Barnsley, Loverley), two fairly certain cases with *wielle* (Askerswell, Armswell), one certain case with *mylen* (Arfleet Mills), and one certain — though perhaps late — case with *wudu* (Oakers Wood). It may be noted in particular that among the 80 Dorset place-names compounded with a terminal denoting some kind of height (*beorg, clif, cnoll, dūn, hlinc, hyll,* and *hrycg*) we have found only one safe instance of a *full-name* compounded with *beorg* (Symondsbury) and one with *hyll* (Osehill), and it may well be that the latter place-name is of comparatively late origin. It should be added that among these hill-names we have noted only two cases, both doubtful, of compounds with a *short-name* (Brownshall Hundred, Chebbard).

It need hardly be pointed out that the Scandinavian influence on the place-names of Dorset is extremely slight. Two Anglo-Scandinavian pers. names (*Grim* and *Croc*) enter into Grimstone and Cruxton, and Godderthorn (Hundred) may contain a third. It should be mentioned, however, that several originally Scandinavian personal names have *via* Normandy found their way into Dorset place-names.

The Norman-French and feudal influence, on the other hand, has been of the greatest importance for the place-nomenclature of the county. Anglo-Norman peculiarities in spelling occur on almost every page of the book, and traces of French influence of various kinds are found on the modern map. It is true there is no instance of a purely French name in Dorset of the type Beaumont or the like, but we find manorial names such as Font le Roi, Chantmarle and Matravers, and the feudal names of the type Okeford Fitzpaine and Turners Puddle are remarkably common, probably more so than in any other county in England. One type of feudal names is worthy of special note. There is an unusually large number of post-Conquest names ending in -*ton*[1], the first part of which is an early ME personal name or surname, mostly, though not always[2], of Norman-French or Continental-Germanic origin. Most, though not all[3], of the places in question originally derived their names from the rivers on which they stand (Winterborne, Tarrant, Piddle, Cerne and Frome). Many of these, such as Winterborne Clenston and Tarrant Keynston, still bear their characteristic "double-barrelled" names, others, such as Quarleston and Bhompston, have dropped the river-name and cannot in their present form be distinguished from the ordinary type of names in -*ton*, a few, such as *Auntyocheston*, *Turbervileston* and *Marlewardeston* (*infra* 61, 71 f., 73) are now lost. It should be mentioned that these late compounds in -*ton* are not found in the western part of the county, where, instead, we find the numerous late compounds in -*hay*.

Latin influence has also left some marks on the place-names of Dorset. Names containing Latin designations of former ownership, such as Compton Abbas and Bere Regis, are numerous, the appendages Magna and Parva are well represented, and even such curious additions as Intrinseca and Porcorum occur on the maps, but they are never used by the people.

Though the present monograph does not claim to deal with problems of dialect, a few observations may here be made on

---

[1] Cf. Tait's list in IPN p. 131, where the majority of these names are included.

[2] Cf. Athelhampton *infra* 170.

[3] Cf. e. g. Bryanston, Shillingstone, Egliston, Godlingston, Chaston.

some dialectal features illustrated by Dorset place-names. The breaking of *a* to *ea* before *l* followed by a consonant (in words like *c(e)ald* and *c(e)alf*), resulting in the palatalization of *c* (> *ch*), has long ago been shown by Ekwall to be characteristic of the old West Saxon territory.[1] The material *infra*[2] corroborates the results obtained by Ekwall. Another dialectal feature, viz. the development of OE *ie* (< *i*-mutated *ea*) is represented by a great number of Dorset names containing *wielle* 'well, spring'. Ekwall has shown[3] that the genuine ME Dorset form of that word was *wulle* (*wolle*), i. e. a form with [u]. The fresh material brought to light *infra*[4] again confirms Ekwall's results.[5] In this connexion it may be noted that two names *infra* (Woodbury, Woodstreet), both containing *wind-*, would seem to point to a tendency of *wi-* to become *wu-* in Dorset.

The ME development of OE *īe* (< *i*-mutation of *ēa*) is illustrated by place-names containing *stīepel* 'steeple'. Miss Serjeantson has already pointed out[6] that in Dorset place-names this word appears fairly often as *stupel*, i. e. [y]. The fresh material *infra*[7] shows an overwhelming majority of *u* spellings, particularly in the forms for the two places situated in the east of the county.[8] OE *eo* fairly commonly becomes *u*[9], as illustrated by the early forms of many place-names *infra*.[10]

---

[1] Contrib. to the Hist. of OE Dialects, chapter I.

[2] See Belchalwell, *Chaldecote, Chaldecots*, Chaldon.

[3] Op. cit., chapter II.

[4] Names containing *wielle* are enumerated under that word *infra* 318.

[5] Matters are however somewhat different when the vowel appears in a stressed and in an unstressed position. In a stressed position (Wool, Woolbridge, and the two Woolcombes) I have found about 50 *wulle* (*wolle, Owel*) spellings (against two *wille* forms in DB), whereas in an unstressed position I have noted 20 *wulle* (*wolle*) against 25 *wille* (*wylle*). It should be mentioned, however, that no less than 16 of these *wille* spellings occur in the names of the three places which are nearest Devon (Elwell in Netherbury, Askerswell and Gorwell), cf. also Ekwall, op. cit. pp. 47, 60.

[6] English Studies IV, 192.

[7] Steeple, Steepleton Iwerne, Winterborne Steepleton.

[8] Steeple and Steepleton Iwerne.

[9] Cf. e. g. Wyld in IPN p. 137, and Miss Serjeantson in English Studies IV, 195, 197.

[10] Cf. e. g. Durweston, Sturthill, Hursey, Barnsley, Hartley, *Coringdon*, Swyre, Preston (107), Fleet, and the names containing *neoðera*.

The intricate question of the development of OE y in Dorset[1] requires a special investigation and cannot be entered upon here. Only that much may be said that u forms are very numerous.[2]

Other dialectal features may be briefly mentioned. Voicing of f to v occurs in many names and is preserved in Venn, Black Venn, (Frome) Vauchurch, and Verwood. The ME tendency of raising e to i before certain consonants is seen in the early forms of such names as Redhone Hundred, Redlane Hundred, and Silton. There is at least one name which shows development of a prothetic i (Yetminster), and one which seems to preserve traces of a medial inflexional syllable (Radipole). A late development of a to o has taken place in Notton and Rodden. Finally, the early history of the names of Stafford, Stallen, Stoborough, (High) Stoy, and (probably) Oborne will show that the tendency of dropping n before a labial consonant, dealt with by Ekwall[3], was characteristic of Dorset, too.

A few words may be added on the material from which the early forms have been collected. The OE charters relating to Dorset are fairly numerous, but unfortunately very few are originals. The great Shaftesbury Register (MS Harl. 61), which has yielded the majority of the charter forms *infra*, appears to have been written in the 15th century. That attempts to check the forms in BCS (and KCD) with the spellings of the manuscript in the British Museum are not without interest, may be seen from the discussions in connexion with Sixpenny, Blynfield and Combs Ditch (*infra* 19, 21, 63). Part of the manuscript is still unpublished. That also this part may be of value for the interpretation of place-names, is shown by the name of Winterborne Zelstone (*infra* 73).

The other early sources, from DB up to the end of the ME period, do not call for much comment. Volume I of VCH for Dorset is still unpublished, and the identifications of DB forms made by Eyton have therefore been accepted in most cases. The index to the Book of Fees, which was published a couple

---

[1] Cf. e. g. Wyld in ESt XLVII, 147 ff., 159 f., and Brandl, Zur Geogr. d. altengl. Dialekte p. 50.

[2] In order to illustrate this and several other dialectal features I have included a great number of early forms.

[3] Klaeber Celebr. Volume pp. 21—27.

of years ago, has been inaccessible to me, and I am, therefore,
solely responsible for the identifications of the numerous forms
taken from that valuable document. Such is *inter alia* also the
case with the Feet of Fines for Dorset, the indexer of which
has made no attempts to identify the many place-name forms
occurring in that priceless record. Valuable material has been
obtained from two unprinted sources, viz. the Subsidy Rolls and
the Assize Rolls, the former having been transcribed by Mr J.
E. B. Gover, the latter by myself.

During my stay in Dorset I had ample opportunity to study
the topography of a great many places in the county, to collect
a number of local pronunciations of place-names, and to go
through the proceedings of the Dorset Field Club and other
publications of local interest. Hutchins' monumental county
history has, of course, been carefully studied and has proved
to be of the greatest value for the interpretation of many names,
especially those connected with the feudal history of the county.
I have myself paid great attention to such names, and much
trouble has been taken in the endeavour to trace the persons
or families whose names appear in the early forms of the place-
names.

The etymological part of my book is, I regret to say, not
altogether satisfactory. Many names have withstood all attempts
at a reasonable explanation, and I have therefore thought it best
to leave these names without any etymological suggestion. In
defence of this I may be allowed to quote a word by Zachrisson[1]: "It is of greater importance to have safe and complete
material, than to offer tentative explanations of *all* the names
dealth with."

The general arrangement of the present monograph follows
practically the same lines as those adopted in the publications
of the English Place-Name Society. With very few exceptions,
however, only those names have been included for which early
forms have been found before the year 1500, and which I have
been able to identify with names occurring on the modern Ordnance Survey maps (1″ and 6″). A fairly large number of names
now no longer current have also been included and have been

[1] Englische Studien LXII, 97.

marked as "lost". These names are printed in italics when referred to elsewhere in the volume. Local pronunciations are frequently given in phonetic script within square brackets. The phonetic symbols are practically the same as those used by the English Place-Name Society and the British Broadcasting Corporation.

Dorchester and Dorset[1]

Dorchester is *Dornuuarana ceaster* 847 (orig.) BCS 451, other charter forms being *Dornwerecestre* 833 (c. 1400) BCS 410, *Dornwaracester* 863 (12th) BCS 508, *Dornwaraceaster* 864 (copy) BCS 510, (*æt*) *Dornwara ceastræ* 868 (12th) BCS 520, *Dornace(a)ster*, *Dorneacester* 937 (12th) BCS 716, 718, 719, *Doracestria* c. 939 BCS 738, 739.[2]

Other spellings are *Dorecestre* 1086 DB *et passim* (with later variant *Dorcestre*), *Dorsestre* 1244 *Ass* (201 m. 12), *Dorchestre* 1334 Cl *et passim*.

Dorset is *Dorset* 891 (14th) BCS 564 (: *Dornsetan* KCD 319); *Dorseteschire* 940-6 (14th) BCS 817, *Dorseteschyre* 955 (14th) BCS 913; (*to, on*) *Dorsæton* 955 (14th) BCS 912[3], n. d. (orig.) KCD 704, c. 1006 (12th) KCD 1302, 1046 (12th) KCD 1334, (*on*) *Dorsætan* n. d. KCD 841, 871.

The form (*mid*) *Dornsætum* occurs twice in ASC (s. aa. 837, 845, MS A), otherwise the forms there are (*mid, on*) *Dorsætum*, *Dorsæton*, *Dorsætan*, *Dorseton*.

Other forms are *Dorsetscira* 1066-78 (1269) Ch; *Dorsete* 1086 DB (*Dorseta* Exon) *et passim* (later also *Dorset'*, *Dorset*), *Dorsette* 1154-5 (etc.) RBE, 1235-6 Fees (455, 562), *Dorsat'* 1174-5 P, *Doreseta* 1178-9 P, *Dorsett(a)* 1179-80 P, *Dorsetha* 1190 (1330) Ch, *Dorsit* 1194 Cur (P XIV).[4]

The Romano-British name of Dorchester was *Durnovaria* (Antonine Itinerary). To this name was later added *ceaster*, and

---

[1] The local pronunciations are [dɑːdʒestə] and [dɑːzet].

[2] These two charters from the Milton Register (now lost) must be very late copies.

[3] Cf. (*de comitatu*) *Dorsetensi* BCS 914.

[4] Layamon has *Dor(e)sete* and *Dorchestre seten*, Sim Durh *Dorseta scire*, France *Dorseta scira*, *Dorsetasire*, *Dorset(h)*, *Dorscete* (all 11th cent.); cf. also the Latinized forms *Dorsetia* (Sarum) and *Dorsetania* (Flor Worc). On the form *Thornsæta* in Asser (repeated in Flor Worc) see W. H. Stevenson, Asser p. 250. On the spelling *Torsete* in Wace see Zachrisson, AN Infl. p. 43 n. 1.

we thus get OE *Dornuuarana ceaster* and *Dornwaraceaster*[1] which ultimately resulted in Dorchester.[2] The people in and about *Dorn(wara)ceaster* were called *Dornsæte*, *sæte* meaning 'dwellers, inhabitants'; hence· the name of the county.[3]

The meaning of *Durnovaria* has never been satisfactorily explained. That it cannot contain Welsh *dwfr* (< Brit *dubron*) 'water', as has often been supposed, has been shown by Bradley (Essays and Studies I, 14); and the same author says concerning the etymology (op. cit. p. 21): "Now as *durno-* means 'fist', and *war* is the root of the Welsh *gware*[4], play, it seems possible that the town got its name because it was adjacent to a place set apart for pugilistic encounters". On *durno-* cf. also Watson (Celtic PN Scotland p. 488) who indicates that a certain place Dundurn, 'fort of the fist', may have been called so from its shape. Zachrisson (Romans p. 79 n. 1) carries this further and suggests that, if *durno-* could really indicate the shape of a hill-fort, *Durnovaria* may have been the original name of Maiden Castle, the famous hill-camp just outside Dorchester.

Dorchester in Dorset (the *villa regalis*) has sometimes been mixed up with its Oxfordshire namesake[5] (the *villa episcopalis*) even in very early documents, cf. *Æðelricus Dorccensis aecclesiae episcopus* KCD 737, corresponding to *Ægelric bisceop of Dorsætscire* (sic) in another part of the same charter; cf. also *Dorkecestr'* 1244 Cl, 1292 Ipm, apparently referring to the Dorset town but showing a form which clearly reminds us of the Oxfordshire name.

---

[1] According to Stevenson (Asser p. 250), the West Saxons identified the latter part of *Durnovaria* with their own word *ware* 'inhabitants', hence OE *Dornuuarana ceaster* and *Dornwaraceaster*, showing that word in a weak and a strong genitive plural respectively.

[2] The transition from *Dornwaraceaster* to *Dorn(a)ceaster* (> Dorchester) is perhaps no phonetic development in the ordinary sense of the word, but should probably, as suggested by Ritter (p. 89 f.), be looked upon as an ellipsis.

[3] Bradley (Essays and Studies I, 21 f.) describes the whole process thus: "The Saxons at first called the place Dornwara-ceaster (retaining the contemporary British form of the name unchanged), but afterwards shortened this to Dornceaster, whence the modern form. The inhabitants of the region about 'Dorn-ceaster' were called Dorn-sæte".

[4] The form *Durngueir* in Asser (49, 7) is the regular Welsh development of *Durnovaria*, see Stevenson, Asser p. 250.

[5] Of different origin, see Alexander, PN O p. 94 f.

I. Gillingham Liberty and Redlane Hundred[1]

gelingehã 1084 GeldRoll, *Gellingehã* 1130 PR
Gillingeham 1177-8, 1187-8 P, 1212 Fees (91) *et passim*
Gelingham 1244 *Ass*, *Gillingham* 1252 Ch, 1275 RH, 1285 FA
See Gillingham *infra*.

Ridelawe (sic) 1251-2 Fees (1268[2]).

La Redelane 1252 Pat, 1285 FA, *La Rede Lane* 1270 Pat[3]
la Ridelan 1265 Misc, *Ridelane* 1327 *SR*, 1333 Orig, 1340 NI,
    1354 IpmR, 1428 FA, *Ryde-* 1326 Orig, 1333 *SR*, 1346,
    1431 FA
La Radelawe (sic) 1273 Cl
Redelane 1303 FA, 1303, 1304 Pat, 1329 Ipm, 1334 Misc,
    1390 IpmR, Cl, *Redlane* 1325 Inq aqd, *Reedlane* 1451 FF

This probably means exactly what it seems to mean, viz. 'the red lane', OE *rēad*, *lane*; cf. Zachrisson, Anglia XXXIV, 324. The many *i*, *y* spellings are remarkable, but cf. Redhone *infra* which shows a similar run of forms but which in all probability contains OE *rēad*.

The name of Redlane Hundred long survived as the name of the small hamlet of Redlane, "situated about half a mile south-west from Todbere" (Hutchins); no trace of such a name can be found now in the vicinity of Todber. For an older name of this hundred cf. Farrington *infra*.

Bourton

Bourton [bɔ:tən] 121 G 9
Bureton 1212 Fees (91), t. Edw. II Ipm, *Burton* 1244 *Ass*, t.
    Edw. II Ipm, 1333 *SR* (p), *Borton* 1275 RH (p)

OE *burhtūn*, for the meaning of which see EPN s. v.

---

[1] For practical reasons I have placed these together. Otherwise the old Liberties are included among the hundreds to which they geographically (and sometimes historically) belong. The ancient Dorset Liberties were eighteen in number, and are enumerated here as they appear on Bayly's map (1773): Frampton, Loders and Bothenhampton, Powerstock, Broadwindsor, Fordington, Piddlehinton, Portland Island, Preston and Sutton Poyntz, Upway (often called *Waybyhouse*), Wyke Regis, Gillingham, Alton Pancras, Halstock, Minterne Magna, Piddletrenthide, Ryme Intrinseca, Sydling St Nicholas, Stour Provost.
[2] Note 3: Read *Ridelane*.   [3] Once spelt *Redendale*.

Sandway is *la Sandweye* t. Edw. II Ipm (p), *atte Sandweye* 1333 *SR* (p). Self-explanatory, OE *sand, weg*.

Buckhorn Weston

Buckhorn Weston 121 I 8

Weston(e) 1086 DB, 1210-12 RBE, 1212 Fees (91) *et passim*
Bo(u)keres Weston 1285 FA, 1303 FA *et passim*
Bukereweston 1286 Orig, *Burkereweston* 1301 FF
Bukeres Weston 1289 Orig, 1310 FF, 1348, 1361 Cl
Bo(u)kerne Weston 1346 FA, 1352 FF, 1428, 1431 FA
Bokernesweston 1344 IpmR, *Boukernes Weston* 1398 IpmR
Bokesweston 1423 AD II
Weston Maundevyle, Boukeres Weston 1412 FA
Boukerswaston al. *Weston Maundevile* 1414 IpmR
Bakeres (Bokerys) Weston al. *Weston Moygn(e)* 1486, 1495 IpmR
Weston Bukkehorne 1535 VE

Weston is self-explanatory (OE *west, tūn*), but the additional name is difficult. Presumably it is no pers. name, but the forms are not early enough for an interpretation. — The *Maundevilles* were here as early as the 13th century, and the *Moygnes* (of whom see more under Owermoigne *infra*) at the end of the 14th.

Fifehead Magdalen

Fifehead Magdalen [faif(h)ed mægdǝlǝn] 130 A 9

Fifhide 1086 DB, *Fifhidam* (ack.) 1153-4 (1318) Ch
Lifiden (sic) 1158 France
Fifhyde, Fyfhide 1285 FA, Ch, *Fifide* 1291 Tax, 1428 FA
Vifhide 1316 FA, 1333 *SR*
Fyffehyde Maudlyn 1460 IpmR, *Fighfeld Magdalyn* 1535 VE

Besides this place there are three more Fifeheads in Do, viz. Fifehead Neville, Fifehead St Quintin and Fifehead Sydling *infra*. They were all assessed at five 'hides' in DB[1], which accounts for their names, see EPN s. v. *hīd*. The VE form shows this name on the point of assuming the *Fifield* type, common in other parts of England. The voicing of *f* to *v* (*Vifhide*) will occur again in many Do names. The church is dedicated to St Mary Magdalen (Hutchins).

[1] On the question of the 'five-hide unit' in DB cf. e. g. VCH So I, 386 f.

Gillingham

Gillingham [gilɪŋəm] 121 I 10

Gillingaham 993 KCD 684[1], s. a. 1016 Flor Worc, Sim Durh[2]
wið Gillinga s. a. 1016 ASC(E), *wið Gillinga hâm* ib. (D)
Gelingehā, Gelinge ha 1086 DB (*passim*[3] and Exon), 1209 LibR
Gellingeh, -ham 1155 PR, 1167-8 P, 1212 Fees (90)
Gildingehā 1156 PR
Geldingehā 1157 PR, 1158-9 P, *Goldingehā* 1159-60 P[4]
Gillingeham, -hā 1155-6 RBE, 1160-1 (etc.) P *et passim* up to
   the beginning of the 14th cent.[5], *Gilingeh* 1209 LibR
Gyllingeham (*Ghillinge-*) 1152-8 Montacute, *Gyllingeham* 1236 Cl
Gillengeham t. John RBE, 1229 Cl
Gillingham 1200 FineR, 1201 Cur, 1204 LibR, ClR *et passim*
From the latter half of the 13th cent. onwards forms like
Gyl(l)yngham, Gyllingham, Gil(l)yngham are also common.

It has been suggested that this -*ingahām* name (as well as its
namesakes in K and Nf) contains a pers. name **Gylla*, possibly
an assimilated form of (or a pet-name for) **Gylda*; cf. Ritter
p. 205; Ekwall, PN in -*ing* pp. 128, 133, 136; PN BedsHu p. 60;
Karlström p. 50; PN D p. 85. Wallenberg, however, assumes
(p. 304) that Gillingham (K) should be interpreted as 'the *hām*
of the people living near the pool district', the base being an
OE **gyll, *gill* (cf. MHG *gülle* 'pool'), a word actually evidenced
in Sussex (*atte Gylle*) from 1404, see PN Sx p. 204 (s. n. In-
holms Gill) and Mawer, Problems of PN Study p. 78 f.[6] On
the score of topography a similar interpretation would seem
possible for the Dorset Gillingham, too.

Bugley

Bogeley 1275 RH, 1311 Ipm, *Bogeleigh* 1313 Cl
Buggeleye 1312 Fine, *Buggele(e)* 1316 Inq aqd, 1317 FF (all p[7])

---

[1] The identification is not absolutely certain; the charter (MS Cott. Aug.
II, 38) is starred by Kemble.

[2] Wm Malm has *Gillingeham*.

[3] Once *Gelingham* and once printed *Ingelingehā*.

[4] The *d* spellings (probably errors) occur only in P (four times).

[5] Abbreviated forms like *Gill[ingham]* 1136-7 France, and *Gilling'* 1135-54
1317) Ch, 1204 (etc.) ClR, are also met with.

[6] Cf. also Zachrisson, StNPh V, 17 n. 1.

[7] With the exception of the RH reference, all the forms recorded above
refer to one and the same person (*Wm de B.*).

This would seem to mean 'Bucge's clearing' (OE lēah); on this feminine pers. name cf. Crawford Ch. p. 56 f., Redin p. 115 (with literature) and PN BedsHu p. 253.

Eccliffe

Atteclive, Atteclyue 1244 *Ass* (p), *atte Clyue* 1333 *SR* (p)
Accliff 1811 OM

The *Johannes* 'at the cliff' (OE *æt þǣm clife*) mentioned in 1244 (*Ass*), occurs under Gillingham and in a context that makes the above identification extremely probable. The development must have been *atteclif* > *acclif* > *ecclif*; as late as 1861 the place was called Accliff Mill (Hutchins). Cf. EPN s. v. *æt*.

Ham Common

(the land of *Ghillingeham* called) *Hamme* 1152-8 Montacute
Hampe (*juxta Gillingham*) 1461 IpmR

OE *hamm*, here in the sense of 'land near a river', the place being near the river Lodden, a tributary of the Stour.

Huntingford

Huntingeford (2 ×) t. Hy III (14th) Cerne

Like Huntingford (Gl[1]) this name must originate from an OE *huntena ford* 'ford of the hunters'[2], especially as association with hunting is certain in this case, too. The above references occur among the boundary-marks (which begin and end with Huntingford) of a perambulation of the royal forest of Gillingham, at the end of which the text runs: *Infra vero predictos fines habet dominus Rex venationem suam — — —.*[3]

---

[1] See PN BedsHu p. 261; (Wo) is a misprint for (Gl).

[2] Cf. (*to*) *huntena forda* BCS 764 and Middendorff p. 78 (s. v. *hunta*).

[3] We shall return to this most interesting perambulation when discussing some identifications *infra*. I here, however, take the opportunity of suggesting an explanation of Lyemarsh Fm, just over the Wilts border. The text runs: — — — *ad Marches Dorsetie et Wiltesire. Et sic procedendo sicut Marche tendit inter dictos duos comitatus usque a la Leghe. De la Leghe semper per divisas comitatus — — —.* This is exactly the point where the present Lymarsh Fm is situated, and it is therefore very tempting to assume that the name means 'the boundary clearing', (OE *lēah* >) ME *lege, marche*; on the spelling *Lye-* cf. the local pronunciation of Leigh (2) *infra*.

Langham

Langehā, -ham 1156, 1157 PR, 1173 RBE, 1247 Ipm, 1309
Inq aqd, FF
Langhā, -ham 1158-9 (*et passim*) P, 1251-2 Fees (1268)
Langenham 1303 FA, 1316 FF *et passim* to 1495 Ipm
OE *lang* 'long' and *hām*.

Madjeston

Malg'eston 1205, 1206 ClR
Mager(e)ston 1256 FF, 1275 RH (p), 1303 FA, 1316 Ipm *et passim*
Mauger(e)ston 1266 FF, 1299 Ipm, *Mangirston*[1] 1273 Ipm
Magirstone 1278 Misc, 1285 FA, *Maggerston* 1420 IpmR
Mageston 1360 IpmR, 1361 Fine, 1371 FF *et passim*

I take this to mean '*Mæðelgar*'s farm', thus containing the
same pers. name as is found in Maugersbury (Gl): *mæþelgares
byrig, mæþelgeres byrig* BCS 882, *Mæðelgares byrig, Mædelgares
byrig* KCD 1365, *Malgaresbyr* 1251 Ch, and perhaps also in
Meagre (Hu).[2]
Tait (IPN p. 131) includes Madjeston among the so-called
hybrid pl.-ns in Dorset. It is true that *Malger*, a fairly common
pers. name in DB and later documents, is probably in most
cases of continental origin[3], but since there is nothing to indicate that Madjeston is a post-Conquest name, we are probably
more justified in looking for an OE pers. name in the first
element.

Milton on Stour

Miltetone, Mideltone 1086 DB
Mid(d)elton 1235-6 Fees (426), 1236 (?) ib. (607), 1242-3 ib.
(753), 1244 Ass (p) *et passim, Mildinton* 1287 Cl
Milton 1275 Cl, 1318 FF (*juxta Gillyngham*) *et passim*
Multon super Stoure 1397 IpmR, *Milton upon Stoure* 1429 FF
'Middle farm' (OE *middel, tūn*), probably so called because of
its position about halfway between Gillingham and Zeals.

---

[1] A clear mistranscription for *Maugirston* (which is the form in the index).
[2] See PN BedsHu p. 264 f.; cf. also the discussion (ib. p. 171) of Meppershall (Beds).
[3] See Forssner p. 184 (cf. also note 2).

Park Fm is named from Gillingham Park, often mentioned in earlier documents (1228 Cl, t. Hy III Cerne *et passim*).

Pierston Fm (6″)

  Poereston 1257 FF, *Poerstone* 1270 Hutchins[1], 1285 FA
  Peterstone 1278 Misc, *Petreston* 1316 FA
  Power(e)ston 1303 FA, 1305 Abbr, 1333 FF, 1428 FA
  Powkerston 1346 FA
  Poureston 1396, 1415 IpmR, *Pureston* 1481 IpmR
  Pyryston 1431 FA
  Preston (sic) 1811 OM, *Peeston, Person, Pierston* 1869 Hutchins

The early forms of this name are rather bewildering. If, however, we eliminate the two forms in *Peters-*, *Petres-* as probably due to a conscious attempt at making the name intelligible, it would seem that the first element contains the gen. of a pers. name which — whatever its ultimate origin may have been — had already about the middle of the 13th century coincided in form with the word *poor* (ME *pouere, poer, powere* etc.). *Poor(e)* was not unusual as a surname in ME times[2], and if Pierston is a post-Conquest name, the place may have been named after some owner bearing some such name. Tait (IPN p. 131) looks upon Pierston[3] as a doubtful case of a hybrid place-name.

Sandley

  Sandhull(e) 1316 Inq aqd, 1329 FF, 1330 Ipm, 1333 *SR*, 1346, 1428 FA
  Sandehull 1329 FF, *Sandhill* 1330 Orig (all p)

'Sand-hill', OE *sand, hyll*. The identification is not absolutely certain but very nearly so. For the later development of *-hull* to *-ley* cf. Whetley *infra* (in Broadwindsor).

---

[1] III, 663: Placita Forestæ, 54 Hy III, PRO.

[2] Cf. e. g. the famous Richard Poore, bishop of Sarum 1217-28, and see Bardsley s. n. *Poore* and *Power*. According to Weekley (Romance of Names pp. 99, 212, and Surnames p. 314 f.), the origin of the English surname *Power*, generally from AFr *le poure* 'the poor', may sometimes be OFr *Pohier* 'a Picard' (Weekley quotes Randulf *Puherius* and Roger *le Poher*). Another origin of *Poor(e)* and *Power* (from Latin *puer*) is vindicated by the editor of The Register of S. Osmund (II, LXXXIV ff.).

[3] Tait, misled by the indexer of FA, prints "Preston (?)". It is apparently the wrong form of the earliest OS map (1811) that reappears here.

Thorngrove is *Thorngrave, Thorngrove* 1313 Cl. Self-explanatory, OE *þorn, grāf(a)*.

Wyke Marsh is *Wyke* 1244 *Ass* (p), 1278 Misc, 1329 FF (p), 1414 FF, 1431 FA. OE *wīc* 'dairy-farm'.

Wyndlam Fm (6″)
Windelhā 1086 DB, Exon, *Windelham* 1285 FA
Wyndeleshā, Wyndessam, Wydelesham 1244 *Ass* (p)
Wyndelham 1276 FF, 1285 FA, 1303 FF, 1306 Abbr, 1481 IpmR
Wyndham 1278 Misc, *Wyldenham* 1333 FF

This DB manor has never been satisfactorily identified[1], but there can be no doubt that the above identification is correct. Wyndlam Fm is about half a mile ENE of Silton, very near the Stour. The name seems to be identical in origin with Windlesham (Sr): *Windlesham* 1227 Ch, *Wyndelesham* 1316 FA, *Wyndlesham* 1398 BM II.[2] The second el. may be either *hām* or *hamm* (probably the latter), and the first el. should be interpreted along the same lines as names like Windsor (Berks) and Broadwindsor (Do); see the latter name *infra*.

Hanford
Hanford 130 D 11
Hanford 1086 DB, 1212 Fees (91), 1230 ChancR, 1285 FA
Hamford 1197 FF, 1230 P, 1240, 1242 Ch, 1244 *Ass*, 1251-2 Fees (1268), 1278 QW, 1285 FA, 1291 Tax *et passim* to 1428 FA
Enforde 1210-12 RBE
Haunford 1228 Cl, 1240 FF
Hampford 1241 Ch, 1275 RH

The forms above seem to point to a derivation from OE (*æt þǣm*) *hēan ford* '(at the) high ford'. The exact meaning of a 'high ford' is somewhat difficult to understand. Mawer (EPN p. 34) suggests that *hēah* in some pl.-ns may have had the meaning 'chief' (as in 'high street'); another possibility is perhaps

[1] Hutchins is silent, and Eyton (p. 124) regards the name as lost.
[2] Hopwood (PN Sr p. 52) has apparently mixed up two distinct names under Windlesham.

that a 'high ford' may have been so called in contrast to another
ford lower down the river. — Just to the south, on the other
side of river, are Enford Bottom (1″) and Enford Fm (6″). This
would seem to indicate that the original *hēan ford* has been split
into two names, Hanford and Enford (cf. the form from RBE);
if, of these two places, Enford (Fm) marks the original site of
hēan ford, then the epithet 'high' may, in some way or other, refer
to the almost perpendicularly descending southern river-bank.

Iwerne Courtney

Iwerne Courtney [juːən] 130 D 11/12

  Werne 1086 DB[1], *Ywern(e)* 1212 Fees (91), 1292 Cl
  Iwern(e) 1219 Fees (260), 1242 Cl
  Iwerton' 1242 Cl
  Yuern Curtenay 1244 *Ass, Ywerne Curtenay* 1261 Ch
  Iwern(e) C(o)urtenay 1274 Ipm, 1285 Pat *et passim*

For the name Iwerne see Iwerne Minster *infra*. — There is
a detailed account of the history of the ancient family of *Courtenay*[2] in Hutchins (IV, 85, 88); Hawis(ia) de *Curtenei* (1212
Fees) is the first of that name mentioned in direct connexion
with this place. — The curious from *Iwerton'* (if not a mere
miswriting) is an interesting illustration of the Dorset tendency
of forming names in *-ton* even at a comparatively late period,
or may at least serve as an illustration of how loose the element
ton was; cf. e. g. Shillingstone and Melbury Bubb *infra*.

Iwerne Courtney is also called

Shroton [ʃroːtən]

  Shereueton 1374 FF, *Shereneton* (sic) 1388, 1455 FF
  Shrowton, Shroton 1632-3, 1679 DorchesterR

The editors of Hutchins (IV, 85) are evidently right in suggesting that the name is a "corruption of Sheriffstun from
having belonged to Baldwin the sheriff at the Domesday Survey"; OE *scīr-gerēfa* (ME *scirreve* etc.), *tūn*. This *Balduinus*

---

[1] Other DB references to places along the river Iwerne will be found *infra*
under Iwerne Minster, Steepleton Iwerne, Lazerton, and Ranston.

[2] In all probability originating from the town of Courtenay in France
(Loiret).

vicecomes was sheriff of Devon (not of Dorset)[1], and such was the case with his descendants, the *Courtenays*. Shrewton (W) is identical in origin[2], and so is evidently Shurton (So): *Sureveton* 1246 Ipm, *Shyrreneton* (sic) 1283 FF, *Serreveton* 1284-5 FA, *S(c)herreveton* 1296 Ch, 1303, 1346 FA, *Shereveston* 1316 FA, *Sherveton* 1428, 1431 FA; cf. also Sheriff Hutton (PN NRY p. 31).

Farrington [færiŋdən]

Ferendon(e) 1084 GeldRoll, 1212, 1219 Fees (91, 260), 1285 FA (p)

Ferdon' 1177-8 P (*Ferndone* ChancR)

Farendon(e) 1324 Inq aqd, 1327 Cl, 1333 *SR* (p), 1336 FF (p)

Farindon 1377 IpmR, *Faryngdon* 1412 FA

'Fern-grown down', OE *fearn, dūn*. In this name, as for instance in the identical Faringdon (Berks), the svarabhakti vowel between *r* and *n* has developed further and given a delusive *-ing*-type to the modern name; cf. *Coringdon infra*.

This seems to have been the earliest meeting-place of the Redlane hundred-court, cf. Hutchins IV, 56. The hundred appears under this name (*Ferendone, Ferdon*) up to 1219 (Fees)[3], but some thirty years later (1251-2 Fees) its name is definitely established as Redlane.

Ranston

Iwerne 1086 DB (cf. Eyton pp. 63, 137 f.)

Randolveston(e) 1274 Pat, 1277 Ch, Pat, 1285 FA *et passim*

Randelfestone 1274 Ipm, *Randelveston* 1316 FA

Randulveston(e) 1283 Ch, 1303 FA[4]

Randolfeston 1303 FA, 1350 Cl, 1431 FA, *Randalveston* 1346 FA

Randel(e)ston 1346, 1362 Orig, 1406 IpmR, 1455 FF

Randolfeston al. *Randeleston* 1399 IpmR

Randolston 1428 FA

'*Randolf*'s farm' (*tūn*), a ME pl.-n. of the hybrid type, cf. Tait in IPN p. 131. On the history of the name *Randolf* cf. W. H.

---

[1] See Eyton p. 74 and VCH Do II, 132.

[2] Ekblom p. 148; EPN p. 52.

[3] The four earliest forms above refer to the hundred-name.

[4] Clear miswritings like *Randulneston* (1278) need not be included.

Stevenson in Ancestor XII, 52 f., and Björkman, Nord. Personennamen p. 111. I am not able with certainty to trace the
Randolf after whom Ranston was named, but it is perhaps not
excluded that further investigation would carry us back to
Randulf le Meschin, earl of Chester (whose son and heir was
also called Randulf).[1]

Kington Magna

Kington Magna 130 A 8/9

   Chintone 1086 DB, *Kinton* 1203 Cur, 1206 ClR, 1252 Ch
   Kington(e) 1242-3 Fees (751, 753: *Magna*), 1256 FF *et passim*
   Kyngton(e) 1268 FF (*Magna*), 1274 Cl *et passim*
   Kington Ploket, Kingtonploket 1408, 1429 IpmR
   Machil Kyngton, Machelkyngton 1412 FA

This seems to be from OE *cyne-tūn* 'royal farm' or 'manor',
cf. the discussion in PNWo p. 330 s. n. Kington. *Ploket* from
the ancient lords, the *Plokenets* (*Plukenets, Plogenets*), the first
of whom, Alan *Plogenet*, was here at the end of the reign of
Henry III.[2] *Magna* in contrast to Little Kington in West Stour
parish *infra*. Here, as in so many other Do names, the struggle
between a Latin and an English addition (OE *micel*) ended in a
victory for the Latin word.

Nyland, Higher and **Lower** [nailənd]
   Iland 1086 DB, 1205 RC, *Inlande* 1086 DB
   Liland' 1212 Fees (87), *Lylande* 1236 FF
   [*La Eslond* 1285 FA[3]]
   Lay(e)lond(e) 1303, 1428 FA, *Lailond* 1346 FA

---

[1] In DB the above *Iwerne* was held by Robert Fitz Gerold. When he died
without issue, his estates may have fallen to his brother Roger, whose widow
later on married this *Randulf le Meschin*; cf. Dict. of Nat. Biogr. XLVII, 285.
This is, however, by no means certain, since Robert's estates seem to have
passed, not to Roger himself, but to his son, William de Roumare; cf. Eyton
p. 76, and VCH Do II, 137.

[2] Cf. Hutchins IV, 69; 1273 Ipm (p. 8); 1285 FA.

[3] This identification, given in the index of FA (II), is very doubtful, the
form being in all probability a mistranscription. Zachrisson (Anglia XXXIV,
323), misled by the identification in FA, looks upon the form as an early
instance of *s* having been introduced in the spelling. This view should probably be cancelled; *La Eslond* belongs to an entry under Uggescombe Hundred
(many miles from here) and cannot be identified.

le Ilonde 1420 ImpR, *Le Ylond*, *La Ilond* 1431 FA
Ilond 1477 IpmR, *Neylond* al. *Ilond* 1554 SoDoNQ VI

'Island', OE *īegland*, the word here taken in its extended
meaning of 'land in the midst of marshes'.[1] The modern form
shows an *n* in front of the name, apparently due to a misdivision of (*æt þǣm* >) *atten ilande* into *atte nilande*, see Zachrisson,
AN Infl. p. 131, and cf. Nayland (Sf)[2]: *Neiland* 1227 Ch, *Ley-
laund* 1235 Cl. For the frequent occurrence of the French
definite article[3] see Zachrisson, Anglia XXXIV, 323. The DB
form *Inlande*, if not merely a scribal error, may reflect confusion
with OE *inland* 'land in the lord's own occupation'.

Manston

Manston 130 C 10

Maneston(e) 1086 DB, 1230, 1232 Cl (p), 1244 *Ass et passim*
Manneston(e) 1235-6, 1242-3 Fees (425, 753) *et passim*
Manston(e) 1285 FA, 1297 Pat, 1303, 1346 FA, etc.

'Man(n)'s farm' (*tūn*), *Man(n)* being a well established OE pers.
name; cf. Redin p. 8.

Northwood Fm appears as *Northwode* in 1333 *SR* (p), and is consequently self-explanatory; OE *norð*, *wudu*.

Child Okeford

Child Okeford 130 D 11

Acford(e) 1086 DB, 1155 Montacute *et passim*
Chiltaneford (sic) 1210-2 RBE, *Chiltacford* 1211 Fees (91)
Childacford, *Childakford*, *Chyld Acford* 1227 FF, 1242-3 Fees
(753), 1284 Ipm *et passim*, *Childhacford* 1296 Ipm
Childocford, *Childokford* 1236 FF, 1274, 1307 Ipm *et passim*
Childokeford 1284 Cl, Ipm, *Childeokeford* 1431 FA

---

[1] The watercourses here are "liable to floods" (6"). I have also met people
from Nyland who complained of such troubles, in particular during the winter.
[2] See Skeat, PN Sf p. 76, and (for more forms) Zachrisson, Anglia loc. cit.
[3] The curious mistake made by Miss Serjeantson (Journal of Engl. and
Germ. Phil. XXVI, 357) in interpreting *Lay(e)lond*, *Lailond*, etc., as containing
OE *lēah* (!) shows the importance of identifying a form and of settling the
etymology of a name before drawing any conclusions in regard to ME dialectal
development of a certain OE vowel or diphthong.

Chyldacford al. *Childocford* 1310 Ipm
Childockeford 1396 IpmR

Other small variations in spelling are of little interest.[1]

'Oak ford', OE *āc, ford*. The exact sense of 'child' as the first element in pl.-ns (such as Chilton, Chilcote, etc.) is uncertain; see EPN s. v. *cild*. With regard to this particular name it should be mentioned that the editor of the Register of S. Osmund, W. H. Rich Jones, in his Introduction (Osmund II, LXXXV f.) advances the theory that, since *child* was used in the Middle Ages to denote men of a certain kind of knightly rank (and consequently as some sort of family-name?), *child* in Child Okeford may be a reminiscence of the time when the place was owned by Earl Harold (DB), whose father, the great Earl Godwin, is spoken of in an entry in ASC (s. a. 1009) as the son of Wulfnoth *child*.[2] These speculations are, of course, extremely uncertain, and must for the present be looked upon as mere guesses.[3] As late as the middle of the 12th century this Okeford was apparently in need of an addition to distinguish it from the two neighbouring Okefords, now Okeford Fitzpaine and Shillingstone (earlier *Okeford Shilling*), for whereas, in an entry from 1155 (Montacute and Dugdale), the two last-mentioned places are referred to as *Acforde Aluredi de Lincoln* and *Acforde Roberti Eskilling* respectively, the present Child Okeford is simply called "the other *Acforde*".

Fontmell Parva

Parva Funtemel 1360 FF, *Litil Funtymels* 1412 FA
Lytel Fountemel, Lytelfontemell 1431 IpmR, FA

Se Fontmell Magna *infra.*

---

[1] The following more or less corrupt forms may be noted: *Child Okfeld* 1306 Cl, *Chidocford* 1310 Fine, *Chyldayford* 1291 Tax and *Childeyford* 1428 FA, the last two forms having probably arisen from confusion with the name Hayward (Bridge) *infra.*

[2] *Brihtric Eadrices broðor ealdormannes forwregde Wulfnoð cild þone Suðseaxscian* (MS F: *Godwines fæder eorles*) *to þam cyning* (Plummer I, 138). The entry has been criticized (see Plummer II, 186), but the statement that Earl Godwin was the son of this Wulfnoth *child* seems to have been generally accepted; on Wulfnoth *child* cf. also Freeman, Norman Conquest I, 374 n. 2.

[3] Even if it can be shown that Godwin was the son of Wulfnoth, it remains to be proved *inter alia* that *child* was used not only as a temporary additional description for Wulfnoth but as a real additional name for his family, and that it continued to be used as such by Harold.

Hambledon Hill is (*on*) *hamelendune* (*north ecge*) 932 (15th) BCS
691. The elements are OE **hamel* and *dūn* (EPN), and the
meaning is probably 'scarred hill', as suggested in PN NRY p.
158 for the Yorkshire Hambletons.[1] On *hamel* and place-names
containing that el. see also Middendorff p. 65; Mawer, Namn
och Bygd IX, 56 ff. and English PN Study p. 3 f.; B. T. Suppl.
s. v. *hamel* (?). For Scandinavian parallels and a general discussion of the stem in question cf. Ad. Noreen, Namn och Bygd,
VI, 169 ff.

Hayward Bridge

> *Ryford'* (sic) 1278 QW, *Heyford, Hayford*[2] 1280-1 QW
> *Haifordesbrigge* 1337 DorchesterR
> *Eyford Bridge* c. 1540 Leland

I suppose this means the 'ford where hay grows' (OE *hēg,
ford*) or perhaps where it is transported. OE *hege* 'hedge' may
also be thought of. Cf. Highford in PN D p. 78, and Hayford
ib. p. 295.

Silton

Silton 121 H 9

> *Selton(e)* 1086 DB, 1194 P, 1222 ClR, 1236 (?) Fees (607), 1285
>   FA, 1297 Cl, Pat, 1314 BM I *et passim* to 1415 IpmR
> *Salton* 1291 Tax, 1303 FA, 1319, 1330 Ipm, 1340 NI, 1346,
>   1428 FA
> *Silton* 1333 *SR*, 1431 IpmR, FA, 1466 FF
> *Sylton* 1412, 1428 FA, 1535 VE

I take this to mean 'willow farm', OE *sealh, tūn*; cf. Salton
in PN NRY p. 57. As seen from the history of many Dorset
place-names, there seems to have existed a strong tendency in
this county towards the raising af [e] to [i] before a dental; cf.
Jordan § 34.

Feltham Fm is *Fyletham* 1327 *SR* (p). Probably identical in
origin with Feltham (So) and Fillham (D), see PN D p. 285.

---

[1] The Dorset Hambledon is a very irregular hill, the ground is mostly
rugged and uneven, and the camp is surrounded by several ramparts and
trenches (Hutchins). Viewed from some distance it gives a vivid impression
of something 'scarred'.

[2] Hutchins (IV, 79) gives a still earlier form "Hayford Bridge" from an
unprinted source (54 Hy III Forest Pleas, PRO).

If so, the meaning is 'hay enclosure', OE *filiðe*, *hamm*. Cf. Filford *infra*.

Slait Barn may be *Odeslade* c. 1311 Ipm, the context in which
this reference occurs making the identification very probable
though not absolutely certain. The elements are apparently OE
wudu 'wood' and *slæd*. In OE the latter word meant 'low flat
valley', whereas dial. *slade* has different meanings in different
parts of England (see Middendorff and EPN). In many dialects
(including Dorset) it means 'a valley, dell; a forest glade; the
side or slope of a hill', see NED and EDD. Slait Barn is on
a slope near an affluent of the Stour. The modern form shows
confusion with *sleight* (*slait*) 'a pasture, a sheep-walk' (sheep-
sleight), common in SW dialects; cf. NED (s. v. *sleight*) and
EDD (s. v. *slait*); see also the name Sleight *infra*.

Stour, East and West

East Stour [stauə] 130 A 10, **West Stour** 130 A 9
  Sture 1086 DB, 1304 Pat, *Stures* 1212 Fees (87), 1244 *Ass*
  Stures Cusyn Westou'e 1244 *Ass*
  Sture Cosin (*Cosyn*) 1285 FA, 1314 FF
  Sturewestovere, St(o)ure Westover(e) 1290 Ch, 1327 *SR*, 1412
    FA, 1462 IpmR, *Westouere* 1333 *SR*
  St(o)urewake, Stoure Wake 1327, 1333 *SR*, 1338 FF *et passim*
  Stoure Estouere 1371 FF, *Stoure Estover* 1462 IpmR

These places derive their names from their situation near the
river Stour. The early additional forms *Westovere* (*Westouere*)
and *Estoure* (*Estover*) seem to contain OE *ōfer* 'shore, bank' (ME
over), thus denoting the west and the east bank respectively, cf.
Hutchins III, 632. As appears from a passage in the Cartulary
of Cerne Abbey[1] (*per divisas domini Regis usque ad Boscum
Willelmi Cusin, scilicet de Stures, quod est de feudo Abbatisse de
Sancto Eadwardo.*[2] *De Bosco Willelmi Cusin cuntreval usque a
la Blakeuenne.*[3] — — —), Wm *Cusin* had land here early in

---

[1] Do Field Club XXIX, 196; Hutchins III, 662.
[2] *Abbatissa de Sancto Eadwardo* (i. e. the abbess of Shaftesbury) was the DB
owner of East and West Stour.
[3] See Black Venn *infra* (next name).

the reign of Henry III. The later distinctive name *Wake* is
from Ralph *Wake*, mentioned here in the time of Edward I (FA,
Ch, Pat). His family name survives in Stoke Wake and Caundle
Wake *infra*.

For the river-name Stour cf. Ekwall, ERN p. 379 ff.[1] The
other Dorset places named from the Stour are Stour Provost,
Sturminster Newton, Stourpaine, and Sturminster Marshall (all
infra).

Black Venn is *Blakefenne* 1270 Hutchins (Forest Pleas, PRO),
1275 RH (p), *la Blakeuenne* t. Hy III (14th) Cerne. 'Black fen',
OE *blæc, fenn*. For the voicing of *f* to *v* cf. Fifehead Magdalen
supra 4.

Little Kington Fm
  Chintone 1086 DB
  Parva Kynton 1238 FF, *Parva Kington'* 1242-3 Fees (753)
  Parva Kyngton(e) 1268 FF, 1285, 1303, 1346, 1428, 1431 FA
  Little Kyngton (*Kington*) 1273 Ipm, 1290 Ch, 1366 AD II
  Kyngton Parva 1462 IpmR
  See Kington Magna *supra* 12.

Stour Provost
Stour Provost 130 A 9
  Stur 1086 DB[2], *Stures Pratellorum* 1243 Cl
  Sture Pratell[is] 1285 FA, *Sture P'tell'* 1291 Tax
  Sture Prewes 1297 Pat, *Sturprewes* 1307 FF, *Stoure Prewes*
    1311 Cl
The forms run like this up to the end of the 15th century.
Then we have *Stoure Provys* 1535 VE
  See East and West Stour *supra* 16. This place takes its
distinctive name from the abbey of St Leger of Préaux (*de
Pratellis*) in Normandy, to which it was granted probably even
before the time of DB, cf. Eyton p. 76. The fact that it was
later on given by King Edward IV to (the Provost of) King's

---

[1] The charter forms for the Do Stour are (*on, anlang*) *sture* 944 (15th) BCS
793, (*of, on*) *stoure* 968 (c. 1350) BCS 1214.

[2] With the exception of the DB form, only such early forms are included
here as also contain the additional name.

College, Cambridge, may possibly have contributed to the perversion of its additional name; cf. Hutchins IV, 512 f.

Duncliffe (Hill and Wood)

   (*ad capud de*) *Dunclive* 1270 Hutchins (Forest Pleas, PRO)

   This 'hill-cliff' (OE *dūn, clif*) is a conspicuous topographical
feature (692 ft.) in the northern extremity of Blackmoor Vale.

Sutton Waldron

Sutton Waldron 130 C 12

   (*at, of*) *suttune* 932 (15th) BCS 691

   Sudtone 1086 DB, *Seitone* (sic) 1210-12 RBE (p. 550)

   Sutton(e), Suttun' 1212 Fees (91), 1216, 1222 ClR *et passim*

   Sotton(e) 1285, 1303 FA

   Sutton Walerand 1297 Cl, Pat *et passim*, the additional name
      being variously spelt *Walrond, Walraund, Walrand, Wallerond*

   'South farm or manor', OE *sūð, tūn*. The addition is from its
DB lord *Walerannus* (*Venator*) or perhaps rather from his family,
of whom we know that Walter *Walerand* or *Walerant* was here
at the beginning of the 13th cent., see 1210-12 RBE p. 550 and
1212 Fees p. 91. Cf. Hutchins IV, 107 and Eyton p. 65.

Todber

Todber [tɔdbə] 130 B 10

   Todeberie 1086 DB, *Todeberia* Exon

   Toteberg(a) 1174-94 Bruton, France, *Totebire* c. 1217 Sarum

   Tótdeberia, Totebera 1194 P

   Toddebir 1228 FF, *Toddebere* 1279, 1285 Ipm

   Todeber(e) 1244 *Ass*, 1285 FA, 1291 Tax *et passim* to 1362 Cl

   Todeberwe 1268 FF, *Todebur* 1316 FA

   Toteber(e) 1299 Bruton, 1303 FA, 1338 BM II, 1346 FA *et
      passim* to 1453 IpmR, *Totebeare* 1412 FF, *Totbere* 1479 IpmR

   The first difficulty here is the second element. As has been
shown in PN D p. 107 f. s. n. Shebbear, it is however almost
certain that names from this part of England which show a
series of ME forms like that of Todber, contain OE *bearu* 'grove,
wood'. In the absence of OE forms it seems impossible to be

sure about the first el.; cf. PN Sx p. 108 s. n. Todhurst, and
p. 144 s. n. Todhurst Fm. Se also Zachrisson, StNPh V, 3.

II. Sixpenny Handley Hundred

sexpene 1084 Geld Roll, *Sexpen* 1212 Fees (87), 1303, 1428,
    1431 FA, 15th *Harl. 61*, 1535 VE, *Sexpon* 1265 Misc
Sexpenne 1244 *Ass*, 1275 RH, 1303 FA, 1327 *SR et passim*
Sexepenne 1244 *Ass*, 1316 FA

hanglege 1084 Geld Roll, *Hanlegh(e)*, *Hanleg'* 1244 *Ass*
Henleg 1265 Misc, *Henleye* 1275 RH, *Henlegh* 1303 FA, 1333
    SR, *Henleigh* 1316 FA, *Hennele* 1327 *SR*, *Henle* 1340 NI
    Hanle 1431 FA

These names represent two originally distinct hundreds. From
the 13th century onwards, however, they are mostly mentioned
together and seem at a fairly early date to have been united or
confused (cf. Hutchins III, 534), perhaps owing to the fact that
they both belonged to the abbess of Shaftesbury.

When trying to find out whether there existed any traces of
the name *Sexpenne* on modern maps, I started from Eyton's
assumption (p. 143) that the meeting-place of the hundred-court
was somewhere near Iwerne Minster (130 C 12). I then found
a certain John de *Sexepenne* mentioned in 1340 (NI) under the
parish of Fontmell Magna (130 C 12), and this led me to believe
that the present Pen Hill (356 ft.), a mile W of Fontmell Magna,
might in reality be the old *Sexpenne*. This on the other hand
made me suspect that the boundary-mark *on ðæs lutlen searpennes
suð eke* in BCS 691 (land at Fontmell) belonged here, and that
the word *searpennes* might be a mistake for *seaxpennes*.[1] When
later on (July 1929) I had the opportunity of looking at the MS
(Harl. 61), I found that such was the case, the letter *x* in *seaxpennes* (which in the MS shows a strong resemblance with an *r*)
having been mistaken for an *r* by Birch.[2] Not until that little

---

[1] Not until long afterwards did I notice that this is the reading in KCD
361 (vol. III, 409).

[2] Other mistranscriptions in the same charter are discussed under Blynfield
Fm *infra*.

discovery was made, had I the opportunity of carefully examining the 6″ map for that part of the county, and I then found to my great surprise that, only a few hundred yards W of Pen Hill, there is still a little farm called Sixpenny.

The situation of Pen Hill (and Sixpenny Fm) is roughly in the centre of the ancient *Sexpenne* Hundred, corresponding to the present parishes of Melbury Abbas, Compton Abbas, Fontmell Magna, East and West Orchard, and Iwerne Minster.

Sixpenny (*Sexpene*) has been interpreted by Zachrisson (Romans p. 49) as 'the Saxons' mountain top' (OE *seaxa pen*), the second el. being British *pen* 'head, top'. The absence of a medial vowel in *seaxpennes* and in the majority of ME forms seems however to speak against a base *seaxa* (gen. plur.). I suppose the first el. is OE *seax*. This is recorded only in the meaning 'knife, short sword', but an older sense of 'cliff, stone', preserved in place-names, seems very likely; cf. e. g. Förstemann, Ortsnamen 654 s. v. *sahs*.

For the second part of the hundred-name cf. Handley *infra*.

Cann

Cann [kæn] 130 A 12

Canna t. Hy I (15th) *Harl. 61, Canne* 1323 Inq aqd, 1371, 1437 FF

Cann is situated in the bottom of a deep valley, the sides of which are extremely steep, and it may therefore be suggested that the name goes back to OE *canne* 'can, cup, vessel', used in some topographical sense such as 'valley-basin' or the like; cf. Canwell (St) for the first el. of which Duignan (p. 33) suggests the same derivation.[1] Cf. Canford Magna *infra*.

Anketil's Place (site of) (6″) preserves the memory of the ancient *Anketil* family, cf. the detailed pedigree in Hutchins (III, 61 ff.). My earliest reference is Roger *Anketil* 1244 Ass. *Anketil* is the Norman or normanized form of the common OScand. pers. name *Asketill*, see Björkman, Nord. Personennamen p. 16 ff. The name still survives in Dorset in the form of *Antell*, cf. C. H. Mayo in Do Field Club XV, 43. Cf. also Antell's Fm (6″) in Marnhull.

---

[1] Recently the same derivation has been suggested for a number of Devon names, see PN D p. 481 s. n. Canna.

Barton Hill (6″)

La Bertone 1293 Ch, *Barton* 1535 VE

OE *bere-tūn* 'barley-farm', cf. EPN s. v., and Ekwall, PN La p. 38 (with literature). This was the demesne farm of Shaftesbury.

Blynfield Fm

Blingesfeld(a) c. 1140 BM I, 1154-8 (1340) Ch
Blinchesfeld(a) c. 1140 (1340) Ch, c. 1140 Dugdale[1], c. 1160 (?)
    ib.[2], 1244 *Ass* (p), *Blinchisfeld* 1167-8 P (*Blinchesfeld* ChancR)
Blinchildfeld 1168-9, 1169-70 P
Blinkefeld 1175-6 P (*Blinkisfeld* ChancR)
Blinchefeld 1244 *Ass*, 1275 Cl, *Blynchefeld* 1258 FF (all p)
Blyndefeld 1244 *Ass*, 1274 FF, *Blindefeud* 1244 *Ass* (all p)
Blintisfeld 1333 *SR* (p), *Blyntesfeld* 1340 NI (p), 1360 IpmR
Blyndesfeld 1333 *SR* (p), 1442 IpmR, *Blintesfield* 1811 OM

To this list of forms should in all probability be added (*on*) *blinnesfeld* in BCS 1033 (cf. Hutchins III, 24), and as the boundary-points of that charter coincide to some extent with those of another Shaftesbury charter, BCS 691, the boundary-mark (*to*) *hlinchesfelde* in the latter charter would seem to have something to do with this place, too. An examination of the MS (Harl. 61, 15th cent.) revealed to me that *hlinchesfelde* in BCS 691 is almost certainly a misreading for *blinchesfelde*, and that *hlinches broc* in the same charter is clearly *blinches broc* in the MS. Consequently there can be little doubt that *hlinchesfelde* (i. e. *blinchesfelde*) belongs here, and that also *hlinches broc* (i. e. *blinches broc*) must have some connexion with the origin of Blynfield. But I can offer no plausible suggestion for the etymology of the name.

In the four Pipe Roll forms quoted above Blynfield appears as the name of a hundred, probably another name for Alcester Liberty.

Compton Abbas

Compton Abbas [kɔmtən] 130 B 12

Cumtune (3 ×) 956 (15th) BCS 970[3], *Cuntone* 1086 DB

---

[1] IV, 175 (No. I, late copy).   [2] IV, 177 (No. VIII).

[3] *Cumtune, Kuntune* 871 (15th) BCS 531, 532 should, according to VCH Do II, 73, be identified with Compton Basset (W).

Cu'pton, Cumpton 1278 QW, 1342 Orig

Compton 1278 QW, 1291 Tax, 1327 *SR*, 1330 Cl *et passim*

Cumpton Abbatisse 1293 FF, *Compton Abbatisse* 1340 NI

'Valley farm', OE *cumb, tūn*. I have not found the pronunciation [kʌmtən] for any of the Dorset Comptons (cf. EPN p. 20). There is nothing surprising in that, since Standard English [ʌ] in this position is often rendered by [ɔ] in the Do dialect, cf. Wright, EDG § 101. Compton Abbas belonged to the abbess of Shaftesbury; hence its distinctive name.

Sturkel (lost)

    (*to*) *stirchel* (*an lang streames*, etc.) 932 (15th) BCS 691

    (*to*) *stirthel*, (*ouer*) *stirtel* 939 (15th) BCS 744

    (*on*) *stirchel* (*anlang streames*, etc.) 956 (15th) BCS 970

    Sturkel 1244 *Ass* (p), (aqua de) *Sturkel* 1278, 1280-1 QW

    Sturcul (ident. prob.) 1276 Cl

    (aqua de) *Sterkel* 1280-1 QW, *Sturtel* 1340 NI (p)

Ekwall's suggestion (ERN p. 382) that *Sturkel* is (or rather was) the name of the little stream which rises near Melbury Abbas and runs past West Orchard to the Stour at Manston is apparently correct, for in Hutchins (I, LXXXI) it is stated that some meadows in Twyford (in this parish) are called Sturkel Meadows. No such name, however, can be found on any old or modern map, so the name is probably lost now.

Ekwall (loc. cit.) takes *Sturkel* to contain the river-name Stour (OE *Stūr*), and looks upon *Sturkel* as a diminutive of *Stūr* (*Stȳrcel or the like, possibly from OE *Stȳrincel).

Fontmell Magna

Fontmell Magna [fɔntməl[1]] 130 C 12

    Funtamel (rivus) 704 (15th) BCS 107

    ffuntemel, Funtemel 871 (15th) BCS 531, 532

    Ffuntemel, Funtemel, funtmel 932 (15th) BCS 691

    funtemel, (*anlang*) *funtmeales* 939 (15th) BCS 744

    funtemel (*forð*) 963 (15th) BCS 1115

---

[1] This seems to be the only pronunciation heard nowadays, but old people have told me that pronunciations such as [fʌntməl, fʌməl] were not uncommon in their childhood.

Fontemale 1086 DB
Funtemel 1201 Cur (p), 1278 QW, 1329 Pap
Fontemel(l) 1258 Pap, 1291 Tax, 1303 FA *et passim*
Fontimel 1303, 1346 FA, *Fountymell* 1428 FA
Fountemel(l) 1345, 1346 FF, 1428 FA, *Fountmell* 1535 VE

Fontmell Magna and Parva (*supra* 14) take their names from Fontmell Brook which rises a few hundred yards E of F. Magna and falls into the Stour near F. Parva.

The name has been dealt with by Zachrisson (Romans p. 52) and Ekwall (ERN p. 161 f.) who seem to agree that it is a compound of OE *funta* (or a British form of Latin *fontāna*) 'spring, brook', and OCeltic **mailo-*, Welsh *moel* 'bare, bare hill'.

Bedchester [bedʒestə]
Bedeshurst(e) 1354, 1372, 1374 FF, 1431 FA, 1535 VE
Bedehurst 1392 IpmR, 1412 FA, *Bedcister* 1811 OM

The second el. is OE *hyrst* 'wooded height', and to judge from the above list of forms, the first may possibly be the OE pers. name *Bǣde* (Redin p. 125); cf. Beeson (earlier *Bedeston*) in PN D p. 333. What complicates the thing, however, is that in the unprinted part of the Shaftesbury Register (cf. Hutchins III, 556) we have a form *Butesursta* which probably belongs here.[1] This again leads us to believe that the boundary-mark (*up on*) *beteswirþe sled* in BCS 691 (15th) may have some connexion with the present name, too. But more early forms are needed to establish this possible connexion. For the present the interpretation of the first el. in Bedchester had better be left open.

The late transformation of *Bedeshurst* into Bedchester has a parallel on Dorset territory in the name Hogchester (earlier *Hoggeshurst*) *infra*. Zachrisson, who deals with this interesting analogical transformation in his AN Infl. (pp. 78-82), accounts for the old forms of Penshurst (K), showing vacillation between *Penshurst* and *Penecestre*, in two different ways (ib. p. 81): *Pens(h)erst* > **Pensert* > **Pensetr* (by metathesis of *r*), or *Pens(h)erst* > **Pensestr* (keeping of *s* and shifting of *r*). The list of early forms for Hogchester *infra* shows that the latter of

---

[1] I have checked the form *Butesursta* in the MS (*Harl. 61*) and also ascertained that it occurs at least two or three times there (f. 63).

Anton Fägersten

Zachrisson's alternatives may be applicable to the Dorset names. There is, however, perhaps a third possibility of accounting for the process. In *Bedeshurst* (and *Hoggeshurst*) *r* may have been lost at a fairly late date, as was evidently the case with Holnest (from earlier *Holenhurst*) *infra*; *Bedsest was then a suitable starting-point for an analogical transformation into *Bedsester (*Bedcester*), after which the French spelling *-cester* easily gave rise to its English equivalent *-chester*. Bedchester and Hogchester seem to be the only *hurst*-names hitherto found in England in which the analogical transformation into *chester*-names has been preserved up to the present time.[1]

Hill Fm is *atte Hulle* 1333 *SR* (p). Self-explanatory, OE *hyll*.

Longcombe Bottom may be (*to*) *langencumbes hauede* 932 (15th) BCS 691. At any rate the names are identical in origin. 'Long valley', OE *lang*, *cumb*.

Sixpenny Fm (6″). — See the hundred-name *supra* 19 f.

Woodbridge
   (*on*) *wde brigthe*, (*to*) *wde bricge*, *wdebrige* 932 (15th) BCS 691
   (*oð*) *wdebrige*, (*of*) *wudebricge* 963 (15th) BCS 1115
   Self-explanatory, OE *wudu*, *brycg*.

Handley
Handley 131 B 2
   Hanlee 871 (15th) BCS 531, 956 (15th) BCS 970
   Henlee 871 (15th) BCS 532
   (*at*) *heanlegen* 956 (15th) BCS 970
   Hanlege 1086 DB, *Hanleg(h)* 1244 *Ass*
   Hanleige 1166 RBE (p) (*Hanlege* LN)
   Henle 1181-2 P, 1265 Misc, 1291 Tax, 1340 NI, 1428, 1431 FA
   Henleg', *-legh(e)* 1212 Fees (87), 1249 FF *et passim* to 1428 FA
   Hanle 1230 Cl (p), 1325 FF (*juxta Craneburn*)

---

[1] That such false *chester*-names may deceive people, is shown from a somewhat curious passage in Kelly's Directory of Dorsetshire (ed. 1923, p. 2) where Bedchester and Hogchester together with other Do places of equally humble origin, are spoken of as Roman settlements (!).

OE (*æt þæm*) *hēan lēage* '(at the) high clearing', cf. EPN s. v.
hēah. Cf. Henley *infra* (in Buckland Newton).

Dean is *la Denn(e)* 1278, 1280-1 QW, *Dene* 1333 *SR* (p), 1340
NI (p). OE *denu* 'valley'. Cf. Dean (Fm and Hill) *infra*.

Frogmore Fm (6″) is *Froggemere, Froggem'* 1244 *Ass* (p). 'Frog-
pool', OE *frogga, mere*. The well-known confusion between OE
mere 'pool, (mere)' and OE *mōr* 'swampy ground, (moor)' is particularly common in this name; cf. Frogmore Dairy Ho, Frogmore
Hill and Fm, and Frog Lane Fm, all *infra*.

Gussage St Andrew[1]
Gissic 871 (15th) BCS 531, *Gersicg* ib. 532
Gersiz 1205 RC, *Gessich* 1242 Ch, 1244 *Ass*, *Gesriche* 1244 *Ass*
Gissik St. Andrews 1258 Ch
Gyssich St. Andrew 1260 FF, *Gissiche St. Andrew* 1268 FF
Gussich(e) c. 1270 Sarum, 1303 FA, 1307 Pat *et passim*
Gissich St. Andrews, Gisshych' Sči Andr' 1278 Cl, QW
Gussuch, Gussych(e) 1324 Inq aqd, 1395 IpmR (*Sancti Andree*)
Gussage Sči Andree 1535 VE

Seè Gussage All Saints *infra*. 'St Andrew' from the dedication
of the chapel.

Minchington
Munecheneton 1307 Pat
Gussich Mu(n)chenton 1314 (15th) *Harl. 61* (f. 98 f.)[2]
Gussich Menechenton 1324 Inq aqd
Gissych Monek Hampton 1332 FF
Gussich Monechynton 1340 FF
Gussichmincheueton (sic) 1387 FF

OE *myn(e)cena-tūn* 'the nuns' farm', so called because it belonged to the nunnery of Shaftesbury. It is near Gussage St
Andrew.

---

[1] Gussage St Andrew, Gussage St Michael (in Badbury Hundred), and Gussage All Saints (in Knowlton Hundred) are near each other, and the names
are identical. It is therefore sometimes extremely difficult to be sure to which
of the three places an early form refers when it appears without a distinctive
addition. Doubtful cases have as a rule been included under G. All Saints
infra.

[2] Cf. Hutchins III, 547.

Woodcutts

Wodecote 1244 *Ass* (p), Abbr (p), 1307 Pat, 1396 (etc.) IpmR
Estwodecotes 1387 FF, *Wodecotys* 1456 FF

'Cottages by the wood', OE *wudu, cot(e)*. In Hutchins the
name is still spelt *Woodcotes*, or *Woodcotts*.

Iwerne Minster

Iwerne Minster [juːən] 130 C 12

Ywern 871 (15th) BCS 531, *Hywerna* ib. 532
Iwern (3 ×) 956 (15th) BCS 970
Evneminstre 1086 DB
Ywern(e), Ywerne Minstre 1227 FF, 1303 FF *et passim*[1]
Iwerne, Iwern(e) Menstre (*Munstre, Mynstre, Minstre*) 1278 QW,
    1291 Tax, 1316 FA, 1345 FF *et passim*

Other forms show little variation (cf. next name).

The little river Iwerne rises at Iwerne·Minster and gives
name also to Iwerne Courtney *supra* 10 and Steepleton Iwerne
infra; it is *iwern broc* in 958 (15th) BCS 1033. Ekwall (ERN
p. 222) considers the name to be Celtic, the elements being the
stem **iu̯o-* (W *yw, ywen*) 'yew' and the suffix *-erno* (*-ernā*).
Professor Zachrisson would take it to be English, containing OE
iw 'yew' and *ryne* 'running, flow' (cf. Wallenberg, StNPh II, 95).
In either case the meaning would be 'yew river'.

The church of Iwerne Minster (OE *mynster*) must have been
of importance even in the time of DB.

Hill Fm is *Hill(e)* 1086 DB, 1346 FA (*Parvo*), 1391 IpmR (*juxta
Ywernemynstre*), 1428 FA (*Parva*), *Hull(e)* 1303 FA, 1327 Ipm,
1336 FF (*juxta Ywerneministre*), 1350, 1352 Cl, 1377 Cl (*by
Ywermynstre*), 1412 FA, 1420 IpmR. Self-explanatory, OE *hyll*.

Pegg's Fm is *Pegges* (maner') 1390, 1408 FF, 1469, 1484 IpmR
and takes its name from the *Peg* family, according to Hutchins
(III, 540) mentioned as tenants here in the Shaftesbury Register
(*Harl. 61*). Cf. John and Robert *le Peg* 1317 FF, and Michael
Peg 1340 NI, all under this parish.

---

[1] *Ywerne* is the usual form in the Shaftesbury Register (*Harl. 61*, 15th cent.).

Preston Ho

It is not always easy to distinguish this place from the other Prestons in Do, but in all probability the following references belong here:

Preston(e) 1345 (*juxta Shaftesbury*), 1354 (near *Iywerne Court-ney*), 1372 (*juxta Sheftebury*), 1374 (*juxta Shereueton*) FF, 1376, 1377 Cl (in the parish of *Ywerne Minstre*), 1388, 1455 FF (*juxta Shereneton*). 'Priests' farm', OE *prēost, tūn.* It is near Iwerne Courtney or Shroton, but about 6 m. distant from Shaftesbury.

Melbury Abbas

Melbury Abbas 130 B 12

at *Meleburge imare, on meleberig dune* 956 (15th) BCS 970[1]
Meleberie 1086 DB, (super montem de) *Melebur'* 1251 Cl
Melleber, Melebyr' 1278 QW
Mel(e)bury, Mel(e)bury Abbatisse 1291 Tax, 1303, 1316 FA,
     1329 Ipm, 1333 *SR*, 1340 NI *et passim, Est Melbury* 1495 Ipm

Melbury Abbas belongs to a group of place-names the first el. of which (ME *Mele-, Melle-*) has already been the object of much discussion. Zachrisson's view (Romans p. 52) that this el. goes back to OCeltic **mailo-* 'bare' (cf. Fontmell Magna *supra* 22) has been criticized by Ekwall (Namn och Bygd XVII, 168) who takes it to be an OE adj. **mǣl(e)* 'variegated' (cf. *un-mǣle* 'spotless').[2] Recently the problem has been discussed again by the editors of PN D (p. 203 f. s. n. Meldon) who come to the same conclusion as Ekwall. To this may be added that one would have expected an OE (*æt*) *mǣlan beorge* to have been shortened at a fairly early date, and the almost total absence of ME *Male*-spellings is therefore hardly in favour of the etymology suggested. It should further be noted that the charter forms for the place-name (Mill Barrow in Hants, SW of Kilmeston) which is generally supposed to give the clue to this group of names, are in themselves conflicting: *to meolæn beorge* BCS 620 (Harl. 43), *to meolan beorge* ib. 621 (Cod. Wint.; copy of BCS

---

[1] (*on*) *mealeburg* (*norþewarde*) ib. may be identical in origin but would seem to refer to some spot near Handley (131 B 2), about 8 or 9 miles E of Melbury Abbas.

[2] Melcombe (Regis, Horsey) may be a different case.

620), *on mælan beorh*[1] ib. 622 (Cod. Wint.), *(on) melan beorh,*
(of) mælan beorge ib. 731 (Cod. Wint.), *(neah) mælan beorge, (bæ
supan) melan beorge* ib. 1077 (Cod. Wint.).[2] The whole problem
of *Mel*-names should probably be reconsidered, but I can myself
give no contribution to a solution. The second el. of Melbury
is apparently OE *burh*. Like Compton Abbas *supra* 21 this
place belonged to the abbess of Shaftesbury; hence its distinctive name.

Motcombe

Motcombe 121 I 11

Motcumbe 1244 *Ass* (p), t. Hy III (14th) Cerne, Edw II Ipm
Motecumb 1244 *Ass* (p), *Mot(t)ecombe* 1413, 1430 IpmR
Moucumb 1275 RH (p), *Motcombe* 1535 VE

It has been suggested that Motcombe (Sx) is a compound of
OE *(ge)mōt* 'meeting-place' and *cumb* 'valley'[3], and it is evident
that the same explanation must be true of the Dorset name too.
In charter material the word *(ge)mōt* is particularly common in
compounds with *lēah* and *beorg*, e. g. *(in) gemotleage* BCS 476,
(to, of) Motlege ib. 610, *(to) gemot leage* ib. 1213; *(on þæne) gemot
beorh* ib. 392, *(on) gemot biorh* ib. 702, *(on) Motbeorh, (of) Mot-
beorge* KCD 741 (Do); cf. Middendorff p. 58. Two places called
Modbury *infra* apparently go back to OE *(ge)mōtbeorg*. Cf. Mutley
and Modbury in PN D pp. 235, 279.

Bittles Green, about a mile N of Shaftesbury, should probably
be associated with the boundary-mark *(on) bytelesmor, (of) biteles-
more*[4] 958 (15th) BCS 1026, interpreted by Middendorff (p. 23)
and van Zandt Cortelyou (p. 13) as containing (the genitive of)
OE *bitel(a)* 'beetle'; see also Björkman, ESt LII, 178 (with a long
list of names of this type). Ritter (p. 191 n. 3) takes the gen.

---

[1] It is from this charter form that B. T. Suppl. postulates the adj. *mǣle*
'marked, spotted'.

[2] The editors of PN D (loc. cit) are themselves uncertain as to what authority
should be given to the form *meolæn (meolan)*. Is perhaps Grundy's assumption
(Arch. Journal LXXVIII, 150 n. 1) that *eo* is a corruption due to the previous
meoluc cumbe, worthy of consideration?

[3] PN Sx p. 431.

[4] According to Hutchins (III, 6), the form *Bytellesmore* occurs in a 15th
cent. court-roll.

-es rather to speak in favour of a pers. name[1]; on this intricate question cf. also Mawer, MLR XIV, 233 ff.[2]

Cowridge Copse (6″) is *Kurhigge* (2 ×) t. Hy III (14th) Cerne (cf. Hutchins III, 662). Self-explanatory, OE *cū, hrycg.*

Enmore Green is probably to be associated with Johannes de *Enedem'e* (i. e. *Enedemere*) 1275 RH, one of the many small land-holders under Gillingham manor mentioned in RH I, 101 f. The name means 'duck-pool', OE *ened, mere.* For the modern form *-more* cf. Frogmore Fm *supra* 25.

Fernbrook Fm is *Fernbroc, Farnbroc'* 1251 Cl, *Ferenbroken* 1275 RH (p). Self-explanatory, OE *fearn, brōc.*

Frog Lane Fm is to be compared with *vroggemere* t. Hy III (14th) Cerne, *Froggem'e, Froggesmere* 1275 RH (p), *Frogmere* 1340 NI (p). See Frogmore Fm *supra* 25.

Kingsettle Fm is *Kingessetle* 1270 Hutchins (Forest Pleas, PRO), t. Hy III (14th) Cerne, *Kaingessetle* (sic) t. Hy III (14th) Cerne, *Kynggessecle* (sic) 1275 RH (p), *Kingessettle* 1285 FA (p), *Kynges-settle* 1327 *SR* (p), 1340 NI (p), *-setle* 1333 *SR* (p). Literally this means 'king's seat' (OE *setl*), but, as suggested in PN D p. 201 s. n. Kingsett, places-names of this type may originally have been hill-names, 'king's seat' signifying perhaps a lofty spot. Kingsettle Fm is on the slope of a prominent hill. A tradition that King Alfred the Great rested here on his way from Athelney to *Epan dune* (cf. ASC s. a. 878) should probably not be taken too seriously.[3]

Sherborne Causeway

I have not found any reference to this old *chaussée* between Sherborne and Shaftesbury earlier than in Leland (V, 110): *the*

---

[1] Cf. the discussion in PN NbDu p. 21 s. n. Biddlestone.

[2] For the evidence of a pers. name **Byttel* (or **Bittel*), not on independent record, cf. e. g. PN Bk p. 41 f. s. n. Biddlesden, Karlström p. 157, and PN D p. 187 s. n. Beechcombe; I am not convinced that all the pl.-ns adduced there contain a pers. name.

[3] Cf. J. J. Reynolds, The Ancient History of Shaftesbury p. 7.

causey that ledithe to Scheftesbyry (cf. Hutchins IV, 296). See NED s. v. *causey*.

Woodsend Fm is *Wodeshende* 1275 RH (p), *atte Wodeheynde* 1333 *SR* (p). Self-explanatory, OE *wudu, ende*.

Orchard, East and West

East Orchard 130 B 11, **West Orchard** 130 C 10
    Archet 939 (15th) BCS 744, 963 (15th) ib. 1115, 1175-6 P (p)
    (*on*) *archet hamm* 939 (15th) BCS 744
    (*on*) *arcetham*, (*of*) *archethamme* 958 (15th) BCS 1033
    Orchet 1330 Cl (p)
    West Orcharda 1535 VE

This name has been dealt with by Ekwall (Anglia Beiblatt XXXVI, 149), who takes it to contain Brit *cēt* 'wood' (W *coed*), the whole name thus being identical with W *argoed* 'shelter of wood' (literally 'on-wood'). *Archet* regularly developed into *Orchet* (1330 Cl), and popular etymology apparently did the rest.

Hartgrove has been confused with Yardgrove *infra* (in Marnhull) and possibly also with Hargrove *infra* (in Stalbridge). The only references which certainly belong here are *Harcgrave* 1254 FF, and *Hargrove* 1535 VE. The material is scanty, and it is difficult to be sure whether the first el. is OE *hār* 'grey' (possibly in its transferred sense of 'boundary') or *hara* 'hare', cf. EPN s. v. *hār*. The fact that Hartgrove is on the bounds of East Orchard and Fontmell Magna would seem to speak in favour of the former alternative. The second el. is OE *grāf(a)* 'grove'. The *t* of the modern form is apparently a very⁄late intrusion, Hutchins (in 1868) still calling the place *Hargrove*.

Key Brook
    cagbroc, (*anlang*) *cagbroges* 939 (15th) BCS 744

This would seem to contain OE *cǣg*, but in what sense is impossible to say.[1] That OE *cǣg* 'key' may have had some unrecorded earlier sense is suggested by Ekwall in PN La p. 100

---

[1] Middendorff (p. 23) takes *cagbroc* to contain the dial. word *cag* 'a small cask, keg'. This supposition is contradicted by the modern name of the brook.

s. n. Cayley; cf. the river Key in Wilts, of which the earlier name *Worvinchel* is a derivative of *Worf* 'the winding stream', see Ekwall, ERN p. 470.

Shaftesbury

Shaftesbury 130 A 11/12

Shafton(e) 833 (15th) BCS 410, 860 (15th) ib. 499

Sheftesbury (rubr.), *Sceaftesburi* 871 (15th) BCS 531, *Scepto-niensis* (eccl.) ib. 532

Schaftesbiry 932 (15th) BCS 691, *-buri* 935 (15th) ib. 708, 984 (15th) KCD 641, *-bury* 966 (15th) BCS 1186

Shaftesbury (rubr.) 942, 956, 958 BCS 775, 970, 1026 (all 15th)

Sceafnesbirig 955 (14th) BCS 912, *Schaftysbury* ib. 913, (monast.) *Septoniæ* ib. 914

Sceaftesburi 956 (15th) BCS 970, *-byrig* s. a. 982 ASC (C), c. 995 (orig.) KCD 1290, s. a. 1036 ASC (E), *-byriȝ* 979-1015 (14th) LibHyda, *-byri* s. a. 1035 ASC (D)

Sceaftesberi, Scaftesberi 958 (15th) BCS 1026

Scæftes byrig s. a. 980 ASC (E), *Sceftesbirio* 1001 (15th) KCD 706, *Sceftes byrig* s. a. 1035 ASC (C)

(ad) Sceftoniam s. a. 980 ASC (F), Sim Durh[1]

Sceaftesbirig, Sceftesbyrig, Scæftesbyrig c. 1000 Saints

scæftenesbyrig 1015 (orig.) Earle p. 225, *Sceaftenes byrig* c. 1015 BM II, *Sceaftenesbyrig* n. d. (12th) KCD 722

Sceptesberie, Sceftesberie 1086 DB

Sceftesbiry, Scaftecbyria, Seftesbiria 1154-5 (etc.) RBE

Shaftesberia 1155 (etc.) PR, 1158-9 (etc.) P *et passim*

Saftesbur', Saftisbur' 1194 Cur (P XIV), *Saftesberi* 1201 Cur

Later forms show only slight variation. *s*-less forms like *S(c)hafte-, S(c)hefte-* are fairly common from 1186-7 (P) onwards. Latinized forms occur frequently: *S(c)hefton(ia)* 1260 FF, 1265 Misc, 1275 RH, 1278 Misc, QW *et passim*, *Schaftona* 1275 RH, *S(c)hafton(ia)* 1275 RH, 1278 QW, Cl, 1282 BM I *et passim*,

---

[1] Other forms in ME chronicles are *Sceftesburg* (Asser, Sim Durh), *Sceaftes-byrig* (FlorWorc), (Hereluve) *Sceaftesbyriensis* (ib.), *Scestoniæ, Sceafstesbyrig* (Sim Durh), *Sephtonia* (GeoffrMon), *Cestebire* (Wace), *Septonia, Septuna* (Higden), *chasterbury, Septone, ssaftesbury, -buri* (RobGl), *Sceofoniense* (monast.), (apud) *Sceftoniam, Scephtoniam* (WmMalm), *Scef(f)tonia* (WmMalmP); cf. also (— — — urbem) *Septoniæ* quod est *Shaftisbiri* (LibHyda), (monasterio) *Septoniense* (ib.).

S(c)haston 1275 RH, 1304 Pat, 1311 FF, 1368 Orig, 1380 Cl[1],
(burgus) *Shastonie* 1426 BM I; rare spellings are *Scheston* 1275
RH, 1291 Tax, *Sefton* 1293 Ipm, and *Shapton* 1313 Cl.

Shaftesbury has recently been dealt with by Ekwall (Studies
on PN p. 12), who assumes that there must have been two forms
of the name, (1) *Sceaftesburg*, containing **Sceaft*, the name of the
founder of the place, and (2) *Sceaftenesburg*, containing the longer
name **Sceaften* (< **Sce(a)ftīn*), used as a hypocoristic side-form.
For a few pers. names of this latter type Ekwall considers it
possible that they may go back to *-wine*[2] (*Cuþenes* < *Cūþwines*),
and in a review of Ekwall's book (Namn och Bygd XIX, 168 ff.)
Tengstrand has tried to show that derivation of *-en* names from
older *-wine* names may be considered for a few more of the pl.-ns
dealt with by Ekwall, *inter alia* in the case of Shaftesbury,
which might consequently be interpreted as '*Sceaftwine's burh*';
cf. *Sceftwine* BCS 111.

It has however also been assumed[3] that the first el. in Shaftesbury may be a topographical term (OE *sceaft* 'pole, shaft')[4],
Shaftesbury being situated on a prominent, very abruptly descending hill which might possibly have been called a *sceaft* in
OE times; cf. the similar case of Pilsdon *infra*. That OE *sceaft*
was used in pl.-ns is shown by the name Shebbear (PN D p. 107)[5],
but if such was the case here, it seems difficult to account for
the original forms *scæftenes-* (*Sceaftenes-*). Professor Zachrisson,
however, would take these forms to go back to an *-in* extension
of *sceaft*, resulting in OE *sceafte(n)-*.

The Latinized forms of Shaftesbury have been discussed by
Zachrisson, Latin Infl. on Engl. Place-Nomenclature pp. 11 and
13. His first explanation of *Sceftonia*, *Scestonia* (adding of the
usual ending *-onia* to *Sceaft-*, *Sceaftes-*) is very probably correct,
whereas his second suggestion (an unrecorded OE **Sceaftestun*)
seems more doubtful.

---

[1] The form *Shaston* is still used locally.
[2] Cf. Zachrisson, PN and RN p. 26 n. 2.
[3] See C. H. Mayo in Do Field Club XV, 37.
[4] Cf. Zachrisson's assumption (StNPh V, 8 n. 3) that *sceaft* (in *sceaftes hangran* BCS 629) may have had the meaning of 'crag'.
[5] It should be noted that Shebbear is also on a hill which slopes very abruptly towards a brook.

For a plausible explanation of the relation between the names Shaftesbury and *Dun Paladyr* cf. Zachrisson, Romans p. 55 n. 1.

Alcester

Among the early endowments to the abbey of Alcester in Warwick, founded in 1140, was apparently land in two different parts of Dorset, viz. in or near Shaftesbury (cf. Blynfield *supra* 21), and near Wimborne Minster; cf. the discussion in connexion with the name Chilbridge *infra*. The possessions near Shaftesbury are referred to sporadically in later documents[1], and there can be no doubt that Alcester here is a transferred name.

III. Brownshall Hundred

bruneselle 1084 GeldRoll
Brumishill 1174-5 P (*Brimeshulle* ChancR)
Bruneshill 1212 Fees (89), 1219 ib. (260), 1244 *Ass*, 1265 Misc,   *-hull(e)* 1244 *Ass*, 1285 FA
Broneshille 1244 *Ass*, *-hull* 1275 RH, 1303 Pat *et passim* to   1428 FA, *Breoneshull* 1316 FA, *Bronshill* 1431 FA

This looks like *'Brūn's* hill' (OE *hyll*), *Brūn* being a well-evidenced OE pers. name (Redin p. 11), but Professor Zachrisson would compare the first el. with the hill-name *Brūne*, to which Ekwall has drawn attention in his Studies on PN p. 63.

The name of the hundred is apparently preserved in Brunsell's Fm (6″) and Brunsell's Knapp (6″) (OE *cnæpp* 'top, summit of a hill'), both in Stourton Caundle parish *infra*. Brunsell's Knapp is almost exactly in the centre of the hundred; the height just N of that spot is called 'Browns Wheel' on the OS map of 1811.

Holwell

Holwell 130 D 6/7
    Holewal(e) 1194, 1195 P[2], 1207 PatR (*in Blakemor*), 1210-12   RBE, 1212 Fees (79), 1216 ClR, 1225 FF, 1230 P, 1251

---

[1] See Dugdale IV, 172 ff., Hutchins III, 54, and VCH Wa II, 59 (from 1307 Pat); cf. *semper per diuisas inter dominum Regem et Abbatem de Alcestre* from the Perambulation of Gillingham Forest (t. Hy III Cerne; also in Hutchins III, 662).

[2] *Holewala* 1186-7, 1187-8 P may belong here too.

Misc (*in Blakemore*), t. Hy III (14th) Cerne, 1291 Tax, 1305 FF, 1323 Inq aqd, 1336 Ch, 1340 NI, 1412, 1428, 1431 FA
Holewall(e) 1208 PatR (*in Blakamor*), 1244 *Ass*, 1301 Ipm, 1316 FA
Holewell' 1239 FineR

The first el. is probably OE *hol(h)* 'hollow'. The second may be OE *walu* 'ridge, bank' (OE *æt þære holan wale* 'at the hollow ridge')[1], though OE *weall* 'wall' is perhaps equally possible. -*well* in the isolated form *Holewell'*[2] may be due to association with names containing OE *wielle* 'spring, well', cf. the old forms of Bestwall (OE *weall*) *infra*.

Note. That the present name cannot contain OE *wielle* is clear from a comparison with the numerous Do names *infra* in which the identity of the element *wielle* can be proved beyond all doubt: those names exhibit no *a* spellings. This is exactly what was to be expected on this old West Saxon territory and tends to confirm Ekwall's results in chapter II of his Contributions to the History of OE Dialects. Ekwall's list of Do names containing OE *wielle* (op. cit. p. 46 f.) includes, however, also one *a* spelling, *Holewale* 1428 FA. Ekwall suggests that this may be a bad spelling, but the true explanation is that, since it refers to this Holwell, it does not contain *wielle*. It may be added that the early forms of Holwell (*Holewale* 1210-12 RBE, 1431 FA, *Holewalle* 1316 FA) in Ekwall's list of Somerset names (op. cit. p. 45) refer to this Dorset place, too.[3]

Blackland (lost) is *Blakelond(e)* 1379 (etc.) BM I, 1421 FF, 1431 FA *et passim*, *Blakelondes* 1412 FA, *Blaklond* 1439 FF. Self-explanatory, OE *blæc, land.*

Buckshaw Ho

Two references in P, (boscus de) *Buggechage* (1194) and (boscus de) *Bugehag'* (1195), have been identified with this place. The early forms are not easily compatible with the modern form of the name, which suggests OE *sceaga* 'small wood, thicket', (dial. *shaw*) in the second element.

---

[1] Cf. the meaning of Horridge in PN D p. 476.
[2] The form *Holewella* 1194 P possibly also refers to this place.
[3] The parish was a detached part of Somerset (Horethorne Hundred) up to 1844, a fact that seems to have escaped the attention of indexers of even quite modern editions of records.

Cornford Hill Fm (6″) is *Querneford* t. Hy III (14th) Cerne. The
elements are apparently OE *cweorn* and *ford*, but the exact
meaning of the compound is not quite clear. *cweorn* 'quern,
hand-mill' is usually compounded with *dūn* 'down, hill' in pl.-ns
(cf. *Coringdon infra*), and it has therefore been suggested that
cweorndūn denotes a hill where mill-stones were quarried, *cweorndūn* being possibly an ellipsis for *cweornstāndūn*, cf. EPN p. 20.
cweornford may have been the ford by the *cweorn(stān)dūn*; a
quarry is marked just near on the 6″ map. If, on the other
hand, *cweorn* was used also of water-mills (cf. Ekwall, PN La
p. 46 s. n. Quarlton) — there is still a mill about a hundred
yards from the farm — *cweornford* may be interpreted simply
as the 'mill-ford'.

Note. The above form *Querneford* is taken from the Cartulary of
Cerne Abbey, called "The Red Book of Cerne", printed in Do Field
Club, vols XXVIII (1907) and XXIX (1908), from the MS in Cambridge University Library; an important part of it[1] has also been
very accurately transcribed in Hutchins III, 662 f. I have already
had occasion to quote several forms *supra* from this very interesting
document. For different reasons I find it convenient here to reprint
the part (the perambulation of Blackmoor Forest) which is of particular interest for the pl.-ns in this district (MS f. 16 b, Do Field Club
XXIX, 196 f., Hutchins loc. cit.[2]):

*Hec sunt mete de Foresta de Blakemore. A capite de Rocumbe[3]
ex occidentali parte versus Boream inter Crockeresrewe[4] et boscum, et
Holenhurste[5] et boscum. Et sic Levre de Bosco ex orientale parte de
Holenhurste usque Deoulepole[6] juxta aquam. Et de Deoulepole usque
Querneford. Et de Querneford juxta predictam aquam usque Bradeford
sub molendino de Candel.[7] De Bradeford per divisas de Holewale[8]
usque ad magnum iter quod venit de la Wdebrigge.[9] Et de itinere illo
semper per divisas de Holewale usque ad truncum qui stat in tribus
divisis.[10] Et de trunco illo usque ad aquam de taleford. Et de taleford
usque ad domum Waremanni in Levre de bosco. Et a domo Waremanni usque ad Grangias monachorum de Binnedune.[11] Et a grangiis
usque ad ecclesiam de Pulham[12] semper in Levre de bosco versus austrum.*

---

[1] The perambulations of the forests of Gillingham and Blackmoor.

[2] Cf. also ib. IV, 516 f.   [3] *Rocombe infra* (in Hermitage).

[4] Cf. foot-note to *Crockern Stoke infra* (in Haselbury Bryan).

[5] Holnest *infra*.   [6] Cf. Poll Bridge Fm *infra* (in Caundle Marsh).

[7] Cf. foot-note to Stourton Caundle *infra*.   [8] Holwell *supra* (this parish).

[9] Woodbridge *infra* (next name but one).   [11] Grange Fm *infra* (in Pulham).

[10] Cf. Kingstag *infra* (in Pulham).

[12] Pulham *infra*.

Et de ecclesia de Pulham usque ad Sandhulle.[1] *Et totum boscum de
Sandhulle. Et de Sandhulle per divisas inter Pulham et Dunethis*[2]
*usque Timberhurste. Et de Timberhurste usque ad caput alneti quod
vocatur Netelbede versus Boream. Et inde usque Bissupesbrigge. Et
de Bissupesbrigge per aquam usque ad Molendinam de Heortleghe.*[3]
*Et de Molendino illo usque la Rode. Et de la Rode per magnum iter,
usque Staweius jwinde.*[4] *Et de Staweius jwinde versus occidentem in
Levre de bosco usque ad caput de Rocumbe ubi mete incipiunt.*

Sandhills

  (ad, de) *Sandhulle* t. Hy III (14th) Cerne

Self-explanatory, OE *sand, hyll.* The present Sandhills is perhaps not exactly on the spot indicated by the perambulation
printed above, but, to judge from the text, *Sandhull* may once
have been the name of a fairly large wood (*totum boscum de
Sandhulle*).

Woodbridge is *Wudebrige* 1194 P, *Wudebruge* 1251 Misc (p),
Wodebrigg' 1256 FF (p), *la Wdebrigge* t. Hy III (14th) Cerne.
Self-explanatory, OE *wudu, brycg.* Cf. the same name *supra* 24.

Stalbridge

Stalbridge 130 B 8

  (*in*) *Stapulbreicge* 998 (12th) KCD 701 (cf. Thorpe p. 294)
  Staplebrige 1086 DB, *-brig(g)* 1297 Cl, Pat, *-brugg* 1286 Abbr
  Stapelbrig(g)e 1191 (etc.) Sarum, 1244 *Ass et passim* with
    variant spellings *Stapil-* and *-brugg(e), -bryg(g)e*
  Stapulbrigg 1316 FA
  Stalbriggh 1346 FA *et passim* (with variant spellings *-brugge,
    -brygg*), *Stalbrigg* al. *Stapelbrigg'* 1415 IpmR

'Staple-bridge', OE *stapol, brycg* (EPN).

Antioch Fm (6") takes its name from the *Antioch* family, for
which see more under Tarrant Rawston *infra*. Roger, Robert
and William de *Antioche* are mentioned in connexion with Stalbridge in 1244 (*Ass* 200 m. 10; 201 m. 6, ib. m. 12), and John
de *Antioch* was party to a fine here in 1267 (FF). The manor
is mentioned several times (as *Ontioche, Antioches, Antiokes*) from
1361 onwards (IpmR, FF, AD VI).

---

  [1] Sandhills *infra* (next name).   [2] Duntish *infra*.   [3] Hartley *infra*.
  [4] High Stoy *infra*. Hutchins (III, 663) prints *Staweius Iwinde*.

Bibbern Fm (1″) and **Brook** (6″)

(*on*) *bydeburnan* 933 (12th) BCS 696

(aqua de) *Biddeburn'* 1244 *Ass* (201 m. 6)

It is suggested by Ekwall (Studies on PN p. 52 n. 1) that the first el. is identical with the river-name Boyd (Gl), for which Ekwall (ERN p. 46 f.) assumes British origin. It seems more likely to me that the first el. in Bibbern is an English word (second el. OE *burna* 'stream, brook'), probably OE *byden* 'bushel, tub', cf. Middendorff p. 22. For the use of that word in pl.-ns, presumably in the sense of coomb-like depression, cf. Blomé p. 44 s. n. Bidna (and p. 34 s. n. Bideford), Karlström, StNPh II, 67, and PN D pp. 102, 398, 430, 410, 573 s. nn. Bidna, Betham, Bennah, Bidwell Barton, and Bidwell. Near Bibbern Fm the brook runs through a small valley.

Note. As I had occasion to suggest at an earlier date[1], and as has also been pointed out by Ekwall (Studies on PN p. 52 n. 1), there can be no doubt that BCS 696 refers to Dorset and to land in this parish. (*æt*) *Westune* is Stalbridge Weston[2] *infra*, (*on*) *bydeburnan* is Bibbern, and among the boundary-marks we can further identify *stanbroc* with the present Stanbrook (6″) *infra*. Moreover, (*on hean*) *wifeleshylle* survived in 1244 (*Ass* 201 m. 12) in the name of Wm de *Wyueleshill*, in 1285 (FA II, 8) in Johannes de *Viveleshulle*, in 1317 (Inq aqd p. 250) in J. de *Wyneleshull* (sic), and in 1333 *SR* as *Wyueleshull* (p). Finally, the boundary-mark (*of*) *Cirichylle*, (*on*) *ciric hylle*, is probably not lost. I have seen no forms of it in ME records, nor can I find the name on maps, but in Kelly (ed. 1923, p. 199) one of the private residences in Stalbridge is called Church Hill (or Churchill) house. This may of course be quite a modern name, but very likely it goes back to the *Cirichyll* of BCS 696. Ekwall's assumption (op. cit. p. 51 f.) that this boundary-mark contains *cirice* 'church'[3] would thus seem to be corroborated. The church of Stalbridge stands on the slope of a well-marked hill.

Callow Weston (lost) is *Calweston* (*in Nywenham*) 1431 FA. From what is stated in Hutchins (III, 754) this lost place was named after a family called *Le Calewe* (OE *calu* 'bald', cf. Ekwall,

---

[1] See Karlström p. 164 (s. n. *Beorreding mæd*).

[2] BCS 696 is one of the charters of the Sherborne Register, and (Stalbridge) Weston belonged to the bishop of Sherborne in DB.

[3] Cf. PN Wo p. 108.

Contrib. to the Hist. of OE Dialects p. 13), holding land in "Dunes Weston" in the time of Edward I.[1]

Frith Fm is *la Frithe* 1244 *Ass* (p), *atte Frythe* 1333 *SR* (p). OE *fyrhþ(e)* 'wood, wooded country'.

Gummershay Fm is *Gommeresheye* 1315 FF, *Gummeresheye* 1327 FF, *Gomershaye* 1327 *SR*, 1415 IpmR, *Gomeresheye* 1333 *SR*, *Gummersey* 1765 Taylor. The first el. is probably the pers. name *Gummǣr*, recorded in the form *Gummar*, the name of a Yorkshire undertenant in DB (Ellis, Intr. II, 333). The second el. is OE *(ge)hæg* 'enclosure'. Do pl.-ns ending in -*hay* are otherwise confined to the west of the county, where they abound.

Hargrove Fm is *Haregrave* 1285 FA (p), *Haregraue* 1333 *SR* (p). See Hartgrove *supra* 30.

Marsh Fm is (*in*) *the M'ssh* 1327 *SR* (p). Self-explanatory, OE *mersc*.

Newnham (lost) is *Newenham* 1244 *Ass* (p), *Nywenham* 1315, 1327 FF, 1431 FA. '(At the) new farm', OE (*æt þǣm*) *niwan hām*; cf. Newnham Fms *infra*. The name seems to have been in use as late as 1869 (Hutchins).

Stalbridge Weston

(*æt*) *Westune*, (*apud*) *Westonam* 933 (12th) BCS 696
Westun 998 (12th) KCD 701, *Weston* 1086 DB, etc.

Self-explanatory, OE *west*, *tūn*. The place was sometimes distinguished as *Weston Abbots* (1334 FF), or *Weston Abbot* (1439 BM I, FF, 1442 IpmR); it belonged to the abbot of Sherborne.

Stanbrook (6″) is *stanbroc* 933 (12th) BCS 696. 'Stony brook', OE *stān*, *brōc*.

Thornhill is *Thornhill* 1244 *Ass* (p), 1431 FA, *Thornhull(e)* 1285 FA (p), 1333 *SR*, 1340 NI (p), 1377 FF (*juxta Caundel Haddon*) *et passim*. Self-explanatory, OE *þorn*, *hyll*.

---

[1] Two members of that family, Radulphus *le Calewe* (5 Edw I) and John *le Calewe* (25 Edw I), are mentioned in Hutchins; cf. also the account given in SoDoNQ III, 81 ff.

Stourton Caundle

Stourton Caundle [stɔ:tən kɔ:ndl, stə:tən kændl][1] 130 C 7
Candel, Candele, Candelle 1086 DB
Candel Malherbe 1202-3 FF
Candel 1206 RC, 1212 Fees (89) *et passim, Kandel* t. Hy III
   BM I
Kaunvel (sic) 1210-12 RBE, *Caundel* 1212 Fees (89)
Caundel Haddon 1275 RH *et passim, Candel Haddon* 1285 FA

Stourton Caundle, Bishop's Caundle (with Caundle Wake) and
Caundle Marsh are on different arms of Caundle Brook (an
affluent of the Lidden), whereas a fourth place, Purse Caundle,
is on another stream, a brook that falls into the Yeo.[2] Ekwall (ERN p. 72) assumes that Caundle is no original river-
name, and suggests instead that it may be an old hill-name, the
Caundle villages being situated on both sides of a chain of hills.
Ekwall leaves the name unexplained, and I can offer no suggestion.

Robert *Malherbe* granted land here to Henry de *Haddon* in
4 John (see 1202-3 FF, and Hutchins III, 664), the name of the
Haddon family being preserved in **Haddon Lodge**. Stourton
Caundle derives its present distinctive name from the Lords
Stourton, whose property it was from the time of Henry VI up
to 1727 (Hutchins). Part of the place seems once to have been
called *Caundle Lydelinche* (1306 Ch).[3] A mill here is referred
to as *Candel Joce* in 1256 FF.[4] A *Candel Henrici Budde* (1177-8
P) cannot be identified. A *Caundle Pyle* (1335 BM, FF) may
be preserved in the name of **Pile Lane** (6″) near Stalbridge
Weston; cf. Wm de *la Pile* 1244 *Ass* (Brownshall Hundred), and
John *atte Pyle* 1333 *SR*, 1340 NI (under the adjacent parish of
Haydon); these references apparently contain OE *pīl* 'stake', cf.
Pilsdon *infra*. — On the AN spelling *aun* for *an* see Zachrisson,
AN Infl. p. 153 ff.

---

[1] A third pronunciation [kɑ:ndl] has been kindly communicated to me by
Mr G. W. L. Fernandes of Haddon Lodge.

[2] The other Caundles are to be found under Sherborne Hundred *infra*. The
DB forms, except for Purse Caundle, are included here.

[3] Lydlinch (*infra*) is about two miles distant.

[4] Cf. *sub molendino de Candel* t. Hy (14th) Cerne.

Brunsell's Fm (6″) is *Bruneshull* 1244 *Ass* (p), 1284 Pat (p), *Broneshull* 1340 NI (p). See Brownshall Hundred *supra* 33.

Cockhill Fm is *Cokhull'* 1333 *SR* (p). Probably self-explanatory, OE *cocc*, *hyll*. Cf. Cockle Spinney in PN BedsHu p. 38, and Cogdean (Hundred) *infra*.

Woodrow Fm is *Woderewe* 1327, 1333 *SR*. The elements are OE *wudu* 'wood' and *rēw* (*rāw*) 'row, line', and the compound probably means 'a row of trees, a thin wood', as suggested in PN Wo p. 239. Cf. Woodrow *infra*.

IV. Sturminster Newton Hundred

Neuuentone 1084 GeldRoll
Niwetona, -ton(e) 1130 PR, 1168-9 (*et passim*) P, 1212 Fees (87), 1236 FF, 1265 Misc, *Harl. 61* (15th)
Niwenton' 1159-60 P, *Nieweton'* 1167-8 P
New(e)ton 1244 *Ass*, 1316, 1428, 1431 FA
Nyweton 1303 FA, 1340 NI, 1346 FA, *Nyentone* 1327 *SR*

Self-explanatory, OE (*æt þǣm*) *niwan tūne*. Newton (or Newton Castle) is the little village on the south side of the river Stour, opposite Sturminster (Newton), see *infra*.

Note. The fact that in some early documents the two hundreds of Sturminster Newton and Buckland Newton (*infra*) were placed together, probably because both belonged to Glastonbury Abbey, has caused much confusion and several wrong identifications in indexes and local histories. A closer investigation reveals, however, that *Neweton* (etc.) in early records always refers to the hundred of Sturminster Newton, whereas that of Buckland Newton is always called *Bocland* (etc.). This frequent combination of the hundreds of (Sturminster) Newton and Buckland (Newton)[1] seems, finally, to have led to the curious result that 'Newton' was attached to Buckland, first probably in the name of the hundred, later on to the place itself, the distinctive name of which seems earlier to have been 'Abbas'; cf. Buckland Newton (hundred and parish) *infra*.

[1] Cf. e. g. 1265 Misc, 1333 *SR*, 1340 NI, 1316, 1431 FA.

Hinton St Mary

Hinton St Mary 130 C 9

(at, to) Hamtun(e) 944 (15th) BCS 793[1], 958 (15th) ib. 1033
Hainton(e) 1086 DB, 1212 Fees (87)
Henton 1212 Fees (91), 1244 *Ass*, 1291 Tax, 1303 FA *et passim*
Heynton 1327 *SR*, *Henton Mary* 1535 VE

'(At the) high farm, OE (*æt þǣm*) *hēan tūne*, the place being situated on an eminence in Blackmoor Vale. It belonged to the abbey of St Mary of Shaftesbury, and the suggestion in Hutchins (III, 547) that it owes its additional name to that fact and not to the dedication of its chapel, seems very plausible. *Hamtun(e)* is apparently due to confusion with OE *hāmtūn*; for *ai* in *Hainton(e)* cf. the early spellings for Heanton Punchardon, Hennock and Broadhembury in PN D pp. 45, 471, 557, and Wallenberg, StNPh II, 86; on the development of *e* to *i* before *n* cf. Jordan § 34.

Hewstock (lost)

Half a mile S of Hinton St Mary is a place called *Hewstock* marked on the OS map of 1811. In an ancient perambulation of Sturminster Newton, printed in Hearne's edition of Adam de Domerham[2] (vol. II, 670-72) there is a boundary-mark *la Hendestok*[3], apparently identical with this *Hewstock*; see Hewstock Fm *infra* (in Beaminster).

Margaret Marsh

Margaret Marsh 130 B 10

I have found no certain forms for this name in ME records[4], but Hutchins (III, 549) is apparently correct in stating that it takes its name "from its low and moist situation, and the saint

---

[1] Birch leaves the *Hamtun(e)* of this Shaftesbury charter unidentified but tentatively suggests (II, 543 n. 3) that it may be Hammoon (Do). This is no doubt incorrect, the place referred to being evidently Hinton St Mary.

[2] Cf. Hutchins IV, 338, where this interesting perambulation is reprinted.

[3] Hutchins (loc. cit.) prints *la Handestock*.

[4] A form *la Marshe*, quoted in Hutchins (III, 556) from 1310 probably belongs here, and so does with certainty a 16th century form *le Marsh* (ib. p. 548).

to whom its chapel is dedicated". It is called *St. Margarets Marsh* on the earliest OS map (1811). OE *mersc*.

Gore Fm

Gora 1282 BM I, *atte Gore* 1327 *SR* (p)
the Gore (by Shaftysbury) 1390 Cl
La Gore (juxta Shaftesbury) 1390 IpmR, *la Gore* 1551 BM I
(cantaria de) *Gore* 1431 FA, *le Gore* 1811 OM

'Triangular piece of land', OE *gāra*; cf. Gorewood *infra*. There was formerly a chantry here.

Marnhull

Marnhull [mɑ:nəl] 130 B 9

Marenhull 1274 Pat, 1308 FF, 1327 *SR*, *Marenull(e)* 1291 Tax
Marnhull(e) 1303 Pat, 1316 FA, 1330 Ch, 1333 *SR et passim*
Marmhull 1340 NI, *Marmehull* 1369 Cl
Marnehull 1417 IpmR, 1572 BM I, *Marnehill* 1428, 1431 FA
Marnell(e) 1426 IpmR, c. 1540 Leland
Marnhyll, Marnhill 1490 Ipm

The second el. is OE *hyll* 'hill', but the first is a mystery to me.

Burton (6″) is *Buretune, -tone* 13th Glaston C, *Burton(e)* 1338
FF, 1347 Cl *et passim*, *Burton atte Nasshe* 1348 Misc, 1361, 1372,
1391 Cl, *Bourton atte Nass(h)e* 1371 Cl, AD III, *Burton Ash*
1348 IpmR, *(Asshe &) Burton* 1350 Orig, *Borton'* 14th Glaston F,
Naysshe Burton 1477 IpmR. OE *burhtūn*, cf. Bourton *supra* 3.
atte Nasshe, Ash (etc.) refer to Nash Court *infra*.

Kentleworth (lost)[1]

Kenteleswurth 1236 FF, *-wrth(e)* 13th Glaston C
Kentelesworth(e) 1313, 1333 FF, 1384, 1407, 1417 IpmR, 1431
    FA, 1451 IpmR, *Kentlesworth(e)* 14th Glaston F (*passim*)
Kenlesworth 1490 Ipm

The editors of PN D p. 564 suggest that a pers.name *Cæntel* (cf. OE *Centwine, Centweald*) may enter into Kentisbeare (D)[2],

---

[1] The exact site of *Kentleworth* is unknown, but cf. (*in*) *Kentlesworth'*, *qui modo dicitur Marnhulle* (Glaston F, p. 30), *Kentlesworth Burton' vel Marnhulle* (ib. p. 31), *apud Yerdegrove* (now Yardgrove Fm *infra*) *in Kentlesworth'* (ib. p. 34).

[2] On that name cf. also Blomé p. 95, and Ekwall, ERN p. 228. A river-name

earlier *Kenteles-*, and the same may be true of the present name,
too. The second el. is OE *weorþ* 'enclosure, farm'. A probably
lost *Kentelesworth* in So is mentioned in 1303, 1346, 1428 FA.

King's Mill is *Kingesmulun* 13th Glaston C (p). Self-explanatory,
OE *myln*.

Knightstreet (lost)[1] is *Kyngestrete* 1308 FF, *Knightestrate* 1324
Inq aqd, *Knyghtestrete* 14th Glaston F (*in Kentlesworth'*), 1431
FA, *Knyghtstrete* 1379 FF, *Knightstrete* 1396 FF, *Kingstete* (sic)
1479 IpmR. The elements are OE *cniht* and *stræt*, for which
see EPN.

Lymburgh's Fm is *Linberg* 1244 *Ass* (200 m. 4), *Limbergh* 1244
Ass (201 m. 12), *Lymbergh* 1333 *SR*, 1345 FF, *Lymborgh* 1431
FA (all p), *Lumbreys* 1811 OM. Probably 'flax-hill', OE *līn*,
beorg; cf. Limbury Fm *infra*.

Moorside is *atte More* 1333 *SR* (p), 1345 FF (p), 1362 Cl (p) *et
passim*, *la More* 14th Glaston F (*in Borton'*), 1384 IpmR (*in par.
de Marnhull*), *More* 1412 FA, 1426 IpmR *et passim*, *Moore* al.
Moorside al. *Moore Court*[2] 1672 SoDoNQ X. Self-explanatory,
OE *mōr*.

Nash Court

The early forms have been given under Burton *supra* 42.
The name means 'at the ash-tree', OE *æt þǣm æsce* > *atten Ashe*
> *atte Nashe*, showing the common misdivision of the definite
article; cf. Nash Fm *infra*.

Ram's Hill Fm is possibly to be identified with (*on*) *Rumanhelle*
958 (15th) BCS 1033, which would seem to mean 'roomy (spacious) hill', OE *rūm*, *hyll*.

---

is apparently out of the question in the case of *Kentleworth*, for there is no
stream in the whole parish of Marnhull with the exception of the upper part
of Chivrick's Brook (which may possibly be identical with *chelbrichtes dich* in
BCS 793).

[1] The house that bore the name of *Knightstreet*, and which stood by itself
about a mile from the church of Marnhull, was pulled down probably about
the middle of the 18th century (Hutchins).

[2] "Here is still a farm-house, called More Court" (Hutchins).

Thorton Fm[1]

(æt) *þorntune*, (at) *þortune*[2] 958 (15th) BCS 1033
Torentone 1086 DB, *Torntone* 1210-12 RBE (p. 546)[3]
Thornton(e) 1212 Fees (91), 1285, 1316 FA *et passim*
Thorenton 1242 FF, *Thorinton* 1242 Ch
Thorneton 1266 FF, 1384 Cl, 1401-02, 1428, 1431 FA

The elements are OE *þorn* 'thorn-bush' and *tūn*, the compound probably meaning 'enclosure made of thorn-bushes'; cf. EPN s. v. *þorn*, and PN NRY p. 24. On the AN rendering of initial *þ* with *t*, cf. Zachrisson, AN Infl. p. 39 ff. and IPN p. 108.

Walton Elm

Walton' 13th Glaston C (*passim*[4]), 1333 SR (p)

Probably 'wall-farm', OE *weall*, *tūn*. For a detailed treatment of this name-type, see Zachrisson, Romans p. 39 ff., and for probable meanings of *weall* in pl.-ns, cf. ib. p. 44. Alternatively the first el. may be OE *weald* 'wood' (there is a Woodlands Fm about a mile away), cf. Ekwall in StNPh I, 106 ff.

Yardgrove Fm

la Wrdegrove 13th Glaston C
Herdegrove [*Erdegrave*] 1303 FA
Erdegrove 1346, 1428, 1431 FA
Yerdegrove (*in Kentlesworth'*) 14th Glaston F
Yeargrove 1811 OM

The above forms from FA have been identified by the indexer of that document with Hartgrove (in East Orchard) *supra* 30.[5] This is no doubt wrong. Hartgrove was (and is) in the hundred of Sixpenny Handley and belonged to the abbot of Shaftesbury, whereas the above FA forms refer to a place situated in the hundred of (Sturminster) Newton and belonging to the abbot of Glastonbury; other reasons, too, make it almost absolutely certain that they refer to the same place as the two Glaston

---

[1] A tithing in Redlane Hundred.
[2] KCD 474 (vol. III, p. 453) has (at) *Ðorntune*.
[3] The identification in the index (p. 1331) with Taunton (So) is a clear mistake.
[4] Once spelt *Valton'*.
[5] The same mistake is found in Hutchins (III, 550).

forms above. The identification of these latter forms with the present Yardgrove is beyond all doubt.

The second el. is of course OE *grāf(a)* 'grove, copse', but the early forms seem too conflicting to allow of any certainty as to the origin of the first element.

Okeford Fitzpaine

Okeford Fitzpaine 130 D/E 10

Adford (sic) 1086 DB

Acford(e) t. Hy I BM I, c. 1165 Montacute *et passim*, *Akeford* 1264 FineR, Ipm, *Ocford* 1303 FA *et passim*

Acforde Aluredi de Lincoln 1155 Montacute (Dugdale V, 167)
Acford Alvredi 1281 Ipm, *Acford Auveray* 1287 Misc, *Acford Aufri* 1297 Pat, *Acford Alfred* 1323 FF, *Akforde Alfridi* 1340 NI

Okeford Nichol 1282 Ch, *Acford Nicholas* 1337 Ch

Ocford Fitz Payn 1321 FF, 1412 FA, *Hakford Fitzpayn* 1381 Cl, *Okford Fytz Payn* 1431 FA, *Ackeford Fitzpayn* 1490 Ipm

'Oak ford', OE *āc, ford*; cf. Child Okeford *supra* 13. For a detailed account of the mighty family of *de Lincoln*, to which the place owes its earliest distinctive name, see Hutchins IV, 327 ff. The first known Dorset member of that family was presumably the *Alfred de Lincoln* who appears in a grant of Henry I (Montacute Cart. No. 132[1]), and who had, in all probability, obtained his extensive Dorset barony by marrying the widow of Hugh Fitz Grip (DB).[2] The place owes its present additional name to its succeeding lords, the *Fitz Payns*, the first of whom, Robert *Fitz Payn* (*filius Pagani*)[3], is mentioned as one of the heirs of the last Alfred de Lincoln, who died in 1264 (Ipm).

Some of the forms above (*Auveray* etc.) show AN features. The dissimilated form *Nichol* (and *Nicholas*!) for *Lincoln* has been dealt with by Zachrisson.[4] It may be worth mentioning that

---

[1] SoRecSoc VIII, 167. This charter belongs to the period between 1107 and 1122, see ib. p. 250.

[2] See Th. Bond in Do Field Club XI, 142 ff. and XIV, 114 ff.

[3] Cf. Wootton Fitzpaine and Elworth *infra*.

[4] AN Infl. pp. 122, 130.

the intermediate form *Nincole*, found once by Zachrisson in a purely French document[1], appears at least once in a 13th century English record, viz. 1212 Fees (p. 90), where one of the members of this Do family is called Alvred de *Ninchol'*.

Belchalwell[2]

The present name is an amalgamation of two earlier names:
1. *Belle* 1286 Ch, 1291 Tax, 1297 Pat, 1303 FA *et passim*
2. *Chaldewelle* 1109 Dugdale, 1316, 1412 FA, *Cheldewell'* 1205 Cur, *Chaldwell* 1286 Ch[3]

The first of these names is probably the word *bell(e)* 'hill', discussed in PN Bk p. 163. The steep hill-ridge, Bell Hill, just SE of the present Belchalwell, reaches a height of 846 ft.

The second name means 'cold well', OE *ceald*, *wielle* (EPN), and belongs to the material treated by Ekwall in his Contrib. to the Hist. of OE Dialects (p. 13).

Fiddleford

Fitelford(e) 1244 *Ass* (p), 1315, 1345 FF, 1364, 1365 Cl, 1402 IpmR, 1412 FA, 1456 IpmR
Fytelford 1350 IpmR, 14th Glaston F, 1418 IpmR

This may be the 'ford of *Fitela*', an OE pers. name occurring in Beowulf; cf. also *(on) fitelan sladæs crundæl* BCS 705, Fittleton in PN W p. 83, Fittleworth in PN Sx p. 126, and Fiddlecott in PN D p. 364. What makes one somewhat doubtful about the correctness of the etymology suggested, however, is the total absence of a medial vowel in the early forms of Fiddleford. That there must have existed an OE word **fitel* seems clear from the compound *fitelfōta* 'white-footed' (B. T. Suppl.), cf. *fitelfot* (1325), an old name for the hare (NED). For the difficult question of the meaning of *Fitela* and **fitel*, cf. Björkman, Eigennamen im Beowulf pp. 27-40.

Hile Fm (6″) is *Hyla, le Hyle, la Hyla* 13th Glaston C, (terra q. voc.) *Westhyla* 13th Glaston C. Both the old forms and the

---

[1] Op. cit. p. 130 n. 1.

[2] Earlier a distinct parish (in Cranborne Hundred), but now for civil purposes added to the parish of Okeford Fitzpaine (Kelly).

[3] The identification in Ch (vol. II) and FA (vols II and VI) with Holywell in Frome St Quintin is a curious mistake.

modern one forbid us to assume derivation from OE *hyll* 'hill'. The existence of an OE **hygel* 'hill' (corresponding to German *Hügel*) has been assumed by Ekwall (PN La p. 82 n. 1), and it seems plausible that we have that word here. The farm is on the slope of a small but conspicuous hillock, Banbury Hill (possibly identical with *bosc. de Ban'ber'* 13th Glaston C p. 91). Hyle Fm *infra* must be identical in origin.

Lowbrook Fm is *Lollebroc* 1264 FineR, *Lollebrok(e)* 1264 Ipm *et passim* with later (1327) variant spelling *-brouk(e)*, *Lullebrouk* 1358 BM I, *Lullebrok* 1383 FF, *Lolbroke* 1535 VE. This may possibly mean '*Lulla*'s brook' (OE *brōc*), this OE pers. name being very well evidenced (Redin p. 100). There seem, however, to be very few cases in which the el. *brōc* is with certainty compounded with a pers. name (there is no other case in Do); as a matter of fact *brōc* appears in a remarkable way to favour a descriptive word as the first el. of compound pl.-ns (cf. e. g. Middendorff s. v.), and the interpretation of the first el. in the present name had therefore better be left open. — The modern form Lowbrook shows vocalization of *l*, cf. PN Sx p. 133 s. n. Lowfold.

Southgarston (lost) is *Southgarston* (*in Okeford*) 1316 Ipm, *Suthgarston* 1321 FF, *Southgarston* (*juxta Acford Alfred*) 1323 FF. OE *sūð* 'south' and *gærs-tūn* 'grassy enclosure'.

Sturminster Newton

Sturminster Newton 130 C/D 9

  Sture minster (*-mynster*) 880-5 (c. 1000) BCS 553, 554, 555
  Nywetone (rubric), *at Stoure* 968 (14th) BCS 1214
  Newentone 1086 DB, *Neutone* 1210-12 RBE, *Niweton'* 1212 Fees (87), *Nywteon* 13th Glaston C, *New(e)ton* 1316 FA, 14th Glaston F
  Sturmanstr' 1275 RH, *-mynstre* 1332 Ch, *Sturministr' Nywteon* 1291 Tax, *Sturmenistre by Niweton Castel* 1297 Ipm
  Sturmenstre (*Stormenstre*) *Abbatis* 14th Glaston F
  Sturmynstre Neutoncastell 1437 FF

  Cf. the name of the hundred *supra* 40, and see also Sturminster Marshall *infra*.

Sturminster derives its name from its situation on the river Stour (see East and West Stour *supra* 16) and from its church, OE *mynster*. Newton is, strictly speaking, a place in itself on the opposite side of the river, and the name has evidently been added to that of Sturminster to distinguish the latter place from Sturminster Marshall; its castle is now swept away (Hutchins). The manor of Newton (including *inter alia* Sturminster) was since 968 (BCS 1214) the property of the abbot of Glastonbury; hence the earlier distinctive name *Abbatis*.

Bagber [1]

Bakebere 1205 FF, 1211-2 RBE (p), 1242-3 Fees (750), 1244 *Ass*, 1264 Ipm (p) *et passim*, *-ber* 1264 Ipm, 14th Glaston F

Backebere, *Bakkeber(e)* 1244 *Ass* (p), 1303 FA (p), 14th Glaston F, 1428 FA

Baggeber' [*Baggebur'*] 1303 FA, *Bakepere* 1316 FA (p)

Estbakeber(e), *West-* 1363 FF, IpmR, 1412 FA, 1438 FF

Bakebeare 1412 FA, *Bagbere* 1475 IpmR, 1535 VE

The second el. is probably OE *bearu* 'grove, wood'; cf. Todber *supra* 18. The first may formally be the OE pers. name *Bac(c)a* (Redin p. 83), but other possibilities may also be thought of, cf. e. g. Middendorff p. 9 f., and Wallenberg p. 22. I must refrain from adding anything to Wallenberg's discussion, as I am not familiar enough with the topography of Bagber.

Colber Crib Ho (6″) [2]

Colesberie 1086 DB, *Colesbreia* Exon

Colber(e) 1244 *Ass*, 1262 FF, 1309 Ipm, 1333 *SR*, 14th Glaston F [3]

Colbeare Iryssh 1412 FA

For the second el. cf. the preceding name. Since the DB form(s) cannot easily be reconciled with the later forms, we may here have a case of "loose" *s*, a phenomenon discussed by

---

[1] One part of Bagber belonged to Cranborne Hundred, the other to the abbot of Glastonbury's manor of (Sturminster) Newton.

[2] Near the railway-line half a mile NW of Sturminster Newton.

[3] On p. 38 of Glaston F we find the spelling *Cowere* (cf. the form *Cobere* in Glaston C p. 231, which may also belong here), probably reflecting a vocalic pronunciation of *l*.

Zachrisson in AN Infl. (p. 118 f.); if so, the first el. may be
OE *cōl* 'cool'.[1] Why the name got the temporary addition *Iryssh*,
I cannot say.

Perry Fm (6″) was probably the home of John *atte Purye* 1331
FF (*passim*), i. e. 'at the pear-tree', OE *pirige*.

Piddles Wood

Puttekwurth (sic) 1244 *Ass* (p)
Puttelesw(u)rthe (bosc. de) 13th Glaston C (*passim*)
Putteswurthe 13th Glaston C (p)
Puctelesworth[2] 14th Glaston F (p)
Puddlesworth or *Puddlewood* 1582 Hutchins (IV, 338)

This may possibly be '*Pyttel*'s farm' (OE *weorþ*)[3], but if so,
one should have expected some *i* (*y*) spellings among the early
forms. An OE word (or pers. name) **puttel* is not on record,
and the etymology had therefore better remain open. The transition to *Puddle(s)-*, *Piddle* may partly be due to association with
the many Do pl.-ns in *Puddle*, *Piddle*.

V. Pimperne Hundred

pinpre 1084 GeldRoll, *Pinpre* 1212 Fees (87)
Pimper 1244 *Ass*, *Pinpern* 1265 Misc
Pymp'ne, *Pymperne* 1278 QW, 1316 FA, 1327, 1333 *SR et
    passim*
Pimperne 1285, 1303 FA, *Pynperne Forinsecus* 1290 Pat

See Pimperne *infra*. *Forinsecus* denotes the 'out-hundred', cf.
Beaminster Forum *infra*. The original hundred of Pimperne was
considerably smaller than the present one (cf. Eyton p. 138 and
Hutchins I, 214) but must soon have absorbed the greater part
of the pre-DB hundred of *Hunesberge* (cf. Eyton p. 131 n. 3),
which comprised an area corresponding to the present Pimperne
parishes of Bryanston, Durweston, Fifehead Neville, Hammoon,

---

[1] OE *col* 'coal' is apparently out of the question here.
[2] Hutchins (IV, 341), who quotes the MS, has *Puttelesworth*.
[3] For the pers. name *Pyttel* cf. Redin p. 143, and PN D p. 207 s. n. Pitts-
worthy.

Haselbury Bryan, and Winterborn Stickland.[1] It also absorbed
a large portion of the ancient hundred of *Longbarrow (langeberge*
1084 GeldRoll, *Langeberga* 1159-60 P, *Langeber(g)', -burgh* 1212
Fees p. 87 f.), which comprised the present parishes of Langton
Long Blandford, Steepleton Iwerne, Tarrant Hinton, Tarrant
Keynston, Tarrant Launceston, and Tarrant Rawston (all now in
Pimperne Hundred), Chettle and Tarrant Monkton (now in Upwim-
borne Hundred), and Ashmore, Farnham, Tarrant Gunville, and
Tarrant Rushton (now in Cranborne Hundred); cf. Eyton p. 132.[2]

Blandford Forum

Blandford Forum 130 F 12

    Blæneford 1086 Exon

    Bleneford(e) 1086 DB, 1191 to 1195 P, 1222 ClR, 1278 QW

    Blaneford(e) 1086 DB[3], 1182-3, 1184-5, 1185-6 P, 1198-9 FF,
        1216 ClR, PatR, 1219 Fees (261), c. 1226 Osmund *et passim*

    Blendfort 1101-18 France (late MS)

    Beneford 1189 France, 1200 (1280) BM I

    Bleinefort 1201 (1231) BM I

    Blaneford super Stur (upon Stures) 1279 Pat, Fine

    Cheping Blaneford 1288 FF, *Chuping Blaneford* 1310 FF,
        Chepingblanford 1319 FF, *Chepyngblan(e)ford* 1330 FF, 1342
        Cl *et passim*, *Chupyngblaneford* 1344 FF, *Chepingblandford*
        1409 Inq aqd

    Blaneford Forum 1291 Tax, 1297 Pat, 1346 Cl, 1428, 1431 FA

    Chepyngblanford al. *Blanford Forum* 1466 FF

    Blandford Forum 1535 VE

Ekwall (Studies on PN p. 62) suggests that the first el. of
this difficult name may be the gen. plur. *blǣgna* of OE *blǣge*
'gudgeon'. The whole name would thus mean 'the ford where
gudgeons were seen'.

---

[1] The old hundred of *Hunesberge* (called *Hundesburg*' 1212 Fees p. 87) also
included Okeford Fitzpaine *supra* (Sturminster Newton Hundred), and Shillingstone and Turnworth *infra* (Cranborne Hundred); cf. also the foot-note to
Plumber Fm *infra*.

[2] *Longbarrow* Hundred probably took its name from what is now called
Pimperne Long Barrow, about halfway between Tarrant Hinton and Pimperne,
cf. Hutchins, loc. cit.

[3] Some of the DB forms (as well as some of the other early forms) refer
to Langton Long Blandford, Blandford St Mary, and Bryanston (cf. Eyton pp.
131 f., 121 f.) but have for practical reasons been included here.

Blandford Forum seems early to have been distinguished as a market town[1], as seen from the distinctive additions *Cheping*, *Chuping* (OE *cīeping* 'market') and *Forum*, of which the Latin word ultimately prevailed.

Damory Court Fm

Dame Marie place de Chepyngblaneford 1363 Orig
Dame Mary Place de Chepyngblaneford 1363 Inq aqd
Damerie (Damery) Court next Blandford 1616 DoIpm

The history of this name seems to be a rather complicated affair. According to Coker[2] and Hutchins the place was owned by and probably named from Roger *Damory*, the Constable of Corfe Castle in the time of Edward II. The editors of Hutchins' History (I, 222) maintain that this is founded on no authority and probably wrong. In an Inquisition of 1283, printed in SoDo NQ VIII, 192, we find however that a certain *Monsieur Damori* held land in Stubhampton (in Tarrant Gunville). As that place is only about 5 miles from Damory Court Fm, there may be some truth in the assertion of the old Dorset historians. If so, the earliest references given above must involve a piece of popular etymology. Yet it seems more likely that these references give a true picture of the origin of the name, and a further clue may be supplied from the text in Inq aqd (p. 334), where the owner is stated to have acquired this manor "de abbatissa Fontis Ebraudi", i. e. the Abbey of St Mary, Fontevrault (Anjou). How that abbey had acquired land in Blandford, Pimperne, etc., see Calendar of Documents preserved in France, Nos 1085 and 1089; cf. also Hutchins loc. cit.

Bryanston

Bryanston 130 F 12

Blaneford Brion n. d. (Hy III) Osmund, *Blaneford Brian* 1271 Ipm
Brianeston 1285 FA, 1291 Tax *et passim* with variant spellings *Bryan(e)ston*, *Bryenston*, *Brieneston*, etc.

Bryanston derives from its one-time owner *Brianus* de Insula, who was here in the early reign of Henry III, cf. Hutchins I,

---

[1] The fair at Blandford is often mentioned in medieval records.
[2] John Coker, Survey of Dorset, London 1732 (not accessible to me).

248; he is referred to as *Brianus de Insula de Blaneford* in 1232 Pat (p. 522). Cf. also Bradford Fm *infra*, the earlier name of which, *Bradford Brian*, derives from the same man.

Durweston

Durweston [dʌrestən][1] 130 E 11

Dervinestone 1086 DB (*Deruinestona* Exon), *Derwinestone* ib.
Deruunestuna 1100-22 (1270) Ch, *Derewineston* 1203-4 FF,
    Derweneston 1242 Ch, *Derwyneston* 1244 *Ass*
Dirwinestun 1091-1106 (*et passim*) Montacute, *Dyr-* 1135-7 ib.,
    Dire- 1135-66 ib.
Darwinestone 1166 RBE (p) (*Durwinestona* LN)
Durewneston' 1212 Fees (92), *Durewineston* 1242-3 Fees (750),
    1280 Ch (p) *et passim* with variant spellings *Dur(e)wynes-*,
    Dur(e)wenes-
Dirrewyneston 1283 FF, *Dyrweneston* 1338 FF
Dorwyneston 1398 IpmR, *Dorwinestan* 1425 IpmR
Durweston 1412 FA, *Dorweston* 1428 FA, *Durwyston* 1431 FA

'*Dēorwine*'s farm', OE *tūn*. For the appearance of OE *eo* as ME *u* in Dorset, cf. Miss Serjeantson in English Studies IV, 195, 197. For this name alone I have noted about 30 *u*-spellings between 1212 and 1490.

Knighton Ho is *Knicteton'* 1212 Fees (87), *Knyhteton'* 1242-3 Fees (753), *Knytteton* 1277 FF, *Knytheton* 1283 FF, *Knyghteton* 1303 FA, 1316 FF *et passim*, *Kyngtedon* 1316 FA, *Knyghton* 1346 FA *et passim*. OE *cnihta-tūn*; for the meaning of *cniht* in pl.-ns cf. EPN s. v.

Note. One of the places called Durweston in DB (*Dervinestone* f. 79 b), consisting of 2 ½ hides and held by Willelmus (de L'Estre), is identified by Eyton (p. 131 f.) with the present Knighton. The identification finds support in the fact that Ricardus de Estre held 2 ½ hides in *Knicteton* in 1212 (cf. first reference above). The *Dervinestone* in question was held TRE by 5 *taini*, and the present name would thus seem to add a further example to the three cases already pointed out by Mawer[2], in which we can actually trace the freemen ("knights") in DB.

---

[1] The pronunciation given in BBC.
[2] PN and History p. 27; cf. EPN s. v. *cniht*.

Fifehead Neville

Fifehead Neville 130 D 9

Fifhide 1086 DB, 1235-6 Fees (425), *Fifide* 1244 *Ass* (p),
  Vifhide 1316 FA
Vyfhyde Nevyle [*Fyfhide Nevile*] 1303 FA

Among later forms may be noted *Fyfede Nevyle* 1428 FA,
Fyfed Nevyll 1491 Ipm, *Fyfhed Nevell* 1535 VE.

See Fifehead Magdalen *supra* 4. The only bearer of the
Nevill name that I have come across in connexion with this
place is Wm de *Nevill'* (1235-6 Fees). According to Tait (IPN
p. 127 f.) the place did not belong to one of the greater Nevill
families.

Fifehead St Quintin[1]

Fifhide 1086 DB, 1205 Cur, 1217, 1222 ClR, 1346 FA[2]
Fifhyde Johannis de Sancto Quintino 1242-3 Fees (750)
Fifhide Seint Quyntyn 1323 FF, *Fyffed Quiteine* 1480 IpmR
Only one form with *v* for *f* (*Vyfhyde* 1303 FA) has been noted.

See the preceding name. On the *St Quintins*, who have left
their name both to this place and to Frome St Quintin *infra*,
see Hutchins II, 643. The first members of that family that I
have found in direct connexion with this place (and with Frome
St Quintin) are Ricardus and Herebertus de *Sancto Quintino*
(1205 Cur).

Woodrow is *Woderove* 14th Glaston F (p) and apparently identical
in origin with Woodrow Fm *supra* 40. There is a third Woodrow
(in Haselbury Bryan) about a mile away.

Hammoon

Hammoon [həmuːn] 130 C 10

Hame 1086 DB (*ham* Exon), *Hamme* 1228 FF, 1252 Pat *et
  passim* to 1331 Fine, *Hama* 1235-6 Fees (424)

---

[1] Formerly a portion of the parish of Belchalwell (and consequently in
Cranborne Hundred, cf. *supra* 46 n. 2) but transferred to Fifehead Neville
in 1920.

[2] *Fifhida* 1109 Dugdale (II, 70) probably belongs here, too.

Ham Galfridi de Moiun 1194 P, *Hamma Galfridi de Moun*
1195 P

Amme Moyun 1297 Pat, *Hamme Mohun* 1303 FA *et passim* with
the distinctive name also spelt *Mooun, Mown, Hame Mohoun*
1340 NI

Hammemown(e) 1408 FF, 1428 FA, *Hammoun* 1428 IpmR

The site of Hammoon is an excellent illustration of OE *hamm*
in its sense of 'low-lying land in the bend of a river', the whole
parish being surrounded by the Stour; cf. Hampreston *infra*.
The place was held in the time of DB by the mighty Wm de
Moion (who derived his name from Moyon in Normandy), and
his family was in possession of the manor for centuries. After
their name had ultimately become fixed to the principal place-
name, a remarkable shifting of stress took place.

Haselbury Bryan

Haselbury Bryan[1] 130 E 8

Hasebere 1201 Cur, 1311 Ipm, 1333 *SR*, *Haseberg(e)* 1201 Cur
Haselber 1237 FF, *Haselbere* 1281, 1282 Cl, 1282, 1297 Ipm,
    1298 FF, 1305 FF (*juxta Stokewak*) *et passim*, *-beare* 1412 FA
Asalber 1291 Tax, 1428 FA, *Hasilbere* 1479 IpmR

The first el. is OE *hæsel* 'hazel', and the second is probably
OE *bearu* 'grove, wood'; cf. Todber *supra* 18. Guy de *Bryene*,
the first Haselbury member of the family whose name was later
on attached to this pl.-n., was here in 1361 (FF).

Crockern Stoke (lost) and **Turberville Stoke** (lòst)

1. *Crokkere Stokke* 1309 Ipm, *Crockerestoke* 1318 FF, *Crokkere-
    stok(k)e* 1340, 1370 FF, *Crokerstok* 1361 FF
    Stokkecrokkere 1340 NI, *Stock Crockerne* 1346 BM I
    Stok' et Crokkern', Stocke et Crockern' 14th Glaston F
    Crokkernestoke 14th Glaston F, *Crockernestoke* 1385 FF, 1435
    IpmR, *Crokkernstokke* 1386 FF

---

[1] This name has often been mixed up with Haselbury Plucknett (So), cf.
Hutchins I, 275. Dorset and Somerset appear under the same heading in
several early records (e. g. P, RBE, Fees), and it is therefore sometimes very
difficult to distinguish between similar names in the two counties. In this
case the So name is probably identical in origin (*Haselberga* 1086 DB, *Hesel-
bere* 1268 Ch, *Haselbere* 1284-5 FA).

2. *Stocketurbervylle* 1318 FF, *Stoketurberville* 1370 FF
Turberevilistokke 1340 FF, *Turbervilstok* 1361 FF, *Turber-vylestoke* 1385 FF, 1435 IpmR

OE *stoc* 'place'. *Crockern Stoke* probably contains the word *crockern*, a compound of OE *crocc* 'pot, crock' and *ærn* 'house', cf. Crockern Tor and Crockernwell in PN D pp. 193, 428.[1] The second place takes (or rather took) its distinctive name from the *Turbervilles* (cf. Johannes de *Turbervill'* Glaston F p. 37), the well-known Dorset family of which we shall find better evidence in connexion with Winterborne Muston, Bryants Puddle, and Melbury Sampford *infra*.

Locketts Fm takes its name from the family of John *Loket* 1386 FF; cf. also Hutchins I, 276 and IV, 533. Near this place is a Stockfield Fm (6″) which may possibly preserve the 'Stock' that enters into the two preceding lost names.

Park Gate is *atte ghate* 1327 *SR* (p), *atte Yate* 1333 *SR* (p). Self-explanatory, OE *geat*.

Langton Long Blandford

Langton Long Blandford 130 F 13, **Langton Ho**
Longa Bladeneford 1179-80 P
Longam Blaneford' 1212 Fees (88), *Longa Blaneford'* 1228 Cl, *Longeblaneford* 1242 Ch, *Lange Blaneford* 1244 *Ass et passim*
Blaneford' Michael' Belet 1217 ClR, *Blaneford' Belet* 1242-3 Fees (752)
Langeblaneford' Tilly 1242-3 Fees (752), *Blaneford Philippi de Tylly* ib. (753)
Langeton Botiller 1303 FA *et passim* with the distinctive addition spelt variously *Botelir, Botyler, Boteler*
Langeton Blaneford 1310 Cl
Langgeton Gulden 1333 *SR*, 1340 NI
Langeton Latile 1334 Cl, Ipm, 1421 IpmR, 1431 FA (*Latyle*)

---

[1] That *Crockern Stoke* contains the word *crocker* 'potter' seems less likely, but the word is found in *Crokeresle* 1394 IpmR and in *Crockeresrewe* (OE *ræw* 'row') t. Hy III (14th) Cerne, the latter referring to a place somewhere near Holnest and possibly preserved in the present Crocker's Knap *infra*. Cf. Crockerhill (with parallels) in PN Sx p. 66.

Langblaneford al. *Langeton Botiler* 1421 IpmR
Lang Blaneford al. *Langton Latile* 1422 IpmR
Langeton Blaneford al. *Langeton Latyle* 1426 IpmR
*Langton, Langton Latell, Langton Butler, Langton Longe Bland-
ford* 1598 AD VI (C 8001)

See Blandford Forum *supra* 50. Langton is self-explanatory,
OE *lang* 'long' and *tūn*. The distinctive names refer to different
manors, cf. Hutchins I, 281 ff. *Michael Belet* is mentioned in
connexion with Blandford in 1216 (ClR). The *la Tillys* had
possessions both here and in the adjoining parish of Blandford
St Mary (*infra*), where their land was distinguished as *Parva
Blaneford* or (*Parva*) *Blaneford Martel*, because held of Wm
Martel (1210-12 RBE p. 548), cf. 1205 ClR (Robert de *Tilli*),
1225 ClR (Oliva de *Tylly*), 1236 Fees p. 581 (Richard de *la
Tille*), and Hutchins I, 163; as early as 1166 (RBE p. 216) Thomas *Latille* held two fees in Dorset. It is difficult to determine
which of the two parishes the above *Blaneford Philippi de Tylly*
refers to. In 1316 (FA) Langton was held by Johannes de
Latille and Johanna *le Botiller*; the family of the latter had
then been here since 1280 (John *le Botyler*, Misc I, 361). Henry
le Guldene held at his death in 1334 Long Blandford and Langton *Latile*, see Ipm VII, 415; for more details cf. Hutchins I,
282 f.

Littleton is *Liteltone* 1086 DB, *Lytleton* 1303, 1346 FA, *Littleton
juxta Blaneford Martel* 1310 FF, *Littel-* 1316 FA, *Litle-* 1333
SR (p), *Lytel-* 1421 IpmR, *Lyttel-* 1431 FA. Self-explanatory,
OE *lytel, tūn*. Langton (Long Blandford) is on the opposite
bank of the Stour.

Pimperne

Pimperne 130 E 13

(*to*) *pimpern*, (*of, to*) *pimpernwelle* 935 (15th) BCS 708
Pinpre 1086 DB (*Pinpra* Exon), 1177-8, 1186-7, 1187-8, 1194
    P, 1212 Fees (87)
Pimpre, Pimpr' 1178-9 P, 1189 France, 1220, 1221 ClR, 1223,
    1224 Pat, 1225, 1227 FF, 1233 Lib, 1238 Pat, *Pinipre*
    1204 ClR
Pympr(e) 1200 (1280) BM I, 1262 Ipm, *Pempre* 1290 Cl

Pimpern(e) 1210-12 RBE, 1234 Cl, Pat, 1242 Ch *et passim*

Pynperne 1290 Pat

Pymperne 1290 Fine, 1291 Tax, 1296 Ipm, 13th AD II *et passim*

Cf. also the forms given under the hundred-name *supra* 49.

Pimperne is possibly an old stream-name, but the etymology is obscure. For different suggestions cf. Ekwall, ERN p. 326, and Wallenberg p. 317 (who starts from a suggestion made by Zachrisson in StNPh II, 65).

Nutford Fm

Nortforde 1086 DB, *notforda* Exon, *Nodford* 1086 DB

Nu[t]ford 1189 France, *Nutford* c. 1191-7 (p), 1222 ClR, 1225, 1227, 1234 FF, 1238 Ch, 1242-3 Fees (753) *et passim*

Nuford 1200 (1280) BM I, *Neudfort* 1201 (1231) BM I

Blakenotford 1319 FF, 1344 FF (*juxta Blaneford*), 1352 Orig

Notforde 1339 Cl, 1346, 1428 FA

'The ford where nut-trees grow', OE *hnutu, ford*. Some of the early forms show AFr spellings. Among the references given above some may belong to what is now called France Fm (earlier *Nutford Lockey*) *infra*, half a mile to the west.

Steepleton Iwerne

Steepleton Iwerne 130 D 12

Werne 1086 DB, *IWerna* Exon

Stepelton(e) 1210-12 RBE, 1235-6 Fees (426), 1316 FA, 1327, 1341 Cl, *Steple-* 1234 Pat, 1550-3 BM I, *Stepil-* 1412, 1428 FA

Stupelton 1244 *Ass* (p), 1279, 1285 Ipm, 1291 Tax, 1303 FA, 1340 NI, 1346, 1431 FA, *Stuple-* 1278 QW, 1333 *SR*, 1428 FA

Stipelton 1291 Tax, 1412 FA, 1428, 1431 IpmR

Stapelton(e) 1316 FA (p), 1331 Ipm (or *Stepelton*)

Iwernestapelton 1346 FF

Iwerne Stupelton 1359 FF, *Iwerne Stupleton* 1431 IpmR, *Iverne Stupulton* 1435 FF

See Iwerne Minster *supra* 26. Steepleton contains OE *stiepel* 'steeple' (EPN). In the case of Winterborne Steepleton *infra* it can be proved that 'steeple' refers to the church steeple, and such may be the case in the present name, too, although there is no church steeple here now. Otherwise Hutchins I, 298.

In order to illustrate the ME development of OE īe (ēa—i) in Dorset (cf. IPN p. 136) a fairly comprehensive list of early forms for this name has been given, cf. also Steeple and Winterborne Steepleton *infra*.[1]

Stourpaine

Stourpaine [stauəpein] 130 E 12

    Sture 1086 DB, *Stures* 1208 Cur, 1212 Fees (87, 88), *Sture(s),*
    -is 1245 Sarum

    Stures Paen 1242-3 Fees (753), *Sture Payn* 1278 QW

    Stoure Payn 1303 FA *et passim, Stourepayn* 1379 FF *et passim,*
    Stowrepayne 1481 IpmR, *Stowerpayne* 1550-3 BM I

Stourpaine derives its principal name from the river Stour (see East and West Stour *supra* 16) and its additional name from the *Payns*. Berthinus *Payn* held the manor in 1303 (FA), but the family must have been here considerably earlier. Cf. also Hutchins I, 304.

Ash is *Aisse* 1086 DB, *Esse* 1244 *Ass* (p), *Assh(e)* 1278 QW, 1346 FF, *Ayssh* 1431 FA. OE *æsc* 'ashtree'. It is doubtful whether *Esse* 1303, 1346 FA, *Esshe* 1428 FA, and *Assh* 1431 FA (Newton Hundred) refer here (as suggested by the indexer of FA) or to Nash Court *supra* 43.

France Fm (earlier *Nutford Lockey*) is *Natford Lok* 1278 QW, *Notforde Locki* 1288 FF, *Notford Lokky* 1303 FA *et passim* (with variants *Loky, Locky*), *Nutford Lokky* 1316 FA, *Nutford Lokke* 1428 FA, *Nutford Lockey* al. *France* 1587 Hutchins. See Nutford Fm *supra* 57. For the distinctive name cf. the mention of a Jord' *Locky* in 1275 RH under the adjacent hundred of Badbury. Can the modern name of the farm possibly be due to

---

[1] The many *e* spellings must, at least partly, be due to the fact that the etymology was transparent to the King's scribes who consequently often used their own method of spelling 'steeple'. The late *a* spellings, on the other hand, should apparently be explained from confusion with the word 'staple', cf. EPN s. v. *stapol*.

the fact that the abbey of Fontevrault in France once had a holding in Nutford?

Hod Hill

In 1302 AD I (A 249, A 251) there is mention of a *Hod* meadow in Shillingstone parish, evidently referring to the low-lying piece of land at the foot of Hod Hill. This must be OE *hōd* 'hood', the hill having been so called from its resemblance to a gigantic hood; cf. Hood in PN D p. 297. For the phonetic development cf. EDG § 163.

Lazerton Fm (6″)

Werne 1086 DB (cf. Eyton p. 137 f.)
Lathirton' 1235-6 Fees (425), *Latherton'* 1242-3 Fees (753)
Lasceton 1244 *Ass* (p) (ident. probable)
Lacerton t. Hy III Ipm, *Laterton* 1278 QW
Lazerton 1288 Orig, 1316, 1428 FA
Lasarton 1327 Cl, Ipm, *Laserton* 1341 Cl
Laston 1333 *SR*, 1340 NI (prob. for *Las'ton*)
Iwernelazerton 1346 FF

I am unable to suggest any etymology for the first element of this name. The farm stands on the river Iwerne.

Tarrant Hinton

Tarrant Hinton 130 D 14

(*at*) *Terente* 871 (15th) BCS 531, (*in*) *Tarente* ib. 532
(*ad*) *Tarentam*, (*ad*) *Terentam* 935 (15th) BCS 708
Tarente 1086 DB, *Tarent'* 1212 Fees (87)[1]
Tarente Hyneton 1285 FA *et passim*, *Hynetone* 1327 *SR*
Tarente Hynton 1340 NI, 1435 FF, *Tarent Henton* 1428 FA

---

[1] In a great many cases the early references to places along the river Tarrant (mostly to the old Tarrant Abbey) appear without a distinctive addition. The following list of variant spellings includes also the instances where the reference is to the river itself: (*to*) *terrente* 935 (15th) BCS 708, (*on*) *terente dene* 956 (15th) BCS 970, *Tarent(e)* 1086 DB, 1166 RBE (p), 1181-2 (etc.) P, 1212 (etc.) Fees, 1227 (etc.) Ch, 1233 Cl, 1237 Pat *et passim*, *Tarrent* 1237 Ch, Cl, *Tarrente*, (*super*) *Tarentam* 1237 Pat, *Tharent(e)* 1237, 1240 Ch, 1242, 1243 Cl, *Tarante* 1270 Ch.

Tarrant Hinton takes its principal name from the river Tarrant, for which see Ekwall, ERN p. 416 ff. The same river gives name also to T. Keynston, T. Launceston, T. Rawston, T. Crawford, T. Monkton, T. Gunville, T. Rushton (all *infra*). Hinton, as pointed out in PN Wo p. 107, is from OE *hĭgna-tūn* 'farm of the community', a usual name for monastic possessions; cf. Hinton Martell and Parva *infra*. Tarrant Hinton belonged to Alfred the Great's endowments to Shaftesbury Abbey (BCS 531, 532).

Hyde Fm is *Hida* 1242 Ch (p), *Le Hyda juxta Blaneford* 1316 FA, *atte Hude* 1327 SR (p), *la Hyde* 1333 SR (p), *De la Hide maner' in Tarent Hynton* 1402 IpmR; cf. also (*Stoke and*) *Hide* 1366 FF, *Stokehyde* 1483 IpmR. OE *hīd* 'hide' (EPN), a common name in Dorset.

Tarrant Keynston

Tarrant Keynston [keinstən] 130 G 14
  Tarente 1086 DB, 1201-2 FF *et passim*
  Tarente Kahaines 1225 Osmund, Sarum (*Kaaignes*) *et passim*
    with the distinctive name variously spelt *Kahaynes, Kay(g)nes*
  Kayneston 1278 Pat, 1361 IpmR, 1431 FA, *Cayneston* 1333 SR
  Tarente de Kaynes 1285 FA, *Tarentekenes* 1291 Tax
  Tarente Keyneston 1303 FA *et passim* (variant -*ay*-)

See Tarrant Hinton *supra* 59. For a detailed account of the family of *Kahaignes* (*Chahaines* etc.), the name of which is preserved also in Coombe Keynes *infra*, see Hutchins I, 319 ff. When that family name was first attached to Tarrant (c. 1225), both places were held by Wm de *Kaaines*, but an ancestor of his, Ralph, was apparently here (and in Coombe Keynes) as early as 1166. Cf. Horsted Keynes in PN Sx p. 336.

Tarrant Launceston

Tarrant Launceston 131 E 1
  Tarente 1086 DB (f. 79 a)[1]
  Tarente de Lowyneston 1285 FA

---

[1] What is now called Tarrant Launceston belonged in the time of DB to the Abbey of the Holy Trinity, Caen; cf. the following forms in (Cal. of Doc. preserved in) France: *Tarent* (1082), *Tarenth* (t. Hy I), *Darent* (1180-87).

Tarente Lowyneston 1288 FF, *Tarrente Louwynston* 1316 FA,
Lowynston 1333 *SR*, *Tarente Lowynston* 1417 FF
Tarent Loweston 1390 Cl, IpmR, *Tarent Louston* 1446-8 Inq
aqd, t. Hy VI, 1467 IpmR
Tarent Launston 1397 IpmR, *Tarent Loneston* 1412 FA, *Launston* 1431 FA, *Tyrant Launceston* 1472 IpmR

See Tarrant Hinton *supra* 59. The distinctive name means
'*Lēofwine*'s farm'; it is difficult to say whether this is a post-Conquest place-name or not.

Tarrant Rawston

Tarrant Rawston 130 F 14

Tarente 1086 DB, *Tærenta* Exon
Tarente Willelmi de Antioche 1242-3 Fees (751)
Tarente Antioch 1291 Tax, 1299 Ipm *et passim* with the distinctive name variously spelt *Auntioche*
Annchiatheston (sic)[1] 1340 NI, *Auntyocheston* 1399, 1404 FF
et passim with variants *Auntyches-*, *Antyoches-*
Tarente Auntyocheston 1399 FF
Tarrant Rawston al. *Antyocke* 1535 VE

See Tarrant Hinton *supra* 59. The above Wm de *Antioche*
is the first member of that family found in direct connexion
with this place, but other members are frequently mentioned
under Dorset in the Pipe Rolls of Henry II, and Robert de
Antiochia occurs as one of the witnesses of a 12th cent. Dorset
charter (Montacute No. 119). Cf. Antioch Fm *supra* 36.

The present additional name *Rawston* may contain the pers.
name *Ralph* (cf. Rawstone in PN D p. 384), but earlier forms
are needed to support this suggestion. Curiously enough the
DB under-tenant here was called *Radulfus* (Eyton p. 131 f.).

Winterborne Houghton

Winterborne Houghton [hautən] 130 F 10

Wintreburne 1086 DB[2], *Winterburn* 1229 Ch, 1234 Fees (401)

---

[1] The form should apparently be read *Aunthiacheston*. NI is full of similar
mistranscriptions.

[2] The Dorset part of DB contains no less than 35 Winterbornes, spelt
Wintreburne 34 times, and *Wintreborne* once; corresponding forms in Exon (not

Winterborn (etc.) *Hueton(e)* 1247 Ipm, 1294 Misc, 1302 AD I
  W.[1] *Hugheton* 1279 Ipm, 1305 AD III, 1428 FA, *W. Hugeton*
  1291 Tax
W. Huweton al. *Howeton* 1285 Ipm
W. Hutton 1297, 1311 FF, *W. Huton* 1301 Cl
W. Houton(e) 1302 AD I *et passim*, *Howeton* 1303, 1412 FA,
  W. Howeton 1316 FA *et passim* to 1439 BM I, *Hoton* 1428 FA
W. Hoghton 1311 Ipm, *Hogheton* 1333 *SR*, 1346 FA
W. Hough(e)ton 1327 Misc, 1331 Ipm, 1439 FF, *Houghton* 1431 FA

There are two small streams called Winterborne in Dorset,
both of which give name to a great number of places. This
one[2] rises at Winterborne Houghton and runs past W. Stickland, (W.) Quarleston, W. Clenston, (W.) Whatcombe, W. Whitchurch, W. Kingston, W. Muston, (W.) Anderson, W. Tomson,
and W. Zelstone (all *infra*). Both streams are typical of their
names (OE *winter*, *burna*), being often dry in the summer; cf.
EPN s. v. *winter*.

The distinctive name *Houghton* should apparently be compared
with similar names in Devon, cf. the discussion in PN D p. 267
s. n. Houghton. Can the first el. here be the ME pers. name
Hugh (*Hugo*)? If Eyton's identification (p. 121 f.) is correct,
one of the DB under-tenants of this manor was *Hugo* (de Bosc-
Herbert), and about 1300 it was held by *Hugh* le Despencer,
earl of Winchester.

Winterborne Stickland

Winterborne Stickland 130 F 11
  Winterborna 1068-84 France, *Wintreburne* 1086 DB
  Winterburn Stikellane 1203 France, *W. Stikelan(e)* 1223 Osmund,
    1225 ClR *et passim* to 1341 Orig, *W. Stykelane* 1347 Cl
  W. Stikeland 1205 ClR, 1316 FA, *W. Sticland* 1310 Inq aqd
  Stykelane 1333 *SR*, 1431 FA, 1535 VE, *W. Stokelane* 1428 FA

See the preceding name. The additional name means 'steep

---

included here) are always spelt *Wintreborna*. As to the identification of the
different DB forms I must content myself with referring to Eyton.

  [1] Since the ME spellings (*Wynterbourne* etc.) are of little interest, I have frequently used a *W.* instead of printing the whole word.

  [2] The charter forms are: *Winterburne* 942 (15th) BCS 775, *Winterburne*,
winterburne ford 943 (15th) BCS 781.

lane', OE *sticol, lane*. The river Winterborne flows here in a
deep valley, surrounded by steep hills.

Broadley Wood[1] is *Bradeley* (*in Stykelane*) 1431 FA. 'Broad
clearing', OE *brād, lēah.*

Normandy Fm may derive its name from the fact that Winterborne Stickland once belonged to the canons of the Cathedral
of Coutances in Normandy.

Quarleston Fm[2] is *Winterburn Quarel* 1232 Pat, *Winterborn' Quarel*
1242-3 Fees (751), *Quareleston* 1303 FA, *Wynterburne Quareleston*
1316 FA, *Quarelston* 1346 FA *et passim*, and derives its name
from the family of Wm *Quarel*, first mentioned here in 1232
Pat (pp. 513, 519). An ancestor was probably Osbert *Quarel,*
frequently mentioned under Dorset in the Pipe Rolls of Henry II.

VI. Combs Ditch Hundred

(*anlang*) *cunucces*[3] *dich* 942 (15th) BCS 775
(*on*) *cinninces dic* (sic) 943 (15th) BCS 781
concresdie (sic) 1084 GeldRoll
Cunkesdiche 1244 *Ass*, -*dik* 1300 Ipm, -*dych* 1303 FA, *Cunkis-
    dych* 1428 FA
Conkesdich 1244 *Ass*, 1307 Ipm, 1316, 1346 FA, 1387 Cl, -*dyche*
    1431 FA, *Coukesdiche* (sic) 1401, 1408 FF, -*dyche* 1486 Ipm
Cunkediche, Cuniḡedych 1244 *Ass*
Conewesdich' (sic) 1251-2 Fees (1267)

---

[1] Part of W. Stickland parish was annexed to Bryanston in 1897, and the
wood is now in the latter parish.

[2] There is another Quarleston c. 2 miles NE in Bryanston parish. I have
found no certain early forms for that place. It is not by the Winterborne
stream.

[3] Birch gives this form only as an alternative reading in note 5: "Or *cunucces*, MS". In the text itself he prints *cinincces*, probably as an attempt at
getting some meaning out of the word. The later forms collected above show,
however, that *cunucces* is the correct reading, and they also suggest that *cinninces* in BCS 781 should be read *cunnuces*. A careful examination of the MS
has convinced me that this assumption is correct. The two charter forms
refer of course to the 'ditch' itself, not to the hundred.

Kunekesdich 1265 Misc, *Chunekesdich* 1296 Ipm, *Cunekesdych*
1300 Ipm, *Conekesdych* 1333 *SR*, 1340 NI, *-dich* 1343 Cl
Comingesdich 1269 FF, *Cumebusdich* 1275 RH, *Cokesdich* 1275 Cl

The second el. is of course OE *dīc* 'ditch, dike'. The first is
apparently the genitive of a word *cunuc*, but the question must
be left open whether that word is a pers. name[1] or a topographical term; cf. Mawer, PN NbDu p. 51 f. s. n. Consett, and
Ekwall, ERN p. 92 s. n. Cong Burn. Ekwall may be right in
suggesting that *cunuc* is a hill-name.

Combs Ditch is the name of an ancient earthwork or dike
beginning a little S of Winterborne Clenston church (130 G 11)
and running in a south-easterly direction for about three miles
until it loses itself in Great Coll Wood. It appears to have
been of still larger extent in earlier times (cf. Hutchins I, 192).

Anderson

Anderson 130 I 12
Wintreburne 1086 DB

It is called *Wynterbourn Fiveesse* 1284 Cl, *Wynterburn Fivesses*
1285 Cl, *W. Fifaysches* (*Fisaisshe*) 1285 Pat, and the like up to
1451 IpmR, with the additional name variously spelt *Fifhasse*,
Fifheysse, *Fyhasse*, *Fifhassh*, *Fifayssh*, *Fyf(f)ayssh*, *Vifhache*,
Vif(h)assh, *Vyfass(c)he*, *Vifaysshe*. See Winterborne Houghton
supra 61. The distinctive name means 'five ash-trees', OE *fif, æsc*.
In earlier references that name always refers to the manor.

The early forms of the present name are *Andreweston* 1331
FF, 1340 NI, *Andruston* 1377 Cl, *Anderston* 1428 FA, *Wynter-*
borne Andreston 1469 IpmR. The name is probably due to the
dedication of one of the churches here to St Andrew. That
church (now disused) is in the present parish of Winterborne
Tomson but only a few hundred yards from the manor house
of Anderson. The name *Andreweston* (etc.) seems in earlier references always to denote either the church or the parish (not
the manor). Not until 1469 is the manor referred to as *W. An-*
dreston.

---

[1] Cf. Crawford, Arch. Journal LXXVII, 145, who points to the pers. name
Conuc in the Book of Llandaff.

Blandford St Mary

Blandford St Mary 130 F 13

Parva Blaneford 1205, 1225 ClR, 1236 Fees (581), *Parva Blaneforde Martel* 1210-12 RBE, *Blaneford Martel* 1302, 1339 FF

Blaneford St Mary 1262 FF, 1265 Misc, *Sancte Marie de Blaneford* 1291 Tax, *Blaneford Marie* 1340 NI, *Blaneford Beate Marie* 1421 IpmR, 1431 FA, *Seynt Mary Blanford* 1489 Ipm *Blaneford Mon(i)alium* 1316 FA

See Blandford Forum *supra* 50. *St Mary* "either from the dedication of its church, or because it belonged to the nunnery of St. Mary in Clerkenwell, London" (Hutchins). The latter fact accounts for the temporary addition *Monialium* (Latin *monialis* 'a nun'). For (*Parva*) *Blaneford Martel* cf. the discussion under Langton Long Blandford *supra* 55.

Thorncombe is *Tornecome* 1086 DB, *Tornecumba* 1160-62 (1336) Ch, *Turnecumb(a)* 1203 RC, 1234 Cl, *Thor(e)cumbe* 1234 Pat, 1244 FF, *Thorncumbe* 1236 FF, *Thornecombe* 1398 IpmR. 'Thorn valley', OE *þorn* (with temporary confusion with *þyrne*), *cumb*; cf. Thurnworth *infra*.

Bloxworth

Bloxworth 130 I 12

(*in*) *Blacewyrðe* (sic) 987 KCD 656 (copy, perhaps spurious) *Blocheshorde* 1086 DB, *-borda* Exon

Blokeswrth' 1200 Cur (p), *-wurth(e)* 1201-2 FF, 1213 ClR, 1260 Pat (p), *-worth(e)* 1303, 1316, 1346 FA

Blokeswrd' 1212 Fees (92), *Blokeswerdi* 1250 Pap

Blockeswurth, -worth 1223 Pat (p), 1291 Tax *et passim*

Bloxworth 1481 IpmR

Probably '*Bloc(c)*'s homestead', OE *weorþ*. This pers. name is not on independent record in OE but has been postulated from good place-name material, cf. e. g. PN Wo p. 98 s. n. Blockley. In ME times it occurs as a surname (Robert *Bloc*) as early as 1199 Cur (Wilts).

Marsh Fm is *atte Mershe* 1333 *SR* (p). Self-explanatory, OE *mersc*.

Stroud Bridge is *Strode* 1333 *SR* (p). OE *strōd* 'marshy land overgrown with brushwood'.

Winterborne Clenston

Winterborne Clenston 130 G 11

Wintreburne 1086 DB, *Winterburn* 1232 Pat
Winterborn' Clench 1242-3 Fees (750)
Wynterborn Cleyngestone 1274 Ipm, *W. Clencheston* 1303 FA *et passim*, *W. Clencheton* 1318 FF, *W. Clyncheston* 1370 FF
Clengeston 1316 FA, *Clencheston* 1333 *SR*, 1340 NI
W. Clenston 1535 VE

This Winterborne takes its distinctive name from Robert *Clench*, mentioned twice in 1232 Pat (pp. 513, 522).[1] Three entries from 1232 Pat (pp. 513, 519, 522) have thus helped us to trace the origin of the names of the three adjacent places Bryanston *supra* 51, Quarleston *supra* 63, and Winterborne Clenston.

A second manor here is called *Wynterborne Nicholestone* 1283 AD VI *et passim* (with the distinctive name also written *Nicholaston*, *Nicolston*), *W. Nicole* 1286 Ipm, Cl, *Nicholeston* (alone) 1340 NI, and *W. Nicholai* 1428 FA. It is stated to have been called *Winterborne St. Nicholas* in later records and possibly received its additional name from the dedication of its church (Hutchins). In 1340 (NI) *Nicholeston* and *Clencheston* denoted two distinct parishes.

A third manor here, *Winterborne Philipston*, appears as *Wynterburn Philip*'s 1244 FF but has otherwise not been met with in medieval records. The names of both these manors are now lost.

Winterborne Tomson

Winterborne Tomson 130 I 12

Wintreburne 1086 DB, *Winterborn' Thom'* 1242-3 Fees (753)
Wynterbourn Thomaston 1280 FF *et passim*, *W. Thomston* 1428 FA
Thomaston 1316 FA, *Thomaseston* 1340 NI, *Thomston* 1428 FA

---

[1] No other person bearing the name *Clench* has been found in connexion with Winterborne, but a family so called resided for many generations in the nearest town, Blandford Forum, and the name is still met with in the county.

There is no church here dedicated to St Thomas (cf. the discussion in connexion with Anderson *supra* 64), so the distinctive name should probably be derived from some unknown *Thomas*.

Den Wood (6″) is to be associated with the boundary-mark (*anlang*) *standene* 943 (15th) BCS 781, which means 'stone valley', OE *stān*, *denu*.

Winterborne Whitchurch

Winterborne Whitchurch 130 H 11

Wintreburne 1086 DB, *Winterborn' Rocheford'* 1242-3 Fees (751)
W. Albi Monasterii 1202 FF, 1206 RC, 1269 Sarum, 1297 Ipm
Winterburn and Blauncmuster 1249 FF
W. Bla(u)ncmuster 1253, 1256 FF, *W. Blauncmusters* 1280 Ch,
  W. Blaumuster (*Blauncmoster*) 1303 FA
Winterburn and Witchirch 1294 Misc, *Wytchurche* 1316 FA,
  Whitchurche 1333 *SR*, 1431 FA
W. Whytchirche 1294 Cl *et passim* with the distinctive name
  spelt variously *W(h)ytchurch*, *Whitchirche*, *-churche*, and once
  (1331 Ipm) *Withcherche*[1]

The distinctive name means 'white church' (or possibly 'stone church', cf. PN Bk p. 86), OE *hwīt*, *cirice*; cf. Whitchurch Canonicorum *infra*. The dates of the above Latin and French forms of the name possibly suggest that *Whitchurch* is simply a translation. The *Rochefords* had apparently been here for more than half a century when first mentioned in 1294 (Cl, Misc), cf. Hutchins I, 196 f.

La Lee Fm [ləli:] is *la Le, la le* 1244 *Ass* (p), *La Leye* 1291 Tax, *La Lea* 1310 Inq aqd, *La Lee* 1535 VE, *Lalee* 1811 OM. OE *lēah*. The French definite article is of interest here, as this seems to be the only case hitherto noted where that article is preserved as an independent word in front of an English place-name. For cases of the French article coalescing with the noun,

---

[1] A *Winterburne Gurewambe* found in two 12th cent. Montacute charters (No. 118 f.) has been identified by Bond (Do Field Club XI, 146) with Winterborne Whitchurch. An equally obscure *Winterburn' Guahebon* (*Guah'bon*) in 1235, 1236 Cl is identified by the indexer of that record with Whatcombe (*infra*) in this parish.

cf. PN Bk p. 51 s. n. Lamua Hundred, PN Wo p. 355 s. n. Lifford, and PN D p. 490 s. n. Lawell Ho.

Whatcombe

(*on*) *hwete cumb* 943 (15th) BCS 781
Watecumbe 1316 FA, *Watcoumbe* 1363 Cl, *Whatecombe* 1412 FA
Wynterborn Watecombe 1370 FF, *W. Whatecombe* 1402 IpmR
'Wheat valley' (EPN), OE *hwǣte, cumb*.

VII. Bere Regis Hundred

bere 1084 GeldRoll, *Bera* 1169-70, 1170-1 (etc.) P
Bere 1244 Fees (1387), 1265 Misc, 1275 RH, Cl *et passim*
Byre 1333 *SR*, 1346 FA, 1365 Cl, 1431 FA, *Beere* 1428 FA
See next name. The pre-DB hundred of *Bere* comprised *inter alia* also what was later called *Hundredesberg* (now Barrow Hundred *infra*).

Bere Regis

Bere Regis 130 I 11

Bere, Bera(m) 1086 DB, Exon, 1091, 1158 Osmund, 1195 P, 1204, 1205 (etc.) ClR, 1207, 1213 PatR *et passim*
Beere 1242 Sarum, 1314 Ipm, 1428 FA, 1578 BM I
la Bere 1248 Cl, 1255 Pat, 1365 Cl
By(e)re, Bi(e)re 1259, 1306 Pat, 1314 Ipm *et passim* to 1412 FA
Kyngesbyre, -bere, -biere, Kingesbere 1264 Orig, 1280 Ch, 1303 FA, 1308 FF, 1316 FA, 1319 FF *et passim*
Bire (Byre) Regis 1495 Ipm

OE *bǣr(e)* 'pasture' according to EPN, but after the discussion in PN D p. 107 s. n. Shebbear (cf. Todber *supra* 18) we should probably take Dorset names of this type to go back to OE *bearu* 'grove, wood', instead; several of the forms above refer to Bere Wood. The place belonged to the old crown demesnes (DB); hence *Kynges-* and *Regis*.

Chamberlayne's Fm is probably to be associated with the family of Nicholas *le Chaumberlayn*, mentioned under this hundred in 1244 *Ass* 201 m. 2.

Dodding's Fm is *Bere* 1086 DB, Exon, *Dogdyngbire* 1320 Ch, *Doddyngbyre* 1348, 1419 FF, *Dodyngbeare* 1412 FA, *Dodding Bere* 1811 OM. A pers. name *Doding* is recorded in DB (cf. Redin p. 169), and has been met with as a surname (Robert *Dodding*) in 1244 *Ass* (201 m. 7) under Knowlton Hundred (Do). *Dodding* in the present name, however, has probably another origin. Ekwall (ERN p. 210) has drawn attention to a (mol. de) *la Doddingg'* from an unprinted Do Ass Roll of 1268. A similar reference, *Kyngesbere apud la Doddinge*, is found in Hutchins I, 140 (charter without date), and it seems fairly clear from the context of the latter of these two references (*Kyngesbere* = Bere Regis) that they both refer to the present Dodding's Fm. Ekwall regards *la Doddingg'* as being very likely an original stream-name. It is true Dodding's Fm is on a stream, but it is also at the foot of a well-marked hillock, and one is therefore at least equally inclined to interpret *la Doddingg'* (*la Doddinge*) as a hill-name. Cf. Wallenberg (p. 3) who connects *doddinghyrnan* BCS 3 with *inter alia* Mod. Engl. dial. *dod(d)* 'a rounded summit or eminence'.

Foulcombe (lost) is *Fulcume* 1316 FA, *Foulecomb* 1483 IpmR. 'Dirty valley', OE *fūl, cumb*.

Hyde Ho is *Hyde* 1285 FA, *Hyda* 1291 Tax, *La Hyde* 1316 FA. OE *hīd* 'hide'.

Philliols Fm is named after the *Filiols*, for whom see Hutchins III, 151 ff. William and Hugh *Filol* are mentioned in connexion with this parish in 1354 (FF), and John *Filoll* (1403 IpmR) had land in Stockley, the adjoining farm.

Roke Fm is apparently identical with *Rokemede* (*in Kyngesbere*) 1478 FF. The form is late but indicates that the original meaning was 'meadow haunted by rooks', OE *hrōc, mǣd*.

Shitterton
   Scetre 1086 DB, *scetra* Exon
   Schitereston 1285 FA
   Shiter(e)ton 1300 FF, 1316, 1431 FA, 1431, 1484 IpmR
   Shyterton 1333 *SR*, 1420 FF, *Chiterton* 1456 IpmR

Names of this type have been dealt with *inter alia* in PN Wo
p. 32 (from where also the above identification of the DB form
is taken) and by Ekwall in ERN p. 362 ff. Shitterton apparently
contains an OE *scitere* (derived from OE *scītan* 'cacare' or OE
*scite 'dung')

Southbrook is *Suth(e)brok* 1300 FF, 1316 FA, *Bysouthbrouk* 1352
FF, *Southbrook* 1419 FF. Self-explanatory, OE *sūð*, *brōc*.

Stockley Fms is *Stocle* (*juxta Kyngesbere*) 1308 FF, *Stockley* 1403
IpmR, *Stokkele* 1415 IpmR. 'Stump-clearing', OE *stocc*, *lēah*.

Woodbury Hill
   (*on*) *windee bergh* 943 (15th) BCS 781
   Windebyre 1242 Sarum (p. 277)
   Wodeburyhyll 1535 VE

The form *Windebyre* is taken from a Sarum charter containing
an endowment of the vicarage of Bere Regis, and from the context in which it occurs ("*cum omnibus oblationibus de Windebyre
in festo Nativitatis beatæ Mariæ Virginis*") I have drawn the
conclusion that it must refer to the present Woodbury Hill.[1]
This identification, on the other hand, clearly indicates that the
boundary-mark *windee bergh* in BCS 781 refers to this hill, too.

The second el. of the name is OE *beorg* 'hill', and the first
may be either OE *wind* 'wind' or *windig* 'windy'.[2] *wi-* was apt
to become *wu-* in Dorset, and popular etymology has done the
rest. Cf. Woodstreet Fm *infra*.

Milborne Stileham
Milborne Stileham 130 I 10
   Meleborne 1086 DB, *-bourne* 1305 Ipm, *Melborne* 1398 IpmR
   Mileburn' 1225 ClR, *Milborne* 1361 Cl

---

[1] This hill (near Bere Regis) has since hundreds of years been the scene of
a very considerable fair, which begins on the Nativity of the Virgin Mary,
Sept. 18; cf. e. g. Hutchins I, 135, and Thomas Hardy, Far from the Madding
Crowd, chapter 50.

[2] Pl.-ns meaning 'windy hill' are fairly common in England, cf. (*on*) *wind-
berghes* BCS 564 (Do), Windle (PN La p. 109), and the parallels adduced there.
Windy Bank (PN La p. 58) and Windybank (PN SWY p. 302) seem to contain the adj. *windig*.

Muleborn(e) 1285 FA, 1291 Tax
Mulleborne Beek 1326 BM I, *Milbournebek* 1436 IpmR
Little Meliburne 1332 Ch, *Parva Melebourn* 1340 BM I
Milborn Stylam 1431 FA

'Mill-brook' OE *myln, burna*. The same stream has also given name to Milborne St Andrew *infra*. *Be(e)k* because earlier belonging to the abbey of Bec-Hellouin in Normandy. *Stileham* must for the present remain unexplained. It may possibly contain OE *stīgel* 'stile', but the scanty material does not allow of any certainty.

Winterborne Kingston

Winterborne Kingston 130 I 12

Wintreburne 1086 DB, *Wynterburn, -born* 1233 Cl, 1431 FA
Kingeswinterburn(e)[1] 1194 P, 1206 RC, 1212 Fees (89), 1234
    Cl, FineR, 1242 Sarum, 1244 Fees (1387) *et passim*
Winterborne Kingston, Wyntreburn Kyngeston 1310 Inq aqd,
    1316 FA *et passim, Kingeston Wynterborn* 1459, 1462 IpmR
Wynterborn Regis 1312 Ipm, *Kyngeston juxta Byre* 1468 IpmR

See Winterborne Houghton *supra* 61. For the distinctive name cf. entries like 1212 Fees (89)[2] and 1244 ib. (1387); see also Hutchins I, 145.

Abbot's Court Fm is *Abescourte* 1550-3 BM I, the name probably preserving some reminiscence of the time when the *abbess* of Tarrant had a concern here; cf. Hutchins I, 150.

Whitwell (lost) is *Whitwell* (*in Kingeston Wynterborn*) 1459, 1462 IpmR, *Whytwell* 1473 IpmR. A manorial name. The *Wytewells*, the 13th cent. owners of Winterborne Kingston, came from Norfolk (Hutchins).

Winterborne Muston

Wintreburne 1086 DB, *Winterburn* 1204 RC, FineR, 1228 FF
Vinterburne et Turberville, Winterburne Turbereville 1242 Sarum,
    W. Turbervill' 1242-3 Fees (753), 1262 FF, 1275 RH

---

[1] Also spelt *Kingiswinterburn, Kyn(g)geswynterburn(e)*, etc.

[2] *Rogerus de Millirs tenet in Kingeswinterburn' c. solidatas terre de dono domini Regis Johannis.*

Winterborn' Musters 1242-3 Fees (751), *W. Mosters* 1286 Ipm
Winterborne Mousterston 1310 Inq aqd, *Musterton* 1331 FF,
W. Mustereston 1354 FF, *W. Musterton* 1403 IpmR, 1535 VE
Turbervileston (-*vyles*-) 1316 FA[1], 1333 *SR*, 1431 FA[1], *Winter-
born Turbervileston* 1416 IpmR
W. Mustereston al. *W. Turbervyleston* 1468 IpmR

Walter de *Turbervill* received land here in 1204 (RC, FineR).
Among the witnesses to his son's, Bartholomew de *Turbervill's*,
charters concerning grants in Bere Regis and *Winterburne Turbereville* (see Sarum p. 278 ff.) there is a certain Walter de
Musters (*Mustries*), also mentioned in 1244 *Ass* (201 m. 13)
under Combs Ditch Hundred (Walter de *Monast'us*). Cf. also
Melbury Sampford, Bryants Puddle, and Muston Fm, all *infra*.

VIII. Rushmore Hundred

(*an lang*) *riscemeres* 943 (15th) BCS 781
Rys(s)emore 1275 RH, 1285 FA, *Rysshemore* 1278 QW, 1425
IpmR
Russhemore 1278 QW, 1327 *SR*, *Russchemore* 1307 Ipm, *Russh-
more* 1333 *SR*, 1431 FA, *Russehemour* 1340 NI
Risshemore 1315 Ipm, *Risemore* 1316 FA

This is a compound of OE *rysc* 'rush' and *mere* 'pool, (mere)',
the second el. showing later confusion with OE *mōr* 'swampy
ground, (moor)'; cf. Frogmore Fm *supra* 25. The boundary-mark
riscemere in BCS 781 must refer to the small brook that rises
at Botany Bay Barn (130 I 12) and joins the Winterborne stream
a little E of Winterborne Zelstone. The ground here is marshy.
The name *Rushmore* is not to be found on the maps, but the
description in Hutchins (I, 336) of the spot so called takes us
to the immediate neighbourhood of the upper part of that brook.
Rushmore is the smallest hundred in Dorset, containing only

---

[1] The identification in FA (II, 595) with Bryants Puddle is a mistake, cf.
Tait, IPN p. 131 n. 6. *Turbervileston* occurs under the hundred of Combs
Ditch in FA, Winterborn Muston being a tithing in that hundred, whereas
Bryants Puddle (*Pidele Turbervyll* or *Turbervylespudele*) is, and always was, in
Barrow (*Hundredesberg*) Hundred.

the parish of Winterborne Zelstone (and West Morden in Morden parish in Loosebarrow Hundred).

Winterborne Zelstone

Winterborne Zelstone 130 I 13

Wintreborne 1086 DB, *Wynterburn* 1227 FF

Wynterburne Malreward' 1230 P, *W. Maureward* 1242-3 Fees (750), 1278 QW, 1285 FA *et passim*[1], *W. Marleward* 1285 FA

Marlewardeston 1275 RH

Wynterbo(u)rn Selyston 1350 FF, 1431 FA, *W. Seleston* 1403 IpmR, 1422 FF, *Selston Wynterborne* 1484 IpmR, *W. Selston* 1535 VE

Wynterborn Seleston al. *Wynterborn Maureward* 1468 IpmR[2]

The first of the *Maurewards* (Fr 'mal regard') that I have found in connexion with this place is Wm *Maureward* in 1227 (FF); the family remained here for several generations. The solution of the present distinctive name is apparently to be found in an unprinted Shaftesbury charter (*Harl. 61, f. 28*) connected with the adjacent village of Almer. In that charter there is mention of three *capellani Henrici de Seles*, and there can be little doubt that Zelstone contains the family name of this Henry de *Seles*, about whom nothing is otherwise known. He may have come from Zeals (earlier *Seles*) in Wilts.

Huish is *atte Ywyssch'* 1333 SR (p), *Hywyssch* 1340 NI (p), *Wynterbourn Hywyssh* 1350 FF, *Hywyssh* 1462 FF. OE *hīwisc* land for one household'.

IX. Loosebarrow Hundred

Luseberge 1130 PR, *Luseberga* 1169-70 *et passim* to 1184-5 P, *Luseberg(h)* 1219 Fees (260), 1227 ib. (378), 1244 *Ass*, 1251-2 Fees (1267), 1321 Ipm, *Luseberehe* 1265 Misc, *Lusbergh* 1303, 1428 FA, *Lus(e)burgh* 1315, 1344 Fine

---

[1] Occasional spellings are *W. Maylward* 1291 Tax, *W. Maryward* 1383 IpmR, *W. Maurewod* 1416 IpmR, *W. Maleward* 1428 FA.

[2] As late as 1626 (Do Ipm) we have mention of "the manors of Winterborne Marwood and Winterborne Zelston".

Loseberge 1212 Fees (88), *Losebergh(e)* 1315 Ipm, 1316 FA,
   1340 NI, 1361 IpmR, *-burgh* 1323 Inq aqd, 1346 FA, *-bargh*
   1431 FA

Louseberouwe 1306 Ipm, *Lousebergh* 1333 *SR*, 1343 Orig, *Lous-
   berghe* 1376 FF, *Louseburgh* 1388 FF

The elements are apparently OE *lūs* 'louse' and *beorg* 'hill,
barrow', cf. *lusa beorg* BCS 699, *lusebeorg* BCS 748 (orig.), and
PN NRY p. 80 f. s. n. Loose Howe. The hundred was called
celeberge in the Geld Roll (1084), from Charborough *infra*. Loosebarrow is somewhere west of that place, but the barrow is now
almost levelled (Hutchins), and the name is not to be found on
the maps.

Almer

Almer 130 H 13

(of, on) elmere 943 (15th) BCS 781, *Elmer* 1211 Cur
Elmerham 1166 RBE (cf. Hutchins I, 711)
Almere 1212 Fees (87), 1227 FF, 1228 Cl, 1231 FF, 1235-6
   Fees (426), 1246 Ipm *et passim*, *Au(e)mere* 1244 *Ass*
Estalmere 1290 Ipm, 1391 FF, *West Almere* 1408 FF

This means 'eel-pool' (OE *ǣl, mere*), as suggested in PN Sx
p. 142 s. n. Elmer Fm. The form *Au(e)mere* shows AN vocalization of *l*.

Mapperton

(at, to) Mapeldertune 943 (15th) BCS 781
Mapledretone 1086 DB, *Mapeldorthon, Mapeldureton* 1244 *Ass*
Maperton 1212 Fees (87), 1385 FF
Mapellerton 1316 FA, *Mapelerton* 1326 Ipm, 1327 Cl *et passim*
'Maple-tree farm', OE *mapuldor, tūn*. Mapperton *infra* is iden-
tical in origin.

Morden

Morden, East and **West** 130 I 13

Mordune, Mordone 1086 DB (*Mordona* Exon)

Other forms are without interest except to mention *Mordon'
Roberti* 1242-3 Fees (751), cf. *Robertus* de Porton Fees p. 378.
Est- is prefixed from 1250 (Fees), *West-* from 1275 (RH), and
the spelling *Morden* occurs from 1280 (Pat) onwards. *Mourdon*
is rare (1340 NI, 1346 FA).

The elements are of course OE *mōr* 'barren land, (moor)' and *dūn* 'hill, down'. Morden is at the northern extremity of the great Dorset heath.

Charborough Ho[1]

Cereberie 1086 DB, *Cereberia* Exon, *Cereberg* 1253 FF, *Cerberge* 1274 Cl (*passim*)

Cheleberge 1204 PatR, 1215 ClR, 1251 Ch, *Chelebir'* 1227 Fees (379)

Chereberge 1212 Fees (88), *Cherebergh* 1274 Ipm

Chernebrug' 1219 Fees (260)

Cherlegh' (sic) 1251-2 Fees (1267)

Cherberwe 1274 Cl, Fine, *Chereberwe* 1275 Cl, 1280 Pat

Cherbergh 1316 FA, 1333 *SR*, 1334, 1337 FF, 1341 Cl, 1490 Ipm

Cherburgh 1389 IpmR, 1396 FF, 1428 FA

Charburgh 1431 FA, *Charborughe* 1535 VE

I take the meaning of Charborough to be 'the barrow (OE *beorg*) by the river *Cherne*'. The river near which Charborough is situated is now called *Winterborne*. Certain facts, however, would seem to indicate that *Winterborne* was formerly the name only of the upper part of that stream. The many Winterbornes (*supra*), scattered along its upper course, come to an end with Winterborne Zelstone, and the boundaries of BCS 781 also tend to show that the stream was called *Winterborne* only up the point E of Winterborne Zelstone where it joins the *riscemere* discussed under Rushmore *supra* 72, or at any rate not farther north-east than Almer. From Almer (where the stream becomes considerably broader and probably could not appropriately be called a 'winter-burn') and up to the point near Sturminster Marshall where it falls into the Stour, it may once have been called *Cherne*. I do not base this suggestion barely on the evidence of the above form *Chernebrug*, but chiefly on a comparison with Charminster *infra*. That place undoubtedly takes its name from the river *Cerne*, although only two of the early forms clearly suggest this (*Cerneministr'* 1223 ClR, *Chernminstr'* 1291 Tax); all the other forms (*Cer-, Cere-, Cher-, Char-*) show loss of *n*, thus affording a good parallel to the early forms of Char-

[1] Indexers have often confused this name with Chalbury *infra* and Chelborough *infra*. Cf. also Chilbridge *infra*.

borough. Another parallel is Charmouth (*infra*) 'mouth of the *Cerne*', in which name, however, the *n* was preserved throughout the ME time, probably because the meaning of the compound was easy to understand.

On the spelling *c* for *ch*, cf. Cerne Abbas *infra*. *l* for *r* is another AFr feature (dissimilation of *r—r* to *l—r*), cf. Zachrisson, AN Infl. p. 120.

Marsh Bridge (1"), Marsh Wood (6")

In 1274 Ipm there is mention of a common pasture in Charborough called *Brodermerse*, and the pers. name *in the Merssh*, *atte Merssh*, is found repeatedly in 1333 *SR* under this hundred. OE *mersc*.

Sherford is *Sireford* 1244 *Ass* (p). The meaning is evidently 'clear ford', OE *scīr, ford*.

Whitefield is *Wytefeld* 1244 *Ass*. The meaning is clear (OE *hwīt, feld*)[1], but the identification is not absolutely certain.

Spettisbury

Spettisbury [spetsbəri] 130 G 13

   Spesteberie, Spehtesberie 1086 DB, *Speftesberia* Exon
   Poststeberia, Posteberies (-bere, -beri) 1087-1100, 1099, 1166-87,
      1187 France, *Postebiri, Posterbiri* 1219 Sarum
   Spectesb'i 1161-2 P, *Spectesbury* 1294 Pat, 1385 IpmR
   Spetteberi 1242 Ch, *Spettebury* 1294 Pat *et passim* to 1360 Fine
   Spectebury 1291 Tax *et passim* to 1428 FA, *Spectbury* 1346 FF
   Spestesbyry 1301 Ipm
   Espeghtebury 1312 Inq aqd, *Speghtebury* 1313 Inq aqd, Orig
      et passim to 1390 FF, *Speyghtebury* 1340 NI
   Speghtesbury 1399, 1401 FF, *Speytesburi* 1435 FF
   Spetisbury 1535 VE, *Spittesburye* 1571 BM I

The second el. is OE *burh* (dat. *byrig*), the reference being to the ancient earthwork now called Spettisbury Rings. The first el. looks like an unrecorded OE **spe(o)ht*, corresponding to OHG *speht* (German *Specht*), and possibly the origin of the

---

[1] For the meaning of 'white' here, cf. EPN s. v. *hwīt*.

obsolete Modern English *speight* 'the green woodpecker' (NED). The German word seems to enter into *Spessart* (earlier *Spehtes-hart*) 'Spechtwald' and possibly a few more German place-names, cf. Kluge, Etym. Wörterbuch s. v. *Specht*, and Förstemann, Orts-namen s. v. *Speht*. For the loss of *s* before *p* in some of the earliest forms, cf. Zachrisson, AN Infl. p. 67 ff.

Middlestreet (lost), now **South Fm**
   Middelstrete 1278 FF *et passim* to 1451 FF, *Middlestrete* 1385
      IpmR, *Middelstreet* 1811 OM
Self-explanatory, OE *middel*, *strǣt*. Three minor roads run parallel in a south-westerly direction from Spettisbury, and this farm evidently got its name from its situation by the middle road.

X. Badbury Hundred[1]

(æt) Baddan byrig s. a. 901 ASC(A)
bedeb'ie 1084 Geld Roll
Badeberi 1181-2, 1184-5 P, *-bir'* 1212 Fees (91), 1244 *Ass*
Baddeberi 1219 Fees (260), *Baddebir'* 1230 P, 1244 Fees (1388)
   et passim with variant spellings *-byr'*, *-bur(y)*
Badbir' 1286 (1313) Ch, *Badbury* 1428 FA

This means 'the *burh* of *Badda*', a well recorded OE pers. name (Redin p. 44), the reference being to the famous camp (in Shapwick parish) now called Badbury Rings. This is sup-posed by some scholars to have been the scene of the battle of *Mons Badonicus*, an identification first suggested by Guest (Origines Celticae II, 189). The theory has been subjected to severe criticism (cf. e. g. W. H. Stevenson in EHR XVII, 633 f.) and seems now to have been generally given up, cf. Antiquity III, 297.

---

[1] The name of the pre-DB hundred of *canendone* (1084 Geld Roll), which according to Eyton (pp. 117 f., 143) comprised parts of the present hundreds of Badbury and Cranborne, has been met with three times in later records, viz. in the form *Canedon'* in 1212 Fees (88) and 1244 *Ass* (201 m. 13), and in the form *Kenedun'* in 1219 Fees (260).

Chalbury

Chalbury [tʃɔːlbəri] 131 F 3

(ouer) chelesbergh' [1] 935 (15th) BCS 708

(on) cheoles burge (eastgeat) 946 (13th) BCS 818

(an) cheoles byrig (east gete) 956 (13th) BCS 958

Chelesbyr' 1244 *Ass, Chelesbury* 1297 Cl, Pat, 1318 FF, 1324
Inq aqd, 1340 NI, 1341 FF

Cheselbury 1291 Tax, *Chesebury* 1428 FA

Chalesbury 1386 IpmR, *Chelbury* 1428 FA

Chaldebery 1432 BM I, *Chalbery, Chelkesbury* 1535 VE

'The *burh* of *Cēol'* (cf. Gevenich p. 38).[2] For this pers. name
cf. Redin p. 5. Since we should have expected a development
to *Chel(s)-* rather than to *Chal-* [ɔː], the modern form should
probably be explained as due to confusion with *chald* (< OE *ceald*
'cold'), cf. the form *Chaldebery* above. The situation of Chalbury
on the top of a high hill speaks in favour of such an assumption.[3] *Cheselbury* (1291 Tax) may reflect confusion with another
element, OE *ceosol* 'gravel'[4], but is probably best explained as a
metathesis. *Chesebury* (1428 FA) occurs in a list of churches
which seems to be a mere copy of Tax.

Didlington Fm (6")

(æt) Didelingtune, (into) dydelingtune 946 (13th) BCS 818

Dudelingtone, (æt) Dydelingtune ib. (rubrics)

(æt, to) Dydylingtune 956 (13th) BCS 958, *(æt) Dydylingetune*
ib. (rubric)

Dedilintone 1086 DB, *Dedlyngton* 1327 *SR*

Didlington' 1229 Cl

Dudelinton, Dudlington, Dodelinton 1244 *Ass*

Dudelyngton 1285 FA *et passim, Dudelington* 1318 FF

This *-ing* name may be derived from the OE pers. name
Dyddel (Redin p. 140), see Karlström p. 73, but the possible

---

[1] The identification of this boundary-mark with Chalbury is not quite certain.

[2] Or could possibly OE *cēol* 'ship' have been used as a topographical term?

[3] The forms given by Hutchins (III, 117 f.) in a list of Chalbury rectors
will strengthen this supposition: *Chelesbury* (1306), *Cheldebury* (1420), *Chaldebury*
(1473), *Chellesbury* al. *Chaldebury* (1494); once also *Cheselbury* (1509).

[4] The soil here is chalk and gravel.

existence of an OE topographical term *dȳdel, suggested by Zachrisson (StNPh V, 18) makes this derivation somewhat uncertain. The first element is repeated in the boundary-marks *on dydelingdune. of dydelingdune* BCS 818, and *on dydeling dune middewearde. 7 of dydeling dune* BCS 958. Karlström (p. 34 note 80) is probably right in suggesting that these are more likely to mean 'Didlington Down' than 'down of the *Dydelingas*'.

Colehill

The three parishes of Colehill, Holt and Pamphill in this hundred were formed in 1898 out of the old parish of Wimborne Minster. I have found no ME forms for Colehill (131 G 13).

Leigh [lai]

Lege 1086 DB, n. d. France, *Leg* 1249 FF
Legh(e) 1261 FineR, 1291 FF (*juxta Wymborn'*) *et passim*
Leye, Leya 1285 FA, 1287 FF, 1289 Abbr
Leygh(e) 1321 FF, 1326 Ipm *et passim*, *Leigh* 1363 FF
Lyeghe 1479 IpmR, *Lye* 1487 Ipm

OE *lēah* (dat. sg. *lēage*) 'clearing' etc. There is ano ther Leigh in Yetminster Hundred *infra*, and the two places are not always easy to distinguish. The modern pronunciation of both is [lai]; cf. Jordan § 97.

Wilksworth Fm

Wedechesworde 1086 DB, *Wudotheswurde* 1107 (1300) Ch
Wudekesworth, -wurth 1244 *Ass*
Wodekesworth 1244 *Ass*, 1284, 1293 *et passim* FF, 1388 IpmR,
Wodokesworth 1293, 1449 FF, *Wodkysworth* 1448 FF
Wodekokkesworth 1412 FA, *Wodcockesworth* 1535 VE
Wodecotesworth 1425 IpmR (*juxta Winborneminstre*)
Wodecokesworthy 1433 IpmR, *Lytel Wodekyworthy* 1484 IpmR

The second el. is OE *w(e)orþ* 'homestead'. The two last forms above show confusion with the expanded form *worðig* which is otherwise almost unknown in Dorset; cf. Hamworthy *infra*. The first el. is difficult. A pers. name *Wuduc* is unrecorded, and consequently very doubtful, but would be a regular diminutive formation of *Wud(d)a* (Redin p. 58). Professor Zachrisson would take *wuduc* to be a topographical term, a derivative of *wudu* 'wood'; cf. **pearr* (dial. *par*) and *pearroc* (EPN).[1] — Some of the later forms for Wilksworth show popular association with the word *woodcock*. The modern form of the name is noteworthy.

More Crichel

More Crichel 131 E 2

Mor Kerchel 1212 Fees (92) *et passim* with variant spellings
More and *Kerchell (Kerechel)*, *More Kerchhulle* 1285 FA
Kerchil Sifrast 1242-3 Fees (753), *Chruchil* 1252 FF
Mor(e)kirchil 1356 Cl, FF, *Mo(u)rekurchell* 1387, 1391 IpmR,
Mourekyrchel 1438 FF, *Mourkyrchull* 1450 IpmR

See Long Crichel *infra*. *More* is evidently ME *more* (< OE *mōr*) 'moor, swampy ground', the valley here being marshy (Hutchins). Richard de *Sifrewast* held the manor in 1212 (Fees).

Chetterwood is *Chetred* 1215 ClR, *Cettred(e)*, *Cetred* 1242 Ch, *Chetreth* 1243 FF, *Chettered* 1869 Hutchins. The first el. is apparently Brit *cēt* 'wood' (cf. Orchard *supra* 30), see Zachrisson, Romans p. 52. There is woodland here now, and in all the above 13th cent. instances the reference is to a wood. As tentatively suggested by Zachrisson (loc. cit.), the second el. may be OE *riþ* 'small stream, brooklet'. Another possibility is perhaps that it may be an OE *harad (harað)* 'wood', for which see Middendorff p. 66 and Ekwall, StNPh I, 99.

Little Crichel (lost) is *Kerchel Freinel* 1212 Fees (91), *Parva Kerchil* 1244 *Ass*, *Parva Kerchel* 1244 Abbr *et passim* to 1309 Ipm (*Little Kerchel*) with variant spellings *Kerchell(e)*, *Kerechel; Little Curchull* 1271 Ipm, *Parva Curchell* 1300 Abbr, *Litel Kurchel* 1345 FF; *Parva Kyrchel(l)* 1291 Tax, 1431 FA, *Little Kirchul(l)* 1295 Pat, *Parva Kirchel* 1346 FA, *Parva Kirchile* 1428 FA; *Little Kerchehull* 1297 Cl; *Parva Crichull* 1428 FA. See Long Crichel *infra*. No person bearing the name *Freinel* is known here, but cf. Roger *Fraynel* noted in connexion with Studland in 1288 (Hutchins).

---

[1] For similar formations cf. also Olson, De appellativa substantivens bildning i fornsvenskan, p. 268 f. (with literature).

Gussage St Michael

Gussage St Michael 131 D 2

Gersich 1167-8 P, *Gersiz* 1212 Fees (92), *Gissic* 1219 Fees (260)
Gessiz Dinant 1212 Fees (91), *Gussich Dynaunt* 1275 RH,
   Gussiche Denaunt 1291 Tax, 1428 FA
Gissich Sancti Michaelis 1285 FA, *Gyssich St. Michael* 1292 Ipm,
   Gussich St. Michael 1297 Cl *et passim*
Gissiche Bount 1387 IpmR, *Gussych Bohun* 1420 IpmR
Gussage Mich'is 1535 VE

See Gussage All Saints *infra*. Roland de *Dinan* was here
as early as 1167-8 (P), cf. also 1212 Fees p. 92 (*Gersiz que fuit
Rolandi de Dinant*). The *de Bohuns*, earls of Hereford and
Essex, were in possession of this Gussage for about a century,
the first of them mentioned here being Milo de *Bohun* in 1275
(RH). The church is dedicated to St Michael.

Hinton Martell and Parva

Hinton Martell 131 F 3, **Hinton Parva** 131 F/G 2

Hineton(e) 1086 DB *et passim* with variant spellings *Hinetun,
   Hyneton*, later *Hynton* (1323), *Henton*, *Hinton*[1]
Hineton Martel 1226 FF, *Parva Hyneton* 1285 FA

OE *hĭgna-tūn* 'farm of the community'[2] (EPN), cf. Tarrant
Hinton *supra* 59. Eudo *Martel* held the manor of Hinton in
1212 (Cur p. 268), cf. the discussion under Broadmayne *infra*.
Hinton Martell is sometimes called Great Hinton (or Hinton
Magna).

Stanbridge is *Stanbrig'* 1230 Cl, *Stambrigge* 1262 Pap, *Stanbrigg*
1291 Tax, 1428 FA, *Stanebrigg* 1297 Cl, Pat, *Stanbrugge* 1428 FA.
'Stonebridge', OE *stān*, *brycg*. Stanbridge is the old name of
the chapel of Hinton Parva. The indexer of FA has mixed up
this name with Stoborough *infra*.

---

[1] Occasional spellings are *Hunton* 1272 Ch, *Hynington* 1311 Orig, *Hynetton*
1327 Cl, *Henyton* 1428 FA; cf. *Little Hynyngton* al. *Hyneton* 1486 Ipm.

[2] In 946 (13th) BCS 818 the boundary between Hinton Martell and Chalbury
is referred to as *(to) þare hina gemære (on cheoles burge eastgeat)*, whereas in the
same charter the boundary of the people of Horton (*infra*) is called *hore tuninge
gemære*. Does this indicate that Hinton was not a stabilized place-name at
that date? Cf. Piddlehinton *infra*.

Holt

Holt 131 G 3

Winburneholt 1184-5 P, *Wynburneholt* 1221 ClR *et passim*[1] with later *Wim-, Wym-; Wumburnehold* 1252 Misc *Holte* 1286 (1313) Ch, *Holt* 1307 Pat

'The wood near Wimborne', OE *holt.* The *foresta de Winburne* is already mentioned in DB (f. 78 b).

Bothenwood Fm is *Bothenwode* 1462 FF and probably means the 'wood in the valley', ME *bothem*, OE *wudu*; cf. Bothenhampton *infra.*

Grange is *atte Graunge* 1327 *SR* (p). Cf. Creech Grange *infra.*

Honeybrook Fm is *Honybrouk* 1333 *SR* (p). See EPN s. v. *hunig* 'honey'.

Mannington is *Manitone* 1086 DB, *Manton* 1237 Ch, *Maniton* 1242 Ch, 1244 *Ass*, *Mayton* 1242 Ch, *Manyton* 1374 Orig, IpmR, 1390 Cl, *Manyngton* 1376 FF, 1387 IpmR. An -*ing* name derived from the OE pers. name *Mann* (or *Manna*), see Karlström p. 108.

Petersham Fm

Petrishesham 1086 DB
Pitrichesham 1086 DB, 1199 CurR, 1236 Cl, 1242-3 Fees (750)
Pitrechesham t. John Abbr, *Pidrischesham* 1219 Fees (261)
Pitericesam c. 1217 Sarum, *Pitherichesham* 1244 *Ass*, *Piteriches-ham* 1264 Ipm *et passim* with variant *Piteryches-*
Petrichesham 1230 Cl *et passim* with variant spellings *Petrethes-, Peteryches-, Peteriches-*
Pytrigesham 1260 FF, *Pytrickesham* 1282 Ipm, *Pyt(e)richesham* 1303 FA, 1321 FF *et passim* with variant *Pytreches-*
Pitericheham 1303 FA
Putrichesham, Putresham 1346 FA
Petrisham 1398 IpmR, *Peytresham* 1428 FA, *Petresham* 1431 FA

---

[1] Cf. also mistranscriptions like *Winberncholt* 1199 (1233) Ch. In Ch Wimborne Holt is frequently mentioned together with a place, the modern name of which would be *Wishley*. The early forms are *Wsselay* 1199 (1233), *Wysselay* 1199 (1236), *Wisceley* 1267, *Wysselay* 1267 (1309), and the meaning is 'marsh clearing, damp (forest)land', OE *wisc, lēah*. The place was probably in Dorset, but its exact site is unknown.

This would seem to mean '*Peohtrīc*'s farm', OE *hām*. The pers. name is not on record, but other *Peoht-* names are well evidenced in OE (see Searle p. 387). Cf. Petersham (Sr), *Piterichesham* BCS 39, 697, 1195, KCD 812.

Thorn Hill Fm (6") is *Tornehelle* 1086 DB, *Thornhill'* 1212 Fees (88), *þhorhull'* 1219 Fees (260), *Thornhull'* 1226 ClR, 1227 Fees (378) *et passim*, *Tornhull'* 1250 Fees (1240), *Thornhell* 1260 FF. OE *þorn, hyll*; cf. Thornhill *supra* 38.

Uddens Ho

   (æt) Uddingc, (æt) udding 956 (13th) BCS 958

   Uddyng 1331 Cl, Misc, *Uddynge* 1331 Misc

   Uddyng al. *Oddyng* c. 1333 BM I

   Uddings c. 1669 Hutchins[1]

An *-ing* name of the uncompounded type, possibly to be derived from a pers. name *Udd(a)*, see Ekwall, PN in *-ing* p. 14; the existence of such a pers. name seems however to be rather doubtful, cf. Redin p. 37 and Zachrisson, StNPh V, 7 (with foot-note 5). The *s* in *Uddings* is presumably pseudo-possessive, and the development of *-ings* to *-ens* should in my opinion be compared with the dialectal pronunciation of *shillings* as *shillens*. Otherwise Ekwall (loc. cit.) and Ritter p. 116 n. 1.

Horton

Horton 131 E 3

   hore tuninge gemære Ᵹlang hore tuninge gemæres 946 (13th) BCS 818

   Hortun(e) 1033 (12th) KCD 1318, *Hortune* 1061 (12th) KCD 1341, 1086 DB, *Horton* 1231 Cl *et passim*

'Muddy farm', OE *horh, tūn*. For *hore tuninge gemære* 'the boundary of the people of Horton', cf. the foot-note to Hinton Martell *supra* 81, and Karlström p. 182.

Pamphill

Pamphill 131 H 2

The only early form I have seen is *Peympehull'* 1333 *SR* (p), but that material is too scanty for any suggestion to be made.

---

[1] From a memorial inscription in Chalbury church. Uddens was a detached part of that parish up to 1886.

Abbott Street is *Abbottestrete* 1535 VE. OE *strǣt*. The place belonged to the abbot of Sherborne.

Barford Fm (1"), **Old Barford** (6")
  Bereford 1244 *Ass*, 1333 *SR*, 1340 NI (all p)
  La Bere 1329 Ipm (*Andrew Peverel*), *atte Ber'* 1333 *SR* (p),
    Bere 1375 Orig, IpmR (*juxta Canford*), 1377 Cl, *Beare*
    1431 FA

I suppose the two Barfords had different names originally. Old Barford is by the Stour and may consequently represent the earlier *Bereford*, whereas the present Barford Fm is at some distance from the river and may represent the earlier *Bere*. *Bereford* (Old Barford) would thus mean 'the ford near *Bere*', cf. the parallel (East) Stoke: Stokeford *infra*. *Bere* is probably OE *bearu* 'wood, grove', cf. Bere Regis *supra* 68. For the *Peverels* here (Hutchins uses alternatively the name *Bere Peverel*), cf. Bradford Peverell *infra*.

Barnsley Fm (6"), **Lower Barnsley Fm** (1")
  Bernardeslega 1177-8 P (p), *-lege* 1179-80 P (p), *-le* 1212 Fees
    (91), 1231 Cl *et passim* with variants *-leya*, *-leye*
  Burnardesle 1189 (1313) Ch
  Barnardeslegh 1479 IpmR, *Barnesley* 1536 AD V

'*Beornheard*'s clearing', OE *lēah*.

Bradford Fm
  Bradeford' (de feodo Briani de Insula) 1212 Cur
  Bradeford 1224 ClR (*Brianus de Insula*), 1235-6 Fees (425),
    1244 ib. (1388), 1271 Ipm, 1283 FF (*juxta Wymburne Menstre*)
  Bradeford Brian 1289 FF, 1304 Ipm, 1358 FF *et passim*

'The broad ford', OE *brād*, *ford*. In Hutchins the place is still called *Bradford Brian*, the additional name originating from the same *Brianus* de Insula after whom Bryanston (*supra* 51) was named.

Chilbridge Fm
  Chelebruga c. 1140 (1340) Ch
  Chelbruge c. 1140 BM I

Chellrug' (sic)[1] 1154-8 (1340) Ch, *Chelbrigg* 1326 FF
Chilbrigg(e) 1307 FF, 1365 Inq aqd, *Chilbrige* 1535 VE

The first el. may formally be the OE pers. name *Cēola*, but
the nature of the second el. (OE *brycg*) makes it more probable
that we have here OE *ceole* 'throat, channel, gorge, chasm', cf.
PN Sx p. 49 s. n. Chilgrove. The whole name would thus mean
'the bridge over the chasm' or the like. Unfortunately I am not
familiar with the topography of the place.

Note. It has, as far as my knowledge goes, hitherto been unknown
that Chilbridge belonged to the Dorset possessions of Alcester Abbey
in Warwickshire. As the Victoria County History of Warwickshire
contains no attempt whatever at identifying these possessions (cf. vol.
II p. 59), a few explanatory words may be of some value.

Alcester Abbey evidently had two groups of possessions in Dorset.
One was just outside Shaftesbury and is now represented by the
modern names Blynfield and Alcester, the latter a name transferred
from the Abbey itself, cf. *supra* 33. The other group was apparently
somewhere near Wimborne Minster. In Nos I, II, V, VI and VIII
of the Alcester charters printed in Dugdale (vol. IV p. 175 ff.) there
is repeated mention of two places called *Walte(s)ford* and *Chelebruga*
(*Chelbruge*, etc.).[2] The former of these names has (in BM I and Ch)[3]
been correctly identified with Walford *infra* in the parish of Wimborne
Minster, whereas the latter name has only caused confusion. In BM I
(p. 157) it is tentatively identified with Chalbury *supra*, in Ch (vol.
IV p. 529) with Chelborough *infra*. Both identifications are no doubt
wrong. *Chelebruga* (etc.) is constantly mentioned together with Walford and once also with *Winburna*, i. e. Wimborne Minster, and it is
clear that it should be sought in the vicinity of these places. Walford
is just to the north of Wimborne Minster, and hardly two miles to
the north-west of that town is the present Chilbridge Fm. When
we then find that the 14th cent. forms for that place agree so well
with the forms in Dugdale, Ch and BM I, we must draw the conclusion that the latter refer to Chilbridge.

Cowgrove is *Cugrove* 1321 FF, *Cougrove* 1358 FF, *Cowgrove* 1479
IpmR. Self-explanatory, OE *cū, grāf(a)*.

---

[1] Dugdale (IV, 177; No. VI) prints *Chelbrug*.

[2] The forms *Cunbruge* in No. I and *Craubruge* in No. VIII are, if they really
belong here, apparently corrupt. Both charters are evidently late copies, the
originals of which should probably be dated 1140 and c. 1160 respectively.

[3] No. V is reprinted in Ch vol. IV p. 482, and No. VI ib. p. 483. No. II
must be the Add. MS 21494 quoted in BM I and dated c. 1140.

Hogford (6″) is *Hoggesford* 1333 *SR* (p). Probably self-explanatory, OE *hogg*, *ford*; see Hogchester *infra*.

Kingston Lacy

   Kyngeston 1176-89 AD VI, 1275 RH, 1284 Pat *et passim*
   Kingeston' 1191 (etc.) P, 1212 Fees (91), 1230 FF *et passim*
   Kyngeston Lacy from 1335 (Ipm, Cl) onward

'The King's farm', OE *tūn*. In DB, where it is not mentioned by name, it was included among the Wimborne group of royal demesnes (cf. Eyton p. 87), the whole of which was later on granted by King Henry I to Robert, count of Meulan, see 1212 Fees (91) and Eyton p. 89. From the earls of Leicester it then passed to the *Lacys*, earls of Lincoln, the first of whom, John de *Lasey*, constable of Chester, was lord of the manor in 1230 (FF p. 151).

Tatten is probably *Taddehauene* 1333 *SR* (p), but no suggestion can be made on the base of this scanty material.

Shapwick

Shapwick 130 G 14

   Scapeuuic 1086 DB, *escapewich* Exon
   Schapewyk 1176-89 AD VI *et passim* with variant spellings
     Shap(e)-, *Schap-* and *-wick*, *Chapwyk* 1253 FF
   Sepewich . 1191, 1192, 1193 P, *Sepewic* 1195 P, *Sepwik* 1235-6
     Fees (425), *-wyk* 1265 Pat; *Shepwyk* 1238 Pat, *Schepwyk*
     1244 *Ass* (p), *Shep(e)wic* 1256 FF, *Scepwyk*' 1275 RH; *Schep-*
     ike 1265 Misc
   Sap(e)wic 1212 Fees (91 f.), *Sapewyc* 1242 Ch (p), *Sapwyk*
     1244 *Ass*, 1285 FA, *Sabwyk* 1267 Ipm
   Shapewik Plecy 1417 IpmR, *Shapwike Champayn* 1469 IpmR

   'Sheep-farm', OE *scēap*, *wīc*; cf. Shipton Gorge *infra*. Members of the *Champaine* family are first mentioned here in 1212 (Fees). Another manor was held by John *Plecy* at his death in 8 Henry IV (IpmR), cf. Hutchins III, 160, 165.

Tarrant Crawford

Tarrant Crawford 130 G 13/14

   Craveford 1086 DB, *Craueford* 1274 Ipm, 1367 Fine

Cramford' (sic) c. 1236 Fees (607)

Crauford 1242 Ch, 1243, 1253 FF, 1258 Ch *et passim*

Craweford 1242-3 Fees (753), 1274 Ipm *et passim*

Parva is prefixed from 1291 Tax onward, *Magna* (or *Great*) from 1308 FF onward, *Craford Magna* 1386 (etc.) IpmR, *Parva Croweford (Crawford)* 1428 FA, *Craford Parva* 1469 IpmR

'Crow-ford', OE *crāwe, ford*.[1] Parva Crawford is an older name for the present Tarrant Crawford (Hutchins), to which *Tarrant* was prefixed in analogy with the names of the other places on the river Tarrant; the ancient Tarrant Abbey, now represented by **Tarrant Abbey Fm** (6″), was in this parish, cf. Tarrant Hinton *supra* 59. Magna Crawford (now lost as name) was in the adjoining parish of Spettisbury.

Wimborne Minster[2]

Wimborne Minster 131 H 3

(æt) Winburnan s. aa. 718, 871, 901 ASC, *(æt) Wimburnan* s. a. 962 ib.

(æt) Winburnan mynster s. a. 871 ASC (E), *(on) Winburnan mynstre* c. 1000 Saints

Winburne, Winborne 1086 DB (*-borna* Exon), *Winburna* 1154-8 (1340) Ch, *Winburn* 1184-5 P *et passim* to 1265 Pat

Wimburn(e) c. 1165 Osmund, 1214 ClR *et passim*, interchanging (from 1229 Pat) with *Wymburn(e)*, later *Wymbo(u)rne*

Wymburneminstre 1236 FF, 1244 *Ass et passim* with the additional name variously spelt *Mynstre, Ministre, Menstre*

Wumburn Ministre 1256 Pat, *Wymburn Monaster'* 1281 FF

Wymburnysmynster 1305 Cl

'The monastery (OE *mynster*) by the river *Wimborne*', the place being referred to as *(in) monasterio quod juxta fluvium qui dicitur Winburna situm est* in 705 (12th) BCS 114.[3] The second el. of

---

[1] *(at) crawan forda* 956 (13th) BCS 958 possibly belongs here.

[2] According to Eyton (pp. 88, 113 f.) two DB places called *Odeham* and *Selavestune*, of which no traces have been found in later records, were in the old parish of Wimborne Minster (which was much larger than the present one). *Odeham* probably contains OE *wudu* 'wood', *Selavestune* possibly the OE pers. name *Sǣlāf*.

[3] For other charter references to this river (always called *winburna*) see BCS 818, 958, and KCD 1318.

the river-name is of course OE *burna* 'stream, burn', and Ekwall
(ERN p. 461) is inclined to take the first el. to be an OE *winn*
'meadow', a word for which there are good parallels in other
Germanic languages; cf. also Middendorff p. 154.

Note.   **The River Allen**

The stream which gave name to Wimborne Minster and to three
other places higher up on the river, viz. Wimborne St Giles, All
Hallows Fm (earlier *Wymborne Omnium Sanctorum*) and Monkton Up
Wimborne, is not called *Wimborne* now; it is called Allen. Ekwall
has a short note on that name in ERN p. 4. He quotes the form
Alen from Holinshed (1577, 1586) and regards the name as late. He
then adds that it may have been suggested by the name of the bridge
mentioned 1278 QW (*Alwynesbrugg' subtus Wymburn'*) and by Leland
(*Aleyn Bridge*). I had arrived at the same conclusion some time
before Ekwall's work appeared, and I will try and show why I think
it must be correct.

The name *Allen* (for this stream) does not occur in any OE or ME
records, and even Leland (c. 1540) uses the name *Winburn* (I, 257).
Leland gives an interesting account of Winborne Minster and its en-
virons which is recognized in Hutchins (III, 182) as "a very just one,
except in one instance, where he speaks of his passing over Aleyn
bridge; whereas the bridge he passed over in his way from Poole
to Wimborne was never called Aleyn, but Canford bridge". There
can, however, be no doubt that this detail in Leland is correct, too.
It is true the bridge in question is *now* called Canford Bridge (6")
(named after Canford Magna, a mile to the east), but from the detailed
descriptions in Leland, where the bridge is mentioned five times
(I, 256, 258, 303, 305), it is clear that it must at his time have been
called *Aleyn Bridge*.

As pointed out by Ekwall, there is also mention of an *Alwynesbrugg' subtus Wymburn'* in 1278 QW (p. 185), the reference being taken
from a 13th cent. version of an old perambulation of Cranborne Chase.
As a matter of fact the bridge is mentioned again on page 773 in
1280-1 QW, which page contains two more versions of the same perambulation. We here find, besides the form *Alwynesbrigg'*, the interesting variants *Aldwynesbrigg* and *Aldwinesbrigg*, telling us that the
bridge contains the OE pers. name *Ealdwine (Aldwine)*.[1] The boundaries
of the part of the perambulation that refers to the neighbourhood
of Wimborne Minster are so clear that there can be no doubt that

---

[1] It seems a strange coincidence that one of the landowners in *Winburne*
in the time of Edward the Confessor (DB f. 83 b) bears the name *Alduin*.
This *Winburne* is identified by Eyton (p. 111 f.) with Wimborne St Giles, but
I am not sure that the identification is correct.

Al(d)wynesbrigg is the bridge which Leland calls *Aleyn Bridge* and which is now called Canford Bridge. That bridge, which is one of the largest and most important in the county, is built over the Stour just below the spot S of Wimborne Minster where the Allen joins that river.[1]

The 13th cent. name *Al(d)wynesbrigg* had in Leland's time consequently been worn down to *Aleyn Bridge*, the name of the bridge having thus by chance received a form which showed a striking resemblance to certain well-known English river-names. A misunderstanding was then near at hand: *Aleyn Bridge* was supposed to mean 'the bridge over *Aleyn*', and the result was a new name (*Alen* 1577) for the river which falls into the Stour just above that bridge.

Walford Bridge and Fm (6″)

Walteford 1086 DB, c. 1140 (1340) Ch, 1225 FF (p), 1275 RH
  (p), 1307, 1326 FF, 1365 Inq aqd
Waltesford c. 1140 BM I, 1154-8 (1340) Ch
Waldeford 1278, 1280-1 QW (6 times)
Walford 1535 VE, *Walleford bridg* c. 1540 Leland

The numerous *t* spellings and the persistent medial *e* forbid us to take the first el. to be OE *weald* 'wood', but the *Walde*-forms in QW (from the perambulation mentioned in the preceding note) may possibly have been influenced by that word. There was an OE noun *wealte* 'ring' and probably an OE adj. *wealt* 'shaky, unsteady' (cf. OE *unwealt* 'steady, stable'), but neither of them has been evidenced in pl.-ns (cf. Ekwall, StNPh I, 98), and both would leave us with the *Waltes*- forms unexplained. The etymology had therefore better remain open.

XI. Knowlton Hundred

chenoltune 1084 Geld Roll
Cnolton 1167-8 P, 1212 Fees (88, 91), 1244 *Ass*, 1246 Ch,
  1251-2 Fees (1268) *et passim*, *Cnoutone* 1244 *Ass*
Knolton 1258 FF, 1274 Ipm, 1285, 1316 FA *et passim*
See Knowlton *infra*.

---

[1] In Hutchins (III, 407) *Aldwynesbrigg* is wrongly identified with Julian's Bridge (6″), another large bridge over the Stour. It is to the west of Wimborne Minster (not *subtus Wymburn*').

Long Crichel

Long Crichel 131 E 2

chircelford 935 (15th) BCS 708
Circel 1086 DB, *Chirce* 1086 DB, Exon
Kerichel, Kerechel 1202-3 FF
Kerchel 1208 FineR, 1233 Cl, 1235-6 Fees (426, 427[1])
Longcherchel 1219 FF, *Longa Ker(e)chel* 1258 FF, 1285 FA
Curchel 1244 *Ass* (p), *Lange Curchille* 1325 Ipm
Longa Kyrchyl (*Kyrchile*) 1291 Tax, 1428 FA
Kerchehull 1297 Pat, *Kyrchhylle* 1378 Cl
Langecrichel 1297 Pat, *Langecriechill* 1316 FA
Kirchil, Kirchull, Kyrchil, Lang(e)- 1298 Pat, 1303 FA, 1346
    Fine, FA *et passim, Langkyrchel* 1333 *SR*
Crouchull' 1333 *SR* (p), *Cruchell Longa* 1366 IpmR
Lanchirchull 1388 IpmR, *Lanchrichull* 1428 FA
Churchell, Churchill 1411 IpmR

Cf. the forms given under More Crichel and *Little Crichel supra* 80.

Crichel is Brit *cruc* ('hill, barrow'), to which was added the explanatory OE *hyll* 'hill', see EPN p. 16. The boundary-mark *chircelford*[2], which heads the above list of forms, has been identified in PNWo p. 107[3] with the point where Week Street (next name) crosses the little stream on which lie Long Crichel and More Crichel. As pointed out loc. cit., *chircelford* as well as Long, More, and Little Crichel were named from the neighbouring hill now called Crichel Down.

Week Street

an lang wic herepaþes 935 (15th) BCS 708

Cf. the discussion under the preceding name. For different meanings of OE *wic* see EPN s. v. OE *herepæþ* 'army-path, military road' had about the same sense as OE *(here)strǣt*.

---

[1] On p. 427 also the mistranscription *Kertel*; 1263 Ipm has *Churethel*.
[2] *an lang wic herepaþes to chircelford.*
[3] In PNWo p. 106 ff. there is a detailed discussion of the *circ-* names in OE charters. The same problem has recently been dealt with by Ekwall in his Studies on PN pp. 33—54, Crichel being discussed on pp. 43, 45.

Gussage All Saints

Gussage All Saints [gʌsidʒ, gisidʒ] 131 D/E 2

(*æt*) *Gyssic* 1012 (12th) KCD 721 (= Thorpe p. 553)

Gessic 1086 DB

Gersic 1091-1104, 1107-22, 1135-7, 1152-8 Montacute

Gersich(e) 11Q0-18 Montacute, 1100-22 (1270) Ch, 1107-22, 1155 (*Omnium Sanctorum*), 1189-99 Montacute, 1227 ClR, 1230 FF, 1232, 1233 Cl

Gessich(e) 1182-3 P, 1205, 1215 ClR, 1240, 1242 Ch, 1242-3 Fees (752; *Omnium Sanctorum*), 1244 Cl, 1282 Pat (p), *Gessich Gentil* 1236 FF [1]

Gersiz 1183-4, 1184-5, 1185-6, 1186-7, 1187-8, 1194, 1195 P

Gessing 1195 P, 1231 Cl, *Gersigg̃* 1221-2 ClR

Garsic 1207 ClR, *Gersy* 1232 Cl, *Girsech'* 1239 Cl [2]

Gussich(e) 1211 ClR, 1244 FF, 1254 Ipm, 1285 FA *et passim*

Gessiz 1212 Fees (91), *Gessigh' Omnium Sanctorum* 1245 Cl

Gissich(e) 1217 ClR, 1227 Fees (378), 1244 *Ass*, 1288 FF

Gussich All Saints 1245 Ch, 1276 FF, 1332 Cl, Ipm

Gissik All Saints 1258 Ch, *Gissich All Saints* 1280 Ch

Gussich(e) (*Gussuch, Gussick, Gussych*) *Regis* 1285 FA, 1291 Tax, 1340 NI, 1383 FF, 1428 FA, *Gyssych* 1300 Pap

Gussych Allhallows 1384 Cl, *All Hallow Gussege* 1466 IpmR

Gyssege 1476 IpmR, *Gussage Omnium Sanctorum* 1535 VE

Cf. the forms given under Gussage St Andrew and Gussage St Michael *supra* 25, 81.

As pointed out by Ekwall (ERN p. 187), there can be no doubt that Gussage is an old name for the stream which rises at Gussage St Andrew and runs past Gussage St Michael and Gussage All Saints. Ekwall regards the name as English and takes the second el. to be OE *sīc* 'a water-course'. The first el. is considered by him to be a word corresponding to OHG *gusi* 'water suddenly breaking forth' (the OE form of which would be **gyse*, from a base **gusi-*), derived from the stem found in ON *giósa* 'to gush forth', *gusa* 'to gush', *Geysir* 'a hot spring'. Zachrisson in his review of Ekwall's work (ZONF VI, 245)

---

[1] *Kissich Gentil* 1242 Ch also belongs here.

[2] I have also noted *Gutsich'* (1233) and *Cussigh* (1237) from Cl.

takes the name to be Celtic and connects it with Irish *gus* 'force, violence' (Welsh *gwst*) < **gud-tu*. Zachrisson, who bases his suggestion on the seven early forms collected by Ekwall, adds the reservation "if *r* is excrescent in the late spelling *Gersicg*" (cf. Gussage St Andrew *supra*), and it is clear that Ekwall's interpretation is based on the same assumption. The numerous early forms collected above show, however, that *r* cannot be excrescent, and that we must look for an etymology which explains this *r* as well.

It seems to me very likely that the name is English, and that Ekwall is right in suggesting that the second el. is OE *sīc* 'small, stream, water-course'. It would be tempting to suggest that the first el. is OE *gærs* (*græs*) 'grass', but a development along the line **gærssīc* > *gersic* > *gessic* > *gissic* > *gussich* (1211) would involve too great phonological difficulties. Above all, however, the suggestion would hardly be in conformity with the chronology of the material, which rather points to an original form **gyrsic* or the like, the many (always early) *e* spellings being probably due to AN influence. Professor Zachrisson agrees with this argumentation and suggests that the first el. is OE *gyr* 'filth, mud, marsh'.

Robert *le Gentil* was lord of the fee of *Gessich Gentil* in 1236 (FF p. 62). The manor of *Gissich*' was the king's escheat in 1227 (Fees p. 378); hence apparently the earlier distinctive name *Regis*. It would seem that these were two different manors. The church is dedicated to All Saints.

Bowerswain Fm[1] [bouswein, bousən]
    Baresfeld 1091-1104, 1100-18 Montacute, 1100-22 (1270) Ch,
        1135-7 Montacute, *Baresfelt* c. 1155 Montacute
    Boresfeu[d] c. 1155 Montacute
    Boressen 1316 FA, *Boresfen* 1333 *SR* (p)
    Boreswain 1545 Hutchins

'Wild boar's open land (field)', OE *bār*, *feld*. The second el. has undergone a curious corruption, and in later times popular etymology has apparently been at work.

---

[1] The article on this name in Hutchins (III, 490) has been of great help to me with regard to identification.

Brockington Fm

Brocheṁtune 1086 DB

Brochamton 1204 FineR, 1225 FF, *Brochampton* 1225 FF, Pat,
1262 FF, 1316 FA, *Brokhampton* 1324 Cl *et passim*

'Home farm by the brook', OE *brōc*, *hāmtun*. The brook here
is the river Allen.

Loverley Fm (6″) [lʌvəli]

Loverlay 1091-1104 *et passim* Montacute (once *-lai*)[1]

Luverlay 1100-22 (1270) Ch, 1135-7 Montacute, *-lea* 1285 FA

Louerleygh, Lowerleygh 1341 FF, *Loverle* 1383 IpmR

Leverley 1462 IpmR

This may be '*Lēofwaru's* enclosure', OE *lēah*. For the evidence of this OE feminine pers. name, cf. Searle p. 333.

Woodlands

Woodlands [wudlændz, udlənz] 131 E 4

Wodelaunde 1244 *Ass* (p)

La Wodelond 1303 FA *et freq* to 1412 FA, *La Wodelande*
1345 FF

Woodland 1321 Inq aqd, *Wodelond* 1346 FA *et passim*

Wudlond 1486 Ipm

Self-explanatory, OE *wudu, land*.

Baggeridge (lost) is *Bag(g)herug'* 1250 Fees (1182) (p), *Bagerughe*
ib. (1240), *Bageregge, -rug(h)'* ib. (1240 f.) (p), *Bargarich'* (sic)
1251-2 ib. (1268) (p), *Bagerig* 1274 Ipm (p) *et passim* with
variant spelling *Baggerigg(e)*. It also appears with the addition
'street' (OE *strēt*) as in *Bagrichstrete* 1251-2 Fees (1268), *Bage-
richesstrete* 1274 Ipm, *Baggerugestrete* 1274 Ipm *et passim* with
variant spelling *-rigge-*, *Bagrigstret* 1325 Inq aqd. The second
el. is of course OE *hrycg* 'ridge'. From a formal point of view
the first el. may be the OE pers. name *Bacga*, but cf. Karlström

---

[1] In the Montacute Cartulary there is frequent mention of a *Hunecroft* (once
spelt *Hunescroft*). Nothing further is known about that croft, but as it is
constantly mentioned between Gussage All Saints and Loverley, it may have
been somewhere in this district. The first el. is apparently the pers. name
Huna (Hun).

p. 130 and Blomé p. 48, where good reasons are given for a topographical interpretation of the first el. in *Bag-* names. It may be worth noting that in 1305 (Ipm) there is mention of a wood in the neighbourhood called *Baggeham*, and also that the boundary-mark (*to*) *bacging berghe* BCS 708 (cf. Karlström loc. cit.) cannot have been more than two or three miles distant. Cf. Baglake *infra*.

Charlton Dairy Fm (6″) is *Charleton* 1432 BM I. OE *ceorla-tūn* 'farm of the peasants'.

Knowle Hill is *Cnoll(e)* 1212 Fees (88), 1346 FA, *Knol* 1242 Ch, *Knolle* 1318 Ipm, 1324 Cl, 1428 FA. OE *cnoll* 'rounded hilltop, hillock'. Cf. next name.

Knowlton [1]

> *Chenoltone, -tune* 1086 DB, *Chenoltona* Exon
> *Cnolton* 1212 Fees (91 f.), 1236 Cl, 1246 Ch *et passim*
> *Gnolton* 1214 ClR, *Chinouton'* 1217 ClR
> *Cnowton* 1237 Ch, *Cnouton* 1237 Ch, 1239 Cl, 1244 *Ass*
> *Knolton* 1242 Ch, 1242-3 Fees (750), 1244 *Ass et passim*
> *Chnoldon'* 1250 Fees (1182), *Cheltun'* (sic) ib. (1240)

'Farm by the hillock' (OE *cnoll*, *tūn*), the reference being probably to the neighbouring Knowle Hill (preceding name). The above list of forms is a good illustration of two typical AN features, viz. insertion of a vowel in the initial consonant-group *kn*, and vocalization of *l* before a consonant, cf. Zachrisson, AN Infl. p. 49 f. and p. 146 ff. *G* for *C* may be a third AN peculiarity (op. cit. p. 137 f.). Cf. Church Knowle *infra*.

XII. Upwimborne Hundred

Upwynburn, Upwimburne 1244 *Ass*
Upwymbo(u)rn 1275 RH, 1285 FA, 1340 NI *et passim*

See Wimborne St Giles *infra*, now in the hundred of Wimborne St Giles.

---

[1] Formerly a hamlet and manor (giving name to the hundred), now only a church-ruin.

Chettle

Chettle 131 D 1

Ceotel 1086 DB, 1107 (1300) Ch
Chettel 1233 Lib, *Chettell'* 1235 Cl
Chetel 1234 Cl, 1237 Lib, Cl, 1238 Lib, Cl, 1239 Lib, 1241 Cl, 1291 Tax, 1294 Pat *et passim*, *Chetul* 1333 *SR*
Chettille, Chetelle 1390 Cl[1]

Zachrisson (Romans p. 52) has interpreted this name as 'the forest-hill', OE *cēthyll*. Chetterwood (*supra* 80) is not more than three miles distant.

Tarrant Monkton

Tarrant Monkton 131 E 1

Tarente 1086 DB, *Tarenta* 1107 (1300) Ch
Tarent(e) Monachorum 1291 Tax, 1390 Cl, 1428 FA
Tarente Monketon 1333 *SR*, 1340 NI

Named from its situation on the river Tarrant, see Tarrant Hinton *supra* 59. It belonged to the priory of Cranborne (DB) and the abbey of Tewkesbury; hence its distinctive name.

Luton Fm

Tarente Loueton 1323 FF, *Tarant Loveton* 1435 FF
Loueton 1323 FF (p), 1376, 1408 FF, *Loveton* 1412 FA
Loffeton 1478 IpmR, *Luffeton* 1486 Ipm

Probably '*Lufa*'s farm', *Lufa* being evidenced both as a masculine and a feminine pers. name in OE, cf. Redin pp. 51, 40.

XIII. Wimborne St Giles Hundred

This seems to be a modern hundred, see Hutchins III, 578.

Wimborne St Giles

Wimborne St Giles 131 D 3

Winburne 1086 DB, *-burna* Exon (Eyton p. 111 f., cf. next name)

---

[1] Two early forms from ClR may also belong here, viz. *Chatell'* (1215) and *Chatele* (1217). The boundary-mark *Chettlesheved* (once), *Chetelesheved(e)* (3 ×) 1278, 1280-1 QW apparently refers to some part of the old Chettle wood.

Upwinburn(e) 1179-80 P (p), 1199 Cur, 1207 PatR, 1212 Fees
  (91), 1214 ClR, 1227 FF, 1230 Cl, *Upwynborne* 1359 Cl
Uppingburn' 1186-7, 1187-8, 1194 P, 1230 Cl
Opwinburne, Upwinborne 1212 Fees (92)
Upwymburn(e), Upwimburn 1213 ClR, 1231 Pat *et passim*
  Vpwymburne Malemayns 1296 FF, *Upwymborn Malemeyns* 1301
  Ipm *et passim, Uppe Wynbourne Malmayns* 1428 FA
  (parochia) *Sancti Egidij de Upwymbourn* 1340 NI
Upwymburn Pleycy 1347 Cl, *St. Giles Upwymborn Plecy* 1375 Cl

See Wimborne Minster *supra* 87 with the note on the river
Allen. Nicholas *Malemains* was here in 1227 (FF), and by 1259
(FF) the manor had passed into the hands of Robert *de Plassetis*
(*Plecy*), cf. Hutchins III, 578 ff. The church is dedicated to
St Giles (*capella Sancti Egidii* 1291 Tax).

All Hallows Fm

Opewinburne 1086 DB, *Obpe Winborna* Exon (cf. Eyton p. 89)
Wymborn Karentham 1291 Tax, *Wymborn Carentham* 1340 NI,
  Upwimborn Karntham 1408 IpmR
Vpwymburne All Saints 1294 FF, *Upwymburne All Saints* 1310 FF
Wymborne Omnium Sanctorum al. *Upwymborne* voc. *Brytysplace*
  1430 IpmR

See the preceding name. No person bearing the name *Karentham* (*Carentham*) has been noted in direct connexion with
this place, but several members of a 13th cent. family so called
are mentioned under the neighbouring parishes, cf. Alice de
Karenthem 1242 Ch, William de *Carentham* 1243 FF and Henry
de *Carenteym* 1251 FF. Johannes *Bryt* held the manor called
Brytysplace at his death in 1430 (IpmR); Thomas and William
le Bret were here as early as 1294 (FF), cf. Hutchins III, 601.
The ancient church here, which seems to have been the mother
church in 1291 (Hutchins), must have been dedicated to *All
Saints*.

French's Fm (6″) is *Frensshes* 1412 FA, *Frenches* (maner') 1422
IpmR, and the editors of Hutchins (III, 601) are apparently
right in connecting it with the hide of land in *Upwinborne* which
Ricardus *le Franc'* held in 1212 (Fees p. 92). Wm *le Fraunceys*

(le Frenche) mentioned as landholder in *Upwymburne All Saints* in 1310 (FF) was probably a descendant of this Richard.

Monkton Up Wimborne is *Winburne* 1086 DB (f. 77 b), *Wymburne Abbatis* 1316 FA *et passim*. It belonged to the priory of Cranborne (DB) and the abbey of Tewkesbury; hence the distinctive name.

Oakley Fm
  (to) acclei (MS H: *Aclei*) 940-46 (14th) BCS 817
  on litlen ac lee estward of aclee 956 (15th) BCS 970
  (eft to) anclee (sic) BCS 970, *Ocle* 1333 *SR* (p)
  'Oak clearing', OE *āc*, *lēah*. For *Aclee* in the Durham Ritual, cf. the discussion under Woodyates (next parish).

Philipston (lost)
  Philipeston' 1206 Cur
  Felipston' 1235-6 Fees (426), *Felipeston* 1239 Cl
  Phelippeston 1236 FF, 1316 FA, 1318 Ch, 1324 Misc, Cl
  Phelip(e)ston(e) 1244 FF, 1285, 1303 FA *et passim*
  Phelpeston 1318, 1356 FF *et passim*, *Phelpyston* 1431 FA
  Philippeston 1351 Cl, *Phillipston* 1535 VE
  '*Philip*'s farm', OE *tūn*; cf. Tait's list of hybrid pl.-ns in IPN p. 131. *Philip* is early found as *Phelip*, cf. Bardsley s. n. *Phelps*.

Sutton Holms is possibly to be identified with *Suddon* in some 15th cent. references in Ipm(R). *Suddon* means 'south down', OE *sūð*, *dūn*.

Woodyates, East and West[1]

Woodyates [wudiəts, udiəts] 131 B 3
  (at) Wdegeate 869 (15th) BCS 525, *(at) wudegate* ib. 526
  (to) wideyate 940-46 (14th) BCS 817, *Widiate* 1199 FF
  Odiete 1086 DB, *Wudiete* 1199 FF (p), *Wodiet'* 1244 *Ass*
  Wudegat' 1199 Cur (p), *Wodegat(e)* ib., 1242 Ch *et passim*
  Wud(e)iate 1217 ClR, 1232 Pat, Cl (all p), 1233 Cl
  Wodeyate 1244 *Ass* (p), 14th Glaston F *et passim*
  Wudesate 1251 FF, *Wodezete* 1291 Tax, *Wodeyats* 1535 VE
  This apparently means 'gate in the wood', OE *wudu*, *geat*.

---

[1] East Woodyates is, strictly speaking, in Cranborne Hundred.

Note. What possibly complicates this etymology is a suggestion by W. H. Stevenson (in Asser p. 178) that the entry *Be Suðan Wudigan Gǽte ǽt Aclee on Westsǽxum* in the Durham Ritual (a note written in 970) may in reality refer to the two Dorset places Woodyates and Oakley *supra* 97.[1] Stevenson takes *Wudigan Gǽte* to contain the pers. name *Wudiga* (cf. *Widia, Wudia* in Redin p. 159). This assumption seems however quite unnecessary, as we may here have the adj. *wudig* 'wooded', later reduced to or confused with *wudu* 'wood'.

Denbose Wood (6″) must take its name from a family called *Denebaud*, mentioned several times as landholders in Woodyates in the 13th and 14th centuries: Philip *Denebaud (de Denebald', de Denebaud)* 1233, 1234 Cl, 1244 *Ass* (200 m. 3), Wm *Denebaud* 1316 FA, 1317 FF, John *Denebaude* 1390 Ipm, etc.; cf. also Do Field Club XLIX (1928).

Note. I suppose *Denebaud* goes back to a pers. name *Denebeald. It is remarkable, however, that in one entry in 1233 Cl (p. 349) we find the name twice with a *de* in front of it (*de Denebald', de Denebaud*). We should of course not have expected to find *de* before a surname which originally comes from an OE pers. name, *de* being used exclusively before (a surname derived from) a place-name. *Denebaud* can, however, hardly be an original place-name, for Philip *Denebaud* also occurs without *de* several times in the 1231-34 Cl vol. as well as in 1244 *Ass*. It is true this *de* before a surname was later on dropped, a fact which sometimes led to confusion between the two types, but since this does not seem to have happened till about the end of the 13th cent. or the beginning of the 14th[2], one must draw the conclusion that, in the two examples mentioned, *de* in front of the name is a mere blunder. Cf. also Ewen, History of British Surnames p. 175 f., where such errors are drawn attention to.

---

[1] Oakley (about a mile SW of Woodyates) would consequently, as suggested by Stevenson, have been the scene of the battle *ǽt Aclea* in the Anglo-Saxon Chronicle (s. a. 851), usually identified with Ockley in Surrey.

[2] In the volume just referred to (1231-34 Cl) I have at least found no instance of *de* having been dropped, the different types of surnames being strictly kept apart: Richard *Siward* (< OE *Sigeweard*, pers. name), Wm *Lungespee* (Fr. *longue épée*) etc., on one side, Thomas *de Sampford*, Gilbert *de Lescy* etc., on the other.

XIV. Cranborne Hundred[1]

Craneburn(e) 1167-8 P, 1244 *Ass et passim*, later *-borne*
Crambourne 1428 FA
See Cranborne *infra*.

Alderholt

Alderholt 131 D 6

Alreholt(e) 1315 Ipm, 1333 *SR*, *Areholt* 1398 IpmR
Alberholte (sic) 1425 IpmR, *Alderwood* 1535 VE

'Alder wood', OE *alor, holt*.

Vale Acre Fm (6″)[2] is possibly to be identified with *Vellak* 1315
Ipm, but the material is too scanty to allow of any suggestion.

Ashmore

Ashmore 130 B 13

Aisemare 1086 DB, *Aisemara* Exon
Essemera, -mere 1107 (1300) Ch, 1181-2 P, 1230 Cl, 1289 Pap,
   Essemor(e) 1247, 1250 Cl, *Eshmere* 1398 IpmR
Assemere 1235 Cl, 1291 Tax, 1303 FA
Aysmere 1242-3 Fees (750), *Aysshmer* 1412, 1431 FA
Asshemere 1305 FF *et passim* to 1428 FA, with variant spellings
   Ash(e)-, Assh-, As(s)ch-, Asshemore 1316 FA

The first el. is OE *æsc* 'ashtree'. The second is probably OE
mere 'pool', but it should be mentioned that Ashmore is on the
Wilts border, so OE *(ge)mǣre* 'boundary' is perhaps not excluded[3];
the situation of the village is about 700 ft. above sea-level. For
the confusion with 'moor' cf. Frogmore Fm *supra* 25.

Well Bottom is *(atte) Welle* 1333 *SR* (p). OE *wielle* 'spring'.

---

[1] The name of the pre-DB hundred of *albretesberge* (1084 GeldRoll), which
according to Eyton (pp. 111 f., 143) comprised parts of the present hundreds
of Cranborne, Upwimborne and Wimborne St Giles, has only been met with
once in a later record, viz. in the form *Alvredesberge* in 1212 Fees (92), under
which rubric are enumerated pl.-ns from widely different parts of the county.
Cf. also the discussion under Pimperne Hundred *supra* 49, and the foot-note
to Badbury Hundred *supra* 77.

[2] The 1″ map has Vate Acre Fm, which seems to be a misprint.

[3] Cf. *Æscmere* BCS 508 and *(be) Æsc mere* BCS 678, referring to a place near
Buttermere (W) where the boundaries of Wilts, Hants and Berks meet.

Cranborne

Cranborne 131 D 4

Creneburne 1086 DB, *Creneburna* Exon

Craneburna, -burne 1162-3 (etc.) P, 1200 RC, 1204 ChR, LibR, 1205 ClR *et passim, Cranneburna* 1164-5 P *Craneborn(e)* 1233 Lib, 1237 Ch *et passim* (later *-bourn*) *Cranebroke* al. *Cranbourn* 1398 IpmR *Cramborn* 1398 IpmR, *Cramburn* al. *Cranborne* 1483 IpmR 'The cranes' stream', OE *cran, burna*. The modern name of the river — the Crane — is a typical back-formation, cf. Ekwall, ERN p. 102.

Biddlesgate Fm is *Butelgate (juxta Cranebourn)* 1332 FF, *Buttelgate (juxta Cranborn)* 1386 FF, *Buttylgats* 1535 VE, and is possibly to be associated with the boundary-mark *bi talajate* in BCS 817 (in which, however, *bi* seems to be the preposition). The second el. is of course OE *geat* 'gate', but the first is doubtful. Could it be OE *bietl* 'beetle, hammer'? For the *u* spellings cf. Steeple *infra*. Just over the Hants border is Bittlegate Copse (6″) which probably preserves a more correct form of the name.

Blagdon Fm (and **Hill**) is *Blakedon'* 1234, 1235 Cl *et passim* to 1398 IpmR, *Blagdon* 1535 VE. 'Black down', OE *blæc, dūn*. Cf. *(on) blacan dune* KCD 1318, referring to another 'black hill' a few miles to the south-west.

Boveridge [bɔvəridʒ] is *Bovehric* 1086 DB, *Bewerugg'* 1245 Cl, *Boverig, Boverug* 1256 FF, *Boucrigg'* (sic) 1329 FF, *Boueryg'* 1333 *SR*, *Boveregge* 1390 IpmR, *Boueregge* 1390 Cl, *Bonerigge* (sic) 1436 FF, *Bowrigge* 1535 VE, *Bowridge* 1811 OM. This may mean 'above the ridge' (OE *bufan, hrycg*), as suggested by Mawer in EPN p. 10. See Bowood *infra*.

Castle Hill. In 1385 Cl and 1393 FF there is mention of a *Castelfeld(e)*, probably referring to some spot near this ancient earthwork S of Cranborne (for which see Hutchins III, 381).

Holwell Fm [houlwel] is *Holewell(e)* 1333 *SR*, 1335 Orig, 1385 Cl, *Holwelle* 1378 Cl, *Holewyll* 1393 FF. 'Spring in the hollow', OE *holh, wielle*.

Horsith (lost) is *Horsyth(e)* 1249, 1256, 1331 FF, 1338 Cl, IpmR, 1381 IpmR, *Horseth* 1256 FF, *Horsith* 1311 Cl, *Horsiche* 1330 FF, *Horshide* 1412 FA, *Horsetts* 1535 VE. It is difficult to make a definite suggestion with regard to the etymology, in particular as the exact site of the place is unknown.[1] A second el. *hȳð* 'landing place on a river' is perhaps not very likely here, as it may be questioned if there is any river in this part of the county large enough to give rise to a name in -*hȳð*. A name *hors-hȳð* 'landing place for horses' would however find good parallels in names like Rotherhithe and Lambeth (Sr).

Leftisford[2] (lost) is *Levetesford* 1086 DB, *Luuedesford* (ident. probable) 1169-70, 1170-71 P (p), *Leftesford* 1244 *Ass* (200 m. 2), *Lestisford* 1329 FF, *Lestesford juxta le Fairewode* 1416 IpmR, *Leftisford* 1436 FF. This may be '*Lēofgēat*'s ford', but the early forms are not quite conclusive. The site of the ford must have been near Verwood (*infra*).

Edmondsham

Edmondsham [edmənʃəm, enʃəm] 131 D 4

Amedesham 1086 DB

Medesham 1086 DB (*medessan* Exon), c. 1150 Montacute

Ædmodesham 1175-6, 1185-6 P (p), *Edmodesham* 1226, 1236 FF, *Emodesham* 1251 Ch, 1303 FA

Agemodesham 1176-7 P (p)

Edmundesham 1195 P (p), 1249, 1286 Ipm *et passim* with variant spelling *Edmondesham*; *Edmonsam* 1535 VE

Eymondesham 1316 FA, *Emundesham* 1378 Cl, *Emondesham* 1393 FF

Edmondesham al. *Ensham* al. *Edynsham* 1563 Hutchins

This can hardly be anything else than '*Ēadmund*'s farm' (OE *hām*) with early confusion between the terminals -*mund* and -*mōd* in the pers. name. For similar confusion cf. e. g. Amersham in PN Bk p. 209 and Hamsworthy in PN D p. 156.

---

[1] *Horsith* (which Hutchins calls *Horsych*) and the equally lost *Leftisford* (next name) were in the old and much larger parish of Cranborne.

[2] It is difficult to tell what was the real form of the name just before it was lost. Eyton (p. 112) calls the place *Lestisford*, but I have preferred the youngest form noted.

Romford may possibly be identical with *Roughford* 1407 IpmR, *Rougeford* 1417 IpmR and *Runggeforde* 1490 Ipm. The two earliest forms suggest that the meaning is 'rough ford', OE *rūh*, *ford*; if so, the modern form must be corrupt.

Farnham

Farnham 131 C 1

Ferneham 1086 DB, Exon, 1281 Cl, c. 1333 BM I, *Fernham* 1086 DB, 1201 Cur, 1201-2 FF *et passim*, *Fernam* 1431 FA *Farnham* 1199 CurR, *Farneham* 1205 RC, *Farnam* 1263 Ipm *Fornham* 1314 Cl, *Fyrnham* 1324 FF

'Fern (bracken) homestead', OE *fearn*, *hām*. Cf. Farrington *supra* 11.

Hampreston

Hampreston 131 H 4

Hame 1086 DB (*passim*), *Hame*, *hama* Exon, *Hames* 1204 Cur *Hamma* 1107 (1300) Ch, 1264 Ipm, *Hamme* 1204 Cur, 1216 ClR, 1258 FF *et passim*, *Esthamme* 1333 BM I *Hammes* 1208 FineR, 1275 RH, *Hammespreston* 1244 *Ass* *Hamme Preston* 1244 *Ass*, 1283 FF *et passim* with variant *Hammepreston*; *Hamme et Preston* 1327 *SR* *Hamme Chamberlayn* 1291 Tax, 1321 FF, 1428 FA (*-leyne*) *Hammedaumarle* 1298 FF, *Hamme Aumerle* 1479 IpmR

OE *hamm* 'low-lying land near a river' (the Stour), the site of Hampreston being fairly like that of Hammoon *supra* 53 f. Both the abbot of Tewkesbury and Wimborne College had land here, which may account for the additional name *Preston*; cf. Hutchins III, 433 f. *Chamberlayn*, as suggested in Hutchins, probably from the fact that a certain portion of *Hame* was held at the time of DB (f. 82 b) by Aiulfus *Camerarius* (the Chamberlain). *Hammedaumarle* (*Hamme Aumerle*) must have taken its additional name from one Galfridus de *Albemarle*, mentioned in connexion with *Hamme* in 1216 ClR (p. 277).[1]

Little Canford is *Parva Caneford* 1321 FF, *Lytill Canford* 1479 IpmR. See Canford Magna *infra*.

---

[1] I have afterwards found a few remarks on (*Ham*) *Aumerle*, "now probably Long Ham", in Do Field Club XXII, 127; **Longham** is a mile SE of Hampreston and may be the *Esthamme* of 1333 (BM I).

Parley, West
West Parley 131 I 5

Perlai 1086 DB, *Perlea* 1186-7 P, *Parlea* 1194 P
Perlee 1228 FF, *Perle* 1244 *Ass et passim* with variant spellings
-ley, -legh, Perlyghe 1315 Ipm
Westperele 1305 FF, *Westperle(e)* 1331 Cl *et passim*

This is apparently a compound of OE *peru* 'pear' and *lēah* 'enclosure', as suggested in PN Sx p. 152 s. n. Parham; cf. also Parnham *infra*. 'West' in contrast to East Parley just over the Hants border.

Dudsbury is *Dodesberie* 1086 DB, *Dudesbir'* 1235-6 Fees (426), *Duddesbury* 1312, 1393 FF, 1479 IpmR. This would seem to mean '*Dud(d)*'s *burh*', the reference being to the earthwork just near; *Dud(d)* is a common OE pers. name (cf. Redin p. 16). Alternatively the first el. may be a topographical term **dud* or **dūd*, for which cf. Wallenberg pp. 271, 291, 303.

West Moors

la More 1364 Cl, *Moures* 1407 IpmR, *Le Moure* 1412 FA

Self-explanatory, OE *mōr*. There is an East Moors Fm just over the Hants border.

Pentridge
Pentridge 131 B 3

Pentringtone 940-46 (14th) BCS 817
Pentric 1086 DB, 1107 (1300) Ch, 1236 Cl, *Pentrice* 1244 *Ass*
Pencriz 1186-7, 1187-8, 1194 P, 1234 Cl (twice)[1]
Pentrich 1264 Ipm, 1291 Tax, 1303 FA *et passim* to 1428 FA
Pencrich 1297 Cl, Pat
Pentrech 1316 FA, *Pentryssh* 1346 FA, *Pentrych* 1431 FA
Pencrych vel *Pentrich* 1398 IpmR, *Pentryge* 1535 VE

I take this to be a compound of Brit *penno-* (Welsh *pen*) 'head, top', and Brit **crouk-ā* (Welsh *crug* 'mound, hill', Cornish *cruc*), OE *cric, cryc* 'hill'[2], the name being thus etymologically

---

[1] Also *ecclesia de Pencrico*.

[2] The village of Pentridge is on the NW slope of the mighty Pentridge Hill, the highest part of which is called **Penbury Knoll** (600 feet).

identical with the Romano-British *Pennocrucium* = Penkridge (St).[1]
Pentrich (Db) is another pl.-n. of identical origin.[2] The development of *Pencric(h)* to *Pentrich* may have been facilitated by
the common orthographical confusion of *c* and *t*. For the form
Pentringtone, see Karlström p. 15. — Cf. Hutchins III, 441;
Duignan, PN St p. 115 ff.; Ekwall in IPN p. 27; Mawer, EPN
p. 16 f.; Zachrisson, Romans p. 49 f.

Shillingstone

Shillingstone[3] 130 D 10

Alford (sic) 1086 DB, *Akeford* 1199 Cur

Acforde Eskelin c. 1150, 1298 Montacute (*passim*)

Acforde Roberti Eskilling c. 1155 Montacute (Dugdale V, 167)

Acforde Eschellinch 1189-99 Montacute

Acford Eskelling 1215 ClR, 1227 FF, 1285 Cl

Akeford Skelling 1220 ClR, *Acford Skelling* 1297 Pat

Acford Eschelling 1236 FF, *Akford' Eschelling* 1242-3 Fees
(750), *Hakeford Eskellyng* 1268 FF

Acforde Scillinge 1268 Montacute, *Acfordshillyng* 1336 Cl

The forms run like this[4] till we come to

Skyllyng Ocford 1412 FA, *Shilling Okford* 1418 IpmR

Swillingysokford (sic) 1426 IpmR, *Shillyngesokeford* 1453 IpmR

Shillyngeston 1444 Ancient Indictments[5]

Shinington (sic) c. 1540 Leland V

See Child Okeford and Okeford Fitzpaine *supra* 13 and 45.
Of particular interest is the additional name *Eskelin* (*Eskilling*,
Eskelling etc.), out of which the modern name of the well-known
hybrid type was ultimately formed (*Acford Shillyng* > *Shilling
Okford* > *Shillyngesokeford* > *Shillyngeston*). The name of the DB
tenant in chief was *Schelin*[6], and Hutchins (III, 444) and Eyton

---

[1] Professor Zachrisson kindly gave me the opportunity of suggesting this
etymology some years ago (see Romans p. 49 n. 2).

[2] Zachrisson, Romans p. 49. For earlier forms see Walker, PN Db s. n.

[3] The older name *Okeford Shilling* or *Shilling Okeford* has now disappeared
from the OS maps, but is still found on Philip's map of Do.

[4] Cf. e. g. the forms in BM I: *Acford Eskylling* (1303), *Okford Eschylling* (1319),
Acford Skillyng (1328), *Acford Shillyng* (1389), *Ocford Skylling* (1405).

[5] Quoted from EPNS III, xxxvii (Addenda et Corrigenda to vol. I, part I).

[6] DB f. 83 a; the same man is called *Eschelin(us)* in Exon p. 31; cf. Eyton
p. 112 n. 7.

(p. 112 n. 7 and p. 131 n. 5) agree in suggesting that the place
owes its additional name to him.[1]

Note. Tait (IPN p. 122 f.) seems inclined to believe in the same
derivation of *Shilling* but adds a "probably". For my part I think
we need not hesitate in identifying the DB lord as the ancestor of
the *Eskellings* of this place, of whom John *Eskelingh'* held *Akeford*
as early as 1199 (Cur).[2] Note in particular the evidence found in the
Montacute Cartulary. Among the gifts to the priory of Montacute,
granted and confirmed in charters 8 and 9 of that cartulary, both of
which are from about 1155, there is mention of "a moiety of the church
of Acforde of Robert Eskylling" (No. 8[3]; No. 9 has "Robert son of
Scilling, a moiety of the church of Acforde"). Charter 121[4], which
contains the very text of this grant of Robert's ("Robert son of
Eskelin, grants to the church and monks of Montacute, half a hide
of land, and a moiety of the church of Acforde Eskelin") must consequently be earlier, perhaps considerably earlier, than 1155[5], and one
may therefore venture the suggestion that *Eskelin,* Robert's father,
was the DB lord himself. — For this name (Exon *Eschelinus*) see
Björkman, Nord. Personennamen p. 19 f. The dropping of the initial
e in the DB form *Schelin* (and in the later *Skelling*) is apparently due
to the general uncertainty as to the orthographical use of *e* before *sc*
at that time; cf. Zachrisson, AN Infl. p. 55.

Bere Marsh Fm (6")

La Bere (*in parochia de Acford Shillinge*) 1384 IpmR
Bere 1412 FF (*juxta Okford Fytz Payn*), 1412 FA *et passim*
Bere al. *Bere Marsh* 1611 Hutchins

See Bere Regis *supra* 68. *Marsh* because in a low-lying
position near the river Stour.

Tarrant Gunville

Tarrant Gunville 130 D 14, **Gunville Ho**
Tarente, Terente 1086 DB, *Tarente* 1180-1 P, 1233 FF

---

[1] Cf. also J. H. Round in VCH So I, 416.
[2] He and other members of the *Eskelling* family are mentioned under Do
and often in connexion with *Acford* in several records from about the same
time, cf. e. g. 1227 FF p. 36 ("John Eskelling grandfather of John son of
Robert"); cf. also 1175-6 P (p. 160), 1200 FineR (p. 50), 1220 ClR (p. 411:
Johannes Eskelling junior), etc.
[3] Cf. Dugdale V, 167 (: *Acforde Roberti Eskilling*).
[4] This charter also proves that *Eschelinus* (Exon p. 31) and *Schelin* (DB f.
83 a) are identical.
[5] I have printed c. 1150 in the above list of early forms.

Tarente Gundevill 1233 Ch, Cl, 1236 FF *et passim*, the distinctive name being also spelt *Goundevill* etc.

Gondevileston 1264 Ipm, *Gundevyleston* 1303 FA
Goundeville maner' 1466 IpmR, *Tarant Gunvile* 1476 IpmR

See Tarrant Hinton *supra* 59. The first member of the *Gunville* family that I have found in direct connexion with this place is Robert de *Gundeuill'* who held one fee here in 1180-1 (P); a somewhat later Hugh de *Gundeville* occurs in 1211-2 RBE, 1212 Fees (87) and 1233 FF. Two of the above forms (and I have found only these two) show the hybrid type, cf. Tait p. 131.

Stubhampton

Stibemetune 1086 DB

Stubehampton 1233 FF, *Stubhamtune* 1263 Ipm, *Stubhampton* 1278 QW *et passim*, *Tarentestubhampton* 1324 FF
Stebhampton 1276 FF (p), *Stibhampton* 1280 Ch (p)

'The home farm by the stump', OE *stybb*, *hāmtun*. The hamlet is a little N of Tarrant Gunville, and the river Tarrant rises near it.

Tarrant Rushton

Tarrant Rushton 130 F 14, **Rushton Fm**

Tarente, *Terente* 1086 DB, *tarenta*, *Tærenta* Exon
Tarente 1194 Cur (P XIV), 1198-9 FF, 1226 ClR, 1227 FF
Tarente Petri de Russell' 1242-3 Fees (750)
Tar' Russ' 1264 Ipm, *Tarente Russeals* 1289 Orig, 1290 Fine
Tarente Vileres 1291 Tax, *Tarente Vylers* 1297 Cl, Pat *et passim* (the distinctive name also spelt *Vil(l)ers*)
Tarente Russchnes 1296 Ipm, *Tarente Russeaux* 1314 Cl *et passim* with dist. name also spelt *Russeux*, *Russeussh*
Tarente Russcheweston 1307 Ipm, *Tarente Russeauston* 1308 Ipm, *Tarrante Russeaston* 1316 FA, *Tarente Russeauxton* 1338 Fine *et passim*, *Tarente Russheston* 1344 FF
Russeauston 1315 Ipm, *Russheston* [al. *Russheton*] 1326 Ipm
Tarente Russhton 1340 NI, *Tarente Rousshton* 1359 FF
Tarent Rissheton 1383 FF, *Ryssheton* 1463 IpmR

See Tarrant Hinton *supra* 59. Rushton is delusively like the common English pl.-n. which goes back to OE *rysc* 'rush' and *tūn* (cf. Rushton *infra* in East Stoke), but the above list of forms shows that it is a post-Conquest name of the hybrid type. The feudal history of the place is as follows. Wm de *Vilers* held land in *Tarente* in 1194 (Cur) and 1198-9 (FF), and is mentioned under Dorset as early as 1175-6 (P). In 1216 (ClR) the king conceded to Peter de *Rusceaus* the land which belonged to Roger de *Vilers* (in Dorset, Somerset and Hants), and in a Dorset fine of 1227 Roger de *Vilers* acknowledged the manor of *Tarente* to be the right of Peter de *Russeous*. In ClR the name of the latter is also spelt P. de *Russea(u)ls* (1224), P. de *Russell'* (1226) and P. de *Russels* (1227).

Preston Fm is *Prestetune* 1086 DB, *Prusteton* 1212 Fees (87), *Preston(e)* 1285 FA *et passim, Tarent(e) Preston* 1318, 1359 FF, 1367 Cl, 1383 FF. 'The priests' farm', OE *prēost, tūn.*

Turnworth

Turnworth 130 F 10

Torneworde 1086 DB

Turnewordam 1204 (1313) Ch

Turnewurth 1234 Cl, Pat, 1237 FF, 1436 IpmR, *-worth* 1291
    Tax, 1428 FA (also *Tourneworth*), *Turnet* 1412 FA

Thorneworthe 1316 FA, *Torneworth* 1327 *SR*, 1340 NI

The second el. is OE *weorþ* 'enclosure, farm', and the first must be OE *þyrne* 'thorn-bush' rather than *þorn* 'thorn', but it seems clear that confusion between these two cognate words has taken place. Initial *t* for original *th* (*þ*) is due to AN influence, cf. Zachrisson, AN Infl. p. 39 ff. and IPN p. 98. The place belonged to an important Norman family, the *de Lincolns* of Okeford Fitzpaine (the adjacent parish).

Verwood

Verwood [və:wud, və:rud] 131 E 5

Fairwod 1329, 1436 FF, *Fayrwod* 1436 FF

Fairewode 1412 FA, *Le Fairewode* 1416 IpmR

'Beautiful (fair) wood', OE *fæger, wudu,* the modern form showing the common voicing *f* to *v*. It is probably no mere chance that the family which resided here in the 14th century was called *de Bello Bosco* (*Beauboys*), cf. Hutchins III, 421 n. b.

Potterne Fm

Poterne 1283 SoDoNQ VIII (p)

Wymbourne Poterne 1384 IpmR, *Wymborne Potterne* 1430 IpmR

Poterneswimborn 1396 IpmR

'Pot-shed', OE *pott*, *ærn*, the name being thus identical in origin with Potterne (W), cf. EPN s. v. *ærn*. The nearest Wimborne (W. St Giles) is about five miles distant.

Witchampton

Witchampton [witʃǽmtən] 131 F 2

Wichemetune (twice) 1086, *Wichamatuna* Exon

Wichamton' 1216 ClR, *Wichhampton'* 1242-3 Fees (750), *Wichehampton* 1271 Pat (p), *Wichampton* 1338 BM I

Wychampton 1264 Ipm, 1278 QW *et passim* with variant spellings *Wychehampton*, *Wychamton*

Wykehampton 1375 IpmR

The elements are apparently OE *wīc*, *hām* and *tūn*, but it is difficult to be sure whether the original form of the compound was *wīc-hāmtūn* 'the home farm near the *wīc*' ('dairy-farm'), or *wīchǽma-tūn* 'farm of the *wīc(hām)* dwellers'; Shilvinghampton *infra* offers the same difficulty. Cf. e. g. the article in Crawford Ch p. 116, and note the early forms for Ditchampton (W) collected by Ekblom p. 71.

Dean Fm is *La Dene* 1243 FF, 1409 Inq aqd, *Dene* 1412 FA. OE *denu* 'valley'.

Hemsworth, East (1″) and **West** (6″) [hemzud]

Hemedesw(o)rde 1086 DB, *Emmedeswurtha* 1179-80 P (p)

Hemmesdeswurda 1194 P, *Hemmedeswrda* 1195 P

Hemeleswurth, *-worth* 1224 ClR, 1290 FF (*West*), 1302 Ch, 1303 FA, 1304 Ch (*Est*), 1312 Cl, 1340 NI, 1346, 1428 FA

Emeleswurth, *-worth* 1224 ClR, 1303, 1346, 1428 FA

Hendesworth 1235-6 Fees (426)

Emedeswurth 1238 Ch, *Hemedeswurth* 1243 FF

Hamelesw(o)rth 1257 FF, 1303 Ch (*West*)

Emmeswurth, *Hemdeswurth* 1278 Pat

Hemelisworth 1337 FF, *Hemblesworth Giffard* 1348 FF

Elmesworth, West Hemelsworth 1412 FA
Hammesworth, Hemmesworth 1428 FA

The second el. is of course OE *weorþ* 'homestead, enclosure'. The first may be a pers. name, but the curious interchange of *d* and *l* spellings (*Hemedes-, Hemeles-*) in the early forms makes it difficult to suggest a plausible derivation. *Hemele*, a well-recorded OE pers. name (Redin p. 149), would suit the *l* spellings but would leave the *d* forms unexplained. The interpretation of the first el. had therefore better remain open.

The family name *Giffard* occurs in Dorset in the 13th and 14th centuries but has not been noted in direct connexion with Hemsworth.

XV. Cogdean Hundred

Cocdene 1084 Geld Roll, 1212 Fees (90), 1244 *Ass*, 1265 Misc *et passim* (variant *Cok-*), *Kocdene* 1249 FF
Chogden' 1181-2 P, *Cogdene* 1244 *Ass*, 1247 FF
Cockeden(e) Cokkeden 1244 *Ass*, 1303, 1431 FA
Cokeden(e) 1307 Pat, 1346 FA, 1347 IpmR *et passim*

The elements are probably OE *cocc* 'cock' and *denu* 'valley', cf. Cockhill Fm *supra* 40. The meeting place of the hundred-court was at **Cogdean Elms** (6″) in the parish of Corfe Mullen.

Canford Magna

Canford Magna 131 H 3

Cheneford 1086 DB, *Keneford'* 1180-1 P (p)
Caneford(e) 1200 RC, 1211 LibR, 1212 Fees (90), 1221 ClR, 1230 P, 1239 FF, 1244 *Ass*, 1248 Pat *et passim*
Kaneford 1213, 1214 PatR *et passim* to 1327 Ipm
Canford 1307 Pat, 1428 FA, etc.

A pers. name *Cana* is recorded in DB (cf. Redin p. 87) and has been supposed to enter into several pl.-ns, cf. e. g. Karlström p. 166 with literature. Canford may possibly[1] be another instance. Cf. however Cann *supra* 20, where the possibility

---

[1] Zachrisson has recently (StNPh V, 20) expressed strong doubts about the existence of a pers. name *Cana* in English pl.-ns.

of OE *canne* 'can, cup, vessel' being used as a topographical
term in pl.-ns was pointed out.[1] — Little Canford (*supra* 102) is
on the other side of the Stour.

Ashington is *Esseton* 1242-3 Fees (753), 1396 IpmR (*juxta Wymbourne*), 1415 IpmR (*juxta Wynterbourne*). 'Ash-tree farm', OE
æsc, tūn. *Wynterbourne* in the last reference is apparently a
mistake for *Wymbourne*. Wimborne Minster is only a mile distant.

Lake Fm is *atte Lake* 1333 *SR* (p). OE *lacu* 'stream, water-
course'.

Oakley is *Ocle* 1333 *SR* (p), 1475 FF (*in the parish of Canford*).
'Oak clearing', OE *āc, lēah*.

Charlton Marshall

Charlton Marshall 130 G 13

   Cerletone 1086 DB, *Cerletona* Exon
   Cerlentone, -tonia 1087-1100, 1099, c. 1165 France
   Cherlentona, -tune 1166-87 France, *Cherlintone* 1219 Sarum
   Cheorleton 1187 France, *Cherelton* 1244 *Ass*
   Cherleton 1244 *Ass* (p), 1256 FF (p), 1258 Ch, 1266 FF (*juxta
   Wymburn*), 1275 RH *et passim* to 1428 FA
   Charleton 1337 Fine, 1345, 1386 Cl, 1390 FF (*juxta Speghte-
   bury*) *et passim, Charleton Prioris* 1340 NI

OE *ceorla-tūn* 'farm of the peasants', cf. s. v. *ceorl* in EPN.
For the forms *C(h)erlen-, Cherlin-* see PN Wo p. 105 (s. n.
Charlton), where it is suggested that such forms may go back
to an OE *ceorlena-tūn*, with weak gen. plur. *Prioris* probably
because belonging to the abbey of Préaux in Normandy. I can
find no particular reason why the place is called *Marshall*, un-
less it be as a counterpart to Sturminster Marshall *infra*, about
four miles distant.[2] — Its situation is near Spettisbury and not
very far from Wimborne Minster.

---

[1] On Dorset territory two other names show a similar first el., viz. the pre-
DB hundred called *canendone* (see *supra* 77 n. 1) and a lost field-name (bosc.
de) *Canewic* (1231 Cl) in Gillingham Forest.

[2] Cf. however Hutchins III, 522 ("looks as if part of this vill had some
relation to one of the manors in Sturminster Marshal").

Charisworth is *Kaerswurth* 1227 FF (twice). The identification is almost a mere guess; the place was a member of *Acford* (*Shilling*). I can do nothing with the first element; OE *cærse* 'cress' would phonetically suit the early form *Kaerswurth*, but could not possibly have become *Charis-*.

Corfe Mullen

Corfe Mullen 131 H 2

Corf 1086 DB, 1212 Fees (90), 1244 *Ass* (p)

Corf le Mulin 1175-6, 1176-7 P

Corfmulin t. Hy III Ipm, *Corf Mulyn* 1283 Misc, 1353 Cl

Corf Molyn 1282 Cl, 1282, 1302 Ipm *et passim*, with the additional name also spelt *Molin*, *Molen*, *Moleyn(s)*

Corf Huberd (*Hubert*) 1303, 1346, 1428, 1431 FA, *Corff Hubert* 1478 FF, *Corfe Hubert* 1487 Ipm

See Corfe Castle *infra*. According to Eyton (p. 120 n. 9) the place owes its additional name to its valuable mill, and the form *Corf le Mulin* leaves no doubt that this is correct.[1] *Huberd* (*Hubert*) must refer to *Hubertus de Burgo*[2], who held *Corf* in 1212 (Fees), cf. Eyton loc. cit.

The Knoll is *atte Knolle* 1333 *SR* (p). OE *cnoll* 'hillock'.

Sleight is *atte Sleyte* 1333 *SR* (p). This must be the dialect word (see EDD *slait* sb. 2, NED *sleight* sb. 3) meaning '(sheep-) pasture', often in the compound *sheep-sleight*. The first reference in NED is not earlier than 1670 (from Wilts).

Kinson

Kinson 131 I 4/5

Chinestanestone 1086 DB, *Kinestaneston* 1238 Pat

Kynestanton 1231 FF, *Kynstanton* 1259 FF

Kunestonston 1244 *Ass*, *Knustanstone* (sic) 1314 Ipm

Kynsten(e)ston 1303 FA, 1327 Cl, Ipm, 1363 FF

Kyngeston [1303], 1346, 1428 FA

---

[1] The entry in Liber Niger: "*Hubertus de Burgo tenet Croft molendina*" is according to Eyton to be read — — "*Corfe Molendina*". The Liber Niger (ed. Hearne) is not accessible to me, but the passage is reprinted in RBE p. 235 n. 15.

[2] Chief justiciar, earl of Kent, see Dict. of Nat. Biogr. VII, 315.

Kenstaneston 1326 FF, *Kynstaneston* 1393 FF
Kinstanton 1407 IpmR, *Kyneston* 1431 FA
'The farm (*tūn*) of *Cynestān*', a well-recorded OE pers. name.

Lytchett Matravers

Lytchett Matravers [litʃət mətrǽvəz] 131 I 1
Lichet 1086 DB, 1297 Ipm, *Litsed* 1235-6 Fees (426)
Lischet 1242-3 Fees (753), *Liscete* 1244 *Ass*
Luchet Mautravers 1291 Tax, 1349 Fine, 1428 FA
Lyc(c)het Mautravers 1303 FA, 1306 Ch, 1346 FA *et passim*
Lischet Mautrauers 1333 *SR*, *Lechet Mautravers* 1351 Fine

Cf. the early forms for Lytchett Minster *infra* (next parish).
Ekwall (Anglia Beiblatt **XXXVI**, 149) takes the second el. to
be Brit *cēt* 'wood' (cf. Orchard *supra* 30), and looks upon the
whole name as probably identical with Brit *Letocetum* 'grey
wood'. For that word see Bradley in Essays and Studies I,
20 f.[1] The two Lytchetts are situated in the north-eastern part
of the great ("Egdon") heath, and DB mentions both *silva* and
broca ('brushwood') here. — The place takes its distinctive name
from the *Mautravers* (Fr *mal travers*) who had great possessions
in Do and who have added their name to several Do places.
That already the DB mesne tenant of *Lichet*, Hugo, bore the
surname *Maltrauers*, appears from an entry in Exon p. 410
(So), see Hutchins III, 314 (with further details on the Mautravers
family); cf. also The Complete Peerage VIII, 577.

Dullar Fm is *Dulre* 1333 *SR* (p), 1469, 1484 IpmR, *Doulre* 1421
IpmR. No etymology can be suggested. The farm is on the
slope of a small hill, Henbury Barrow (see Henbury *infra*).
There is no stream in the neighbourhood.

Lytchett Minster

Lytchett Minster 141 D 6
Licheminstr' 1244 *Ass*, *Lyceministr(e)* 1253, 1262 FF
Lechet Ministre 1269 FF, *Lyschet Monaster'* 1281 FF (p)
Lychet ministre (*Minstre*) 1285 FF, 1362 Cl

---

[1] Some of the early spellings of Lytchett show AN influence, cf. Zachrisson,
AN Infl. p. 21.

Liscett 1311 Ipm, *Luchet Mynstre* 1314 FF
Lytchet or *Litchet Mynstre* 1329 Ipm

See Lytchett Matravers *supra* 112. There are no traces of a
monastic house of any kind here, nor did land here belong to
any monastery, and it has therefore been suggested (Do Field
Club XXXVIII, 67) that the place may owe its additional name
Minster to the fact that its church since old is in the position
of a chapelry to Stur*minster* Marshall (*infra*). As suggested
in Hutchins, however, it may have got its distinctive name
simply on account of its chapel; cf. EPN s. v. *mynster*.

Bulbury Fms is *Burlebury*, *Bulrebury* 1306 Ipm, but the material
is too scanty for any etymology to be suggested. Is the first
el. to be compared with that of Birlingham (Wo)? For that
name see PN Wo p. 188 and Karlström p. 111; cf. also Duignan,
PN Wo p. 19.

Newton Fm is *atte Niweton* 1333 *SR* (p). Self-explanatory, OE
niwe, *tūn*.

Slepe is *Slepe* 1333 *SR* (p). See Slepe *infra* (in Arne).

Poole[1]

Poole 141 E 7
  Poles 1179-80, 1183-4, 1184-5, 1185-6 P (p)
  Pole 1182-3 P (p), 1199 Cur (p) *et passim* (variant *Pola*)
  la Pole 1224 Pat, 1227 Lib *et passim*, *La Poule* 1300 Cl
  Self-explanatory, OE *pōl*.

Hamworthy (and Ham Common)
  Hamme 1285 FF (*juxta la Pole*), 1333 *SR*, 1362 Cl (*by Pole*),
    1431 FA, *Southam juxta Poule* 1407 IpmR
  Hãwurthy 1535 VE
  OE *hamm* in the sense of 'low-lying land near a river' (Poole
  Bay). The late addition *-wurthy* (OE· *worðig*) is otherwise prac-
  tically unknown in Do, cf. Wilksworth *supra* 79.

---

[1] Since the town of Poole was a member of Canford in this hundred, the
practical arrangement of including it here may also be historically justified.
In 1905 the boundaries of the borough were extended so as to include *inter
alia* the civil parishes of Hamworthy, Longfleet and Parkstone (Kelly).

Longfleet is (*Villata de Caneforde cum*) *Langeflete* 1230 P. OE *lang* 'long' and *flēot* 'creek, inlet, estuary'.

Parkstone is *Parkeston* 1326 FF, *Parkestone* 1495 Ipm. Probably self-explanatory.

Sturminster Marshall

Sturminster Marshall 131 H 1

> *Sturministris* c. 1080 France, *Sturminstre* 1086 DB, -*ministra* 1154-8 (1390) Ch, -*minstr(i)a* 1162-4 (etc.) France
> *Esturmin(i)stre, Esturminstr(i)a* 1152-66 to 1204 France[1]
> *Sturministre* (-*er*) 1204, 1207 ClR, 1212 Fees (90) *et passim* with variant spellings -*men(i)stre, -mynstre*
> *Stormenistr(e)* 1210-12 RBE, 1216 PatR, *Storemenistre* 1273 Ipm, *Stormenstre* 1290 Pat

The forms run like this, and 'Marshall' is added about the end of the 13th century:

> *Sturmenistre Marescal* 1280 Cl, *Stormenistre Mareschal* 1282 Cl, *Sturministre Marescalli* 1306 Cl, etc.

For the name Sturminster cf. Sturminster Newton *supra* 47. The additional name is from the *Marshals*, earls of Pembroke, of whom Wm *Marescallus* was here as early as 1204, cf. Hutchins III, 336.

Combe Almer is *Cumbe* 1244, 1249 FF, 1271 Pat, *Comb(e)* 1306 Ipm *et passim, Combe Almere* 1327, 1333 *SR, Coumbe by Stormynstre Marchall* 1362 Cl, *Comb Marshal* 1427 IpmR. OE *cumb* 'valley'. Almer (*supra* 74) and Sturminster Marshall are both about two miles distant.

Henbury

> *Hennebyr* 1244 FF, *Hennbyr'* 1244 *Ass*
> *Hembyr, Hymbur* 1249 FF
> *Hymburi, Himburi* late 13th cent. BM I
> *Hymbury* 1327 *SR*, 1352, 1353 BM I, 1383 FF *et passim*

---

[1] *Esturmilistria* 1162 ib. Other forms with prothetic *e* before *st* (cf. Zachrisson, AN Infl. p. 55) are *Estrumenistre* 1204 (?) BM I, *Esturmenistre* 1266 Pat, *Esturminstre Mareschal* 1327 BM I.

The second el. is OE *burh* (*byrig*), the reference being probably to Henbury Barrow just near. The first early form above would seem to point to an original (*æt*) *henna-byrig* 'fowls' *burh*' (cf. Encombe *infra*), but the total absence of a medial vowel in the other forms tells rather in favour of a base (*æt*) *hēan byrig* 'high *burh*', cf. Hembury in PN D pp. 90, 91. For the raising of *e* to *i* cf. Hinton St Mary *supra* 41.

Moorcourt Fm is *Morescourte* (maner') 1469 IpmR, *Morescourts* (maner') 1484 IpmR. Probably self-explanatory.

Newton Peveril is *Niweton* and *Neweton Peverel* 1306 Ipm, and is often referred to as *Neuton juxta Stouremynstre Marchall*' (1375 Orig, etc.). Self-explanatory, OE *nīwe*, *tūn*. The first of the *Peverels* here that I have come across is Andrew *Peverel*, mentioned as landholder in *Stourmistre* in 1244 (FF); cf. Bradford Peverell *infra*.

Westley Wood is *Westleye* (*by Neweton Peverel*) 1306 Ipm. 'West clearing', OE *west*, *lēah*.

Isle of Purbeck

The following two hundreds, Rowbarrow and Hasler, form together what is somewhat incorrectly called the **Isle of Purbeck**, a peninsula bounded on the north by the river Frome and the estuary of Poole, on the east and south by the Channel, and on the west partly by a tributary of the Frome called Luckford Lake. The so-called Purbeck Hills divide the country into a northern part, consisting mostly of comparatively low-lying heath-land, and a southern part which is decidedly hilly. I have collected the following early forms for the name Purbeck:

(pars telluris) *Purbicinga* 948 (15th) BCS 868
Porbi, (Hundret) *Porbiche* 1086 DB
Porbica 1107 (1300) Ch, *Purbica* 1109 Dugdale II
Purbic c. 1170 Montacute, 1200 Cur (p), 1206 PatR, 1206, 1207 ClR (p) *et passim*, *Purbicc*' 1205 PatR
Purbik(e) c. 1170 Montacute, 1216 ClR (p), 1239 Lib, 1262 Ipm, 1264 FineR *et passim* (up to c. 1400)
Purbich 1189 (1313) Ch, 1199 Cur (p), *Porbich* 1190 (1332) Ch
Purebic 1237 Lib, 1240 Lib, Cl, *Porbik*' 1249 Cl
Purbyk(e) 1258 Ch (p), 1306 Pat, 1315 Ipm, 1315, 1318 Fine, 1324 Cl, 1357 Fine (*Estpurbyk*), 1374 (etc.) Cl, 1412 FA

Purbecke, -bek(e) 1326 Inq aqd, 1377 (etc.) IpmR
Pourbyk 1398, 1425 IpmR

It has been tentatively suggested by Ekwall (Studies on PN p. 80 f.) that the first el. of this difficult name may be OE *pur* 'a bittern', a word supposed by Ekwall to enter into Purleigh (Ess) and Purley (Berks). As regards the second el. Ekwall makes the assumption that there may have been an OE word (**becc*?) meaning 'a point, a headland', derived from the base found in OE *becca* 'a beck, a pick-axe, mattock' (with German parallels), and that, consequently, Purbeck may mean 'bittern headland'. — For the DB form *Porbi* cf. Zachrisson, AN Infl. p. 27 n. 1.

XVI. Rowbarrow Hundred

Rug(g)eberga 1182-3, 1183-4, 1184-5 P, *Ruberge* 1195 P
Ruggebergh, Rugheberg, Rougeberghe 1244 *Ass*
Rueberghe 1265 Misc, *Ruber'* 1275 RH
Roweberwe, Rowberge 1278 QW, *Rowebergh* 1412 FA
Rugheburgh 1289 Orig, 1290 Fine, Pat
Rouzberwe 1303 FA, *Rousebergh* 1316 FA
Rouberg(h) 1307 Ipm *et passim, Robergh, Rouburgh* 1346 FA,
    Roubargh 1425 IpmR, 1428 FA, *Rouborgh* 1431 FA

OE *(æt) rūgan beorge* '(at) the rough barrow', a common name, cf. e. g. *(on) Ruanberghe* BCS 564, *(on) ruwan beorg* KCD 1322 (both Do). Hutchins writes (I, 629): "Near Tapers or Talbot's hill in Woolgarston[1], and south of it, is a lane called Rowbarrow Lane, and in a ground near it the Hundred Court was formerly held. It is about a mile south-west from Aylwood which formerly gave name to this hundred."[2] The name *Rowbarrow* is not to be found on the maps.

Corfe Castle

Corfe Castle 141 G 6
    Corf 955 (15th) BCS 910, 1161-2 P, *Corf(e)* 1166 RBE, 1203
        (etc.) PatR, 1204 (etc.) ClR, 1209 LibR *et passim*

---

[1] This must be **Tabbit's Hill** (Fm) on the 6″ map, apparently named after the *Talbot* family of Godlingston (2 miles SE), a younger branch of which had a small tenement in Woolgarston; cf. Hutchins I, 532, 662, 713.

[2] Cf. the first reference given under Ailwood *infra*.

(æt) Corfes geate[1] s. a. 979 ASC (E), *(at) Corf geate* ib. (F),
Porta Corf ib. (F; Latin)
Corff(e) 1217 Pat, 1227 Lib, 1261 Pat *et passim*
Corfcastel(l) 1309 FF, 1333 *SR*, 1380 Cl *et passim*

Place-names containing an el. *corf* have been collected and
discussed by Ekwall (ERN p. 96 f.), and I need not, therefore,
enter upon the question of such names again, in particular as
the parallels I had collected before Ekwall's work appeared
coincide almost wholly with the material adduced by him.[2]
Like Mc Clure (p. 276), Ekwall takes *corf* to mean ʻa cutting,
a passʼ (to OE *ceorfan* ʻto cutʼ), the ʻpassʼ here being the conspicuous cut in the long ridge which, as described above, runs
through the Isle of Purbeck from east to west (the Purbeck
Hills). For the forms *Corfes geate, Corf geate (Porta Corf)* in
ASC, cf. Coryates and Corscombe *infra*. — The castle (*castellum
de Corfe* 1166 RBE onwards) is referred to in DB (f. 78 b 2)
as *castellum Warham* (i. e. Wareham c. 4 miles NW), cf. Eyton
pp. 43 and 111 n. 2.

Afflington Fm

Alvronetone, Alveronetune, Alvretone 1086 DB
Alfrunetone 1086 DB, *Alfrunetona* Exon
Alurinton 1244 *Ass*
Alfrington 1244 *Ass*, 1264 Ipm *et passim* (variant *-yng-*)
Alfington 1307 Pap
Alfrinton(e) 1315 Ipm, 1318 FF, *Alfrynton* 1398 IpmR
Alryngton 1383, 1385 Cl, 1412 FA

ʻ*Ælfrūn*'s farmʼ, see Stenton, PN Berks p. 33, Mawer, PN and
History p. 26, and PN Sx p. 408. It may possibly have escaped
the attention of Stenton and Mawer that the lady in question
is actually mentioned in DB (f. 80 a) as one of the tenants here:
*Idem Rogerius tenet Alvronetone. Alueron tenuit TRE et geldabat
pro II hidis;* see Hutchins I, 527.

---

[1] This form is repeated in Flor Worc *(Corvesgeate)*, Sim Durh *(Corvesgeate)*,
and LibHyda *(Corvesgate)*.

[2] The Dorset examples (besides Corfe Castle) are Corfe Mullen *supra* 111,
Corton Fm and Coryates *infra*, all adduced by Ekwall, to which should be
added Corfe Hill (in Radipole) *infra*. A sixth example in Do is Corscombe
infra, cf. Ekwall, Studies on PN p. 70 ff.

Ailwood [eilud]
aileuesuuode 1084 Geld Roll
Aleoude 1086 DB, *Ailewud'* 1221-2 ClR (p)
Aylethewode 1304 Ipm, 1305 Cl
Aylywood 1585-6 Treswell
The second el. is of course OE *wudu* 'wood', and the first
would seem to be a pers. name beginning with *Æþel-*, possibly
Æþelgȳþ (fem.), but the material is too scanty and conflicting
to allow of any certainty concerning the second part of the
Æþel-name.

Arfleet Mills (6″) [ɑ:fli:t]
Alfledesmulle 1318 FF
Alfletemell 1384 FF, *-mill* 1426 IpmR, *-mulle* 1435 FF
Alfletmill(e) 1408, 1413 IpmR, *Alflete* 1431 FA
Aflet Mills 1585-6 Treswell, *Affleet* 1765 Taylor
'*Æþelflǣd'*s mill'. The inorganic gen. *s* of the earliest form
above has an exact parallel in *Alfledestoft* (13th cent.) recorded
in PN BedsHu p. 297 and containing the same fem. pers. name;
cf. Allweston *infra*.

Blashenwell Fm [blæʃənwel]
(at) Blechenhamwelle 955 (15th) BCS 910
(to) Blechenenwelle 955 (15th) KCD 435 (vol. III p. 433)
(on) Blechene; of ðanen welle ib.
Blakenhamwelle, Blakenwelle (rubrics) ib.[1]
Blackenewell 1227 FF, *Blachenewell* (6 times) 1285 FA
Blachyngwell 1316 FA, *Blachenwoll* 1333 SR
The remarkable 'well' (OE *wielle*) after which this farm takes
its name is an intermittent calcareous spring which formerly deposited tufa and whose limpid water gushes forth from a rocky
cavity at the foot of the hill close to the present farm-house;
see Hutchins I, 526 and Do Field Club XVII, 67 ff. It is
tempting to believe that the first el. may have something to do
with the peculiar character of this spring. Blatchinworth (La)
is assumed by Ekwall (PN La p. 57 f.) possibly to contain an

---

[1] KCD 435 is the same charter as BCS 910, but the addition to the former
charter found on p. 433 in vol. III of KCD seems to have no correspondence
in BCS.

OE *blǣcen 'bleaching', derived from the verb blǣcan. This may be applicable to the present name, too, though Professor Zachrisson would rather take *blǣcen to be an -in extension of the adj. blāc 'bright, shining' and with much the same meaning as that adjective.

Brenscombe Fm [brinskəm]

Brunescume 1086 DB, Exon, Brunescumb 1219 FF
Brundescumb 1244 Ass (p), Bryncescomb' 1286 Abbr
Brunnescorne (sic) 1301 Pat
Bronshyscomb 1443 IpmR, Brenshyscomb 1463 FF

The earliest forms point to the derivation 'Brūn's valley' (OE cumb), but the spellings of some of the later forms are remarkable. Alternatively the first el. may be the same as the one suggested for Brownshall supra 33.

Chapman's Pool

(on) þe schort mannes pol 948 (15th) BCS 868
(on) seortmannes pol 955 (15th) BCS 910

Hutchins (I, 512) is probably right in identifying these two charter forms, meaning 'the short man's pool', with the bay now called Chapman's Pool, but the identity of the 10th century name with the modern one is therefore not quite certain, since the 'pool' may have been renamed after some person whose name was Chapman.[1]

Encombe is Hennecumbe, Henecūbe 1244 Ass (p), Enecumbe 1285 FA, Enecomb 1333 SR, Henna Cumba (passim) 15th Harl. 61 (f. 62), Encombe 1535 VE. Probably OE henna-cumb 'fowls' valley'.

Kingston is Chingestone 1086 DB, Kingeston 1212 Fees (87), 1266 Pat et passim (variant Kyngeston), Kyngeston Abbatisse 1297 FF. Self-explanatory. In 948 (BCS 868) land here was granted by King Eadred to the religious woman Alfþriþ, apparently the then abbess of Shaftesbury, to which Kingston belonged up to the dissolution; hence the additional name. It is sometimes still called Kingston Abbess.

---

[1] Cf. Robertus le Chapman de Purbyk, mentioned in 1321 (Orig) in connexion with Langeton Purbyk, now Langton Matravers, less than 3 miles away.

Lynch Fm

on anne linc reawe. of þane linche 948 (15th) BCS 868
on ðane hlinc; anlang hlinkes 955 (15th) KCD 435
La Linche 1254 FF, 1285 FA (p), *atte Lynch* 1333 *SR* (p)

OE *hlinc* 'bank, rising ground, (dial.) *linch*'.

Ower [auə]

Ore c. 939 (copies) BCS 738, 739, 1291 Tax, 1310 Inq aqd
Ora 1086 DB, Exon, *Hore* 1212 Fees (90)
Oure 1316 FA, 1333 *SR* (p), *Ower* 1535 VE

This is either OE *ōra* 'border, margin, bank', or OE *ōfer*
'shore, bank'.

Note.   **Green Island**

An earlier name for this little island in the estuary of the river
Frome was *St Helens*[1], see Hutchins I, 538. In 1535 (VE), when it
belonged to Milton Abbey (Do), it was called *Insula Sc̄e Helene in
Purbyke*, and among the possessions of that abbey enumerated in Inq
aqd (3 Edw II) we find *Fromouthe*[2] *quod dicitur Insula Sc̄e Elene 2 hid'*,
and *Ore*[3] *maner' 1 hid'*. In King Æthelstan's foundation charter to
Milton Abbey (BCS 739) this corresponds to the *tres (hidas terræ)
apud Fromemuthe apud insulam quæ dicitur la Ye, duas in mari et
unam in terra, scilicet apud Ore*, and in the ME version (BCS 738)
of the same charter the text runs: *þreo (hyde londes) atte Fromemouþe.
atte yle ðan ye to on see. and on on londe þ is to leggende (= seggende)
æt Ore*. The island in question was consequently first called simply
(la) ye (OE *īeg* 'island'). Later on when a chapel was built there
(Hutchins loc. cit.), the island was apparently (re)named after the
saint to whom that chapel must have been dedicated.

Rempstone Hall is probably a transferred name (earliest reference
Remeston 1535 VE), named after the *Rempston* family, the 15th
cent. lords of Godlingston; cf Hutchins I, 533 f.

Rollington Fm

Ragintone 1086 DB, *-tona* Exon
Radelinton' 1236 Fees (581), *Rodlington'* 1242-3 Fees (752)

---

[1] *St Elins Insul* on Treswell's map (1585-6), *St Elyns* in Camden (map from 1695).

[2] Cf. *(into) Frommuðan* s. a. 998 ASC (E), *(to) Fromuðan* s. a. 1015 ib.

[3] *Ower supra* (the preceding name). According to Hutchins (loc. cit.) Ower
and Green Island were formerly joined by a bridge, the remains of which
were still visible in 1774.

Radelington 1256 FF (p), 1290 Cl, 1421 IpmR
Radelyngton 1290 FF *et passim* (later *Radlyngton*)
Rydelington 1303 FA, *Ryadelyngton* 1346 FA
Rikelington 1303 FA, *Rykelyngton* 1428 FA
Redlyngtone 1306 FF, *-don* 1333 *SR*, *Radlyngdon* 1316 FA
Radlintone, Radlyntone 1334 Ipm, Cl
Rudelington 1422 IpmR, *Rollyngton* 1435 FF

Rollington possibly belongs to a group of names (showing
Red(e)ling-, Rid(e)ling- etc.) discussed by Karlström (p. 125) in
connexion with Ringwould (K).[1] The group is very difficult,
and Karlström arrives at no definite conclusion. I can only tentatively suggest that Rollington may go back to an OE *Rǣde-
ling(a)tūn*, thus containing the OE diminutive pers. name *Rǣdel*,
evidenced as the name of a moneyer (t. Edw Conf.), cf. Redin
p. 139. The occasional spellings with *y(a)*, *i* and *u* are bewildering, but cf. Redhone *infra*.

Scoles Fm and **Gate** (both 6″) take their name from the family
of *Scovill* coming from Escoville near Caen in Normandy (Do
Field Club XLIV, xxxviii). Wm de *Scouill* occurs under this
hundred in 1244 *Ass* (201 m. 12), and ten years later (38 Hy
FF p. 101) John de *Scovill* was party to a fine concerning land
in *La Linche*, i. e. Lynch *supra* 120 (the nearest farm). Cf.
also Hutchins I, 525.

Swyre Head [swaiə]
uppe on swuren. þwert ouer swuran 955 (15th) BCS 910
OE *swēora* 'neck, col' (EPN). This is Swyre Head just W of
Encombe. Another Swyre Head 1 ¹/₂ m. W of Lulworth Cove
has apparently the same origin. A third Swyre *infra* in the
west of the county is recorded in a great number of early forms.
The three Dorset Swyres are all on the coast, and the topography is very typical of their name.

Westwood Fm is *Westwode* 1333 *SR* (p). Self-explanatory.

Woolgarston [wulgəstən, wu(:)sən]
Orgarestone 1086 DB, *Wlgareston* 1256 FF

---
[1] For that name cf. also Wallenberg p. 275 f.

Wolgerston 1264 Ipm, 1383, 1404, 1443 IpmR
Wolgareston 1280 FF, *Wolgarston* 1318 FF, 1402 IpmR
'*Wulfgār*'s farm' (OE *tūn*).

Wytch Fm, Wych Channel

Wytch Fm is close to the mouth of the river Corfe, near the point where this stream falls into Wych Channel, one of the arms of the Poole estuary. There can be little doubt that Wytch Fm and Wych Channel preserve an older name of the river Corfe (cf. Hutchins I, 468, 512, 538), called *aqua de Wyche* in *Harl. 61* (f. 122), the present name being a clear back-formation from Corfe Castle. Two Shaftesbury charters, BCS 868 and 910 (KCD 435)[1], contain a great many forms for this stream name:

fram wicanforð — — eft to Wikenforde[2] 948 (15th) BCS 868
on wicun niþer anland wicum streames 955 (15th) BCS 910
on wicum niþer anlang wicunstreames ib.
on Wickenford. on lang Wickenforde ib.
of wikenforde; anlang wiken KCD 435 (III, 433)
on Wicean (twice), *of Wichen* ib.
up anlang Wicean eft on Wichenforde ib.

Unfortunately the spellings of the charters quoted are mostly very bad, and this makes one doubtful as to the best explanation of the above list of forms. Probably we should reckon with a genuine stream-name *wice*, of obscure etymology; if so, forms like *wicum*, *wicun* should be looked upon as false spellings.

Langton Matravers

Langton Matravers 141 H 7

Langeton c. 1165 Montacute, 1276 Pat *(in Purbik) et passim* (later *Langton*), *Langton Purbek* 1321 Inq aqd
Langeton Walisch 1376 IpmR, *Langeton Walsh* 1397 FF *et passim* with the dist. name also spelt *Walysshe*
Lang(e)ton Mautravers 1428, 1431 FA, 1435 IpmR

Self-explanatory, OE *lang*, *tūn*; "the village consists of one street, near a mile in length" (Hutchins). Ing(el)ram *le Waleys* (1276 Pat, etc.) seems to have been the first member here of the family which gave name to the manor of *Langton Wallis*,

---

[1] Cf. the foot-note to Blashenwell Fm *supra* 118.

[2] For the probable site of this ford, see Hutchins I, 512.

cf. also Hutchins I, 634[1]. For the family of *Mautravers* see under Lytchett Matravers *supra* 112; John *Mautravers* was here in 1281 (FF), cf. also Hutchins I, 630.

Acton is *Tacatone* 1086 DB (*-tona* Exon), *Tachetona* 1109 Dugdale II, *Tacton* 1283 FF, *Taketon* 1305 Cl. No certain suggestion can be made about the first el. Probable parallels are Tackley (O), Tackbear (D), and Takeley (Ess), supposed by the editors of PN D (p. 135 f.) to contain an OE pers. name **Tǣcca* (a reduced form of *Tǣtica*).[2] — In this pl.-n. the initial *T* must have been dropped through misdivision (cf. EPN s. v. *æt*), the process giving the modern form the false appearance of going back to OE *āc-tūn* 'oak-farm'.

Coombe (6") is *Come* 1086 DB. OE *cumb* 'valley'.

Durnford Ho (6") is *Derneford* 1275 RH, 1281 Abbr, 1287 FF, *Durneford* 1338 Cl (all p). There is no stream here (and consequently no ford), so this is in all probability a transferred name, perhaps from Durnford in Wilts, as suggested in Hutchins (I, 631). The meaning of that name is 'secret or hidden ford', see Ekblom p. 73 f., and EPN s. v. *dierne*. — Eyton's identification (p. 111 f.) of DB *Torne* (Exon *Torna*) with this place can hardly be correct.

Knaveswell Fm is *Cuaneswelle* (sic)[3] 1285 FF, *Knaveswell* 1535 VE. If the name is late, the first el. may be ME *cnave* (OE *cnafa*) 'boy, servant'; otherwise we may think of a pers. name beginning with *Cēn-* (or possibly *Cyne-*), but more and earlier material is necessary to settle this. The second el. is OE *wielle* 'spring'.

Knitson Fm is *Knyghtwyneston* 1318 FF, *Knyghteston* 1367, 1378 FF *(in Purbyk)*, 1431 FA (II, 109),[4] *Knightwyneston* 1402 IpmR, *Knytteston* 1404 IpmR, *Knyghtweston* 1457 IpmR. This must be the 'farm of *Cnihtwine*', an OE pers. name of which Searle gives one example.

---

[1] The name *Langton Wallis* (or *West Langton*) has now disappeared from the OS maps; cf. however the foot-note to Middlebere Fm *infra*.

[2] Alexander (p. 203; cf. Blomé p. 139) suggested an unrecorded **Tacca*. The occurrence of a certain Robert *Tac* (13th) in Dorset (Burton in Marnhull) may be of little value, but is at least worthy of note; cf. Glaston C p. 96 ff.

[3] Hutchins (I, 532) gives a more correct transcription of this form *(Cnaveswell)*.

[4] Wrongly identified by the indexer of FA with Kingston (Abbess) *supra* 119.

Leeson Ho is (?) *Letsinton'* 1236 Cl, *Lesseton'* 1242-3 Fees (750), *Leston* 1305 Cl, 1431 FA, *Leuston* 1333 *SR* (p). '*Lēofsige's tūn'*? The identification of the earliest form, made by the Cl indexer, seems very uncertain.

Priest's Way is *Prestesweye* 1305 Cl. Self-explanatory, OE *prēost*, *weg*. Even nowadays merely a track.

Wilkswood Fm

Wilceswde, Wilchesode 1086 DB (-*uuda*, -*oda* Exon)
Wilcheswode 1304 Ipm, 1416, 1468 IpmR
Wylcheswod(e) 1305 Cl, 1397 FF, 1434 IpmR

The second el. is of course OE *wudu* 'wood'. The farm is close to a small stream, and it would be tempting to take the first el. to be OE *willecærse* 'watercress', but the late ME *ch* spellings would seem to forbid that. Probably we should start from (the genitive of) some word *wilic, but no suggestion can be made as to its origin.

Studland

Studland 141 G 8

Stollant 1086 DB
Stodland 1213 ClR, PatR, 1235-6 Fees (424) *et passim, Stodlonde* 1242-3 Fees (752), 1255 Pap *et passim*
Stodlaund(e) 1274 Cl, 1275 RH, 1286 Pat
Stoudlond 1333 *SR*, 1414 FF, *Stoudelond* 1431 FA

'Grazing-land for horses' (OE *stōd, land*), see Zachrisson, StM Spr V, 17, where also the loss of *d* before *l* in the DB form is accounted for; cf. also IPN p. 111.

Branksea Island[1]

(in portu de) *Brunkes'* 1235 Cl, *Brunckes'* 1276 Cl
Brunkeseye 1275 Pat, 1276 Cl, 1302 Pat, Cl
Broncheshe 1291 Tax, *Brumkeseye* 1318 Ch
Brunkesey c. 1540 Leland I, *Bruncksey* 1585-6 Treswell
Brow'sea, Bro'sey 1545 Hutchins, *Brownecksey* t. Eliz ib.
Brounsey al. *Brunckesey* t. Eliz ib.
Brownsea 1586 ib., *Branksey, Brenksey* 1695 Camden

---

[1] On the 6'' map (ed. 1925) it is called **Brownsea Island**. Both pronunciations occur.

The second el. is of course OE *ēg, īeg* 'island'. Branksea Island is fairly hilly with several steep descents (cf. the picture in Hutchins I, 647), and Professor Zachrisson suggests that the first el. of the name is an OE *brunc*, gradation variant of *brinc*, cf. ME *brink* '(side of a) hill', for which see NED s. v. and Zachrisson, StNPh V, 61 n. For Scandinavian pl.-ns containing *brunk* with the probable meaning of '(side of a) hill', 'steep descent', cf. Lindqvist, Bjärka-Säby Ortnamn pp. 56-62 (s. n. Brunkeberg).

Claywell is *Cleywoll* 1333 *SR* (p). Self-explanatory, OE *clǣg, wielle*.

Dean Hill is *Dene* 1449 FF, 1457 IpmR. OE *denu* 'valley'; cf. the same name *supra* 25, 108.

Goathorn (Plantation) and **Newton**
The solution of both these names should, in my opinion, be sought in the following interesting entry in 1286 Pat (p. 217): "Appointment of Richard de Bosco (etc.) to lay out, with sufficient streets and lanes and adequate sites for a market and church and plots for merchants and others, a new town with a harbour in a place called Gotowre super Mare, in the parish of Stodlaund and on the king's land — — the lands and tenements of which said new town the king is prepared to commit to merchants and others willing to take them and to enfeoff them thereof for building and dwelling purposes." Since the situation of this *Gotowre super Mare* is expressly stated to have been in the parish of Studland, there can be little doubt that the name refers to the tongue of land now called Goathorn Plantation. Immediately S of the plantation is the little hamlet of Newton, apparently the poor outcome of King Edward's attempt to induce people to settle down on this inhospitable spot. A tramway running from the Newton Clay Works[1] to the pier on Goathorn Point tells us of another result of the settlement.

Gotowre must mean 'the goats' shore or bank', OE *gāt, ōfer*; cf. Ower (*supra* 120) on the same shore, about a mile NW of Newton[2]. The later corruption of the name is apparently due

[1] Cf. Claywell *supra* 125, about a mile SW of Newton.

[2] M. Oppenheim, the author of the Maritime History of Dorset in VCH Do II, who has noticed the same entry in Pat, interprets it in a somewhat

to popular etymology[1]. It is spelt *Gothorne* as early as 1585-6 (Treswell's map).[2]

Swanage

Swanage [swɔnidʒ] 141 H 8
(æt) Swanawic s. a. 877 ASC (A, E)
Suanewic, Suanavine (sic), *Suanauuic* c. 1000 Asser
Suuanwic (-uuic), Sonwic (sonuich) 1086 DB (Exon)
Suanewiz 1082-3 to 1185-6 P, *Swanewiz* 1242-3 Fees (751), t. Hy III Ipm, *Swanewyz* 1252 FF, 1285 FA
Suanewik' 1212 Fees (94), *Swanewic* 1228 Ch, 1264 FineR, *Swannewic'* 1230 Cl (p), *Swanewyc* 1264 Ipm
Swaneswic 1213 ClR, *-wich* 1242-3 Fees (750)
Swanwych 1244 *Ass*, 1269 Pat *et passim* (with variant *-wich*), *Swanewich* 1270 AD I *et passim* (variant *-wych*)
Swaynewych(e) 1291 Tax, 1305 Cl

'The peasants' or swine-herds' (dairy-)farm' (or possibly 'bay'), see Mawer, PN and History p. 27, and EPN s. vv. *swān* and *wīc*.

Godlingston Fm

Godlington [al. *Golinton*] 1299 Ipm
Godelyng(e)ston 1345, 1378 FF, 1428 FA, 1457 IpmR
Gedelyngston 1367 FF, *Godelingston* 1408 IpmR
Godelyngton 1381 IpmR, *Godelington* 1426 IpmR
Cothelynston 1383 IpmR, *Golynston* 1412 FA
Godlyngston 1413 FF, 1431 FA

The preponderance of *s* forms (*Godelyngeston*, etc.) shows that this is no *-ing* name. If the name is late, it may contain one or other of the ME (Continental-Germanic) pers. names *Godelena* (fem.) or *Godelen* (masc.), for which see Forssner p. 120.[3]. Cf. *Egliston infra*.

---

different way (p. 181), taking *Gotowre* to refer to this Ower itself. This, however, can hardly be correct, one reason being that Ower is and evidently always was in the parish of Corfe Castle.

[1] "In form somewhat resembling the horn of a goat" (Hutchins).

[2] **Red Horn** (6"), the name of a small point of land on the other side of the right-hand bay (Brand's Bay) is probably also a corruption (presumably due to Goathorn), for on Treswell's map (1585-6) it is called *Red Orde*, which clearly indicates that it contains OE *ord* 'point, corner, spit of land'.

[3] One of the ME examples of *Godelena* in Forssner is taken from 1340 NI

Herston[1]

Herestone, Herstune 1086 DB (*herestona* Exon)
Herston(e) 1318 FF, 1333 *SR*, 1339 Cl, 1384 FF *et passim*

'*Her*'s farm'. As pointed out in Hutchins (I, 670), this *Her* is actually mentioned in DB (f. 82 b, Exon p. 46) as holding part of this place TRE. — Cf. Redin p. 172 n. 1, and PN Sx p. 127 s. n. Hesworth Common.

Moulham or **Mowlem** [mɔləm] (local)[2]
Moleham 1086 DB
Moulham 1333 *SR* (p), 1340 NI (p), 1376, 1449 FF (p)
Mowtham (sic) 1457 IpmR

The second el. is OE *hām* 'homestead', but the first is difficult, and only tentative suggestions can be offered: (1) An OE pers. name *Mūla*, postulated from *(on) mulantune* KCD 759 (cf. PN NRY p. 286 s. n. Moulton) and being the weak form of the name *Mūl* (Redin p. 21); (2) OE *mūl* 'mule', cf. Mawer, MLR XIV, 242; (3) OE *mūl* used as a topographical term (cf. e. g. OFrisian *mūla*, MLG *mūl(e)*, OSwedish *mūle* 'muzzle, mouth') meaning 'cliff shaped like a muzzle'? Unfortunately the topography of the original *Moulham* is unknown to me.

Newton (6″) is *Nyweton* 1299 Ipm, 1378 FF, 1404 IpmR, 1431 FA, *Nywton Purbyk* 1321 Ipm, *Niweton* 1367 FF, *Newton* 1457 IpmR. Self-explanatory, OE *nīwe, tūn*.

Ulwell is *Ulewoll'* 1333 *SR* (p), *Olewell* 1412 FA, *Olewelle* 1442, 1449 FF, *Owlewill* 1457 IpmR. 'Owl spring', OE *ūle, wielle*.

---

p. 402 (Sx). On the same page in NI there is also a certain *Godelen Daniel*, not noted by Forssner (who instead includes the name *Godelent*). I suppose this *Godelen* (Daniel) represents exactly the name *Godelenus, Godelin* in Förstemann, of which, according to Forssner, *Godelena* is the fem. equivalent.

[1] There was apparently a (now lost) *Westfield* in the neighbourhood called *Lewestfyld* 1449 FF, *Le Westfeld* 1457 IpmR.

[2] "Now only survives in a parcel of ground adjoining the south side of Godlingston farm" (Hutchins). As a place-name it is not found on the maps, but **De Moulham Road** (6″) and **Mowlem Institute** (6″) in Swanage preserve the memory of the family which took their name from this place; cf. also the name of the well-known London building-firm *John Mowlem & Co. Ltd.*

Whitecliff Fm is *Witeclive* 1086 DB (*-cliua* Exon), 1216 ClR, *Whyteclive* 1251 FF, *Wytteclive* 1255 FF, *Wyteclyve* 1287 FF *(juxta Swaneswych in Purbik)*, 1316 FA, *Whiteclife* 1339 Cl. Self-explanatory, OE *hwīt, clif*; the place is near the Channel.

Worth Matravers

Worth Matravers 141 I 6
Orde, Wirde 1086 DB, *orda, Wirda* Exon
Wrde 1086 DB (*Vrda* Exon), c. 1165, c. 1170 Montacute
Worth(e) 1230 Cl, 1291 Tax *et passim, Estworth* 1299 Ipm
Wurthe 1242-3 Fees (752), *Wrthe in Porbik* 1287 FF

OE *weorþ* 'enclosure', etc. John *Mautravers* was here in the reign of Edward III (Hutchins); cf. Lytchett Matravers *supra* 112.

Caplestone [kɔplstən] (6″) is *Cableston* 1431 FA, *Cabulston* 1546 Hutchins. Earlier material is necessary.

Eastington Fm is *Estington* 1259, 1285 FF, *Istone* 1291 Tax, *Eston* 1484 IpmR. 'East farm', OE *ēast, tūn*. "From its position relatively to Worth" (Hutchins). Cf. Weston Fm *infra* (this parish).

Quarr (6″)

la Quarere 1287 FF, *Quarera* 1305 FF
(atte) Quare 1360 Cl, *Quar* 1585-6 Treswell
Quarry Fm 1811 OM

'Quarry', OFr *quarriere*, MLatin *quarer(i)a*. We are here in the centre of the Purbeck marble district, and there are traces of disused quarries all round. The earliest forms above are older than those noted in NED, see *Quarrer* (14th cent.) and cf. *Quarry* sb. 2 (1420) and *Quar* sb. 2 (1485).

Renscombe Fm

Hreminescumbe 987 (copy) KCD 656
Romescūbe 1086 DB, *Romescūba* Exon
Rembescumb' 1212 Fees (92)
Remescumb 1275 Pat, *Remmescumb, Kemescumbe* (sic)[1] 1276 Cl,
    Remescombe 1316 FA, *Remmescomb'* 1333 *SR*
Rennscumbe 1291 Tax

---

[1] The wrong *K* has led the indexer to curious errors of identification.

In all probability this means 'raven's valley', OE *hræfn, cumb*; see Mawer, MLR XIV, 240 f. For a somewhat different view regarding names of this type, cf. PN BedsHu p. 213 s. n. Ramsey.

St Aldhelm's Chapel[1] (6″)
This little chapel *(capella Sancti Aldelmi)*, dedicated to St Aldhelm, first bishop of Sherborne, is mentioned several times in medieval records, the earliest reference that I have found being from 1239 (Lib); cf. Hutchins I, 697 f.

Weston Fm (6″) is *Westeton* 1281 Misc. Self-explanatory, OE *west, tūn*. The site is half a mile W of Worth Matravers; cf. Eastington *supra* 128.

Woodyhyde Fm [udiaid] is *Wodewehide* 1311 FF, 1431 FA. The second el. is apparently OE *hīd* 'hide'. The first may actually be OE *wudig* 'woody', but the material is too late and scanty to allow of any certainty.

XVII.   Hasler Hundred

> *haselore* 1084 GeldRoll,* *Haselor(e)* 1212 Fees (89), 1244 *Ass*,
>   1275 RH, 1279 Ch, 1280 Cl, 1285 FA *et passim*
> *Haselovere* 1210-12 RBE, *Heselore* 1244 *Ass*
> *Hassellor(e)* 1265 Misc, 1412 FA, *Hasellore* 1307 Ipm
> *Haseluor* 1279 Ch, *Aselore* 1285 FA, *Haselehore* 1316 FA

'Hazel-bank', OE *hæsel, ōra* (or possibly *ōfer*). "About a quarter of a mile north-west of Steeple are two or three grounds called Hasler. In one of them is a barrow, overgrown with hazlewood, from the plenty of which hereabout the hundred takes its name. Here the hundred court was formerly kept." The spot thus described in Hutchins (I, 550) still bears the name of Hasler on the 6″ map (Steeple parish).

Arne

Arne 141 E/F 6
> *Harne* (three times), *Harn* (twice) 1285 FA
> *Arn(e)* 1316 FA, 1333 *SR*, 1414 Inq aqd, 15th *Harl. 61*, 1535 VE

---

[1] The promontory on which the chapel stands is called St Alban's or St Aldhelm's Head.

This name should probably be compared with Herne (Beds) and Harome (Y), both of which are taken by Ekwall (in PN BedsHu p. 138) to be dat. pl. forms of an OE *har or the like, for which Germanic parallels (Swedish har 'stony place', MLG hare 'height', etc.) are adduced. Whatever may have been the exact sense of har[1], it seems clear that, in the case of Arne, the topography of the place favours derivation from a word meaning 'height', the church (and the few houses) of Arne being situated on the slope of a small but very conspicuous eminence, rising to 168 feet over the surrounding heath. — It is of course possible, though not very likely, that the H- in the earliest forms of Arne is inorganic. Should such be the case, the name may go back to OE ærn 'house' (cf. Hutchins I, 98), but, as far as my knowledge goes, that word is only found in compound place-names (cf. EPN s. v.).

Middlebere Fm[2] is *Middelber(e)* 1376, 1377 IpmR, 1397 FF, 1416 IpmR, *Middilbere* 1434 IpmR, *Middelbeare* 1468 IpmR. 'Middle grove (or pasture)', OE *middel, bearu* (or *bǣre*). Cf. Todber *supra* 18.

Ridge is *Rygge* 1431 FA. Self-explanatory, OE *hrycg*.

Slepe [slip] is *Slepe, Sleppe* 1244 *Ass.* OE *slǣp* 'slippery place', an appropriate name for a place situated in this muddy district (Poole Harbour). Cf. Slepe *supra* 113 and Slape *infra*.

Stoborough
> *Stanberge* 1086 DB, 1284 Cl, *Stanbe(r)gh* 1293 Ipm
> *Stoburgh(e)* 1315, 1412 FF, 1480 IpmR, 1495 Ipm
> *Stobargh* 1431 FA

[1] It is pointed out by Mansion in English Studies X, 14 (cf. PN NRY p. xliv) that Dutch *haar*, translated by Jellinghaus (Anglia XX, 331) with 'höher liegendes, trockenes Land, Höhenzug', and (Die westfälischen Ortsnamen p. 75) 'mit Holz bewachsene Anhöhe', does not actually exist, Jellinghaus' definition being only an attempt to interpret a place-name element of which the original meaning is obscure; cf. Mawer, Problems of PN Study p. 77.

[2] There is a **Langton Wallis** (6″) in this parish not very far from Middlebere Fm, in all probability a name transferred from the now lost *Langton Wallis* in Langton Matravers *supra* 122, Middlebere being in older times part of the manor of *Langton Wallis*; cf. e. g. the mention of *Langeton Walisch maner' cum salinis de Middelber* in 1376 (IpmR). Cf. also Hutchins I, 101, 636.

'Stone barrow', OE *stān*, *beorg*.[1] Stoborough is a welcome addition to the material in Ekwall's paper on the "Loss of a Nasal before Labial Consonants" (Klaeber Celebration Volume pp. 21—27), the name being a perfectly clear instance of loss of *n* before *b*; cf. Stafford, High Stoy, Stallen, and Oborne *infra*.

Westport Ho (6″)

Bywesteport 1264 Ipm, *Westeport(e)* 1274 FF, 1316 FA
Westport (*juxta Warham*) 1288 FF, 1315 Ipm, etc.

The name is self-explanatory, though it may be discussed whether the exact meaning here of the phrase *bīwestan porte* was 'by the west port (or gate)' or 'to the west of the port'.[2]

Worgret [wə:gət]

Vergroh[3], *Weregrote*, *Wiregrote* 1086 DB
Wergerod(e) 1201-2 FF, 1244 *Ass* (p), *Wergherode* 1244 *Ass*
Werghrode 1227 FF, *Wereghrode* 1266 FF
Wargcherod, *Wirgorod* 1244 *Ass* (p), *Wirgrode* 1285 FA
Wurgrode [al. *Worgrode*] 1312 Ipm, *Wiresrede* 1327 FF
Wyrgered 1316 FA, *Wyrgrede* 1333 *SR*, 1401 FF, 1431 FA
Wirgerede 1337 DorchesterR, *Wirgrede* 1452 FF
Wigred 1366 FF, *Wygrete* 1412 FA, *Wygrede* 1420 FF
Wyrdegrede 1458 FF, *Wyrgrett* 1535 AD V

This name was a mystery to me until Ekwall (Studies on PN p. 91) derived it from OE *weargrōd* 'gallows', basing this etymology above all on the 13th century forms from FF. The fresh material from 1244 *Ass* (201) printed above strongly supports Ekwall's derivation; cf. the boundary-marks (*on*) *þa wærhroda* BCS 959 (So)[4], and (*on*) *þa wearh roda* BCS 998 (W), the latter appearing again as (*on*) *þa wearh rode* in BCS 1053.[5] For a very similar type of name cf. Hewstock *infra* (in Beaminster).

---

[1] A barrow called "King Barrow", at the south end of Stoborough, revealed interesting finds when it was dug down in 1767 (Hutchins).

[2] Cf. the discussion in PN D p. xxxvii; see also Bestwall Fm *infra*.

[3] *uergroh* in Exon.   [4] B. T. s. v. *wearg-rōd*.

[5] Middendorff s. v. *wearh*. Middendorff's correct translation of this boundary-mark has apparently escaped the attention of Grundy (cf. Arch. Journal LXXVI, 214 n. 1).

Church Knowle

Church Knowle 141 G 5

Glole, Chenolle 1086 DB

Cnolle 1086 DB (*Canolla* Exon), 1181-2 P, 1212 Fees (89), 1237 Pat *et passim, Cnol'* 1204 ClR, *Knoll(e)* 1297 Cl *et passim*

Churcheknolle 1426 FF

OE *cnoll* 'knoll, rounded hill-top'. For the AN peculiarities in the DB forms *Chenolle, Canolle, Glole,* cf. Knowlton *supra* 94, and Zachrisson, AN Infl. p. 122 (assimilation of *n—l* to *l—l*). *Church* as distinctive from the other Knowles in this parish[1]; cf. the mention of a priest here in DB f. 80 a (Hutchins, Eyton).

Barnston Fm

Berneston 1333 *SR* (p), 1346 (*et passim*) Hutchins
Barneston 1375 Hutchins, 1426 FF, 1431 FA

'*Beorn*'s farm'. The name of Barnston does not occur in DB, but there can be no doubt that the place is surveyed in that record (f. 82 b) under the name of *Cnolle,* see the preceding name. The name of the owner TRE of that *Cnolle* was *Bern,* spelt *Beorn* in Exon (p. 56), and, as pointed out in Hutchins (I, 579), it is evident that Barnston owes its name to him. It may be worth mentioning that a certain *Beorn faber* occurs in *Harl. 61* (f. 62) in connexion with this district.

Bradle Fm [breidl]

Bradelege 1086 DB, *Bradelegh(e)* 1242-3 Fees (750), 1346 FA
Bradele c. 1170 Montacute, 1285 FA *et passim* to 1399 FF
Bradeley(e) 1285 FA, *Bradelee* 1303 FA
Bradell 1412, 1428, 1431 FA, 1477 IpmR

'Broad enclosure' (OE *brād, lēah*), Bradle being, consequently, a variant of the common pl.-n. Bradley (Broadley).

Bucknowle [bʌknəl, bʌgnəl]

Bubecnolle 1285 FA (p), *Bobeknolle* 1327 *SR* (p)
Bouknolle 1412 FA, *Boveknoll* 1420 FF, *Boueknolle* 1431 FA
Bubbeknolle 1452, 1454 FF
Bucknoll al. *Bubbeknoll* 1594 Hutchins

---

[1] Bucknowle *infra* and Cocknowle (for which I have found no early forms).

The second el. is of course OE *cnoll*, see the parish name.
It has been suggested (EPN p. 10) that the first el. may be
the OE preposition *bufan* 'above', but it is very difficult to reconcile this with the topography of the place, and the early
spellings with *Bub(b)e*, *Bobe-* are decidedly against it. Bucknole
(D), earlier *Bubecnolle* (13th), is taken by the editors of PN D
(p. 628) to contain the pers. name *Bubba*. The Dorset Bucknowle,
which is probably a comparatively late name, may possibly be
interpreted as the (part of Church) Knowle that belonged to
(some ME owner called) *Bubbe*; cf. Melbury Bubb *infra*.
But it is perhaps more likely that the first el. is a hill-name,
for as Zachrisson seems inclined to suggest (StNPh V, 15), there
may have been an OE **bubbe* with the meaning 'eminence,
hillock' or the like.

East Creech [1]

   Crist, *Cric* 1086 DB
   Criz 1086 DB, Exon, 1181-2 P, *Crihz* 1212 Fees (89)
   Crech(e) 1204 ClR, 1244 FF
   Crihc 1264 Ipm, *Chryicht* 1275 RH
   Crich(e), *Crych(e)* 1280 Ch, 1285 FA, 1291 Tax, 1299 Ipm,
      1327 *SR*, 1346 FA *et passim*, *Erlescrich* 1301 Pat
   Cryk 1285 FA, *Crugh* [*Crough*] 1303 FA
   Est Criche 1426 FF, *Estecriche* 1452 FF
   Chryche Grange, *Criche grange* 1535 VE

OE *cryc* (Brit *cruc*) 'hill, barrow' (see EPN p. 16), the three
Creeches deriving their names from the conspicuous conical hill
called Creech Barrow (637 ft.) "resembling in form a volcanic
mountain in miniature"; cf. Long Crichel and Pentridge *supra*
90, 103. The form *Erlescrich* possibly preserves the memory of
the earl of Mortain (the Conqueror's brother) who held the part
called *Crist* in DB (f. 79 b). Creech Grange formerly belonged
to Bindon Abbey; hence the addition *grange* [2]; cf. Grange Fm
infra (in Pulham).

---

[1] I here include also the early forms for West Creech and Creech Grange
in the adjoining parish of Steeple.

[2] "The word *grange* was commonly applied to a farm held in hand by a
monastery, where the abbot and monks deposited their corn" (Hutchins).

Orchard, West (1″) and **East** (6″)

Horcerd 1086 DB, Exon

Orchard(e) 1291 Cl, 1347 IpmR, 1431 FA

(*Purbyke apud*) *La Orchard* 1383 IpmR

West Orchard 1426 FF, *Est Orchard* (*in Purbyk*) 1440 FF

Self-explanatory, OE *orceard*. Orchard (East and West) *supra* 30 is of a wholly different origin.

Whiteway Fm was probably the home of Ric. de *Wyteweye* 1285 FA. Self-explanatory, OE *hwīt, weg.*

East Holme

East Holme[1] 141 F 4

Holne 1086 DB, 1107-22, 1159 (etc.) Montacute, 1242-3 Fees (750), 1281 Misc *et passim* to 1431 FA

Holna 1086 Exon, c. 1106 (*et passim*) BM I, II, 1290 Cl

Holen c. 1172 Montacute, *Holn* 1189-99, 1363 ib., 1285 FA

Holm 1218 FF, 1306 Pat, *Holum* 1287 (1313) Ch

Westholme 1316 FF, *Westholne* 1417 FF, *Est Holne* 1426 FF

'(Place abounding in) holly', OE *holegn*, dial. *holm* (also Do); cf. EPN s. v.

Kimmeridge

Kimmeridge 141 H 4

Cameric 1086 DB, Exon, *Cvneliz* 1086 DB

Kimerich' 1212 Fees (92), *Kemerich* 1230 P (p)

Cumerig(g), Cumerygg(e) 1285 FA

Kymerych, Kymerich 1291 Tax, 1303 to 1431 FA, 1333 *SR,* *Kymerigh* 1303 FA, *Kymershe* 1373 IpmR

Cumerigh [*Cumerich*] 1303 FA, *Cumerych* 1340 NI

Cf. also the forms for Little Kimmeridge *infra*.

I can offer no plausible interpretation of this difficult name. The site of Kimmeridge is at the foot of a steep hill-ridge (not far from the Channel).

Chaldecots (lost) is *Cheldecote* 1244 *Ass* (p), *Kaldecote* 1285 FF, *Chaldecote* 1285 FA (p), 1333 *SR* (p), 1340 NI (p), *Chalcote* 1484

---

[1] I here include also the early forms for West Holme, a mile to the west in East Stoke parish (Winfrith Hundred).

IpmR (p), *Chalcotes in Estkymerche in Insula de Purbek* 1484 IpmR, *Chaldecots* 1765, 1795 Taylor. 'Cold cottage', OE *ceald*, *cot(e)*. The name is now lost, but from the statement in 1484 IpmR we know that the place was in Little Kimmeridge and consequently very near the Channel; cf. another lost *Chaldecote infra* (in Swyre) which must have had a very similar situation, both places having apparently been ruthlessly exposed to storms from the Channel. Cf. the discussion of this type of pl.-ns in EPN (s. v. *cote*).

Little Kimmeridge is *Parva Kymerych* 1316 FF, *Little Kemerych* 1374 Cl, *Estkymerych(e)* 1417, 1421 FF, *Estkymerche* 1484 IpmR. Little Kimmeridge is a good mile SE of (Great) Kimmeridge *supra* 134.

Smedmore Ho
  Metmore 1086 DB, *Smethemore* 1242 Ch
  Smedemore 1244 *Ass* (p), 1285 FA (p), 1324 Misc (p), 1333
    SR (p), 1426 FF, *Smedemour* 1340 NI (p)
  'Smooth moor', OE *smēðe* (EPN), *mōr*.

Steeple

Steeple 141 H 4
  Stiple 1086 DB
  Stuple, *Stupel(l)* 1204 ClR, 1212 Fees (89), 1275 RH, 1291
    Tax, 1296 Ipm, 1303 FA, 1307, 1315 Ipm *et passim*[1]
  Stepel 1222 Pat, 1278 QW, *Steple* 1262 Ipm
  Stypele 1285 FA, *Stepulle* 1385 Cl
  Stupull 1428 FA, 1512 AD IV, *Stipille* 1440 AD VI

OE *stīepel* 'steeple', probably from its situation under a steep hill (Hutchins). Cf. Steepleton Iwerne *supra* 57 and Winterborne Steepleton *infra*.

Blackmanston Fm (6") is *Blachemanestone* 1086 DB, *Blakmanston* 1458 FF. Blackmanstone (K) derives its name from its owner TRE, *Blacheman* (cf. IPN p. 116), and it is evident that this Blackmanston must have been named after a man bearing the same name. Hence '*Blæcman*'s farm'.[2]

---

[1] *Stuple, Stupel(l)* are the common forms throughout the ME period; I have noted about thirty such *u* spellings.

[2] To judge from an entry in the Cerne Cartulary (f. 25) there seems once

West Creech and **Creech Grange.** See East Creech *supra* 133.

Hurpston (6″)

Herpere 1086 DB, *harpera* Exon
la Harpine 1109 Dugdale II, 70
Herpston 1340 NI (p), *Harpson* 1811 OM

Whatever may have been the origin of this name, it seems clear that the DB form was understood as OE *hearpere* 'harper', for the 1109 form is nothing but a French translation of that word. The word 'harper' alone is of course impossible as a pl.-n., but cf. names like Harperley (PN NbDu p. 102) and Harper's Brook (Nth), the latter evidenced as *Harperesbrok*, *le Harperesbrok*, etc. from the 13th century onwards; see Ekwall, ERN p. 191. *-ston* is supposed in Hutchins (I, 609) probably to refer to a remarkable stone just W of Hurpston. If the 1340 form is to be interpreted as *Herperston*, which seems very likely, one may venture the suggestion that *-ston* (*stān*) has simply been dropped in the DB form, and that the name originally meant 'harp-player's stone' (or possibly 'harp-player's farm', if the original terminal was *-tūn*). But I feel more inclined to turn the interpretation the other way round and suggest that the DB form is a perversion of an older unintelligible name which by popular etymology was understood as 'harper', and that, thanks to the existence of the above-named stone in the neighbourhood, the terminal *ston(e)* was added at a later date to bring the name into conformity with the ordinary type of pl.-ns; cf. Hutchins loc. cit.

Hyde Cottage (6″) is *Longa Hyda* 1244 *Ass* (p), 1285 FA, *La Langehide* 1288 Misc, *Langehyde in Purbyk* 1315 FF, *La langehide in Stuple* 1399 BM I. OE *lang*, *hīd*; cf. Hyde Fm *supra* 60. 'Long' refers to the form of the strip of land (Hutchins).

Tyneham

Tyneham [tainəm] 141 H 3

Tigehā (twice) 1086 DB, *Tigeham* 1184-5 P (p)
Tingehā (twice) 1086 DB, *Tiham* 1194 P, 1244 *Ass* (p)

---

to have been a *Blakemanneston* (and a *Blakemanneslond*) somewhere in the vicinity of Weymouth, too.

Tynham 1280 Ch, 1291 Tax, 1316 FA *et passim* (with later
prefixing of *Est-* and *West-*)
Esttynam, Es(t)tinam, Westtynam 1285 FA
Cherestinam, Churchetinam 1285 FA

The second el. is apparently OE *hām*. The first should
possibly be compared with (*to*) *teninge faledun* BCS 459, now
Timbold Hill (K)[1], for which Karlström (p. 147) assumes derivation from OE *tȳning* 'closing, fencing'. The early material for
Tyneham is however not illustrative enough to allow of any
certainty.

Baltington is *Baltingeton* 1287 FF, *Baldyngton* 1329 Orig, *Bal-
tyngton* 1333 *SR* (p), 1426 FF, 1431 FA. The name had better
be left unexplained until more and earlier material has been
brought to light.

Egliston, North and **South** [eglstən]
Egelineston 1201-2 *Ass* (1171 m. 10), 1285 FA
Eggleneston 1285 FA, *Eglineston* 1290 Pat
Eglynyston 1333 *SR*, *Eggleston* 1765 Taylor

"The name of Egliston dates from a period subsequent to the
Conquest, for it is manifestly derived from Engelin or Eglin,
who owned it before the 3rd of King John, in which year
Agatha, his widow, recovered one-third of it (*villæ de Egelineston*)". This interesting statement in Hutchins I, 620 (where the
document from which it is taken is called Plac. aᵒ 3 Joh. No. 10)
has been very kindly verified by Dr A. H. Smith, who found
the reference in an early Assize Roll (for Co, So and Do) in
PRO; cf. the first reference above. The substance of the entry
is accurately given in Hutchins, and the names are (*uille de*)
Egelineston and *Agatha qui fuit ux. Engelini*.[2] For the Continental-Germanic pers. name *Engelin*, cf. Forssner p. 73.

Povington [pɔviŋtən] is *Povinton(e)* 1086 DB, 1212 Fees (89),
1285 FA, *Puninton* (sic) 1223 FF, *Povington* 1285 FA, *Poryngton*

---

[1] See Wallenberg p. 191.
[2] When some time ago I had the opportunity of seeing the MS at PRO,
I found the pers. name written again at the bottom of membrane 11, where it
is spelt *Egelin*.

(sic) 1291 Tax, *Peiuynton* 1316 FA, *Pouynton* 1333 *SR*, *Povyng-ton* 1436 IpmR.   There seems to be very little to connect this difficult name with, and the etymology must therefore be left open. A possible parallel is perhaps *Povenden* (K), for which see Wallenberg p. 217.

XVIII. Winfrith Hundred

Winfrod(e) 1084 GeldRoll, 1130 PR, 1195 P, 1204 Cur, 1212 Fees (87, 89) *et passim* to 1279 Ch, *Windfrod* 1177-8 P
Wilfrod 1194 P, *Wilfrord* 1195 P
Winfred' 1205 FineR, *Winfrot* 1212 Fees (89)
Wynfrod 1244 *Ass*, 1285 FA, *Wynefrod* 1279 Ch
Wymfrod(e) 1244 Fees (1387), 1279 Ch, *Wimfrod* 1244 *Ass*
Wynford, Winford 1269 Ch, *Wyford* 1278 QW
Wynfred 1276 Pat, 1327 *SR et passim, Wymfred* 1280 Pat
Wonfred [*Wonford*] 1303 FA, *Wynfreth* 1412 FA
See Winfrith Newburgh *infra*.

Chaldon Herring

Chaldon Herring or **East Chaldon** [tʃɔːldən] 140 I 9
Calvedone, Caluedone, Celvedune 1086 DB[1]
Chavendon' 1203 Cur, *Chaunedon* 1214 FineR, 1227 FF, *Cha(u)ndon* 1227 FF, *Chauvedon'* 1242-3 Fees (750)
Chalvedon, Chaluedon 1224 ClR, 1234 BM I, 1234 (1279) Ch, 1244 *Ass*, 1269 Ch (p), 1275 RH *et passim*
Chavedon' Hareng 1235-6 Fees (425), *Chavedon* 1269 Ch
Chaluedon Hareng (Harang), Chalvedon Harang (Heryng) 1243 FF, 1279, 1280 Ch, 1306 FF[2], 1332 Ch, 1431 FA
Chandon Hareng 1258 FF, *Chandon Haryngg* 1291 Tax[3]
Estchalvedon 1269 Misc, 1280 Ch
Calvedon Harang 1297 Pat, Cl, *Chalvesdon Heryng* 1428 FA
Chaldon, Est Chaldon 1535 VE

---

[1] Exon: *Caluedona, caluedone, Cealuaduna*.

[2] Corrected from *Chalnedon Harang*; cf. *Chalnedon' Haryng* 1291 Tax, *Chalnedon Harang* 1340 NI.

[3] Corresponding to *Chaudon Haryngg* 1428 FA. It is clear that *n* in all such forms (*Chandon, Chaundon,* etc.) is a mistranscription for *u*.

OE *cealfa-dūn* 'calves' down', see Ekwall, Contributions to the Hist. of OE Dialects p. 13, and EPN s. v. *c(e)alf*. The family of *Harang*, whose name is also preserved in the pl.-ns Winterborne Herringstone, Herrison (in Charminster), and Langton Herring (all *infra*), appear as land-holders in Chaldon from the time of Henry II, cf. Hutchins I, 340, II, 521.[1] — Chaldon Herring is also called East Chaldon in contrast to

West Chaldon

Westchalvedon, West Chalvedon 1269 Misc, 1280 Ch
Chau(e)don Boys 1270 FF, 1285 FA, 1299 Ipm[2]
Chalvedon (Chaluedon) Boys[3] 1280 Ch, 1292 Pat, 1294 FF,
    1313 Ch, 1346, 1428 FA, *Chalwedonboys* 1293 FF
West Chaldon 1535 VE

The old distinctive name comes from the family of *de Bosco* (or *Boys*); Robert *de Bosco* was here in 1269 (Misc), cf. also Hutchins I, 343.

Fossil Fm

Foresteshull 1227 FF (p), *Forsteshull* 1254 FF, 1280 Ch
Forteshull 1227 FF, 1280 Ch, *Forstehull* 1280 Ch
Forshull(e) 1244 *Ass* (p), 1275 RH, 1279 FF, 1300 Ipm, 1313
    Inq aqd, 1329 Orig, 1381 IpmR
Estforshill[4] 1456 IpmR, *Forsehill* 1535 VE

I suppose this means 'frosty hill', OE *forst* 'frost' and *hyll*, though -*es*- in some of the earliest forms (*For(e)stes, Fortes-*) is noteworthy; cf. the early forms of Fosbury (W) in Ekblom (p. 85). If the etymology suggested is correct, the present name has an exact parallel in Forest Hill (O), see Alexander p. 108 f.

---

[1] Terricus *Harang* 1203 Cur (p. 273) seems to be the first member of the family mentioned in direct connexion with Chaldon.

[2] Cf. also the mistranscriptions *Chandoneboys, Chandeneboys* 1291 Tax; the latter form is repeated as *Chaudeneboys* in 1428 FA. It should be remembered that the list of churches in 1428 FA is little more than a repetition of 1291 Tax with much the same mistranscriptions.

[3] Mistranscribed as *Chalnedon Boys* in 1291 Tax, 1310 Inq aqd, 1340 NI.

[4] East Fossil Fm (6″) is in the parish of Winfrith Newburgh.

Coombe Keynes

Coombe Keynes 141 G 2

Cōme 1086 DB, *Cume* 1086 DB, Exon
Cumba, Cumb(e) 1166 RBE (p), 1210-2 ib., 1212 Fees (87),
     1222 ClR *et passim, Combe* from 1276 (Ipm) onwards
The distinctive name *Chaynes* (*Kaynes,* etc.) is added from
1286 (Ipm) onwards.
OE *cumb* 'valley'. For the additional name see Tarrant Keyns-
ton *supra* 60.

Southcombe (lost) is *Suthcumb* 1287 Ipm, *Southcomb(e)* 1403 IpmR,
1412 FA *et passim.* Self-explanatory, OE *sūð, cumb.*

Uphill (lost) is *Hupehill'* 1275 RH (p), *Uppehulle* 1278 QW (p),
Uphulle 1379 IpmR, *Uppehill* 1456 IpmR. Self-explanatory, OE
upp(e), hyll.

West Wood (6″) is *Westwod(e)* 1283 Cl, 1320 FF (*juxta Cumber-
kaynes*) 1483 IpmR. Self-explanatory, OE *west, wudu.*

Lulworth, East and West

East Lulworth 141 G 3, **West Lulworth** 141 H 1[1]

Luluorde 1086 DB, *Luluurda* Exon, *Loloworde* 1086 DB
Lolewurda 1183-4, 1184-5 P, *Lollewurda* 1185-6, 1186-7 P,
     Lolewrdhe 1212 Fees (89)
Lulewurda 1186-8 P, *Lullewurda, -worde* 1194 P, 1210-2 RBE
Lolesworhe 1197-8 FF, *Lolesworth, Lolles-* 1242-3 Fees (751),
     1320 Cl; *Lullesw(o)rth* 1225 Osmund, 1275 Cl (p); *Lilles-
wurth* 1244 *Ass* (p); *Westlullesworth* 1290 FF
Lullewrth, -wurth(e), -worth(e) 1210-2 RBE, 1225 Sarum, 1230
     P, 1232 Cl, Pat, 1234 BM I *et passim*
Lolleworth(e), -wurth 1234 Pat, 1244 *Ass* (p), 1270 Pat *et
passim, Lolleworth* al. *Lollesworth* 1320 Ipm
Est- is common from 1283 (Abbr) onwards, *West-* from 1344 (Cl).

'*Lulla*'s farm', OE *weorþ.* The *-s-* in some of the earlier
forms (about ten in all) is either intrusive or points to early

---

[1] I have heard the following pronunciations for Lulworth: [lʌlwəːþ, lauwəːþ,
lɔlwəːþ, lʌləþ].

confusion with the equally common strong pers. name *Lull*, cf.
Redin pp. 31 f., 100; cf. also Skeat, PN C p. 27 s. n. Lolworth.

Belhuish Fm is *Behylde Hywysche* [*Hiwich*] 1303 FA, *Belehiwich*
1346 FA, *Belhewisch* 1406 AD I, *Belehuyssh* 1428 FA. The
second part of the name is OE *hīwisc*, see Huish *supra* 73. To
judge from the 1303 form, the first part may be the OE fem.
pers. name *Bēaghild*, entering into the boundary-marks (*on*)
beaghildæ byrigels BCS 796, and (*to*) *bæhildestoccæ* (*Behildestocce*)
BCS 1316 (Searle); cf. also the field-name *Beyhyldebrugg* (1288)
in PN Sx p. 563.

Bindon Hill. It was on the southern declivity of this hill, in a
vale near the sea and on the spot now called Little Bindon
(6″), that Wm de Glastonia first began to build the monastery
which in 1172 was transferred by Roger de Newburgh to Great
Bindon near Wool, c. 5 m. NE; cf. Hutchins I, 349, 441, and
VCH Do II, 82. For early forms see Bindon Abbey *infra*.
The original site of the monastery[1] is called *Old Bynedon* in
1279 (Ch), *Litle Bindon* in 1535 (VE).

Burngate is *Bruniethe* 1234 (1279) Ch, *Brunnegate* 1262 Ch,
Brunegat(e) 1279 Ch, *Brun(e)yate* 1280 Ch, 1285 FA, *Bronegate*
1291 Tax, *Brounzate* 1346 FF, *Burnegate* 1535 VE. Probably
'brown gate', OE *brūn, geat*; cf. (*þæt*) *riad geat* BCS 390 '(the)
red gate' (Middendorff).

Gatemerston (6″) is *Gatemareston, -tun* 1236 FF, 1253 Ipm, *Gate-
morestone* late Hy III BM I, *Gatemarston* 1286 Ipm, 1313 FF,
Gatemerston 1303, 1346, 1428 FA, *Yatemerston* 1361 IpmR, *Gat-
meston* 1430 IpmR, *Gatmyston* 1431 FA. The forms are not
early enough for a certain etymology to be suggested, but the
name may go back to an OE *gāta-mæres-tūn* 'goats' boundary
farm'.[2]

---

[1] Marked on the 1″ map (near Lulworth Cove).

[2] The couple of grounds (in East Lulworth) which still bear the name
Gatemerston on the 6″ map are near the boundary of West Lulworth. The
place itself is lost and forgotten, probably destroyed by fire (cf. Hutchins
I, 377).

Hampstead (lost) is *Hampsted* 1234 (1279), 1262 Ch, *Hamsted(e)* 1279 Ch. OE *hāmstede* 'homestead'.

St Andrew's Fm is *St. Andrew* 1284 Cl, *Lulleworth St. Andrew* 1302 FF, *Sanctum Andream* (acc.) 1303 FA, *Seint Andreueschurche juxta Brounzate* 1346 FF, *Sayntandre Westchurch juxta Estlolleworth* 1353 FF, *Seynt Andrewes Churche maner'* 1388 IpmR; in 15th cent. records mostly called *Lulleworth Sancti Andreœ,* see also under East Stoke *infra.* The ancient church, dedicated to St Andrew, which stood quite near the present farm, has now disappeared altogether (Hutchins).

Moreton

Moreton 141 E 1

Mortune 1086 DB, *Morton(e)* 1194 P, 1201-2 FF, 1235-6 Fees (426) *et passim,* later (1333) also *Mourton*

'Moor farm', OE *mōr, tūn.* The great ("Egdon") heath extends all round.

Hurst is *Hurst(e)* 1318 FF, 1402 IpmR, 1412, 1431 FA, 1465 IpmR. OE *hyrst* 'copse, wood', etc.

Owermoigne

Owermoigne [ɔːrmɔin] 140 H 9

Ogre 1086 DB, 1244 *Ass* (also *Oghre*), 1267 Pat

Ogres 1210-2 RBE, 1244 Fees (1387), 1269 Ch, 1278 QW, 1291 Tax[1], 1295 Ipm, *Gres* (sic), *Ogris* 1275 RH

Oweres 1212 Fees (89), *Oares* 1285 FA

Our(e) 1219 Fees (260), 1326 FF *et passim* to 1412 FA, *Ore* 1320 FF, 1327 *SR et passim, Owre* 1431 FA

Oure Moigne (*Moyngne*) 1314 FF, 1315 Cl, Ipm

Ovre Moigne 1375 IpmR, *Owre Moygn(e)* 1486, 1495 Ipm

Owermoigne is at the foot of a steep ridge (on the top of which runs the high-road from Wareham to Dorchester) which, viewed from the village itself, rises to the south like a mighty wall. Connection with OE *ōfer* 'bank' is however evidently out of the question on phonetic grounds. The base seems, instead,

---

[1] Once *Egres*, a mistranscription repeated in 1428 FA.

to be a form *ogre(s)* or the like, but I can find nothing to connect this with, and the etymology had therefore better remain open. It may be added that there is no watercourse in the immediate neighbourhood. The place was held by Radulfus *Monachus* at the beginning of the 13th cent. (1210-2 RBE, 1212, 1219 Fees) and by Wm *le Moyne* (*Le Moine*) in 1244 (Fees, *Ass*) and remained in the possession of that family for about 200 years.

Galton [gɔːltən] is *Gaveltone, Galtone* 1086 DB, *Galdon'* 1212 Fees (89), *Gauton'* 1235-6 Fees (425), *Gauleton* 1244 *Ass, Gaulton* 1244 *Ass* (p) *et passim, Gawelton, Galtone* 1269 Ch, *Gaulwelton* [*Galwelton*] 1303 FA, *Gauelton* 1305 Ipm, *Est-, Westgawelton* 1305 FF. OE *gafol-tūn*, the meaning of *gafol* here being probably the same as in OE *gafolland, gafolmǣd* and *gafolyrð*, which denoted land (etc.) subject to *gafol*, i. e. 'tax, tribute, rent'; cf. PN Bk p. 60 f. s. n. Gawcott, Zachrisson, Namn och Bygd XIV, 56 (with n. 1), and PN D p. 304 f. s. n. Galmpton.

Holworth [hɔləd] is (*at*) *Holewertþe*, (*apud*) *Holewourthe* c. 939 BCS 738, 739 (late copies), *Holverde* 1086 DB (*holuerda* Exon), *Holewrdhe* 1212 Fees (90), *Hol(e)worth* 1275 RH, 1278 QW *et passim*. Probably 'enclosure in the hollow', OE *hol(h), weorþ*.

South Down Fm is *Suddon* 1327 *SR* (p), 1412 FA, 1478 IpmR, 1486 Ipm, *Sudden* 1340 NI (p), *Syddon* 1375 IpmR. The farm is near the Channel on the southern slope of a hill-ridge, and it is clear that the present remodelled form of the name reveals its original meaning; OE *sūð, dūn*.

Poxwell

Poxwell [poukswəl] 140 H 8

Poceswylle (twice) 987 (copy) KCD 656

Pocheswelle 1086 DB, *pochesuuella* Exon

Pokeswell(e) 1187-8 P (p), 1203 Cur (p), 1244 *Ass*, 1285 FA, 1291 Tax *et passim, Pokewell'* 1203 Cur (p)

Pokeswll(e) 1212 Fees (92), 1271 Ch, *Pokeswull* 1340 NI

Pockeswell 1273 Cl, 1333 *SR, Pakeswell* 1428 FA

Poxwell 1535 VE

The second el. is of course OE *wielle* 'spring'. A pers. name
Poc is not recorded in OE, but a corresponding weak name
Poc(c)a has been assumed from names like Pockley, Pockthorpe
and Pocklington (Y), see PN NRY p. 72, where also its probable
connexion with OE *pocc* 'small-pox' is indicated. It may be
added that we have evidence for a ME surname *Poch(e)*, cf.
Ysaach' *Poch'* (Gl) 1181-2 P, Gillebertus *Poche* (Nf) 1183-4 P,
and Wm *Poche* (Do) 1340 NI; the last-mentioned person was,
curiously enough, a parishioner of this very parish (cf. also
Hutchins I, 407, n. a.).

East Stoke

East Stoke 141 F 3
Stoches 1086 DB, *Stokes* 1166 RBE (p), 1291 Tax
Stok(e) 1284 Cl, 1285 FA *et passim*, *Stokke* 1412 FA
Estoke juxta Bynedon 1346 FF

OE *stoc* 'place, dwelling' (or rather the plur. of it). As pointed
out in Hutchins (I, 422), such instances as *Stokes St. Andrew*
(1293 Ipm) and *Stoke Sancti Andree* (1346, 1428 FA) should be
read with a comma after *Stoke(s), St. Andrew (Sancti Andree)*
referring in reality to St Andrew's Fm *supra* 142.

Binnegar [binəgə] is *Bennegere* 1316 FA, *Benegar* 1318 FF,
Beneger 1409 FF. This name should probably be compared
with Binegar (So), earlier *Benhangra* 1300-1 (etc.) FF (So),
Benhangger 1428 FA, the second el. of which is OE *hangra*
'(wooded) slope' (EPN); the first el. can hardly be anything else
than OE *bēan* 'bean'. If the Dorset name is identical in origin,
it would consequently mean 'slope where beans grow'. For the
phonetic development cf. also *(on) heanhangran* BCS 724, now
Henegar (D), see Blomé p. 87, and PN D p. 613.

Hethfelton [hefəltən]
Ælfatune 1086 DB, Exon, *Hafeltone* 1086 DB
Hechfeltun, Hethfelderton 1227 FF
Ethfeld 1234 BM I, 1234 (1279) Ch
Hetfelton 1280 Ch, *Hethfelton* 1280 Ch, 1355 IpmR
Hetfeldyngton 1291 Tax, *Hetherfelton* 1344 Inq aqd
Hethefel(d)ton 1535 VE, *Heath Felton* 1625 DoIpm

Heathfelton al. *Heathelton* 1625 DoIpm
Heathfieldton 1765 Taylor

This is apparently a triple compound of OE *hǣþ, feld* and *tūn*[1], the meaning thus being 'farm on the heath-land'. Hethfelton is on the great Dorset heath.

The editors of Hutchins (I, 417) suggest that Hethfelton should be interpreted as '*Æþelflǣd*'s farm', *Hafeltone* in DB being held TRE by a woman called *Ædelflete*. This derivation, however, is against the evidence of the early forms collected above.

West Holme. See East Holme *supra* 134.

Rushton

Ristone 1086 DB (*-tona* Exon), *Riston* 1218 FF
Rys(s)ton 1251 FF, 1280 Ch, 1303, 1316 FA, *Rysh-* 1330 Ch
Risseton 1299 Ipm, *Rissh(e)ton* 1313 FF, 1332 Misc
Ruston 1304 Ipm (*by Frome*), 1305 Cl, 1318 FF
Rushton, Russh(e)ton 1318 FF, 1344 Cl *et passim*
'Farm by the rushes', OE *rysc, tūn*.

Stokeford is *Stokford(e)* 1244 *Ass* (p), 1318 FF, *Stockeforde* 1535 VE. 'The ford by (East) Stoke' (*supra* 144).

Wool Bridge (1″), **Woolbridge Fm** (6″)

Wullebrigg 1244 *Ass* (p), *Wllebrygg* 1291 Tax
Welebrigg 1303 FA, *Wellebrigge* 1318 Ch, 1343 IpmR
Welesbrigg 1303 FA, *Wellesbrigg* 1346 FA
Wolleberg (sic) 1316 FA, *Wollebrigge* 1343 Misc
Wolbrygge 1428 FA, *Wulbryge* 1535 VE
'The bridge near Wool' (see *infra*).

Wareham Lady Saint Mary
Wareham Saint Martin

Wareham [wɛ:rəm, wɔrəm] 141 F 4/5

The spellings in ASC are *Werham* (*passim*), *Wærham* (*passim*), in FlorWorc, SimDurh, Asser and WmMalmP *Werham*, in Wm

---

[1] The form *Ethfeld* (1234) is probably only an abbreviation. It is printed (*Ethfeld*) in BM I p. 363, but (*Ethfeld.*) ib. p. 699 (s. n. East Stoke).

Malm *Werham, Waram, Werram,* in LibHyda *Warham,* in DB *Warham* (*passim*), *Warhā* (*passim*).[1] From the 12th century onwards *Warham* is the usual form, but the following exceptions may be noted: *Waram* 1152-8 Montacute, (?) 1191-7 France, 1269 Misc, 1428 FA, *Warrhā* 1214 ClR, *Warram* 1300 Cl, 1316 FA, *Worham* 1398 IpmR.

The first el. is OE *wer* 'weir, dam, fish-trap' (EPN)[2], the second is *hām* (or possibly *hamm*). Cf. Hutchins I, 97: "In repairing the works of the hoop-nets, about the middle of the eighteenth century, many large oak posts or piles were discovered in the bottom or bed of the river, the remains of ancient wears there for taking salmon, some of them apparently of great antiquity".

Bestwall Fms (6")

Beastewelle 1086 DB, *Bestwell* 1284 Cl

Biestewalle, Bustewalle 1293 Ipm

Byestewall(e) 1310 FF (*juxta Warham*), 1316 FA, 1331 FF (p)[3]

Byestwall 1412 FF, *Beestwall* 1431 FA, *Biestwall* 1495 Ipm

Biwestwalles (sic), *Biestewalles* 1412 FA

OE *bī ēastan wealle* 'by the east wall' or 'to the east of the wall', Bestwall lying just outside the east walls of Wareham; cf. Hutchins I, 415, Ekwall, Contributions to the Hist. of OE Dial. p. 47, PNWo p. 48.

Note. The type of name represented by Bestwall, common in SW England, has recently been discussed in the Introduction to PN D (p. xxxvii), and it is therefore unnecessary here to add the field-name material of this type which I had collected before PN D appeared. Bestwall is the only Do pl.-n. in which the initial *B-* has survived, but traces of the preposition *bī* can be seen in the early forms for Southbrook and Westport *supra* 70, 131; cf. also the lost *Bestedon infra.* As to the exact meaning of these compounds I entirely agree with the conclusions drawn by the editors of PN D, for it is clear that a name such as *Biestewolstonesbarwe* (found in 13th Glaston C) must necessarily mean 'to the east of Wulfstan's barrow'; cf. also Westbrook *infra.*

---

[1] (*to*) *Weareham* c. 910 (c. 1100) Burghal Hidage should be added (Maitland p. 503).

[2] This derivation seems to have been apparent even to the old Dorset historian Coker, see Hutchins I, 77.

[3] *Brestewalle* (*juxta Warham*) 1315 FF is a clear mistranscription.

Carey [kɛːri] is *Carry* 1318, 1409 FF, *Karry* 1431 FA. Possibly an old river-name to be compared with Carey (D) and Cary (So), for which see Ekwall, ERN p. 70 f. Carey Fm is on the river Piddle.

Holton, East and West
  Holton(e) 1086 DB, 1318 FF, 1333 *SR* (p), 1412, 1431 FA

It is suggested in Hutchins (I, 104) that this means "homestead in the hollow". That may be correct if we are allowed to start from an OE *hol(h)-tūn* but can hardly be so if we must start from OE (*æt*) *holan tūne*, for the latter alternative would almost necessarily have given us some ME forms with medial -*e*-. On the whole I am more inclined to believe that the first el. is OE *holt* 'wood, holt'; cf. Hawton (Nt), Mutschmann p. 66.

Hungerhill (lost)[1] is *Hungerhull* 1318 Ch, *Hungerhill* 1484 IpmR, 1811 OM. Probably self-explanatory (OE *hungor*, *hyll*), 'hunger' being used as a term of contempt for barren land.

Keysworth Fm is *Kisworthe* 1469 IpmR. The second el. is of course OE *w(e)orþ*, but the first must be left unexplained until earlier material has been brought to light.

Warmwell

Warmwell [wɔːməl] 140 H 8
  Warmwelle, Warmemoille, Warmewelle (-*uuella* Exon) 1086 DB
  Warm(e)well(e) t. Steph BM I, 1166 RBE (p), 1203, 1210 Cur, 1241, 1264 FineR, 1264 Ipm *et passim*
  Wermewell(e) 1152-8 (etc.) Montacute, 1204-5 FF, 1210 Cur, 1218 FF, 1244 *Ass*, 1285 FA, 1346 Cl, -*wull(e)* c. 1165 Montacute, 1242-3 Fees (750), -*vill* 1271 Ch
  Warmewule 1201-2 FF (p), *Warmwull* 1340 NI
  Wermwolle [*Wermwelle*] 1303 FA

Self-explanatory, OE *wearm, wielle*.

---

[1] *North Hungerhill* is now called **Trigon Fm**; *South Hungerhill* was on the opposite bank of the river (in East Stoke).

Watercombe

Watercombe 140 H 8

Watrecome 1086 DB, *-coma* Exon, *Watercome* 1280 FF
Watercomb(e), *-cumba*, *-cumb(e)* t. Hy I, t. Steph BM I[1], c. 1165
Montacute, 1242-3 Fees (750) *et passim*
Self-explanatory, OE *wæter*, *cumb*.

Winfrith Newburgh

Winfrith Newburgh 141 G 1

Winfrod(e) 1086 DB (*-froda* Exon), 1212 Fees (89) *et passim*
to 1285 FA, *Winfrot* al. *Winfrod* 1246 Ipm
Wynfrod(e) 1210-2 RBE, 1271 Ch, 1273 Pat, 1278 QW, 1285
FA, *Wynefrod(e)* 1227 FF, 1299 Cl, *Wunfrot* 1289 Cl
Wyn-, *Winford(e)* 1210-2 RBE, 1212 Fees (89) *et freq* to
1275 RH
Winfret, *Winifrat* 1216 ClR, *Wimfrost* 1228 Cl
Wymfrod(e) 1244 Fees (1387), 1279 Ch (also *Wem-*)
Wineford, *Winfroud* 1250 Fees (1183, 1241)
Wynfred(e) 1273 Cl, 1278 QW, 1282 Cl *et passim*, *Wymfred(e)*
1279 FF, Pat, *Wynfreud* 1294 (1313) Ch
Ne(e)uburgh is added from 1288 (FF), and then we have *Wyn-freth* 1412 FA, *Wynfreth Neuburgh* 1431 FA, *Winfrith New-burgh* 1481 IpmR.

Cf. also the early forms of the hundred-name *supra* 138.

Winfrith is apparently an old river-name, according to Bradley (Essays and Studies I, 32) and Ekwall (ERN p. 462 f.) identical with the Welsh name *Gwenffrwd* 'white brook'. Winfrith New-burgh is on a tributary of the Frome. Wynford Eagle *infra* is of the same origin.

The *Newburghs* of this place, of whom Robert *de Novo Burgo* was here in the time of Hy I (cf. Fees p. 89), were originally descended from the earls of Warwick (Hutchins I, 366, 436) and consequently derived their name from *le Neubourg* in Normandy (Eure).

Broomhill is *Bremehull* 1227 FF, *Bromhill* 1244 *Ass*, *Bromhull* 1330 FF, 1333 *SR* (p). Self-explanatory, OE *brōm*, *hyll*; cf. (*on*, *of*) *bromhulle* BCS 564 (Do).

[1] The identification in BM I with Whatcombe (in Winterborne Whitchurch) *supra* 68 is apparently wrong.

Burton (East and **West)** is *Burton(e)* 1210-2 RBE, 1256 FF, 1262
Ch *et passim* (with later prefixing of *Est-*, *West-*), *Bureton'* 1212
Fees (89), *Buriton, Buryton, Estburyton* 1285 FA, *Est Borton,
West Burton* 1333 Misc. OE *burhtūn*, cf. Bourton *supra* 3.

East Knighton is *Knitteton* 1279 FF, *Knytteton* 1280 Ch, *Knyste-
ton* 1285 FA, *Knyghteton* 1294 (1313) Ch (*in Wynfreud*), *Knighton juxta Bynedon* 1313 Inq aqd. OE *cnihta-tūn*, cf. Knighton
Ho *supra* 52. According to Hutchins there is a West Knighton
half a mile to the west, but I cannot find that on the maps;
cf. West Knighton (parish) *infra*.

Woodsford
Woodsford 140 F 8
  Werdesford 1086 DB (*-fort* Exon), 1194 P (p), 1210-2 RBE,
    1212 Fees (88), 1268 FF (*Est*), 1285 FA (*Est, West*), 1299,
    1303 AD IV, V, 1303 FA, 1336 FF, Cl (*Bellet*), 1440 IpmR
    (*Est*), 1445 FF (*Bolet*), 1457 IpmR (*Bolet*)
  Wardesford 1086 DB, 1428 FA, *Wardeford* 1221 Sarum, 1275 RH
  Werdeford 1241 Ch, 1275 RH, 1278 FF, 1280 Ch, 1291 Fine,
    1292 Orig, 1297 Pat, Cl, 1340 NI, 1388 Cl (*Belet*)
  Wyrdeford 1244 *Ass* (p), *Wyrdefforde* 1535 VE
  Wirdesford(e) t. Hy III (14th) Cerne, 1306 Abbr, 1318 FF,
    1320 Ch, 1354 FF (*Belet*), 1367 Cl (*Belet*), 1428 FA (*Wirdis-*),
    1470 IpmR, *Wirdeforde* 1412 FA
  Wyrdesford(e) 1282 Orig (*Belet*), 1291 Tax, 1318 Ch, 1333 *SR*,
    1346 FA, 1367 Cl, 1384 BM I (*Belet*) *et passim*
  E(a)stwordesford 1337 DorchesterR, 1428 FA
  Woddeford Castelle, Woddesford c. 1540 Leland

I can offer no plausible interpretation of the first el. of this
difficult name. There seems to be no topographical feature here
worth noting.
  The part which in DB is called *Wardesford* (= West Woodsford) was held at that time by Wm *Belet*, and the Belets remained here up to the time of Edward II. The manor house
is popularly called Woodsford Castle (1"). The names East and
West Woodsford are found on the 6" map.

Wool

Wool 141 F 2

Well(e) 1086 DB, t. Hy III Ipm, 1275 RH *et passim*
Wille (twice) 1086 DB
Welles 1166, 1210-2 RBE (p), 1212 Fees (89), 1219 ib. (260),
1244 ib. (1387), 1279 Ch
Woll(e) 1249 FF, 1285 FA, 1331 Cl, 1355 Ipm

OE *wielle* 'well, spring', or rather the plural of it. "It seems
to derive its ancient name, Welle, from the springs that abound
there" (Hutchins). The modern form of the name is due to the
rounding of *wy > wu* (*wo*) before *l*, peculiar to SW England
(Jordan § 62, Anm.) and particularly characteristic of Do, cf.
Ekwall, Contributions to the Hist. of OE Dial. p. 46 f. See
also Wool Bridge *supra* 145.

Bindon Abbey

Binad[ona] ? 1191-7 France, *Binadon'* 1204 LibR
Binnedon' 1204 LibR, 1215 ClR, *Binneden'* 1208 ClR, *Binne-
    dun* 1227 FF, 1251 Pat, *Bynnedun* 1229 Pat
Binedon(e), *-dun* 1204 RC, 1207 (etc.) ClR 1209 (etc,) PatR,
    LibR, 1212 Fees (89) *et passim* (very common)
Binendon' 1209 LibR, 1213 ClR, 1215 PatR, 1238 Cl
Bynedon(e) 1210-2 RBE, 1227 Fees (379), 1232 Cl, 1234 BM I,
    1234 (1279) Ch *et passim* (very common)
Binindon' 1214 ClR, 1296 Pat, *Bininndon'* 1219 Fees (260)
Bynendon 1237 Cl, 1276 Pat, *Bynindon* 1296 Pat, Fine, *Bynyn-
    don(e)* 1306, 1309, 1338 Cl, 1320 Ipm
Biningden 1310 Cl, *Binningdon* 1331 Cl, *Bynyngdon* 1335,
    1347 Cl, *Bynyngton* 1360 Cl[1]

It seems very likely that this is from OE *binnan dūne* 'within
(on the inside of) the down'. This aptly describes the situation
of Little Bindon, the original site of the monastery, see *supra* 141.
Bindon Abbey itself is in a level district.

Bovington is *Bovinton(e)* 1086 DB, 1235-6 Fees (425), 1280 Ch,
Bovynton 1280 Ch, *Bonyngton* (sic) 1291 Tax, *Bovyngton* 1312

---

[1] The following occasional spellings have been noted: *Byneton* 1275 RH,
Benendon 1298 Cl, *Benydon* 1362 Cl.

Ipm, *Bobington* 1535 VE. An *ing*-name probably containing the well-recorded pers. name *Bofa* (Redin p. 85). Hence 'farm of *Bofa's* descendants'.

Woodstreet Fm

Windestorte 1086 DB, *Windesteort* 1225 FF
Wudestort 1234 BM I, *Wodestort* 1234 (1279) Ch, *Wodestert(e)*
1280 Ch, 1285 FA, 1319 FF
Wodestrete 1279 Ch, 1291 Tax, 1304 Orig

The second el. is OE *steort* 'tail, tail-shaped piece of land', cf. Sturthill *infra*. The first would seem to be either OE *wind(ig)* 'wind(y)' or *windel* 'something winding', cf. Woodbury Hill *supra* 70 and Broadwindsor *infra*. The development of *wi* > *wu*, popular etymology, and metathesis of *r* have co-operated in giving the name its present quasi-intelligible form.

XIX. Culliford Tree Hundred

cuferdestroue 1084 GeldRoll
Cuiluertestrie 1195 P, *Culuertestrie* 1196 ChancR
Culuerdestre(ue) 1244 *Ass*, *Keuerdestre* 1265 Misc
Culfordestre 1275 RH, 1285 FA, 1388 IpmR, 1412 FA
Cylwardestre 1278 QW, *Culvardestre* 1285, 1346 FA
Kuvesdestre [*Kynewardestru*] 1303 FA
Culfardestr(e) 1311 Cl, 1312 Ipm, 1340 NI
Colyfordestre 1428, 1431 FA, *Culifordestr'* 1435 IpmR

Culliford Tree (6″) in Whitcombe parish, where the hundred-courts were formerly held, is a barrow planted with trees just E of Came Wood (465 feet above sea-level). The local pronunciation is [kʌlivəd].

The second el. of the name is of course OE *trēow* 'tree'. The first presents great difficulties, and no suggestion can be offered. For possible parallels cf. PN NRY p. 103 (s. n. Killerby) and Karlström, StNPh IV, 127.

Bincombe

Bincombe 140 H 6

Beuncumbe 987 (copy) KCD 656
Beincome 1086 DB, *Biemecomma* 1156-7 France

Biencomme 1156-7 France, 1190 (1332) Ch, *Biencoma, Bien-combe* 1174-82 France, *Bincūbe* 1244 *Ass* (p)
Bencumbe 1252 Ch, *Benecumbe* 1376 IpmR
Bynecombe 1327 *SR, Byncomb(e)* 1333 *SR*, 1428 FA

The second el. is OE *cumb* 'valley', but the first must for the present be left open.[1] That it can hardly be the preposition *binnan* 'within' (as suggested in Hutchins II, 278), is shown by a comparison with the early forms for Bindon *supra* 150.

Broadway

Broadway 140 H/I 6

Waia, Wai 1086 DB, Exon, *Veia* 1142 France
Waie 1166 RBE (p), *Waye* 1236 Fees (1468), 1269 Misc
Brode Way, Brodewaye, Brodewey(e) 1242-3 Fees (750), 1269 Misc, 1285, 1303 FA *et passim*
Bradewey(e) 1249 FF, 1291 Tax, 1428 FA (*-way*)
Waye Nichole 1318 FF, *Waye Nich'* 1340 NI

Cf. also the early forms for Upway *infra*.

The river Wey, which gives name *inter alia* to Upway, Broadway and Weymouth, is a name of Celtic origin. Its etymology has been the object of much discussion, see Ekwall, ERN p. 451 ff. — The epithet 'broad' in Broadway is self-explanatory, OE *brād. Nich(ole)* in the two 14th cent. forms must refer to the dedication of the church.

Note. There were formerly several manors along the river Wey, the names of which are now lost. I have found early forms for three such names in Broadway.
1. **Rowaldsway** was *Rowaldeswey(e)* 1299 Ipm, 1436 FF (*Ronwaldesweye* 1303 FF), but usually had its distinctive name added: *Wayernaud* (sic) 1249 FF, *Waye Rewald* 1285 FA, *W. Rouald* 1299 Ipm, *W. Rywaud* 1314 Ipm, *Wayernwaut* (sic) 1316 FF, *W. Rowand, W. Rowaud* 1370 AD I, 1384 Cl, *W. Roel* 1384 AD I, *W. Ruwant* 1391 AD II. — The suggestion in Hutchins (II, 486) that *Rowaldsway* derived its distinctive name from a certain *Rualet de Waie* mentioned in 1166 RBE (p. 218), seems very likely.
2. **Cricketway** was *Kriketesweie* 1371 AD I[2], *Crikettesway* 1412 FA, *Crykettesweye* 1420 FF, and was so called after the family of *Cruket*

---

[1] Some of the early forms show French spellings, and the form *Beuncumbe*, which heads the list, is from a very suspicious charter and probably corrupt.
[2] Cf. also the "lower water-mill called 'Criketesmull' in Weye Ruwant"

from Cricket in Somerset, mentioned as landholders in Broadway
from 53 Hy III (John de *Cruket*) onwards, cf. Hutchins II, 487,
485.
3. **Southway** (*Sutwaye* 1285 FA, *Suthwaye* 1303 FA) is self-explanatory.

Nottington is *Notinton* 1212 Fees (94), *Notingeton* 1234 BM I,
Notington 1234 (1279) Ch, *Notrington* (sic) 1279 Ch, *Nottyngton*
1388, 1397 FF, *Notyngton* 1412 FA, 1436 FF. This would seem
to be an *-ing* name, containing either the pers. name **Hnott*[1] or
the word *hnot* ('bare') itself, used in some topographical sense;
cf. PN D p. 267 s. n. Noddon.

Redlands is *Redeland* 1484 IpmR, *Rodelond* (*beside Brodewey*)
1486 Ipm. The place is only about half a mile from Radipole
(Lake) *infra*, so the two names presumably contain the same
first element.

Chickerell

Chickerell 140 I 5, **East Chickerell**
  Cicherelle 1086 DB
  Chikerel(l), Westchikerel(l), Estchikerel(l) 1227 FF, 1235-6, 1236(?),
    1242-3 Fees (425, 607, 753), 1285 FA, 1293 Ipm, 1303 FA
    et passim
  Chykerel(l), West-, Est- 1285 FA, 1291 Tax, 1302 FF, 1312
    Ipm, 1340 Cl, 1428 FA
  East Chekerell 1375 IpmR

I suspect that this was originally the name of the little brook
which runs from Chickerell in an easterly direction to Radipole
Lake. No etymological suggestion can be offered, but possible
parallels are Chicklade (Ekblom, PN W p. 51) and Chicksands
(PN BedsHu p. 168); cf. also PN D p. 610 s. n. Buckerell.

Putton (6″) is *Podinton(e)* 1237 FF, 1285 FA, *Poditon, Podyton*
1293, 1312 Ipm, 1315 Cl *et passim* to 1366 FF, *Podington* 1293,
1333 Ipm, *Pudicot* [*Pudynton*] 1303 FA, *Podynton* 1333 Ipm,
1339 Fine, Cl, *Podyngton* 1333, 1334, 1362 Fine, *Pydynton* 1360

1391 AD I (C 985). The upper water-mill was called 'Orchardesmull' ib. II
(C 2776); cf. 1384 Cl: "a close in Weye Rowaud called the 'Orchard'."

[1] This pers. name, from OE *hnot* 'bald-headed', is first found on record in
the 12th cent. in the form *Nhott*; see PN D p. 58 s. n. Natsley.

Fine, *Puddington* 1408 IpmR, *Putton* 1430 FF *et passim*. 'Farm of *Podda*'s descendants', *Podda* being a well-recorded OE pers. name (Redin p. 107). The later forms in *Pud-* should probably be looked upon rather as a phonetic development than pointing to a pers. name *Puda*, hardly convincingly evidenced in independent use (cf. Redin loc. cit.) and rare in pl.-ns, cf. e. g. PN Wo p. 65 s. n. Pudford. For interchange of *tūn* and *cot*, cf. e. g. PN D p. 188 s. n. Waddlestone.

West Knighton

West Knighton 140 G 8

Chenistetone 1086 DB, *Cnititon'* 1208 Cur
Knicteton 1226 Pat, *Knittetone* 1285 FA, *Knyghteton* 1294 Pat
et passim (with unimportant spelling variants)

OE *cnihta-tūn*, cf. Knighton Ho *supra* 52. As pointed out by Mawer (PN and History p. 27), this place was held TRE by two *taini*. 'West' probably in relation to East Knighton *supra* 149.

Lewell [luːəl] is *Lewelle* 1086 DB, *Liwelle* 1086 DB, 1201-2 FF, *Liwella* 1194, 1195 P (p), *Lywolle* 1285 FA. The second el. is OE *wielle* 'spring', and the first is possibly OE *hlēow* 'shelter' or the corresponding adj. *hlēow* 'warm, sunny, sheltered' (ModE *lew*); cf. PN D p. 59 s. n. Leeford and ib. p. 396 s. n. Lewdon. Cf. Lewcombe *infra*.

Fryer Mayne is *Maine* 1086 DB, *Mayne* 1275 RH, 1278 QW, 1290 Ch; *Mayne Hospital'* 1244 Ass, *Mayne (Maine) Ospitalis* 1285 FA, *Frarenemayne* 1337 DorchesterR. The three adjoining places Fryer Mayne, Little Mayne (next name) and Broadmayne (*infra* in St George Hundred) have been interpreted by Ekwall as British (Welsh *maen* 'stone'), see IPN p. 28.[1] — The Knights Templars or Hospitallers had land here; hence the distinctive name, cf. Tait in IPN p. 125.

Little Mayne Fm is *Maine* 1086 DB, 1201 Cur, *Parva Maene* 1201-2 FF, *Mayne Syrard, Mayne Sirard* 1285 FA, *Lyttlemayne*

---

[1] The same interpretation has earlier been suggested by Moule, Old Dorset p. 47 (with description of the stones here).

1306 FF. See preceding name. *Little* in contrast to Broad-mayne *infra*. It has been pointed out by Tait (IPN p. 130) that *Scirard* or *Sirard* was a Cheshire tenant of the first earl of Chester, and that the family of *Sirard* which held the present place in 1285 (FA) clearly descended from the Cheshire *Sirard*. It may be added that *Comes Hugo*, the first earl of Chester just alluded to, was the DB tenant-in-chief of *Maine* (Do), and also that, as early as 1201 (Cur, FF), the tenant of *Maine* or *Parva Maene* was Adam *Shirard* or *Syrad*, and that this family (later also spelt *Shyrard*, *Sherard*) held Little Mayne at least up to 1436 (FF).

Radesloe (lost) is *Radesle* 1244 *Ass* (p), 1412 FA, *Radesloe* 1268 FF, 1269 Ch, *Radeslo* 1312 Ipm, 1315 Cl, 1331, 1339 FF, *Redeslo* 1275 RH, 1278 QW, *Radeslowe* 1379 IpmR. 'Red slough', OE *rēad*, *slōh*; cf. Rassler Wood in PN Bk p. 189, and Ratsloe in PN D p. 443. — The name is now lost beyond recovery (cf. *Radeslowe vacua placea* 1379 IpmR), but the place must have been somewhere near Fryer Mayne, probably at the brick works S of West Knighton.

Osmington

Osmington 140 I 7

Osmyntone, Osmingtone c. 939 (copies) BCS 738, 739
Osmentone 1086 DB, *osmentona* Exon
Osminton(e) 1212 Fees (90), 1244 *Ass* (p), 1285 FA
Osmyngton(e), *Osmington* 1291 Tax, 1293 Cl, 1313 Orig (p), 1320 FF, 1333 SR, 1340 NI, -*yn*- 1310 Inq aqd

An -*ing* name containing either *Ōshelm* or *Ōsmund*, well recorded OE pers. names, see Zachrisson, Vising Celebr. Vol. p. 198 f., and Karlström p. 73.[1]

---

[1] Hutchins writes (II, 505): "The vill seems to derive its name from *Osmund*, its patron saint, and most ancient diocesan, the first Bishop of Salisbury." It is true that the church of Osmington is dedicated to St Osmund (cf. Melbury Osmond *infra*), but we need only compare the date of his death (A. D. 1099) with that of the earliest references above to realize that the resemblance between his name and the first el. of Osmington must be due to mere chance. It is, indeed, very probable that the process was the reverse, viz. that Osmington was supposed to contain the bishop's name, and that, for that very reason, the church was later on dedicated to him. Cf. Pancrasweek in PN D p. 156.

Ringstead is *Ringestede* 1086 DB (Exon: *Ringhesteta, -stede*), 1244 *Ass* (p), 1299 Ipm, *Ringsted(e)* 1227 FF, 1264 Ipm *et passim* with variant spelling *Ryng(e)sted(e)* and *Est-, West-* prefixed from 1285 (FA) onwards; *Upringestede* 1293 Cl (p), *Upryngstede* 1303, 1346 FA, *Upperyngsted* 1428 FA. OE *hring* 'ring' and *stede* 'place, site', the meaning of the compound being presumably 'circular site'; cf. EPN s. v. *hring* and PN Nth p. 195.

Upton is *Upton* 1361 Cl (p). Self-explanatory, OE *upp(e), tūn*.

Preston

Preston 140 I 7

  Prestun 1228 Pat, *Preston(e)* 1285 FA, 1291 Tax, etc.

'The priests' farm', OE *prēost, tūn*. It was an old prebend to Salisbury cathedral.

Horyford (lost) is *Horylord* (sic) 1402 IpmR, *Horiford* 1412 FA, 1456 IpmR, *Horyford* 1431 FA. 'Dirty ford', OE *horig, ford*; cf. Holyford in PN D p. 622. The exact site is unknown.

Lodmoor is probably to be identified with *(to) lotomor* c. 988 (12th) KCD 1284, and is spelt *Loddemore* t. Hy III (14th) Cerne, *Lodemor* 1297 Pat (p). The second el. is OE *mōr* 'swampy ground'. This aptly describes what Lodmoor is. The first el. should probably be compared with the river-name *Loddon*[1], for which Ekwall (ERN p. 258) suggests as a base a Brit *lūta* 'mud'; cf. also PN in *-ing* p. 79 f. For a similar compound cf. Crichel *supra* 90.

Sutton Poyntz is *Sutton(e)* 891 (14th) BCS 564, 1218 Fine, 1219 FF *et passim*, *Sutone* 1086 DB (*Sutona* Exon), *Suttun'* 1212 Fees (95), *Sottone* 1285 FA, *Sutton Pointz* 1314 Cl *et passim* (variants *Poinz, Poyntz, Poyntes, Poyns*). 'South farm', OE *sūð, tūn*. For the family of *Poyntz* see Hutchins II, 833 f. Nicholaus *Puinz* was tenant here in 1212 (Fees p. 95); cf. Stockwood *infra*.

---

[1] Another probable parallel is *(to) loddan broces æwylman* BCS 725, cf. PN D p. 108 s. n. Ladford. I do not believe that the first el. here is a pers. name; cf. Lowbrook Fm *supra* 47.

Radipole

Radipole [rædipoul, rædipu:l] 140 I 6
Retpole 1086 DB, *-pola* Exon, *Retpol* 1237 Cl
Redpole, -pola 1166 RBE (p), 1194, 1195 P, 1212 Fees (92),
t. Hy III (14th) Cerne, *Redepol(l)* 1237 Cl, 1244 *Ass*
Radepol' 1237 Cl, 1244 *Ass, Radpol* 1244 *Ass*
Radipol' 1237 Cl, *Radypolle* 1535 VE
Rappele 1280 Pat, 1318 Ch, *Rapely* 1303 FA, *Rappell* 1340 NI
Rippele 1280 Pat
Reppole 1285 FA, 1303 FF
Rappole 1291 Tax, 1311 Pap, 1333 *SR*, 1346, 1428 FA

This is apparently the old name for Radipole Lake, on the
nothern shore of which the village of Radipole is situated, and
the second el. is of course OE *pōl* 'pool'. The first may be
either OE *hrēod* 'reed, rush' or *rēad* 'red'. *hrēod* is perhaps the
more likely alternative (cf. *hreodpol* BCS 451), but the many *a*
spellings speak rather in favour of a base *rēad*. Cf. however
Zachrisson's explanation of such forms with *a*: *hrēod > r(e)ōd >
rŏd > răd*, the change of *ŏ > ă* being, according to Zachrisson,
a common phenomenon in ME dialects, see StMSpv VIII, 131.
What seems to speak against a similar assumption in the case
of the present name is that not a single *o* spelling (*rod-*) has
been noted.[1] If, in spite of that, we start from a base *hrēod*,
the *a* forms are therefore perhaps best explained as due to confusion with names containing *rēad* (> *rad-*), cf. Zachrisson, loc. cit.[2]

Buckland Ripers[3] is *Bocheland* 1086 DB (*bochelant* Exon), *Boclande*
1285 FA, *Boclonde* 1303 FA, *Bouclond* 1340 NI *et passim, Bok-
lond Ripers* 1359 FF *et passim* with the additional name variously
spelt *Riepers, Ryvers, Rippers, Rypers, Repers, Buklond Rivers*
1425 IpmR, *Buklond Rypers* 1495 Ipm. 'Land granted by book

---

[1] The above list includes all the early forms I have found.
[2] Zachrisson (op. cit. p. 132) also mentions Rodwell, the name of a place
just south of Radipole. We have no early forms for Rodwell, but the present
form would seem to point to *hrēod* as the first element. This, on the other
hand, need not imply that Radipole, which refers to a different body of water,
must necessarily contain *hrēod*, too.
[3] An ecclesiastical parish.

or charter', OE *bōcland*; cf. Buckland Newton *infra*. Joh. de *Ripirs* (*Rypirs*) was here in 1285 (FA), but as early as 1235-6 Margeria de *Ripariis* occurs in a Dorset entry (Fees p. 426), and we know that one of her Dorset fees was (West) Chickerell a mile SW of Buckland Ripers, see Fees pp. 605 ff., 753. She was relict of Baldwin de *Reviers*, eldest son of the earl of Devon, see Fees p. 605. It may finally be added that Hawisia de *Ripariis* held Fleet near Chickerell of the earl of Devon in 1212 (Fees p. 93). Cf. Stoke Rivers in PN D p. 69.

Causeway Fm is *Caucesweie* 1371 AD I, *Caus(e)weye* 1380 AD I, 1436 FF, *Causwey*, *Causeway*, *Cauxwey* 1412 FA. Named after the river Wey (see Broadway *supra* 152) and from John de *Kauz* (alias *le Kauz*) who held one third of a fee in *Waye Rouald* 27 Edw I (Ipm p. 414), cf. Hutchins II, 479,

Corfe Hill is *Corfhull* 1303 FF (*juxta Reppole*), 1431 FA, 1436 FF. See Corfe Castle *supra* 116.

Holwell. It has been exceptionally difficult to distinguish the earlier references to this place from those belonging to Elwell *infra* (in Upway), about a mile and a half to the north-east. The two names are hopelessly confused in Hutchins (II, 491, 844) and most indexes, but after a careful examination I venture to give the following series of forms for Holwell.

Halegewelle 1086 DB (prob. ident.)
Halghewell, Holewill 1244 *Ass* (p)
Brodewaye Hallewolle 1285 FA
Halwell [*Hathewelle*] 1303 FA
Halghwell juxta Brodeweye 1307 FF
Halewell 1346, 1431 FA, *Halewolle* 1428 FA

'Holy spring', OE *hālig, wielle*.[1]

Tatton is *Tatetun* 1086 DB, *Tatentone* 1086 DB, Exon, *Tattun(e)* 1212 Fees (93), 1285 FA, *Tatton(e)* 1212 Fees (93), 1262 FF *et passim* with later prefixing of *North-* and *S(o)uth-*. 'Tata's farm', *Tata* being a well recorded OE pers. name (Redin p. 54).

---

[1] Cf. (*on, of*) *halgan wyl(le)* in KCD 741, referring to another 'holy well' not far from Holwell, possibly to this place itself.

West Stafford

West Stafford 140 G 7, **East Stafford** (lost)[1]

Stanford 1086 DB, 1322 Ipm

Staford(e) 1086 DB (*Stafort* Exon), 1264 FineR *et passim* (*West Staford* 1285 FA, etc.)

Stafford(e) 1205 RC, 1227 Fees (379) (p) *et passim*

Stafford' Turberevil' 1242-3 Fees (750)

Stafford Ospitalis 1285 FA, *Estaford* 1303 FA

Stavord(e) 1340 NI (*West*), 1346, 1428 FA

Stofford Byngham 1412 FA

'Stony ford', OE *stān, ford*. For the loss of *n* see Stoborough *supra* 130.

According to Hutchins (II, 512) Henry de *Turbervile* is mentioned 14 John as holding or having held a third of a fee in (West) Stafford. About 1243 Robert de *Bingham* acquired by his marriage with Lucy *Turberville* both this manor and (Bingham's) Melcombe *infra*, see Do Field Club XXII, 136. The addition *Ospitalis* is due to the fact that East Stafford belonged to the Knights Hospitallers; cf. Fryer Mayne *supra* 154.

Frome Billet (lost)[2] is *From(e)* 1086 DB, 1210-2 RBE, 1212 Fees (88) *et passim*, *Froume* 1222 FineR, *Frome Belet* 1285 FA, 1291 Tax *et passim*, *Frome Everard* 1327 *SR*, 1343 Fine. Named after the river Frome [fru:m], for which see Ekwall, ERN p. 166 ff. (with full list of early forms). The river gives name also to Frome Whitfield, Frampton, Frome Vauchurch, Chilfrome, and Frome St Quintin (all *infra*); cf. also Bhompston Fm and Cruxton *infra*. — Wm *Belot* (*Belet*) was DB tenant-in-chief here. Wm *Everard* died seized of *Frome* 7 Edw I (Ipm p. 168).

Upway

Upway 140 H 5

Wai(a) 1086 DB, c. 1201 Sarum, *Waya, Way(e)* c. 1201 Sarum, 1215 ClR *et passim* (later also *Weye*)

Waye Bayouse 1237 Sarum, 1285 FA (*Bause*), 1288 Ipm (*Baiocis*), with variants like *Waye Bayhous(e)* 1316, 1318 Ipm, 1320 Cl, *Way Baihous* 1412 FA

---

[1] According to Hutchins (II, 499) another name for Lewell *supra* 154.

[2] Now Stafford Ho.

Waye Pigace 1242-3 Fees (750), *Wayepigaz* 1246 FF (p), *Pygate-waye* 1272 FF, *Waye Pagace* 1388 IpmR *Waye Hamundevill*[1] 1249, 1311 FF, 1361 IpmR, 1363 Cl *Up(e)weye, Upwaye* 1311 Fine, 1333 *SR*, 1346 (etc.) FA *Weyhamondvyle* al. *Uppewey* al. *Weybayouse* 1456 IpmR

See Broadway *supra* 152. *Bay(h)ouse* from the family of *Baieux*[2], of whom Alanus de *Bayocis* was here about 1200 (Sarum). *Pigace* (*Pigaz, Pygate, Pagace*) probably from some ancient owner who cannot now be traced.[3] *Hamundevill* possibly refers to some branch of the family of *Amundevill*, originally seated at Thorpe Mandeville (Nth). Some member of this family may at a fairly early date have held land here of the Beauchamps just as in Melcombe Horsey (*infra*), cf. Hutchins IV, 364 f.

Elwell. For difficulties of identification see Holwell *supra* 158. The following forms probably belong here: *Helewill'* 1212 Fees (90), *Hellewell(e)* 1256 (1258) Ch, 1275 RH, 1388, 1425, 1433 IpmR, 1449 FF, *Helewell(e)* 1259 Ch, 1275 RH, 1284 (1285) Ch, *Hellewolle* 1285 FA, *Helewoll* 1333 *SR, Halewell* 1412 FA, *Helwell* 1667 BM I. The river Wey rises here, and Elwell probably refers to its spring, the well-known "Wishing Well". Can the name mean 'healing spring' with OE *hǣlu* 'health, prosperity, salvation' in the first element?

Stottingway (local) is *Stokingway* 1235-6 Fees (426), *Scottingesweye* 1249 FF, *Stottynways, Stottyngetone* 1285 FA, *Stottingwaye* 1288 Ipm, *Scottingwaye* 1305 FF, *Stottyngweye* 1346 FF, IpmR *et passim* (variant *Stotingweye*), *Stokkyngweye* 1361 Cl. The second el. is the name of the river Wey (see Broadway *supra* 152). The first and the last of the above forms would seem to point

---

[1] With small variants in spelling (like *Weye Hamundevile* etc.).

[2] *Waye Bay(h)ouse* long survived in the name of the Liberty of Upway, often called *Waybyhouse* (cf. *supra* 3 n. 1); probably it still survives, for among the private residents in Upway there is, according to Kelly, a lady living at *Wabey house* (!).

[3] As a surname I have found the word several times in medieval records, cf. Johannes *Pigace* 1199 RC, Wm *Pigac*', Geoffrey *Pigace* 1210 Cur, John *Pygaz* 1272 FF. Cf. OFr *pigace* 'pointe; instrument pointu, pic; soulier pointu; sorte de parure; femme qui se pare vaniteusement'; also used as a pers. name (Godefroy).

to ME *stocking* 'clearing of stocks, piece cleared of stocks' (cf. EPN s. v.) as the first el., but the other forms are against that, and the name had therefore better be left open. For the form *Stottyngetone* cf. Hutchins (II, 845): *Stotingway* vulgo *Stotton*.

Westbrook is *Westebroke Ospitalis* 1285 FA, *Westebroke* 1285 FA et passim (later *Westbroke*, *Westbrouk*), *Weywestbrok* 1303 FA, *Wey Westbrook* 1428 FA. The meaning here must be 'to the west of the brook' (cf. Bestwall *supra* 146), the brook in question being the river Wey, on the opposite bank of which there is an East-brook (6″). In 1285 (FA) the place belonged to the *prior ospitalis Sancti Johannis Jerusalem*; cf. Fryer Mayne and West Stafford *supra* 154, 159.

Weymouth

Weymouth 140 K 6

Waimouþe, (on ðan) Waymouþe c. 939 (copy) BCS 738
(apud) *Waimudā* 1130 PR, *Waymud* 1243 Pap
Waymue 1152-8 Montacute, 1244 *Ass* (*passim*), 1254 Pat, 1275 RH, 1280 Pat, 1292, 1293 Cl
Weymue 1225 ClR, 1268 (*et passim*) Pat, t. Hy III (14th) Cerne, 1284 (1285) Ch, 1289 Cl, 1290 Fine, 1308 Cl
Waym' 1231 Cl, *Wymue* t. Hy III (14th) Cerne, *Wemue* 1275 Fine, *Waymo* 1282 Cl, *Wyemue* 1293 Pat
Weymuth(e) 1248 Ch, 1258 Pat *et passim*, *Weymothe* 1296 Ipm; from 1307 (Ipm, Cl) also *Waymuth(e)*
Wymuth(e) 1256 (1258) Ch, 1317 Cl
Weymouth, Waymouth 1290, 1299 Cl *et passim*

Self-explanatory, OE *mūþa*. Cf. Broadway *supra* 152. On the Anglo-French spellings (-*mue* etc.) see Zachrisson, AN Infl. pp. 82 f., 93 f.

Bridge (lost)

Brige 1086 DB, (ad) *Brigā* ib. (*Adbrigā* Exon)
Brugi, Bruge(s) near Waymue 1152-8 Montacute

Self-explanatory, OE *brycg*. According to Eyton (p. 122) "probably a name given to the Isthmus which connects Portland Isle with the Mainland". It may be questioned, however, if the name does not refer to some ancient bridge between Weymouth and Melcombe Regis.

Melcombe Regis[1]

Melecumb(e), *-comb(e)* 1238 Cl, t. Hy III (14th) Cerne, 1280 Ch,
   Pat *et passim*, *Mellecumb* 1244 *Ass*
Melcumbe, *-combe* 1314 Ch, 1321 Cl *et passim*
Melecoumbe 1322 Cl, *Melcoumbe* 1325 Cl, *Milcumbe* 1341 Cl
Melecumbe Regis 1340 NI, *Melcombe Regis* 1391 FF

The second el. is of course OE *cumb* 'valley'. The first may
be identical with the first element of Melbury Abbas *supra* 27
(cf. Zachrisson, Romans p. 53), but it seems more likely that
Ekwall is right in suggesting that it is simply OE *meoluc* 'milk',
meoluc cumb occurring as a boundary mark in BCS 620 (and
621), see Namn och Bygd XVII, 168. Cf. Melcombe Horsey
and Bingham's Melcombe *infra*. — *Regis* because anciently a
royal demesne (Eyton p. 82 f.).

Whitcombe

Whitcombe 140 G 7

Widecome, *Wydecombe* c. 939 (copies) BCS 738, 739
Widecome 1086 DB (*Widecoma* Exon)
Widecumb' 1212 Fees (90), *Wydecume*, *Wide-* 1285 FA
Wytecombe 1291 Tax, 1428 FA
Wydecumbe, *-comb* 1291 Tax, 1333 *SR*, 1340 NI, *Widecombe*
   1310 Inq aqd, *Wid-*, *Wyd-* 31 Hy VIII Hutchins

This apparently means 'wide valley', OE (*æt*) *widan cumbe*.
The statement in EPN (p. 40) that the first el. is OE *hwǣte*
'wheat' is not in conformity with the evidence of the early
forms.

Winterborne Came

Winterborne Came 140 G 7

Wittremburna 1174-82 France (p. 162)
Wintreborna 1190 (1332) Ch (p. 271)[2]

---

[1] The towns of Weymouth and Melcombe Regis were united as early as
1571, and since the former name is generally used to designate the whole, the
name of Melcombe Regis has nowadays disappeared from many maps.

[2] This is an *inspeximus* of the important charter of Richard I, specifying
William the Conqueror's and Queen Matilda's grants to the monastery of St
Stephen, Caen (cf. Eyton p. 126 n.). The somewhat earlier form *Wittremburna*
must consequently belong here and not to Winterbourne Monkton (W), as
assumed by the indexer of France.

The additional name appears as *Cham* 1291 Tax, *Caam* 1340
NI, *Came* 1435-6 IpmR, and *Cane* 1436 FF. It is a mere corruption of *Caen* (cf. foot-note), see Hutchins II, 289. This
Winterborne (or some part of it) often appears with another
distinctive name spelt *Hundynton, Huntindon* [*Huntyngdon*] 1303
FA, *Hundingdon* 1305 Abbr, *Huntington, Huntyngton* 1344 Inq
aqd, 1346, 1428 FA, *Houndyngton* 1345 FF, *Honnyngton, Ho-
myngton* 1346, 1428 FA. The only suggestion I can make with
regard to this name is that the earls of Huntingdon, who in 1
Henry V had a grant out of the manor of Frampton[1] (Hutchins
II, 297), may at an early date have had some concern here.
Winterborne Came is named after the little brook called South
Winterborne — the westerly of the two Dorset Winterbornes —
which rises near Winterborne Abbas and runs south of Dorchester, giving name also to W. Steepleton, W. St Martin, (W.)
Ashton, W. Monkton, W. Herringstone, and W. Farringdon (all
infra). Cf. Winterborne Houghton *supra* 61.

Winterborne Farringdon (6″)
Wintreburne 1086 DB

This is *Winterborn' Gemain* 1242-3 Fees (751), *W. Germayn*
(*Germeyn*) 1285 FA, 1286 Ipm, 1329 FF *et passim* to 1428 FA,
W. Germani 1286 Cl, *W. Germaine* 1361 IpmR, and does not
appear until 1431 (FA) as *Wynterborn Faryngdon*. Its former
church[2] was dedicated to *St German* (see Hutchins II, 519);
hence the earlier distinctive name. The present additional name
Farringdon comes from the 14th and 15th cent. owners, of whom
the earliest I have come across, Robert de *Faryndon*, held one
fourth of a fee here in 1346 (FA).

Winterborne Herringstone

Winterborne Herringstone 140 G 6
Wintreburne 1086 DB

It appears as *Winterborn'* (etc.) *Harang* 1242-3 Fees (751), 1268
FF, 1285 FA, 1286 Ipm, as *W. Heryng* (*Hering*) 1333 *SR*, 1343

[1] Winterborne Came belonged to Frampton Liberty.
[2] The place is now entirely depopulated, and a small piece of the church
wall is the only thing that remains.

IpmR *et passim*, as *W. Heryngston* 1372 IpmR, 1431 FA, and as
Heringston alone in 1598 AD VI.

On the family of *Harang* see Chaldon Herring *supra* 138 and
Hutchins II, 520 ff. Philip *Harang* (1268 FF) seems to be the
first of the family mentioned in direct connexion with this place;
cf. Herrison *infra*.

Winterborne Monkton

Winterborne Monkton 140 G 6

Wintreburne 1086 DB, *Winterburne* 1212 Fees (88), 1228 Ch

It is called *Wyntreburn Wast, Winterbornwast* (etc.) 1244 *Ass,*
1255 Pap, 1269 Pat (*Winterburn Sancti Michaelis de Vasto*), 1286
AD III (*de Wasto*), 1291 Tax *et passim*, the reason being that it
belonged to the priory of *le Waast* (*de Wasto*) near Boulogne,
cf. Hutchins II, 530. It appears as *Moneketone* 1285 FA, 1333
SR, but is more commonly called *Winterbourne Monk(e)ton* or
Monachorum (1306 Pat, 1311 Cl, 1370 FF, etc.).

Wyke Regis

Wyke Regis 140 K 5

Uuike, Wike c. 988 (12th) KCD 1284, *Wik(e)* 1212 Fees (90),
   1237 Cl, 1244 *Ass*, 1248 Ch *et passim*
Wyka, Wyk(e) 1236, 1237 Cl, 1244 *Ass et passim, Wykes* 1244
   Ass, Wikes 1263 Pat
Kingeswik 1242 Cl, *Kyngeswyk(e)* 1309 FF, 1365 AD I
Wyke Regis t. Hy VI IpmR, *Weke* 1526 AD II

OE *wīc* 'dairy-farm'. *Regis* for the same reason as Melcombe
Regis *supra* 162.

Small Mouth is *Smalemue* 1244 *Ass* (p), and is spelt *Smalem(o)uth*
(etc.) frequently from 1391 (AD I, FF) onwards. Self-explanatory,
OE *smæl* 'small, narrow' and *mūþa* 'mouth'. The name refers to
the narrow passage between the mainland and the Isle of Portland. The ferry here was superseded by a bridge in 1839
(Hutchins II, 808, 850 f.).

Portland [1]

(*on*) *Port* s. a. 837 ASC (A, E)

Portland(e) s. a. 982 ASC (C), c. 988 (12th) KCD 1284, s. a.
1052 ASC(E), n. d. (12th) KCD 891 *et passim*

Porland(a) 1086 DB, Exon, 1156 PR, 1194 CurR, 1236 Cl,
1243 Pap, 1244 *Ass*, 1258 Pat, 1275 RH

Porlaund 1244 *Ass*, 1258, 1264, 1267 Pat

Port(e)laund 1259 Ch, Pat *et passim* to 1297 Cl

Portlond is common from 1284 (Ch) onwards, *Porlond* has been
found once (1296 Ipm)

port here apparently means 'harbour' (Latin *portus*)[2], and the
whole name should probably be understood as 'land forming
(or giving protection to) a harbour'; cf. Johnston p. 405. The
loss of *t* may be explained simply from its position between
two consonants, but the number of forms without *t* as well as
the date of these forms (1086-1296) indicates a strong French
influence on this name, also to be seen in the numerous -*laund*
spellings.

Note. I have found no OE or ME forms for pl.-ns in Portland.[3]
Chesil Bank, the remarkable beach of pebbles which connects the
"Isle" of Portland with the mainland near Abbotsbury (c. 10 miles
NW), is called by Leland *the Chisil*[4], see EPN s. v. *ceosol, cisel*, and
cf. Cheselbourne *infra*.

XX. Barrow Hundred

Hundredesb'i 1167-8 P

Hunderesberger 1177-8 P (*Hundredisberga* ChancR)

Hundredesberg(h) 1244 *Ass*, 1265 Misc (-*berehe*), 1285, 1316 FA,
1333 *SR*, 1359, 1376 FF

Hondresbergh 1244 *Ass*, *Hundresbergh* 1340 NI

Hundredesberewe 1275 RH

---

[1] For geographical reasons included at the end of this hundred.
[2] Cf. PN Sx p. 430 s. n. *Lamport*.
[3] Cf. however *atte Yate* 1333 *SR* (p), probably to be identified with **Verne
Yeates**; OE *geat* 'gate'.
[4] Also (this) *bank of Chisil*, (this) *Chisille bank*.

Hundredesburgh 1280 Ch *et passim* to 1415 IpmR
Hundesber(e)gh 1303 FA, *Hundredesborgh, -bargh* 1431 FA

'The barrow of the Hundred', OE *hundred, beorg.* **Hundred Barrow** (on the maps) is a tumulus S of Bere Regis and inside that parish and hundred.[1]

Affpuddle

Affpuddle [ɑːfpʌdl] 141 D 1
Affapidele 1086 DB, *Affapidela* Exon
Effipidela 1093-1100 (1313) Ch, *Effepidel'* 1212 Fees (92)
Affepidel(e) 1244 *Ass*, 1285, 1316 FA [2]
Affepudele 1291 Tax[2], 1428 FA, *-pudell* 1535 VE, AD V
Afpudele 1303 FA *et passim, -pidyll* 1428 FA
Pudle 1318 Ch, *Ediuepudle* 1330 Ch

This and several other places *infra* take their names from the river Piddle. For early forms of this river-name and etymological suggestions, see Ekwall, ERN p. 324 f., and Zachrisson, StMSpv IX, 121.

As pointed out in Hutchins (I, 204), Affpuddle should in all probability be identified with the *rus iuxta Pydelan*, consisting of *quatuor cassatos*, which was given to Cerne Abbey by a certain *Ælfriðus*, according to the text in KCD 656 (dated 987). This corresponds exactly to the four hides which the church of St Peter of Cerne held in *Affapidele* at the time of DB. One cannot then help drawing the conclusion that the prefix in Affpuddle derives from the name of the *Ælfriðus* (*Ælffrith*) who — if we can trust the text of KCD 656[3] — gave the place to Cerne. — The form *Ediuepudle* (1330) would seem to indicate confusion with the common fem. name *Ēadgifu*.

Oakers Wood is *Wolgariswode* (bosc') 1465 IpmR. '*Wulfgār*'s wood'.

---

[1] The pre-DB Hundred of *Bere* (Bere Regis) also comprised what was later called *Hundredesberg*, cf. *supra* 68.

[2] 1316 FA and 1291 Tax have the clear mistranscription *Asse-*.

[3] This Do charter is starred by Kemble as liable to suspicion (cf. Crawford Ch p. 88), but, as far as I can see, the details of this particular grant may nevertheless be correct.

Pallington is *Palinton* 1244 *Ass* (p), *Palynton* 1268 FF, *Palyng-ton(e)* 1316 FA, 1318 Ch, 1327 Ipm (p), 1338 FF, *Palington* 1355 IpmR. This should presumably be compared with names like Poling (Sx), earlier *Paling(es)*, probably containing OE *pāl* 'pole, stake', possibly also 'palisade'; cf. e. g. Ekwall, PN in *-ing* p. 61 f.; Karlström p. 170 (with literature); PN Sx p. 171 f.

Bryants Puddle

   Pidele 1086 DB, 1205 FineR

   Prestepidel(a) 1093-1100 (1313) Ch, 1225 FF

   Pidel Turbervill(e) 1238 Cl, 1327 Ch, *Pideleturberevil* 1285 FA,   *Pidele Turbervyll* 1316 FA

   Pudel(e) Turburvile (*Turberville, -wyle*) 1326 FF, 1370 Cl, 1389   IpmR, *Pydele Turbervylle* 1373 Cl

   Turberuyle Pudele 1333 *SR*

   Turbervilespudell 1412 FA, *Turbervylespudele* 1431 FA

   Brianis Pedille 1465 IpmR, *Bryans Pudell* 1480 IpmR

See Affpuddle *supra* 166. The *Turbervilles* here can be traced back to the beginning of the 13th cent. (Hugo de *Turbervill'* 1205 FineR), cf. Winterborne Muston *supra* 71. After having for about two hundred years taken its distinctive name from that family, the place changed its name into "Brian's" Puddle in the latter half of the 15th cent., thus apparently preserving the Christian name of a member of the same family, *Brian(us)* de Turbervill (1316 FA, 1327 Ch). The two early forms beginning with *Preste-* are left unidentified by the indexers of Ch and FF. There can be little doubt, however, that they belong here, for according to Ch (III, 233) *Prestepidela*, which is stated to have been near Affpuddle, was given by King William II to Christchurch Twynham, and in 1225 FF (p. 28) we find the prior of that house and Hugh de *Thurbervill* as parties to a fine concerning land in *Prestepidel*. Since the place apparently had the epithet *Preste-* prefixed to its name before it was given to Christchurch Twynham, the reason for the prefix should presumably be sought in the fact that — if Eyton's identification is correct — this *Pidele* was held in DB (f. 84 b) by a certain Godric who in the GeldRoll of 1084 (Exon p. 21) is referred to as *presbiter*; cf. Eyton p. 115 f.

Roger's Hill Fm is *Rogers Hill, Rogershill* 7 Eliz AD V, and is probably a late and self-explanatory name.

Throop is hardly identical with *Thrope* 1285 FA, as assumed by the indexer of FA II; since the form in FA appears under Puddletown Hundred and immediately after Tolpuddle, it seems very likely that it refers, instead, to the present Southover Ho, earlier *Throop*[1] (in Tolpuddle), cf. Hutchins II, 632. The same is true of the form *Throp* in 1327 *SR*. On the other hand, *Pidele la Trop'* in 1237 Cl, identified by the indexer of Cl with Little Puddle (*infra*), probably refers to the present Throop in this parish, above all if, as is stated in Hutchins (I, 207), this place once belonged to Milton Abbey, cf. the text in 1237 Cl p. 114. OE *þrop* (*þorp*) 'out-lying farm'. The form *Pidre* in DB (f. 78 a) may belong here, too; cf. Eyton p. 115 with foot-note 5.

Turners Puddle

Turners Puddle 141 D 2

Pidele 1086 DB (f. 83 b), *Pidela* Exon (p. 50)

Tunerepidel 1242 Sarum

Pidel(e)tonere 1264 FineR, 1285, 1316 FA

Pydele Tunere (*Tonere*) 1264, 1299 Ipm, 1309 FF

Pydle 1280 Ch, *Pudele* 1303, 1346 FA

Tonerespudele 1333 *SR*, 1366 IpmR, *Toner(e)spudell* 1412, 1431 FA, 1458 FF, *Tonerespedell* 1428 FA, *Tunerspudell* 1484 IpmR

Tournerspedyll 1428 FA, *Turnerspudell* 1535 VE

See Affpuddle *supra* 166. It is Eyton who (p. 115 f.) identifies the above DB reference with the present Turners Puddle, and on p. 40 he also indicates the origin of the distinctive name: "*Turner's Puddle* as the "Pidele" held at Domesday by "Walter Le Tonnerre" under Hugh fitz Grip's widow, has come to be called". Tait objects to this (IPN p. 123): "Turner's Puddle (Do) can hardly, however, be called after the DB undertenant Walter, whom Eyton, on what authority does not appear, describes as Walter le Tonnerre, for as late as 1303 the place was held by Henry Toner of the heirs of William de Gouiz". Tait,

---

[1] *West Thrope* 36 Hy VIII (Hutchins).

however, has apparently overlooked that Eyton's authority is an
entry in the GeldRoll of 1084 (cf. Eyton p. 40) where Walter
is called *uualterus tonitrus* (Exon p. 21), and that in two further
entries in Exon (pp. 50, 55) he is referred to as Walter *tonitruŭ*.[1]
Eyton has thus simply translated Walter's surname into French
(*Le Tonnerre*). That this name enters into Turners Puddle seems
a priori very plausible, but Tait, on the other hand, is quite
right in pointing out that Turners Puddle must contain the
name of the above-mentioned Henry *Tonere* who in 1303 (FA
II, 37) held *Pudele* of the heirs of Wm de Gouiz. As will be
seen from the following discussion, there are strong reasons for
assuming that this Henry Tonere was a descendant of Walter
'Le Tonnerre' (*tonitrus, tonitruum*) in DB.

As was pointed out under Okeford Fitzpaine *supra* 45, there
can be little doubt that the DB tenant-in-chief of this *Pidele*
and a great many other Dorset places, Hugh Fitz Grip's widow,
later on married Alfred de Lincoln, in whose possession we find
many of her DB manors in Dorset and whose family we can
follow for several generations. When the last Alfred de Lincoln
died in 48 Henry III, his possessions were divided between his
three heirs[2], one of them being Wm de Goyz or Gouiz who
inter alia got the place called *Pydele Tunere*, see 1264 Ipm p.
181 f. It was consequently of the heirs of this Wm de Gouiz
that Henry Tonere held *Pudele* in 1303.[3] But it cannot be from
this Henry Tonere himself that the place got its distinctive
name, for when that first appears in 1242, he was not even
born.[4] Since we know that in a great number of cases many
decades elapsed before the name of a tenant was added to a
place-name[5], we are apparently justified in drawing the conclusion that a family *Tonere* must have been undertenants here
probably for a considerable time before 1242. There are also
other reasons for assuming that such was the case. Among the

---

[1] I suppose this should be interpreted as *tonitruum*, both that word and
tonitrus meaning 'thunder'. Eyton (pp. 40, 115) calls him Walterus Tonitruus.

[2] Cf. again Okeford Fitzpaine *supra* 45.

[3] He, or more probably his father, held the place as early as 1280 (Ch
p. 243).

[4] This Henry *Tonere* al. *Toneyre* was forty years old in 29 Edw I, see Ipm
III, 496.

[5] Cf. e. g. Sutton Waldron *supra* 18.

places which in 1303 (FA) were held by Henry Tonere of the heirs of Wm de Gouiz was also Armswell (*infra*), and when we therefore come across an earlier Henry *Toneire* [1] in connexion with Armswell in 1225 (FF), we cannot help believing that he must have been connected with Turners Puddle, too. Finally, there is an important entry in RBE (p. 215) telling us that in 1166 Alvredus *Tonarre* held two knight's fees in Dorset of Alfred de Lincoln. All this tends to prove that the family *Tonere* (*Toneire, Tonarre*) were descendants of the DB undertenant Walter 'Le Tonnerre' (*tonitrus, tonitruum*), and that they had most probably lived here as undertenants all since the time of DB, although their surname is not added to the place-name until more than 150 years after the date of that record. [2]

Snelling Fm is *Snellyng* 1458 FF and *Snelling(e)* 1534, 1565 AD V, but this material is too late to allow of any certain suggestoin. Both *Snell* and *Snelling* are well recorded pers. names in OE (cf. Redin pp. 25, 169).

XXI. Puddletown Hundred

Pideleton(e) 1084 GeldRoll, 1187-8 P, 1212, 1227 Fees (93, 379), 1275 RH, *Pidelton(e)* 1210-2 RBE, 1244 *Ass*, 1265 Misc, 1428 FA, *Pidleton* 1285 FA

Pydelton 1244 *Ass*, 1290 FF, 1346 FA, 1398 IpmR

Pudel(e)ton 1303 FA *et passim*, *Pudeltoune* 1431 FA

See Puddletown *infra*.

Athelhampton

Athelhampton [æþəlæmtən] 140 E 9

Pidele 1086 DB (f. 77 a), 1204 Cur, 1211-2 Abbr, FF, *Pudele* 1303, 1346 FA, *Pudell* 1428 FA

Pidele Aloume (*Aleume*), *Pudele Aleume* 1250 FF

---

[1] Possibly the same man who is called Henricus *Taneire* in 1210-2 (RBE p. 548).

[2] To make this account of the *Toneres* of Turners Puddle complete, it may be added that, according to Hutchins (I, 211), Joan, daughter and heir of Nicholas Tonere, brought this manor to her husband, Wm Turberville of Bere Regis, in the time of Henry VI.

Pidel(e) Athelamston 1285 FA, 1288 Cl, *Pidele Athalamston*
1291 Ipm, *Pydeleathelamston* 1291 Cl
Athelamston 1285 FA, 1365 FF, 1376 IpmR
Athelham(e)ston 1303 FA, 1333 *SR*, *Athelhampston* 1346 FA
et passim, Alamston 1369 Orig

'*Æþelhelm*'s manor (on the river Piddle)', cf. Hutchins II, 580.
The name is interesting *inter alia* because it seems to be a very
rare instance of a post-Conquest pl.-n. in *-ton*, the first part of
which is an originally Old English (not French) pers. name.
There can be little doubt that the addition *Aleume* (for which
Aloume must be a scribal error) stands for *Æþelhelm*, for that
name would easily have become *Alelm* in the 13th century, and
vocalization of the second *l* would exactly have given us the
form *Aleum(e)*.[1]

South Admiston is simply another form of the preceding name
Athelhampton, clearly seen from the fact that in the Dorchester
Records Robert Martyn of *Athelhampston* (so called in 1543) is
referred to as R. M. of *Adelmyston* in 1547; cf. Robert and John
Admyston (1560 ib.), John *Admiston* (1565 ib.). Athelhampton,
the name of the manor, has a more conservative and aristocratic
appearance, whereas Admiston, the name of the farm, has been
more liable to popular development. Cf. also the above form
Alamston from 1369, probably reflecting the true local pronunciation of that date.

Burleston
Burleston 140 E 9
   (*at*) *Burdalueston* c. 939 (copy) BCS 738, (*apud*) *Bordelestone*
   ib. 739[2]
Burdeleston 1212 Fees (90), 1535 VE
Bordesleston 1310 Inq aqd, *Bourdelston* 1354 FF
Burleston 1535 VE

The name of this place has often been confused by indexers
with that of *Bardolfeston*, a now lost place (*infra* in Puddletown),

[1] On the phonetic development cf. Zachrisson, AN Infl. pp. 107 ff., 146 ff.
[2] According to Eyton (p. 135 f.) the DB reference *Pidele* (f. 78 a: *Pidela*
Exon p. 39) belongs here. That may be correct, but Burleston seems otherwise
never to have been called after that stream; cf. *Bardolfeston infra*.

the site of which was only about a mile NW of Burleston. The two names were apparently sometimes confounded even in early records, but since Burleston anciently belonged to Milton Abbey, it is often possible to distinguish between the early references, cf. Hutchins II, 589, 616. Besides the above forms, also *Burdalston* 1285 FA may belong here. Since the name appears already in the foundation charter of Milton Abbey (first examples above), it may be Anglo-Saxon, whereas *Bardolfeston* is a post-Conquest name.

Burleston must be left unexplained. The first el. would seem to be a pers. name, but I can find none that suits the list of early forms.[1]

Dewlish

Dewlish [djuːliʃ, duːliʃ] 130 H 9

Dewlish takes its name from the little stream now called

Devil's Brook: (*on*) *deuelisc*, (*be*) *deuelisc made* 869 (15th) BCS 525, (*on*) *deflisch*, (*wið*) *deuliscmad* ib. 526, (*on, to*) *deulisc stream(e)* 942 (15th) ib. 775, (*on*) *deuelisc stream* 1019 (15th) KCD 730. — Devil's Brook rises on the S slope of Bulbarrow, and, passing through Dewlish, runs in S direction to the Piddle near Burleston. On the N slope of Bulbarrow rises another stream which runs in N direction and falls into the Stour near Sturminster Newton. That is now called

Divelish: (*on*) *deuelisch*, (*of*) *defelich* 968 (14th) BCS 1214. — The name is clearly identical in origin with Devil's Brook. To this may be added some early forms for the village of

Dewlish: *Devenis* 1086 DB, *Deueliz* 1194 P, 1230 Cl, 1244 Ass, 1299, 1300 Ipm, 1316 FA, *Duuelis, Duueliz* 1195 P, *Deueleis* 1204 ClR, *Douelis* 1212 Fees (93), *Deuelich* 1236 Ipm, 1346 FA, *Deuelis, -lys* 1238 Pat, 1241 Cl *et passim* to 1299 Ipm, *Deuelyz* 1244 Ass, 1299 Cl, *Deflis* 1244 Ass, *Douelyz, Douyliz* ib., *Dovelz* 1245 FF, *Deuelisse* 1254 FF, *Deuelliss* 1264 Ipm, *Diuilys* 1264 Ch, *Dyvelys* 1278 QW, *Deuiliz, Dueliz* 1299 Ipm, *Doueliz* 1299 Ipm, *-lich* 1303 FA, *-lysh* 1325 Cl, *Deuelissh*, with variant spellings *-lisch, -lys(c)h* (etc.), from 1300 onwards, *Divelish* 1321 FF.

---

[1] There is a *Burdel* in Searle (p. 120), but that is according to Forssner (p. 42) only a mistranscription for *Bardel*.

These names belong to a large group of English river-names of Celtic origin, dealt with by Ekwall, ERN p. 129 ff. The meaning is 'dark stream'; see also Förster p. 209, Zachrisson, StMSpv IX, 121 and ZONF VI, 246. Devil's Brook runs, at least near Dewlish, in a deep, dark ravine, a fact which seems to account not only for its original name but also for its modern corruption, cf. Ekwall op. cit. p. 133. — On the DB form *Devenis* see Zachrisson, AN Infl. p. 128.

Chebbard Fm [tʃibəd] is *Chebbord* on Taylor's map (1765). I have not found more early forms, but the place should probably be identified with the boundary-mark (*be suðe*) *ceatwanberge* 869 (15th) BCS 526. As this form seems to be of great interest, it is to be regretted that the corresponding entry in another version (BCS 525) of the same Shaftesbury charter only gives us the curious blunder (*be suþe*) *Scaftesbury* (!). On the other hand (*on*) *shete bergh* 1019 (15th) KCD 730 possibly belongs here. If the form *ceatwanberge* is to be relied upon, it may contain a pers. name of a very rare type, *Ceatwa*, of which the corresponding strong form seems to enter into Chaceley (Wo), *Ceatewesleah* BCS 1282, see PN Wo pp. xx and 192. Zachrisson, ZONF IV, 252, looks upon these names as originally Celtic. The second el. of *ceatwanberge* is of course OE *beorg* 'hill, barrow'.

Milborne St Andrew

Milborne St Andrew 130 I 10

(*æt*) *Muleburne*, (*apud*) *Muleborn* c. 939 (copies) BCS 738, 739,
  Muleburne 1264 FineR, 1334 FF, -*born* 1285 FA
Meleburne 1086 DB, 1256 FF, -*born* 1263 Misc
Muleburn(e) St. Andrew 1294, 1307 FF, *Mileburne Sci Andree*
  t. Edw I BM I, *Milborne Seint Andrewe* 1391 FF
Muleburne and Chercheton 1297 FF
Milburnchyrcheton St. Andrew 1318 FF
Mylbourne Churcheton 1417 FF; *Milborne Churcheton* 1436 FF,
  Milbo(u)rne Chircheston 1469 IpmR, 1481 FF
Milborne Churcheston al. *Milborne Sanct' Andreæ* 1484 IpmR

Named from the same brook as Milborne Stileham *supra* 70. *Milborne Churcheston* was the old name of the S part of the village, including the church of St Andrew.

Deverel Fm

Muleborn, -burn 1261 FF, 1264 Ipm, 1303 FA, *Mul(l)ebourne*
t. Edw I-II, 1340, 1358 BM I, *Mul-* 1346 FA
Muleburn Deverel(l) 1316 FA, 1332 Cl, 1347 Cl
Milbo(u)rn(e) Deverel(l) 1332 Misc, 1412, 1431 FA, *Milbourne*
1428 FA, *Mileborne* 1477 BM I
Milborne Deverell al. *Milborne Cary* 1478 FF

See the preceding name. Elyas de *Deverel* held land here in
1303 (FA), but considerably earlier (1261 FF p. 165) we find
Elyas and John de *Deverel* (father and son) as parties to a fine
concerning land *inter alia* in *Muleborn* and *Hulle Deverel*. The
family consequently came from Hill Deverill (W). In 1346 (FA)
Thomas de *Cary* held the land here which was formerly held
oy Elyas de Deverel.

Milborne Michelston (lost)[1] is *Mul(e)born Micheleston* 1316 FF,
1326 Misc, *Muleburn* 1320 Ch, *Muleburn Michelston* 1325 Orig,
1328 FF, *Mulbourne* al. *Milborn Michelston* 1325 Inq aqd, *Milborne Michelston* 1412 FA, *Mylbourne Mycheleston* 1417 FF. See
the parish name. Since there does not seem to have been any
church here dedicated to St Michael, the additional name is
probably feudal in origin. There seems formerly to have been
also a *Milbourne Simondeston* (1481 FF) in this parish, but
nothing is otherwise known about it (cf. Hutchins II, 593).

Piddlehinton

Piddlehinton 130 I 7

Pidele called Hinctune 1082-4 France
Pidele 1086 DB, 1100-6 France, *Bidele* 1100-4 France
Hinepedel, Hinepidel, Hynepide, Pidel Hineton 1244 *Ass*
Hine Pudele 1285 FA, *Hynepudele* 1291 Tax *et passim* to 1431
     FA, *Honi-, Honypedele* 1361, 1363 Cl
Pudele Hynton 1368 Cl, *Pydelhenton* 1440 IpmR

See Affpuddle *supra* 166. *Hine* and *Hin(e)ton* go back respectively to OE *hīgna*, gen. plur. of OE *hīwan* 'members of a family
or of a monastic community', and *hīgna + tūn*; cf. Tarrant Hinton

---

[1] Probably to be kept apart from the equally lost *Michel's Fm* (a modern
name) in Dewlish, cf. Hutchins II, 592, 607.

and Hinton Martell *supra* 59, 81. Piddlehinton belonged to the abbey of Marmoutier (Tours).

Muston Fm

Musterston 1303, 1431 FA, *Mousterston* 1346 FA, *Mustreston* 1412 FA, *Mousterton* 1428 FA
Pudelemusters 1339 FF, *Pudelmusterton* 1364 Cl
Mystereston (*in par.* de *Pydelhenton*) 1440 IpmR

Richard de *Musters* held land in *Musterston* in 1303 (FA), but as early as 1244 (*Ass* 201 m. 10) there is mention of a Ric. de *Musters de Pydel* under this hundred. That the family must have resided hereabout even a century earlier, can be seen from the name of Robert de *Must(i)ers* (*Monasteriis*), witness to three of the Montacute charters (Nos 118, 124, 126) mentioned in connexion with *Bardolfeston infra.* Cf. also Winterborne Muston *supra* 71.

Little Puddle[1] al. **Combe Deverel** (lost)

Litele Pudele, -pidele c. 939 (copies) BCS 738, 739
Litelpidel(e), Litelpidre 1086 DB, Exon (-*a*)
Lit(e)lepidele 1212 Fees (90), 1256 FF, *Littlepidel* 1251 Ch (with later variants *Pudele, Pydele*)
Parva Pidele 1235-6 Fees (425)
Combe Deverell al. *Deverell Combe* al. *Litelpukill* (*Lytylpudyll* etc.) 1456, 1465 IpmR, 1462 FF

Matilda de *Deverel* held a sixteenth part of a fee here in 1303 (FA). She belonged to the *Deverel* family discussed in connexion with Deverel Fm *supra* 174; cf. also Hutchins II, 619.

Puddletown

Puddletown[2] [pʌdltaun, pidltaun] 140 E 8
(*at*) *Vppidelen, uppidele* 966 (15th) BCS 1186[3]

---

[1] Little Puddle Hill (1″), Little Puddle Fm (6″).

[2] To Hardy readers it may be of interest to mention that the ancient camp 3½ m. NE of Puddletown (in Milborne Stileham parish) which is now called **Weatherby Castle** on the maps, appears on the earliest OS map of 1811 as *Weatherbury Castle.* 'Weatherbury' is Hardy's name for Puddletown.

[3] These forms refer to some place on the river Piddle which cannot now be exactly identified. They probably correspond to *Pidele* DB f. 78 b (*Pidela*

Piretone, Pitretone 1086 DB, Exon (*Pidređone*)

Pideltona t. Hy II BM I, *Pideleton* 1212 Fees (93) *et passim*,
   Pideltun, -ton 1219 Fees (261) *et passim*
Pydel(e)ton 1244 *Ass et passim* to 1289 Cl
Pudel(e)ton, -tune 1285 FA, 1290 Ch *et passim*; forms in *-toune*
   occur from 1320 (Ipm) onwards
Pudeltowne 1535 VE, *Puddeltowne* 7 Eliz AD V

'The farm on the river Piddle', cf. Affpuddle *supra* 166; on
the DB spellings *Pire-, Pitretone* see Zachrisson, AN Infl. p. 142.

Bardolfeston (lost)[1]

Pidele 1086 DB, *Pidel* (*Pydele, Pudele*) *Bardolf* 1264 FineR,
   Ipm, 1348 FF, 1384 Ch, *Bardolf Pidel* 1342 IpmR
Pidele Bardolfeston 1257 Ipm, *Pudel(e) Bardolveston* 1339 Cl,
   1385 IpmR, *Puddelbardolveston* 1419 IpmR
Bardolveston 1264 Ipm *et passim, Bardolf(e)ston* 1303 FA, 1333
   SR, Bardolston 1303, 1412 FA
Bardalston, Pidele Bardalston 1285 FA, *Bardalveston* 1346,
   1428 FA, *Bardalfston* 1431 FA
Pudel Barston al. *Bardolfeston* 1594 Hutchins

According to Hutchins (II, 616) this derives its name from
"Drogo de Bardolf, who once possessed a considerable part of
it", the person meant being evidently the Drugo *Bardolf* who
appears here in the time of Edward III. From the above list
of forms, however, it is clear that the *Bardolfs* must have been
here much earlier. An earlier Drugo *Bardolf* is actually found
in connexion with Puddletown in a charter dated 1272[2], and a
still earlier Ralph *Bardolf* occurs in a charter from 1244[3] concerning land in Puddletown; it is clear that a family of this
name resided in the parish in the 13th century. A suggestion
by the editors of the Montacute Cartulary (So Rec Soc VIII,
249) that *Bardulph de Chiselburneford* (see next name) mentioned
in the Montacute charter No. 124[4] (op. cit. p. 164) may have

---

Exon p. 37) which by Eyton (p. 135 f.) is suggested to denote some part of
Puddletown.
   [1] The site is marked on the 6″ map, cf. under Burleston *supra* 171. **Bardolf
Manor,** a little further N, may be a modern restoration of the name.
   [2] Ch vol. III, 231.   [3] Op. cit. p. 228 f.   [4] Probably from about 1165.

given his name to *Bardolfeston*, seems therefore extremely likely.[1]
Other Montacute charters (Nos 118, 119, 126) show that his real
name was *Bardulph Bussel*.[2]

Little Cheselbourne al. **Cheselbourne Ford** (both lost)
>   *Ceoselburne, -a* 1086 DB, Exon, *Cheselbo(u)rn* 1285, 1303, 1346,
>   1431 FA, *Chesylburne* 1428 FA
>   *Chiselburneford(e)* t. Hy I BM I, c. 1165 Montacute
>   *Chileborneford* t. Hy I BM I
>   *Chiseburneforde* c. 1165 Montacute, *-borne-* t. Hy II BM I
>   *Cheseburn(e)ford* 1228 FF, 1244 *Ass* (p)
>   *Chesulbornford* 1244 *Ass* (p), *Cheselbornford(e)* 1285 FA, 1299
>   Ipm, *-burne-* 1300, 1315 FF

See Cheselbourne *infra*. The site of *Little Cheselbourne* or
Cheselbourne Ford was S of that place (sometimes called Long
Cheselbourne). On the form *Chileborneford* cf. Zachrisson, AN
Infl. p. 54; for occasional loss of *l* cf. e. g. IPN p. 113.

Druce Fm is *Drewes* 1431 FA and clearly contains the genitive
of the pers. name *Drew* (*Drugo*). Who this Drew was is uncertain, but Druce Fm is only a good mile from *Bardolfeston*
supra 176, and we know that there were at least two members
of the *Bardolf* family who bore that Christian name. Cf. also
the mention of land in Puddletown belonging to *Al(u)ina uxor*
Drogonis de Monte Acuto in 1219 and 1227 Fees (pp. 261, 379).

Hyde (lost) is *La Hide* 1331 Ipm, Fine, *Hide* 1384 Ch, 1431 FA.
OE *hīd* 'hide'.

Ilsington
>   *Elsangtone* 1086 DB, *Elsindon* 1244 *Ass* (p), *Elsinton* 1260 FF,
>   *Elsyngton* 1333 *SR*

---

[1] Cf. also Do Field Club XIV, 109.

[2] Cf. So Rec Soc VIII, 249, where it is also pointed out that the undertenant
of *Ceoselburna* (i. e. *Cheselbourne Ford*) in DB was Rogerus *Boisellus*, see Exon
p. 47. Bardulph *Bussel* was consequently a descendant of this Roger *Boisell*.
From the charters mentioned we can see that Bardolph Bussel and his brother
Gervase Bussel are also called respectively Bardolph de Chiselburneford and
Gervase de Watercombe. That at least the former gave up his original surname *Bussel* (*Boisell*), is clear from the fact that his descendants (Ralph *Bar-*
dolf, Drugo *Bardolf*) appear with his Christian name as their surname.

Ilsington 1257 FF, *Ilsynton* 1280 Ipm, *Ilsinton* 1285 Ch, *Il(s)-syngton* 1331 FF, 1412 FA, 1483 IpmR[1]

Probably from OE *Elesingtūn* 'farm of the descendants of *Elesa*', a well-established OE pers. name (Redin p. 95). On *e* > *i* before dentals see Jordan § 34.

Lovard (lost)

Pidele 1086 DB, *Pudele Loveford* 1285 FA
Luveford 1235-6 Fees (426), *Loveford* 1285 FA *et passim*, *Lovord(e)* 1331 Fine, Ipm, *Loue(f)ford* 1363 FF
Lufford 1303 FA, *Loford* 1331 Fine, *Lefford* 1346 FA, *Lofford* 1383 FF, 1428 FA, *Loveford* al. *Lofford* 1487 Ipm

Probably '*Lufa*'s ford', cf. Luton Fm *supra* 95.

Waterston

Pidere 1086 DB, (apud) *pidrã* Exon
Pidela Walteri 1212 Fees (93), *Walterton*' 1227 Fees (379)
Pydele Walter(e)ston 1268 FF, 1303 FA, *Pudele Walter(r)eston* 1285 FA, 1319 FF, 1326 Cl, Ipm, 1346 FA
Walter(r)eston 1285 FA, 1326 Ipm, Fine *et passim*

'*Walter*'s farm (on the river Piddle)'. I have not managed to find the *Walter* in question.

Tincleton

Tincleton 140 F 9

Tincladene 1086 DB, *Tingledon* 1201-2 FF
Hincleden, Ingleden 1244 *Ass*
Uptincleden 1257 FF, *Holetincleden* 1260 FF
Tingledene 1291 Pap, *Tyncleden* 1296 Pat
Estynkelden 1304 Orig, *Tynkelden* 1331 FF (*Est-, West-*), 1333 *SR*, 1338, 1430 IpmR (*Est*), 1431 FA
Est Tyngeldon, West Tyngeldon 1483 IpmR
Tynkelton, Tynkelden 1535 VE

The second el. is apparently OE *denu* 'valley', but the first is difficult, and I can only tentatively suggest that it may be OE *tūnincel* 'small farm' with early change of stress.

---

[1] Cf. (a wood called) *Ylsinbr*' 1289 Cl, which by the indexer of Cl is taken to belong here.

Clyffe

Clyue, Clyve c. 939 (copies) BCS 738, 739, 1310 Inq aqd
Clive, Cliue 1086 DB, Exon, 1212 Fees (90), *Clyff* 1535 VE
OE *clif* 'cliff'. The hill-side here is fairly steep.

Tolpuddle

Tolpuddle [toulpʌdl] 140 E 9
Pidele 1086 DB (f. 78 b), *Pidela* Exon (p. 37)
Tolepidele 1212 Fees (92), *Tollepidele* 1269 Misc

Later forms are without interest except to mention that the second part of the name is almost always spelt -*pud(e)le*.

As has long been known to Dorset historians[1], the first part of the name Tolpuddle derives from *Tole* (or *Tola*), the wife of a certain *Orc* or *Urk*, Edward the Confessor's *huscarl* and a great benefactor to Abbotsbury Abbey; cf. 1212 Fees (92): *Abbacia de Abbedesbir' tenet manerium de Abbedesbir' et Portesham — — et Tolepidele et Wdeton', que data fuerunt per Oro* (read *Orc*) *et Tolam uxorem suam.* Several 11th century charters confirm this entry: KCD 841 (n. d.[2]) is Edward the Confessor's permission to *Tole*, widow of *Urc* ("*Tole min man Urces lafe*"), to bequeath her land and other possessions to St Peter's at Abbotsbury, a still earlier charter dated 1024 (KCD 741, orig.) tells us that Canute the Great had given *Orc*[3] seven mansas of land at Portisham, and from KCD 772 (orig.) we see that, in 1044, he had got land in (Abbott's) Wootton. He and his wife apparently gave all their land to Abbotsbury Abbey, to which Tolpuddle (*Pidele*) belonged in the time of DB. According to Dugdale (III, 54), *Tola* was born at Rouen in Normandy.

Southover Ho (earlier *Throop*). See the discussion in connexion with Throop in Affpuddle *supra* 168, where probable early references are adduced. The name Southover itself would seem to mean 'south bank' (OE *sūð, ōfer*), the site of Southover being on the south bank of the river Piddle, whereas the village of Tolpuddle stands on the north. Cf. East and West Stour *supra* 16.

---

[1] Cf. Hutchins II, 630 and 715.

[2] Cf. Thorpe pp. 426 f., 576 f., where the date is given as 1045.

[3] In this charter as well as in KCD 942 (orig.: Thorpe p. 605 ff.) he is called *Orcy*.

XXII. Hundred of St George[1]

This is *dorecestre* (hundr.) in 1084 (GeldRoll) and (hundr.)
Sancti Georgii de Dorecestria in 1166 (RBE). In later records
(1184-5 P, 1212 Fees *et passim*) it is called (hundr.) *Sancti
Georgii* or (hundr. de) *Sancto Georgio* (*Jeorgio*). In 1346 FA we
come across (hundr. de) *Seint Georg*.
As pointed out in Hutchins (II, 533), the hundred seems to
take its name from the church of St George in Fordington.
This is called *eccl. S. Georgii in Dorcestra* in 1091 (Osmund).

Bradford Peverell

Bradford Peverell 140 F 5
   Bradeford(e) 1086 DB, 1200 RC, 1210-2 RBE, 1216 ClR, 1219
      Fees (261), 1221 ClR *et passim*
   Bradefort (?) 1175-6 France, 1212 Fees (88)
   Bradeford Peverel 1244 *Ass*, 1257 Pap *et passim*

'Broad ford', OE *brād, ford*. Robert *Peverell* got ten *libratas
terræ* in *Bradeford* from King John[2] (1200 RC p. 33) and is
frequently mentioned as tenant here up to 1227 (Fees); Andrew
Peverel who had succeeded him here in 1235-6 (Fees p. 425) is
probably identical with the Andrew Peverel noted in connexion
with Newton Peveril *supra* 115.[3]

Muckleford is *Mukelford* 1244 *Ass* (p), 1309, 1315 FF, *Mukleford*
1268 FF (p), *Mokelford* 1333 *SR*, 1372 IpmR, 1384 Cl, 1431 FA.
OE *mycel* 'great' is apparently out of the question here on phonological grounds. The strong pers. name *Mucel* is well evidenced in OE (Redin p. 142 f.), but a corresponding weak name
is not on record, and the first el. of Muckleford had therefore
better remain unexplained.

---

[1] At the end of this hundred I include, for practical reasons, the Dorchester
parishes and Frampton.
[2] Or from Richard I, cf. 1219 Fees p. 261.
[3] *Hiwes*, mentioned immediately after *Bradeford* in DB (f. 80 b), is supposed
by Eyton (p. 123 f.) to have been in this parish. That seems very doubtful.
Hiwes would seem to be from OE *hīwisc* 'land for one household', but it cannot
with certainty be identified with any of the Do names containing that word.

Whitfield Fm (6″) is *Witewell'* 1205, 1222 ClR, 1227 Fees (379), *Witewill'* 1212 Fees (88), *Whitewell* 1231, 1301, 1311 Cl, 1312 Fine *et passim, Whytewelle* 1300 Ipm, *Whetewelle* 1315 FF, *Whittewell* 1318 Fine. 'White spring', OE *hwīt, wielle*; the spring here (marked on the 6″ map) breaks out at the bottom of a chalky hill (Hutchins II, 415).[1]

Broadmayne
Broadmayne 140 H 7
   Maine 1086 DB, 1236 FF (also *Mayne*), *Meine* 1200 Cur (p)
   Brademaene 1201-2 FF, *Brodemayne* 1297 Pat *et passim*
   Mayne (Meyne) Martel 1244 *Ass*, 1280 Ipm *et passim*
   Brodemayne Martel(l) 1368 FF, 1378 Cl

See Fryer Mayne and Little Mayne Fm *supra* 154. For the *Martels* here cf. Hutchins II, 539. Eudo *Martell*, who was party to a fine concerning land in *Parva Maene* and *Brademaene* in 1201-2 (FF), is apparently identical with the first of the Martels found in connexion with Hinton Martell *supra* 81.

Charminster
Charminster 140 F 6
   Cerminstre 1086 DB, 1200-10 Osmund, *Cerminister, -tr(e)* 1091
     Osmund *et passim* to 1275 RH
   Cerneministr' 1223 ClR
   Cermenistra, -e 1223 ClR *et passim* to 1285 FA
   Cermenestre 1242 Sarum, *Cer(e)menstre* 1278 QW
   Chernminstr' 1291 Tax
   Cherministre 1291 Tax, *-mynstre* 1322 Cl *et passim* with variant
     spellings *-minstre, -menstre, -mystre*
   Charmynstre 1386 FF

'The church (OE *mynster*) on the river Cerne', cf. Hutchins II, 543, and Ekwall, ERN p. 72 f. See Cerne Abbas *infra*, and cf. also the discussion in connexion with Charborough *supra* 75.

---

[1] In Hutchins and in several indexes Whitfield Fm is sometimes called *Frome Whit(e)well*. I have never met with that name in medieval records, and, like the modern corruption Whit*field*, it is in all probability due to the fact that another place called Frome Whitfield (*infra* in Stinsford), formerly an important manor and an independent parish, is only a mile distant (on the other side of the river Frome).

Burton

  Burton' 1204 LibR (*sub Dorcestr'*), 1212 Fees (89), 1213, 1222
  ClR *et passim, Borton* 1300 Ipm
  Bourton 1343 FF (*juxta Dorchestre*), 1412 FA

OE *burhtūn*, probably from its vicinity to Dorchester.

Charlton Fm is *Cherleton* 1242 Ch *et passim* to 1346 FA, *Charleton*
1303, 1428, 1431 FA, *Charlton* (*juxta Charmynstre*) 1412 FA.
OE *ceorla-tūn* 'farm of the peasants'.

Forston

  Cerne 1086 DB (cf. Eyton p. 123 f.)
  Fosardeston'[1] 1235-6 Fees (425)
  Forsardeston 1285 FA, 1333 *SR*, 1344 FF[2]
  For(e)shardeston 1303, 1346, 1428 FA
  Fossardeston 1343, 1346 FF, *Forston* 1431 FA

This and the two following names Herrison and Pulston are
of the hybrid type discussed by Tait and included in his list
(IPN p. 131). The three places are on the river Cerne and are
surveyed under that name in DB. Forston was held in 1285
(FA) by Wm *Forsard*, but it is clear that the family bearing
that name must have been here considerably earlier; another (or
possibly the same) Wm *Fossard* occurs under this hundred in
1244 *Ass* (201 m. 12).

Herrison (6″)[3]

  Cerne 1086 DB (cf. Eyton p. 123 f.)
  Harengestun' 1224 ClR, *Haringeston* 1227 FF, *Haringston* 1235-6
  Fees (425), *Harangeston* 1285 FA
  Heryng(e)ston 1303, 1346, 1428 FA, *Lytel Herrynggeston* 1412
  FA, *Lytel Heryngston* 1431 FA
  Heringeston juxta Cherminstr' 1416 IpmR

On the family of *Harang* (or *Hareng*) see Chaldon Herring
supra 138. Philip *Hareng* was here in 1224 (ClR); cf. Winterborne Herringstone *supra* 163; he also appears in 1227 FF when

---

[1] This is the correct reading of the mysterious "*Folardestone*" (from TN) in
IPN p. 131, which should consequently be deleted.

[2] Mistranscribed as *Forfardeston.*

[3] The new county asylum just near is locally known as Herrison House.

Wm *Hareng* granted to him "all the land of Cerne which is called Haringeston"; cf. also Hutchins II, 545.

Pulston (6″)[1]

Cerne 1086 DB, *Cerna Pulli* 1166 RBE
Pulleinston' 1235-6 Fees (424), *Puleyneston* 1244 *Ass* (p), 1268
FF, *Poleynston* 1275 RH *et passim*, *Poleneston* 1285 FA,
Polayneston 1303 FA *et passim*
Pullyngeston 1492 Ipm

The second form above is taken from an interesting entry in RBE (p. 218) called *Carta Bernardi Pulli*, where the text runs: *Ego Bernardus Pullus teneo de Rege feodum unius militis — —. Feodum illud est in Dorsete et in hundredo Sancti Georgii de Dorecestria, et vocatur Cerna Pulli.* The editors of Hutchins (II, 545) have paid due attention to this passage, and they are evidently correct in identifying this Bernardus *Pullus* with the Bernard *Poleyn* (*Polein*, *Puleyn*, etc.)[2] who is frequently mentioned in connexion with Dorset in the time of Henry II (RBE *passim*). A later member of the family is Johannes *Pulein* who held one fee in *Pulleinston'* in 1235-6 (Fees) and who is also mentioned in 1212 Fees (88) and in RBE (*passim*); cf. also Wm *Polein* 1194-5, 1196-7 RBE.

Wolfeton Ho [wulftən, wouvətən]

Wulveton, *Wuluuiton'* 1235-6 Fees (425)
Wlveton 1247 FF, t. Hy III Ipm (p), 1285 FA
Wlfreton 1262 FF, *Wylweton* t. Hy III Ipm
Wolneton juxta Chermunstre 1285 FF, *Wolueton juxta Dorcestre* 1330 FF
Wulfeton 1279 Ipm, *Wolfeton* 1303, 1346, 1428 FA
Wolveton 1303 Inq aqd, 1314 Cl *et passim*
Wolverton 1326-7 Ipm, 1327, 1341 Cl, 1467 IpmR

The first el. is probably some OE pers. name beginning with *Wulf-*. More than that cannot be said, for the identification of

---

[1] Strictly speaking the name is lost. Pulston Barn is marked on the 6″ map [ed. 1903] a furlong S of Forston, but the name is unknown even to people living in the immediate neighbourhood.

[2] Latin *pullus* and *pullanus* both mean 'young animal, colt'.

184 Anton Fägersten

Wlfreton is too uncertain and the *Wolverton* references are too late to be of any real value.

Stinsford

Stinsford 140 F 7

Stiteford, Stincteford 1086 DB
Stinteford 1235-6 Fees (425), 1244 *Ass*
Stintesford 1244 *Ass* (p), t. Hy III Ipm, 1306 FF, 1346 FA
Stinchefford 1285 FA, *Stynteford* 1303 FA, 1363 Cl
Styntesford 1303 FA, 1332 Ipm, 1333 *SR*, 1340 NI, 1343 IpmR,
  1347 Cl, 1364 FF *et passim*

This name is apparently identical in origin with (*on*) *stintes-ford* BCS 567, (*æt*) *stintes forde*, (*on*) *stintes ford* ib. 699, found among the boundaries of North Newnton (W); cf. further Stinchcombe (Gl), earlier *Stintescombe* (Baddeley). Stent Fm (Sx), the home of John de *Stenth* (1332), probably belongs to this group of names, too. It has been suggested (PN Sx p. 524) that in Stent Fm we have the word *stint* (OE **stynt*), denoting first the action of *stinting* or limiting and then what is limited, a piece of pasturage or the like.[1] My own attempts at explaining Stinsford have led me in the same direction.

Bhompston Fm (6″)

Frome 1086 DB, *Frome Bonevile* 1286 Ipm, 1289 Misc
Frome Bonevileston 1285 FA, 1289 Misc *et passim*
Boamston 1811 OM

See *Frome Billet supra* 159. I have not come across any member of the *Boneville* family in direct connexion with this place, but cf. Johannes de *Boneville* 1211-2 RBE (p. 608) and Nicholaus de *Bonevill'* 1242-3 Fees (p. 754). Cf. also Bredy Fm *infra*.

Bockhampton, Higher and **Lower**

(*æt*) *Buchæmatune* 1002-14 (orig.?) KCD 708
Bochehātone 1086 DB, *bochehamtona* Exon
Bocameton 1212 Fees (88), *Buchamt'* 1213 ClR
Bochamton(e) 1228 Ch, 1285 FA, *Bokhampton* 1244 *Ass et passim*, *Bochampton* 1270, 1280 AD I *et passim*
Buketon 1269 Pat, *Bokampton* 1412 FA

[1] Cf. EDD s. v. *stint* (12) 'a limited allowance of pasturage; a cattle-grass.

This would seem to be from OE *buc(c)hǣmatūn* 'farm of the *buc(c)hām* dwellers', where *buc(c)hām* probably means 'buck-farm'.[1] Cf. Witchampton *supra* 108, Buckham *infra*, and Boughton in PN Nth p. 133.

Frome Whitfield is *Frome*, *-a* 1086 DB, Exon, c. 1200-10 Osmund, *Froma Witefeld* 1242-3 Fees (751), *Frome Wytefeuld* 1264 Ipm, *Frome Wyt(e)feud* 1275 RH, 1291 Tax, 1428 FA, *Frome Vitefell* 1285 FA, *Frome Whytefeld* 1294 Ch *et passim* with the distinctive name variously spelt *Whitefeld, Wytefeld*. See *Frome Billet supra* 159. The additional name of this *Frome* comes from its ancient lords, the first of whom, Wm de *Witefeld*, who was married to Matilda de Monasteriis[2], was here about 1200; see Osmund I, 254 and Hutchins II, 410.[3] Cf. the foot-note to Whitfield Fm *supra* 181.

Kingston

Kingeston 1247 FF, *Kyngeston* 1275 RH, 1278 QW
Kyngeston Marlevard, Kyngeston' Marlebard 1280 FF, *Kyngeston Marleward* 1303 FA
Kyngeston Crubbe 1285 FA
Kyngeston Maureward 1329 FF, 1346 FA *et passim*

'The King's farm', because an old crown demesne (Eyton pp. 73, 91). Geoffrey *Mauregard* occurs in connexion with *Kingeston* in 1247 (FF)[4]; in 1285 and 1303 (FA) Robert *Crubbe* was tenant here; cf. also Hutchins II, 561.

Stratton

Stratton 140 E 5
Stratton 1212 Fees (94), 1222, 1226 Osmund, 1275 RH, 1285 FA *et passim, Straton(e)* 1281 Ipm, 1333 SR (p)

---

[1] Derivation from OE *bōc* 'beech', as suggested in EPN (p. 6), is apparently against the evidence of early forms.

[2] This *Frome* was held in DB (f. 83 b) by Wm de Monasteriis (Eyton p. 123 f.).

[3] Hutchins incorrectly calls the family the Whitfields or Whitsends. "Whitsend" is of course merely a misreading for Whit*feud* (= -*feld*).

[4] Cf. the earlier distinctive names of Winterborne Zelstone *supra* 73 and Shipton Gorge *infra*.

'Farm by the (Roman) road', OE *stræt, tūn*, No *e* spellings have been found.

Grimstone

Grimeston 1212 Fees (94), 1285 FA, 1297 Pat, *Grimstone, Grymstone* c. 1226 Sarum, *Grimstan* 1226 Osmund
Grummeston 1275 RH, *Grymeston* 1278 QW, 1344 Inq aqd, *Grymston* 1333 *SR*, 1340 NI

'*Grim*'s farm'. *Grim*, originally a Scandinavian pers.name (cf. Björkman, Nord. Personennamen p. 50), seems to have been common all over England about the time of DB, cf. Ellis, Introd.

Langford Fm (6″) is *Langeford* 1086 DB, 1346, 1412 FA, *Langford* 1333 *SR* (p), 1392 IpmR, 1431 FA. 'Long ford', OE *lang, ford*. The identification of the DB form is perhaps not quite certain, cf. Hutchins II, 571, Eyton p. 111 f., VCH Do II, 70.

Winterborne St Martin

Winterborne St Martin 140 G 5

Wintreburne 1086 DB, *Wynterburn Sci Martini* 1244 *Ass* (p) *et passim*, *W. Seynt Martyn* 1363 Cl
Wynterbourn(e) Martyn 1356, 1386 Cl *et passim*
Martinstowne 1642-3 DorchesterR, *Martins Town* 1811 OM

See Winterborne Came *supra* 162. 'St Martin' from the dedication of its church. The popular local name is Martinstown.

Ashton Fm

Wintreburne 1086 DB, *Winterburn'*, *-born* 1236 Ipm, 1241 Cl
Winterborne Esse 1242-3 Fees (750), *Wynterborne Atthenasse* 1268 FF, *W. Hasse, W. Asse* 1285 FA, *W. Ass(c)he* 1299 Ipm, 1337 FF *et passim*, *W. Osse* [*Esse*] 1303 FA
Ashtone 1333 *SR*, *Asshton* 1431 FA
Wynterbourne Aysshton 1412 FA, *W. Asshton* 1431 FA (p), *Wynterburnassheton* 1445 FF

Cf. the preceding name. The distinctive name is from OE *æsc* 'ash-tree' (ME *atten ashe* 'at the ash-tree') with later addition of *-ton*.

Rew is *La Rewe* 1283 Ipm. From OE *rǣw* 'row', a name which gives a good description of how the houses here are situated. Cf. Woodrow *supra* 40.

Dorchester All Saints and St Peter

Dorchester 140 F 6
See *supra* 1. The parishes are of course named after their churches, cf. e. g. 1244 Fees (1388): *ecclesie Omnium Sanctorum et Sancti Petri*.

Fordington

Fortitone, -a 1086 DB, Exon, *Fortintun'* 1155 PR
Fordinton(e), -tun 1154-5, 1155-6 RBE, 1156, 1157 PR, 1159-60 P *et passim* (with later *-yn-* variants)
Fordington(e) 1155 RBE, 1205 RC *et passim, Fordingeton* 1205 ClR, *Fordyngton* 1312 Fine *et passim*[1]
'Farm of the ford dwellers', OE *fordingtūn*.

Syward Lodge [saiwəd] seems to derive its name from a 14th cent. Do family called *Syward* (< OE *Sigeweard*), of whom Roger *Syward of Dorchestre* is mentioned *inter alia* in 1365 (AD VI) and 1368 (Fine); cf. also Hutchins II, 559 f.

Frampton[2]

Frampton 130 I 4
frontone 1084 GeldRoll, *Fronton* 1252 Ch
Franton(e) Frantona(m) 1086 DB, Exon, 1174-82 France, 1190 (1332) Ch, 1204 ClR, 1351 BM I, Ch
Framton, Franthon 1156-7 France
Fromton 1187-8 P (p), 1204 FineR, 1208 ClR, 1209 LibR, 1212 Fees (94), 1230 Pat, Cl, Lib, 1244 *Ass*, 1252 Ch, t. Hy III Montacute, 1275 RH, *Frompton* 1236 Cl *et passim*

---

[1] A few occasional spellings may be added: *Fodintun'* 1158-9 P, *Forthinton'*, *Forthnton'* 1212 Fees (88, 89), *Forditon', Fodinton'* 1225 ClR, *Forthington'* 1242 Cl, *Forton* 1275 RH, *Fordyngdone* 1291 Tax, *Fardington* 1329 Pap.

[2] Frampton Liberty contains (or contained) the following tithings (Hutchins II, 276): Benville (in Corscombe), Bettiscombe, Bincombe, Burton Bradstock, Winterborne Came, Compton Valence, Frampton.

Frumpton 1242-3 Fees (1135), 1297 Pat, Cl, 1327 Cl
Fremettona 1254 BM II
Frampton 1264 Pat onwards, *Frome toun* c. 1540 Leland
'The farm on the river Frome', cf. *Frome Billet supra* 159, and Ekwall, ERN p. 166 f.

Hyde Fm (6″) is *atte Hyde* 1333 *SR* (p). OE *hīd* 'hide'.

XXIII. Whiteway Hundred

Wichteweia 1169-70 P, *-weie* 1170-1 P
Witewei(e) 1187-8 P, 1212 Fees (90), *-weye* 1265 Misc, 1285,
    1346 FA, *Wytewaye* 1244 *Ass*, *-weya* 1251-2 Fees (1266),
    -weye 1275 RH, 1285 FA *et passim*
Whytewaye 1244 *Ass*, *-weye* 1259 FF *et passim*, *Whitewey(e)*
    1270 Pat *et passim*, *Wytteweye* 1278 QW

Self-explanatory, OE *hwīt, weg.* "This hundred takes its name from the white or chalky road from Bingham's Melcombe to Hilton, where, near the top of the hill, on the left hand of the road, is or was a bush or tree on Newton farm in the parish of Hilton[1], where the hundred-courts were formerly held" (Hutchins IV, 347).[2]

Cheselbourne
Cheselbourne 130 H 8/9
(*juxta*) *Cheselburneam* 869 (15th) BCS 525
Chiselburne 869 (15th) BCS 525, 526, 1242 Sarum, 1293 Ch
Cheselburne 869 BCS 526, 942 (15th) BCS 775, 1019 (15th)
    KCD 730, 1212 Fees (87) *et passim* (later *-borne*)
(*on*) *cyselburnan* 965 (orig.) BCS 1165, (*æt*) *Ceosol burnan* ib.,
    (*in*) *Ceosolburnan* 987 (copy) KCD 656
Ceseburne 1086 DB, *Ches(e)burn* 1250 Fees (p), 1316 FA
Chuselburne 1166 RBE (p), *Chuselbourn* 1338 FF
Long Cheselburn(e) 1297 Cl, Pat, *Lang(a) Cheselborn(e)* 1402
    IpmR, 1431 FA, *Cheselborne Longa* 1456 IpmR

---

[1] For an older name of this hundred see Hilton *infra*.
[2] The editors of Hutchins' History add in a note: "More modern tradition puts this bush on the other side of the footpath in the cottage garden".

OE *ceosol*, *cisel* 'gravel, shingle' (EPN) and *burna* 'stream', some of the charter forms above referring to the stream itself. Cf. *Little Cheselbourne* or *Cheselbourne Ford supra* 177. *Long* here apparently refers to the length of the village.

Lyscombe Fm (and Bottom)

Liscombe c. 939 (copies) BCS 738, 739, 1310 Inq aqd, *Liscome*, *-a* 1086 DB, Exon, *Liscumb'* 1200 CurR (p), 1212 Fees (90), *Luyscombe* 1535 VE

Lyscombe Fm stands on a little stream, apparently the one referred to in 942 (15th) BCS 775 as (*of*) *lisebroke* and in 1019 (15th) KCD 730 as (*on*) *liscbrok*. It is very difficult to find a plausible interpretation for the first element in Lyscombe. Liscombe (Bk) is probably an exact parallel, but the tentative explanation given for that name in PN Bk p. 85 is hardly convincing; cf. also Karlström p. 61 with references to the literature on *Lis*-names.

Hilton

Hilton 130 G 9

haltone[1] 1084 GeldRoll

Eltone 1086 DB, *Heltona* Exon

Helton 1212 Fees (92) *et passim*, this being the constant form up to at least 1602 (BM I)

This is possibly a compound of OE *healh* and *tūn*, the meaning being 'farm on the hillside' or the like, cf. EPN s. v. *healh*. The lack of *a* spellings, however, is noteworthy (cf. Silton *supra* 15) and makes this suggestion very uncertain. Is OE *hēla* 'heel' (in some topographical sense) to be taken into consideration?

Aller is *Alre* 1333 SR (p). OE *alor* 'alder'.

Ansty, Higher and Lower

Anestye n. d. (early Hy III) Osmund (p), 1329 FF (p), *Ansty* 1244 *Ass* (p), *Anesti* 1275 RH (p), *Anstey* 1463 FF

OE *ānstīg* 'narrow path (path for one)', cf. EPN s. v. The *anstig* mentioned in BCS 775 was apparently not far off but can hardly have been this one itself.

---

[1] The pre-DB name of Whiteway Hundred, cf. Hutchins IV, 347, and Eyton p. 129 f.

Hatherly Fm is *Hetherle* 1227 FF. This is almost certainly a compound of the word *heather* and OE *lēah*, though the meaning of *heather* may have been somewhat different from the ordinary one now. Cf. the discussion in PN D p. 142 f.

Ibberton

Ibberton 130 E 9

Abristetone 1086 DB, *Abristentona* Exon
Hedbredinton' 1212 Fees (90)
Edbrichton 1245 Cl, *Edbrighton* 1284 Cl, *Edebrighton* 1303 FA, *Edbryghton* 1327 *SR*, *Edbriston* 1333 *SR*
Ebbrichton 1245 Ipm, *Ebrighton(e)* 1297 Cl, 1340 IpmR *et passim*, *Ebrichton* 1299 Ipm, *Ebriton* 1329 Cl, *Ebryghton* 1375 IpmR, *Ebrithton* 1391 IpmR
Edbrytyngton al. *Edbrichton* 1284 Ipm
Ethbrichinton 1285 FA
Ibrigton 1291 Tax, 1428 FA, *Ybruton* 1340 NI
Iberton 1412 FA, *Iberghton* 1428 FA, *Yberton* 1431 FA
Eberton 1442 IpmR, *Ebberton* 1479 IpmR

'Farm of *Ēadbeorht*'s dependants', OE *Ēadbeorhtingtūn*, this pl.-n. being thus identical in origin with Abberton (Wo), *Eadbrihtincgtun* BCS 1282 (cf. PN Wo p. 184 and Karlström p. 76).

Marsh Fm is *(in) le Merche* 1327 *SR* (p), *atte M'sch* 1340 NI (p). Self-explanatory, OE *mersc*.

Melcombe Horsey

Melcombe Horsey[1] 130 G 8

melecoma 1084 GeldRoll, *Mel(e)come* 1086 DB
Melecomb(ia), -cumb(e) ? 1151-7, n. d. France, 1208 Abbr
Melecum 1152-8 Montacute, *Melecumb(e)* 1198, 1199 Cur, 1205, 1207 FineR *et passim* (the usual spelling)
Melcumba 1210-2 RBE, *Melcom(e)* 1265 Misc
Milecumbe 1229 Pat, *Mellecumbe* 1303 FA
Upmel(e)cumbe 1288 Pat *et passim* (variant *-combe*)

---

[1] Under the parish-name are also included the earlier forms belonging to Bingham's Melcombe (next name), provided they appear without a distinctive epithet.

Overmelecumbe 1296 Ipm, *Overmelcombe* 1431 FA
Melcombe Horsey 1535 VE

See Melcombe Regis *supra* 162. *Up* and *Over* from its situation in relation to Bingham's Melcombe (next name). *Horsey* from its 16th cent. owners (Hutchins IV, 367, 427).

Bingham's Melcombe
Nether Melecumb 1265 BM I, *Nethermelecombe* 1300, 1310 Cl,
  Nethermelcombe 1316 Ipm, 1381 Cl, 1432 IpmR
Nithermelecumbe 1297 Pat, *Nythermellecombe* 1318 Ipm
Bynghammes Melcombe 1412 FA
Melcombe Byngham (*Bingham*) 1431 FA, 1432 IpmR

See the preceding name. The *Binghams* were here from the time of Henry III, see West Stafford *supra* 159 and cf. the detailed account of that family in Hutchins IV, 368 ff. Cf. also Woolcombe Fm *infra* (in Toller Porcorum) and Bingham's Fm *infra* (in Netherbury).

Milton Abbas
Milton Abbas 130 G 10
Middelton(e) c. 939 (copies) BCS 738, 739 *et passim*, -*tun(e)*
  s. a. 964 ASC(A), c. 1000 Saints, 1086 DB *et passim*, -*tona*,
  -*tonia* 1130 PR, 1156 RBE *et passim*
Mideltune 1086 DB (*Miteltona* Exon), -*ton* 1161-2, 1164-5 P,
  1212 Fees (90) *et passim*, *Midleton* 1201-2 Abbr
Middelton Abbatis 1298 FF, 1379 Cl

Other forms are without interest except to mention *Myd(d)elton* 1278 QW, 1291 Tax, *Medelton* 1341 Cl, *Mylton* 1428 FA. 'Middle farm', OE *middel*, *tūn*. *Abbatis* and *Abbas* from its abbey.

Bagber Fm may be *Bakebere* 1310 Inq aqd, but it is doubtful whether this reference belongs here or to Bagber in Sturminster Newton *supra* 48; cf. Hutchins IV, 339 f., 398. The two names are presumably identical in origin.

Chescombe Fm is *Churchecombe* (twice) 1539 Hutchins (IV, 411). Self-explanatory, if this single early reference can be relied upon. The church in question seems to have been that of Winterborne Whitchurch.

Hewish Fm may be *Huyshe* 1539 Hutchins (IV, 411), but since this place and the present Huish Fm in Sydling St Nicholas *infra* probably both belonged to Milton Abbey, it is difficult to be sure about the identification; cf. Hutchins IV, 398, 503. At any rate both names go back to OE *hiwisc* 'land for one household'.

Stoke Wake

Stoke Wake 130 F 8/9
> *Stoche* 1086 DB, *Stok(e)* 1212 Fees (87), 1333 *SR*
> *Stoke Wak(e)* 1285, 1316 FA, 1360 Cl, IpmR *et passim*
> *Stoke Cosin* 1288 FF, *Stock Cofyn* (sic) 1291 Tax
> *Stok in Blakemore* 1290 Ch
> *Stoke Wake* al. *Cofyn* (sic) 1428 FA

OE *stoc* 'place'. For the family names of *Wake* and *Cusin* cf. East and West Stour *supra* 16, Ralph *Wake* being the first of the former family found here, too (1285 FA). Thomas *Cosin* was here in 1288 (FF).

Woolland

Woolland 130 F 9
> *Wonlonde* c. 939 (copies) BCS 738, 739
> *Winlande* 1086 DB, *Winlanda* Exon
> *Wunlanda* 1169-70, 1170-1 P, *Wunland* 1231 FF
> *Wuland'* 1212 Fees (90)
> *Woulond(e)* 1285 FA, 1310 Inq aqd, *Wouland* 1310 Inq aqd,
>   *Woullond, Wullond* 1535 VE, *Wollande* 1539 Hutchins

I am unable to suggest a plausible explanation of the first el.; a possible parallel is Winbrook in PN D p. 185.

Chitcombe Fm (6″) is *Chidecombe* 1327 *SR* (p), *Chidcombe* 1811 OM. This may be '*Cidda*'s valley' (OE *cumb*), the pers. name *Cidda* being on record in Cal. of St Willibrord f. 37 b (cf. Mawer, Problems of PN Study p. 100). *Chide-* (1327) might however have developed from an older *che(o)de*; if so, it should be compared with the el. discussed under Cheddington *infra*.

XXIV. Cerne, Totcombe and Modbury

Under this heading I include what in the Geld Roll of 1084 is called the hundred of *stane* (Exon p. 20)[1], comprising the later hundreds of Cerne, Totcombe and Modbury, and the liberties of Alton Pancras and Piddletrenthide; cf. Eyton p. 143.[2] For early forms of Cerne, see Cerne Abbas *infra*.

Totcombe

Totecumbe 1130 PR, 1160-1, 1167-8 P
Tottecumb' 1207 RC, 1208 FineR, -*comb* 1333 *SR*, 1340 NI
Totcumb(e) 1244 *Ass*, -*combe* 1265 Misc, 1327 *SR*, 1535 VE
Cotescumb (sic) 1278 QW

This must mean '*Tot(t)a*'s valley', OE *cumb*. For this pers. name cf. Redin p. 70 f. Totcombe cannot now be found on the OS maps, but according to Hutchins (IV, 1) it is "a valley west of the great road from Sherborne to Dorchester, near the bounds of Cerne and Nether Cerne". "The court was usually opened at Totcombe, and from thence adjourned to Cerne" (ib. note b).

Modbury

morb'ge 1084 GeldRoll
Modberg(e) 1207 RC, 1230 P, 1244 *Ass*, 1333 *SR*, 1340 NI
Medberg' (sic) 1208 FineR, *Mothberghe* 1244 *Ass*
Motberge 1265 Misc, *Motbergh* 1278 QW
Modbarugh, Madeboroughe 1535 VE

This is in all probability OE *(ge)mōtbeorg* 'barrow of meeting', as suggested in Hutchins (IV, 1 note b), cf. Motcombe *supra* 28, and Modbury *infra* (in Swyre). I cannot find Modbury on the maps, but it is stated in Hutchins to be a barrow "on the hill north-east of Cattistock, between that and Cerne".

Alton Pancras

Alton Pancras [ɔːltən] 130 G 7
Altone 1086 DB, *Alton* 1428 FA

---

[1] The site of this 'stone' is impossible to trace now.
[2] What in 1084 belonged to the hundred of *morb'ge* (i. e. Modbury) is of course also included here.

Aulton 1091 Osmund, c. 1160 Sarum (*-tona*), 1272 FF, 1285 FA, 1291 Tax *et passim* to 1431 FA
Awoltona c. 1160 BM II, *Awelton(e)* c. 1160 (etc.) Osmund, 1216 ClR, c. 1226 Sarum, 1272 FF, *Auelton* 1226 Osmund
Aweltone Pancratii c. 1226 Sarum, *Aulton Pancras* 1372 FF

OE *āewiell-tūn* 'farm by the river-spring' (EPN); the river Piddle rises here. *Pancras* from the dedication of the church to *St Pancratius* (Hutchins IV, 461).

Barcombe Fm is *Berecombe* 1333 *SR* (p). 'Barley-valley', OE *bere, cumb.*

Holcombe Fm
Holancumb 998 KCD 701, (*æt*) *Holancumbe* 1002-14 KCD 708, c. 1006 KCD 1302
(*æt*) *Holacumbe* 1046 KCD 1334, 1050-73 KCD 940, n. d. Thorpe (p. 639), *Holcombe* 1480 IpmR, 1495 Ipm

'(At the) hollow valley', OE (*æt þæm*) *holan cumbe*. I have followed Thorpe in his identifications of the OE forms above[1], but I am not quite sure he is right. The identification of *Holacumbe* in KCD 940 and Thorpe p. 639 is particularly doubtful; the other forms occur in Sherborne charters (12th) and may very well belong here, since this is the only Holcombe in Dorset.

Watcombe Bottom is *whetecombe* 891 (14th) BCS 564. 'Wheat valley', OE *hwǣte, cumb*; cf. Whatcombe *supra* 68.

Cattistock
Cattistock 130 H 3
Cattesstoke c. 939 (copy) BCS 738: *Stoke* ib. 739
Stoche 1086 DB (*Estocha* Exon), *Stok'* 1212 Fees (90)
Cattestok(e) 1291 Pap, Tax *et passim*, *Catestock* 1298 FF, *-stok(e)* 1310 Inq aqd, 1369 Cl, *Catstoke* 1487 Ipm

The second el. is OE *stoc* 'place', but it is difficult to decide whether the first is an unrecorded pers. name **Catt*, as assumed in PN Sx p. 216 (s. n. Catslands Fm), or the name of the animal itself; cf. also Mawer, MLR XIV, 237, and PN BedsHu p. 236 f.

[1] KCD 701=Thorpe p. 294, KCD 1302=Thorpe p. 300, KCD 1334=Thorpe p. 346, KCD 940=Thorpe p. 428.

(s. n. Catworth). What in the present case seems to me to
tell in favour of a pers. name is the fact that Cattistock is
called *Stoke* alone as late as 1212, the form *Cattesstoke* in BCS
738 being in all probability very late. The first el. may consequently have been prefixed during the course of the 13th century when we have evidence of the existence of *Cat* as a surname in England; cf. Robertus *Cat* 1178-9 P, Willelmus *Cat* or
Cattus 1179-80 *et passim* P, Ricardus *le Cat* 1185-6 P. Cf. Catsley
Fm *infra*.

Bestedon (lost) is *Byestedon* 1300 Pat, *Bestedene, Betesdon* 1310
Inq aqd, *Bestedone* 1312 Hutchins (IV, 3). OE *bī ēastan dūne*
'to the east of the down', cf. Bestwall *supra* 146.

Chalmington

> *Chelmyntone* c. 939 (copy) BCS 738: *Chelmingtone* ib. 739
> *Chelminton'* 1212 Fees (90), *Chelmington* 1268 FF
> *Chalminton* 1310 Inq aqd, *Chalmyngton* 1412 FA

An -*ing* name containing either *Cēolhelm* or *Cēolmund*, well
recorded OE pers. names, see Zachrisson, Vising Celebr. Vol.
p. 198 f., and Karlström p. 73.

Chantmarle [tʃɑ:ntmɑ:l] apparently takes its name from a family
called *Chantemerle*. The first of its members that I have met
with in Do is Robert *Chantemerle* (1210-2 RBE, 1219 FF, etc.),
also called Rob. *de Cha(u)ntemerle*.[1] He as well as other members
of the *Chantemerle* family occur from time to time in entries
referring to this part of Do (e. g. in 1244 *Ass* under the adjacent
hundred of Yetminster), and from the beginning of the 14th
century the place itself is called *Chammerle* (1310 Inq aqd),
Chauntemerle (1332, 1384 FF) or *Chauntemerle maner'* (1483
IpmR). Cf. also Hutchins (IV, 4 f.) where, however, the account
is somewhat misleading.

Dudley Moor (lost) is *Dudelesheia* 1206 RC, *Dudleshey* 1268 FF,
Doudeleshegh 1310 Inq aqd. '*Dud(d)el*'s enclosure', OE *(ge)hæg*.
The OE diminutive pers. name *Dud(d)el* is fairly well evidenced
(Redin p. 140).

---

[1] For this name — common as a place-name in France — cf. Schultz-Gora,
Herrig's Archiv 152 (1927) p. 51 f.

Hewdon (lost)[1] is *Hevelden', Heveldan'* 1206 RC, *Heuedon* 1332 FF, *Henedon* (sic) 1384 FF. The second el. is apparently OE *dūn* 'down', but the first must be left unexplained.

Holway Fm is *Holeweia* 1206 RC, *Holewey(e)* 1291 Tax, 1535 VE, *Holloweye* 1310 Inq aqd. 'The way (road) in the hollow', OE *holh, weg*.

Merryfield (6″) is *Murifeld* 1333 *SR* (p). 'Pleasant field', OE *myrig, feld*. Another Dorset *Mirifeld* is mentioned in 1227 FF in the vicinity of Iwerne Minster.

Witcham Fm (6″) is *Witham* (sic) 1310 Inq aqd, *Wicham* 1578 Hutchins. See *wīc* and *wīcham* in EPN.

Cerne Abbas

Cerne Abbas 130 H 5

The place takes its name from the river Cerne (*aqua de Cerne* 1244 *Ass*), for which see Ekwall, ERN p. 72 ff. We should have expected a form *Cherne*[2] (cf. the early forms for Charmouth *infra*) but, instead, the form *Cerne*, showing AN [ts] substituted for English [tʃ][3], is found from DB and up to the present time. By the side of *Cerne*[4], however, there occurs a form *Cernel* (987 (copy) KCD 656, c. 1006 (12th) KCD 1302, 1086 DB *et passim* to 1300 Pap), once spelt *Cirnel*.[5] Zachrisson, who deals with this and similar *l*-formations in his Latin Infl. on English Place-nomenclature (p. 24 ff.), considers them to be the result of an AN addition of *l*; cf. also IPN p. 94. From the form *Cernel* there was at a very early date created a Latin form *Cernelium* (Exon p. 33).[6] The distinctive addition *Abbatis*, re-

---

[1] "The closes called Hewdon, or Chantmarle Farm, adjoin Evershot" (Hutchins IV, 7).

[2] Actually found in Holinshed's Chronicle of 1577 (not accessible to me), see Ekwall, loc. cit.

[3] See Zachrisson AN Infl. pp. 18 f. and 30, with discussion of the etymology in foot-note to p. 19.

[4] A few early forms (from 1086 DB to 1210-2 RBE) show the Latin ending *-a*; cf. also the following spellings with initial *s*: *Sernes* 1265 Misc, *Serne* 1316, 1338, 1360 Cl, 1396 IpmR.

[5] 1190 (1332) Ch (vol. IV p. 271).

[6] This reference corresponds to the form *Cerneli* in DB (f. 77 b); cf. the adjective (abbas) *Cerneliensis* DB, (carta abbatis) *Cernelensis* 1166 RBE (from LN)

ferring to the ancient abbey here, occurs from 1291 (Tax) onwards.

Nether Cerne

Nether Cerne 130 H 6

Nudernecerna 1206 RC, *Nudercerne* 1244 *Ass* (p)
Nithercerne 1291 Tax, 1318 Ch

See the preceding name. The distinctive epithet is from OE *neoðera* (-*i*-, -*y*-) 'nether, lower'; cf. Up Cerne *infra*.

Compton Abbas

Compton Abbas[1] 140 E 2

Comptone c. 939 (copy) BCS 738: *Cumptone* ib. 739
Contone 1086 DB (*Contona* Exon)
Cumbton' 1212 Fees (90), *Cumpton Abbatis* 1291 Tax
Compton(e) 1291 Tax *et passim*, *West Compton* 1811 OM

'Valley farm', OE *cumb, tūn*. This Compton belonged to Milton Abbey; hence the distinctive name.

Godmanstone

Godmanstone [gɔdmənstoun] 130 I 5/6

Godemanestone 1166 RBE, *Godemanston* 1302 Ipm
Godmanneston 1184-5 P (p), 1250 Cl, FF *et passim*
Godmaneston 1201-2 FF, 1242-3 Fees (750) *et passim*
Godmarineston' (sic) 1235-6 Fees (425)
Godmanston 1297 Pat, 1303 FA *et passim*, *Godmastone* 1340 NI

'The farm of *Godman(n)*', a well recorded OE pers. name. Godmanstone is on the river Cerne and is, according to Eyton p. 133 f., assessed under that name (*Cernel*) in DB (f. 79 a). If that is correct, Godmanstone may be a name of post-Conquest origin; cf. Forston, Pulston and Herrison (*supra* 182 f.) further down on the river.

The Cartulary of Cerne Abbey shows the whole series of French and Latin forms: *Cerne, Cernel*, (conventus) *Cernelii, de Cernelio, Cernelien(sis)*; cf. also the forms (monacho) *Cernensi*, (in abbatem) *Cernensem* from 1232 Pat.

[1] There are two places called Compton Abbas in Do. This one is sometimes called Compton Abbas West to distinguish it from Compton Abbas in the NE part of the county near Shaftesbury (see *supra* 21).

Gorewood (130 F 5)

This is an exceptionally small civil parish (51 acres), surrounded by the parish of Minterne Magna. It is — or was at least in 1911 — without population. The wood itself is called **Gore Wood** on the 6″ map. I have seen no earlier form of the name than *Gorewood* 18 Eliz (Hutchins), but there can be no doubt that the first el. is OE *gāra* 'triangular piece of land', the triangular form being clearly seen on the parish maps. Cf. Gore Fm *supra* 42.

Hermitage

Hermitage 130 F 5

The first mention of this priory or hermitage, a house of the friar hermits of St Augustine, is from 1300 Ipm (*Blakemore. A hermitage in the forest*), when Edmund, earl of Cornwall, was its patron; cf. Hutchins IV, 466 f., where a detailed account is given. A few more references may be added: (*Prior*) *Hermitagii de Blakemore* 1329 Orig, *le Hermytage in Blakamore* 1513 Ch, *Ermytage* 1535 VE; cf. also next name. *Blakemore* of course refers to Blackmoor Forest *infra*.

Rocombe (lost) is *Racumba* 1230 Lib, (in bosko de) *Rokcumbe* 1244 *Ass*, *Rocumbe* t. Hy III (14th) Cerne, 1314 Pat, 1315 Orig, Pat, 1321 Cl, *Rocombe* 1314 Fine, 1315 Orig, 1325 Pat, Orig, Inq aqd. This must be OE *rā-cumb* 'roe-buck valley'; cf. Rocombe in PN D p. 461. There is a very tentative suggestion in Hutchins (IV, 466) that *Rocombe* may have been the original name of the valley where the hermitage was founded. From the context of some of the above references there can be little doubt that such was the case; cf. in particular 1315 and 1325 Pat.[1]

---

[1] "Grant to the prior and friars hermits of Blakemore of 8 acres of land — — out of the waste in the king's forest of Blakemore, co. Dorset, in a place called 'Rocumbe' — —. License also for them to enclose the same at their will with a little dyke and low hedge according to the assize of the forest, and to reduce it to cultivation" (1315 Pat p. 336).

Hillfield

Hillfield 130 F 4/5

Hylfelde c. 939 (copy) BCS 738: *Hylefeyld* ib. 739
Hulfeld(e) 1212 Fees (90), 1310 Inq aqd, 1344, 1352 FF
Hul(l)feud 1244 *Ass*, *Hulefeild* 1333 *SR*
Hullefeld 1412 FA, *Hilfeld*, *Hylfeld* 1535 VE

Self-explanatory, OE *hyll, feld.*

Minterne Magna

Minterne Magna 130 G 5

Minterne 987 (copy) KCD 656, 1258 Pap, 1291 Tax, 13th
Glaston C, 1296, 1314, 1315 Pat, 1318 Ch, *Mynterne* 1291
Tax, 1333 *SR et passim* to 1428 FA

If this is an English name, the only suggestion I can make is
that it may be a compound of OE *minte* 'mint' (Latin *mentha*)
and OE *ærn* 'house', the whole name thus meaning 'store-house
for mint'. But can it be supposed that this plant was used to
such an extent that a special shed was needed to keep it?
Alternatively the first el. might be OE *mynet* 'coin, money' (Latin
moneta), but nothing is known of a mint here. *Magna* in distinc-
tion from Minterne Parva *infra* (in Buckland Newton).

Dogbury Gate

(*on doggeneford panen up on*) *doggeneberwe* 941 (14th) BCS 768
Doggebery 1270 Hutchins (Forest Pleas, PRO)

'The dogs' hill', OE *docgena beorge* (dat.), cf. Middendorff p. 42.
It may be of interest to note that *docga* 'dog' is otherwise evidenced only once in OE, viz. in the gen. plur. *docgena* as a gloss
to *canum* (Prudentius Glosses), see B.T. and NED.

Hartley Fm

Herleg' 1212 Fees (88), *Ertleg'* 1227 Fees (379)
Hertlegh(e) 1223 ClR, Pat, 1229, 1231 Cl *et passim*, -*leye* 1313
Ipm, Cl, 1314, 1315 Pat, -*leygh* 1412 FA
Hurtl', *Hertl'* 1238 Cl, *Hertelegh* 1244 *Ass*, 1274 Ipm
Heortleghe t. Hy III (14th) Cerne, *Hartleygh* 1431 FA

'Hart-clearing' OE *heorot, lēah.*

Middlemarsh is *Middelmer(s)sh* 1227 FF *et passim, Middelmers* 1244 *Ass* (p), *Midelmersh* 1318 Ch.   Self-explanatory, OE *middel, mersc.*

High Stoy

Staweyesfote 1270 Hutchins (Forest Pleas, PRO)
Staweius jwinde t. Hy (14th) Cerne[1]
Stowefcte 1300 Hutchins (IV, 517)

This is in all probability OE *stānweg* 'stony road' with the same loss of *n* before a labial consonant as has been noted in Stoborough and Stafford *supra* 130, 159. High Stoy would consequently be of the same origin as the different places called Stowey in Somerset, see Ekwall's paper (p. 22) on this phenomenon in the Klaeber Celebr. Vol. *-fote* in the first and third of the above references is self-explanatory, and *jwinde* in the second is apparently OE *gewind* 'a winding, circuitous ascent', a very appropriate designation for the road which leads up to High Stoy.

Tiley is *Tylly* 1244 *Ass* (p), *Tiley(e)* 1264, 1299 Ipm, *Tyley(e)* 1299 Ipm, Cl, 1325 Cl, 1326 Ipm, *Tilee (juxta Donetish)* 1314 FF, *Tilloye' Tilleye* 1314, 1315 Pat (p), *Tylleye* 1321 FF, *Tylleygh* 1336 IpmR, *Tyle* 1339 FF, 1346 IpmR. This must be a compound of OE *tigel* 'tile' and *lēah* (dat. *lēage*) 'clearing', cf. (*on*) *tigel leage* BCS 764 and (*an, of*) *tihel leahe* ib. 982 (both Ha). It should be noted that Clinger *infra*, containing the word *clay*, is only a mile away. *Donetish* is Duntish *infra*.

Piddletrenthide

Piddletrenthide 130 H 7
Pidrie 1086 DB (f. 77 b), *Pidele* n. d. Dugdale II, 436[2]
Pidele Trentehydes 1212 Fees (92)
Pydele Trentehide 1288 FF, *Pudele Trentehyde* 1323-4 BM I
   (*et passim*), *Pideltrenthide* 1404 Inq aqd, *Pudeltrenthithc* 1412 FA

---

[1] The part of the Cerne Cartulary (Peramb. of Blackmoor Forest) which contains this and several other names in this district, is reprinted *supra* 35 f.

[2] *Emma regina, uxor Adeldredi regis, mater sancti Edwardi London, dedit Pidele cum triginta hidis* ("Ex veteri MS. in Bibl. Cottoniana f. 30'"); cf. Hutchins IV, 485.

Trentehude, Trentehyde 1291 Tax, *Trentehude* 1428 FA
Pydele Thryttyhide 1306 Ch, *Pudele thrittyhide* 1314 FF, *Pudel-
thrntihide* (sic) 1342 Cl, *Pydelthrettyhide* 1348 Cl

Named from its situation on the river Piddle, cf. Affpuddle
supra 166.[1] It was assessed at *thirty hides* in DB (cf. also the
quotation from Dugdale in the foot-note); hence the distinctive
name, see Hutchins IV, 485, and EPN s. v. *hid.* For *r* in the
DB form cf. Zachrisson, AN Infl. p. 142. The struggle between
the French and the English word for 'thirty' (ME *thritti*) resulted
in the victory of the former, cf. Mawer, PN and History p. 22.

Sydling St Nicholas

Sydling St Nicholas 130 H 4

Sidemyntone[2] c. 939 (copy) BCS 738: *Sidelyng* ib. 739
Sidelince 1086 DB (*Sidelincea* Exon), 1244 *Ass* (p)
Sedelinch 1190 (1332) Ch, *Sidelinz* 1200, 1201, 1211 Cur, *Syde-
lich'* 1234 Fees (399), *Sidelinche, Sydelynche* 1291 Tax, *Syde-
linch* [*Sylinche*] 1303 FA
Sideling(e) 1212 Fees (90), 1227 FF, ClR *et passim, Sydeling*
1227 ClR, 1234 Cl, 1256 FF, *Sedeling* 1271 Pat
Brodesideling(e) 1268, 1302 FF *et passim* (with small spelling
variants), *Broad Sidlinch* 1333 Hutchins

OE (*æt*) *sīdan hlince* '(at) the broad hill'.[3] This derivation,
already suggested by Ekwall (PN in *-ing* p. 30), suits the topography excellently, the place being situated at the foot of a
mighty hill-ridge, rising up to c. 700 ft. *St Nicholas* from the
dedication of the church.

Ellston Hill is *Helistun* 1227 FF, *Eliston* 1310 Inq aqd, *Eleston*
1327 *SR, Elyston* 1383 FF. This would seem to mean 'the farm
of *Eli*', but the forms are not early enough to allow of absolute
certainty. The farm itself seems to have disappeared altogether
after having left its name to this hill.

---

[1] The river Piddle has an alternative name *Trent* (at least on the maps).
For the possible connexion between that name and Piddle*trent*hide, cf. Hutchins
IV, 486, 487 (with foot-note), and Ekwall, ERN p. 416.

[2] For this clearly miswritten form cf. Karlström p. 74.

[3] Cf. also some of the earlier forms for Up Sydling *infra* (this parish).

Fifehead Sydling (local)[1] is *Sidelince* 1086 DB (f. 79 b), *Viffhide* 1333 *SR.* See the parish-name, and cf. Fifehead Magdalen *supra* 4.

Halfhide (lost) is *La Halfehid* 1310 Inq aqd, *Helfehide* 1344 FF, *Halfhyde* 1365 Cl, 1489 Ipm, *Halfhide* 1378 FF, *Halfehede* 1455 FF. Self-explanatory, OE *healf, hīd.*

Huish Fm may be *Huysshe* 1535 VE (I, 249), but see Hewish Fm *supra* 192.

Up Sydling

Upsidelinch 1230 FF, 1244 *Ass, Up Sidelinch* 1346 FA
Upseteling 1235-6 Fees (425), *Upsedeling* 1282 Cl
Upsydeling(e), -lyng 1300 Pat, 1333 *SR et passim*
Upsidlinge 1310, 1324 Inq aqd, *Upesydelenge* 1398 IpmR
Other forms are without interest.

See the parish name; Up Sydling is both to the north of and higher up than Sydling St Nicholas.

XXV. Buckland Newton Hundred

bochene 1084 GeldRoll
Bochelande 1086 DB, 1159-60 P, *Bokeland* 1167-8 P, 1212 Fees (94), *Boclaunde, Boklaund* 1244 *Ass, Bocland(e)* 1265 Misc, 1316 FA, *-londe* 1303 FA, 1327 *SR*
Bouclond(e) 1340 NI, 1346, 1431 FA

See Buckland Newton *infra* (next name).

Buckland Newton

Buckland Newton 130 F 6
Boclonde, -lande 941 (14th) BCS 768, 951 (14th) ib. 889, 1242-3 Fees (750), 1264 FineR, 1275 Cl *et passim*
Bok(e)londe, Bokelande 966 (14th) BCS 1177, *Bochelande* 1086 DB, *Bokeland'* 1212 Fees (94), *-lond* 1428 FA

---

[1] Not on the maps but preserved as the name of a tithing in Sydling St Nicholas (Kelly); cf. Hutchins IV, 502: "Up-Sydling is properly the farm, and Fifehide the hamlet adjoining."

Boclaund(e) 1264 Ipm, 1275 FF, 1280 Ch
Buklonde 1330 Ch, *Bouclaund* 1333 *SR*, *-lond* 1346 FA
Buckland al. *Newton Buckland* 1575-6 Hutchins

OE *bōcland* 'land granted by book or charter'; cf. Buckland
Ripers *supra* 157. For the late addition *Newton* cf. the discussion
under Sturminster Newton Hundred *supra* 40. An alternative
addition *Abbas* (Hutchins) is due to the fact that the place anciently belonged to Glastonbury Abbey.

Brockhampton Green is *Brochamtune, -ton'*, *Brechamtune* 13th
Glaston C, *Brochamton* 14th Glaston F, *Brochampton* 1333 *SR*.
'Home farm by the brook', OE *brōc*, *hāmtun* (EPN); cf. Brockington
Fm *supra* 93.

Chaston Fm is *Chawson* 1811 OM and is called *Chawson* or
Chalveston in Hutchins. The clue to this name is apparently to
be found in an entry in Glaston F (p. 47) where we are told
that, about the year 1343, Richard and Wm *Chavel* held one
half of a virgate each of the abbot of Glastonbury in Brockhampton in Buckland, for which Peter *Chavel* paid 2 s. 6 d.
There can be little doubt that the present Chaston Fm, which
lies only ¼ m. from Brockhampton Green, took its name from
that *Chavel* family, this being confirmed by the form *Chalveston*
in Hutchins which evidently stands for an earlier **Chavelston*.[1]

Clinger Fm is *Clehangr'* 1206 RC, *Cleha(n)ger* 13th Glaston C (p),
Cleyhangre 1310 Inq aqd. This is a compound of OE *clǣg*
'clay' and *hangra* '(wooded) slope', a common English pl.-n.,
mostly in the form Clayhanger (EPN). There are two Dorset
Clayhangers on the 1″ map, but I have found early forms for
neither of them.

Duntish
Dunhethis 1249 FF, *Dunethis* t. Hy III (14th) Cerne
Dunetes (*in manerio de Boclande*) 13th[2] Glaston C

---

[1] In their account of the history of Brockhampton the editors of Hutchins
(III, 694) quote the same Glastonbury entry (from the MS), yet without disco-
vering its interesting connexion with the name and history of Chaston.
[2] Probably 1252-61 (cf. Ekwall, Studies on PN p. 73).

Dunedisse, Dunetisse, Duntisse 1264 Ipm (p. 181)
Dundisse 1264 FineR, *Dundys* 1303 FA, *Dundissh* 1346 FA,
  Doundyssh 1428 FA
Dunetys 1280 Ch, *Dontetis* 1284 Pat
Donetis(s)he 1289 Ch, Abbr, *Donetysse, Donetys(s)ch* 1299 Ipm,
  Donetyssh 1300 Ipm, *Donetish* 1314 FF
Duntis(s)h 1299 Ipm, 1314 Pat *et passim*, -*tich* 1315 Pat, 1316
  FA, -*tysh* 1321 FF, 1325 Cl *et passim*
Dountyssh 1299 Cl, -*tis(s)he* 1366, 1381 IpmR
Other small variations in spelling are without interest.

In my opinion this is a compound of OE *dūn* 'down, hill' and
OE *edisc* 'enclosed pasture, (deer-)park', the whole name thus
meaning '(deer-)park on the hill'.[1] The transition of *d* to *t* in
the second element should probably be explained as due to dissimilation, but to the interchange of *d*, *t* and *th* in the earliest
forms may also have contributed the fact that Duntish was for
a long time in the possession of Norman lords.[2]

Henley is *Henele(e), Henle* 1244 *Ass* (p), *Henele(e)* 13th Glaston
C, *Henlegh* 1310 Inq aqd, *Henelegh* 14th Glaston F. This is
probably from OE (*æt*) *hēan lēage* '(at the) high clearing', just
as in the case of Handley *supra* 24, though the absence of *a*
spellings and the appearance of a medial *e* in some of the early
forms might seem to point to a different derivation, cf. Encombe
supra 119. The etymology suggested is, however, decidedly in
conformity with the topography.

Knoll is *Cnolle* 13th GlastonC, 1333 *SR*, *Knolle* 1310 Inq aqd,
14th GlastonF. OE *cnoll* 'knoll, hillock'.

---

[1] It may be of interest to note that the deer-park of Duntish is often mentioned in medieval documents, cf. e. g. 1284 Pat p. 200 ("the persons who
hunted and took deer in the park of William de Gouyz at Dontetis, co. Dorset").

[2] Ekwall (Studies on PN p. 73) considers the second el. of Duntish to be
an unrecorded OE *etisc*, corresponding to Gothic *atisk*, OHG *ezzisch*, G *Esch*,
all meaning 'cornfield', and the *d* spellings (*Dunedisse*, etc.) to be due to association with OE *edisc*. I had written down the above suggestion (OE *dūn-
edisc*) long before Ekwall's Studies on PN appeared, and I do not feel inclined
to change my mind. The actual mention of a deer-park here, probably not
noticed by Ekwall, seems to me to tell greatly in favour of the well recorded
el. *edisc* ('hortus cervorum').

Minterne Parva is so spelt 1314, 1315 Pat and appears as *Parva Myntern* 1431 FF. See Minterne Magna *supra* 199.

Revels Inn Fm. The suggestion in Hutchins (III, 708) that this "seems to be the Terra Ryvel mentioned in Alured de Lincolnia's inquisition 48 Hen. III.", is evidently correct.[1] In the same year we find it called *Dundisse Rivel* (1264 FineR), and there can be little doubt that the place derives its name from a family called *Revel* or *Ryvel*, living here in the 13th and 14th cent. Peter *Revel* is mentioned as one of the seven freehold tenants in Duntish in an inquisition dated 28 Jan. 27 Edw I[2], and in two later Duntish inquisitions (18 Edw II and 10 Edw III) we meet with the names of Richard and Robert *Ryvel*; see Hutchins III, 698, 700, 705.

Buckland Newton (Det.)

Armswell

Ermingewell 1225 FF

Hermingeswll' 13th GlastonC, *Hermyngeswell'* 14th GlastonF

Ermyngyswelle 1303 FA, *Ermyngeswell* 1309 FF, 1431 FA,
    Ermyngeswoll 1346 FA, *Ermyngiswill* 1428 FA

Ermeswell 1362 IpmR

Ermeneswell 1366 IpmR, *Ermeneswill* 1412 FA

I take this to mean the 'spring (OE *wielle*) of *Eormengȳþ'*. The only bearer of this OE fem. pers. name hitherto known seems to be (Saint) *Eormengið*, daughter of Eormenred and granddaughter of King Eadbeald of Kent (7th cent.)

Monkwood Hill Fm is *Munkewod, -wdde* 1244 *Ass*, 13th GlastonC, *Monekwode* 1327 *SR*, *Monkwode* 1333 *SR* (all p). The name probably preserves some reminiscence of the ancient possessions here of Glastonbury Abbey; OE *munuc, wudu*.

Plush

Plyssche, Plusshe, Plisshe 891 (14th) BCS 564

Plyssh', Plussh' 941 (14th) BCS 768

---

[1] In the modern edition 1264 Ipm (p. 182) called "The land of Rivell".

[2] In the modern edition of Ipm this entry is to be found in vol. III p. 414, where, however, all the names of the tenants are left out, and it is therefore only thanks to the detailed account in Hutchins (III, 698) that we happen to know that the name of one of these tenants was Peter *Revel*.

Plys c. 1170 Montacute, *Plyssh'* 1333 *SR*
P'lis[1] 1201-2 FF, *Plis* 13th GlastonC (*passim*), *Plisses* 1291
Tax, *Plissh'* 1327 *SR*
Plush 1340 NI, *Plussh* 14th Glaston F, 1412 FA

This cannot be OE *plæsc* 'shallow pool, dial. *plash*', as supposed in EPN.[2] The forms above suggest instead that Plush goes back to an OE **plysc* (**plisc*), probably a variant of *plæsc* and with similar meaning; cf. ModE *plish* as a dial. variant of the verb *plash*, and Frisian *plis* by the side of *plas(se)* 'pool' (Dijkstra, Friesch Woordenboek). Plush lies in a deep valley.

Stickley Coppice (6″) and **Thorncombe** (6″) should probably be identified with the boundary-marks (*on an*) *Sticholnelniche* (sic) and (*over*) *thorncombe* 891 (14th) BCS 564, the former containing OE *sticol* 'steep', the latter being self-explanatory; OE *þorn, cumb*.

Mappowder

Mappowder 130 F 8
Mapledre 1086 DB
Mapeldra 1088-95 Bruton, 1100-3 (1332) Ch, c. 1155 Bruton, 1155-8 (1332) Ch, *Mapelel* . . 1100-7 France, (apud) *mapeldream* 1121 AC, *Mapoldre* 1189 AD IV, *Mapeldre* 1216 ClR, 1223 FF
Maupod(e)re 1227 FF, 1278 Misc, 1305 Ipm, 1310 Pap, *Maupudre* 1249 FF, 1303 FA, *Maupoudre* 1274 Pat
Mapudre 1227 FF, 1291 Tax, 1428 FA, *Mapodre* 1235-6 Fees (425), 1297 Ipm, *-pp-* 1251 Pap, *-pedre* 1281 Fine, Misc
Mapoudre 1303 FA *et passim*, *Mapowdre* 1447 BM I

OE *mapuldor* 'maple-tree' (Hutchins, EPN). The loss of *l* may be the result of French influence, and the frequent *Mau-* spellings are probably due to false association with French words beginning with *Mal* > *Mau*.

---

[1] Printed as *Perlis* in the modern ed. of FF, but the MS has *P'lis* (see Hunter's ed. of FF, London 1844, p. 83), where the scribble must be a blunder.
[2] EPN (p. 49) calls the Do name Plesh, which would undoubtedly have originated from OE *plæsc*. But there is no such pl.-n. in Dorset.

Pulham

Pulham 130 E 7

Poleham 1086 DB, Exon, 1279 Ch, *Polham* 1234 (1279) Ch,
1251 Cl, 1297 Pat, 1331 Ipm, *Westpolham* 1333 *SR*
Puleham 1130 PR, 1213 PatR, 1291 Tax, 1428 FA
Pullam 1212 Fees (94), *Westpullam* 1244 *Ass*
Pulham 1237, 1251 Cl *et passim* with *West-* prefixed from 1244
(*Ass*) onwards and *Est-* from 1333 (*SR*)

The first el. must be OE *pull* 'pool, stream'[1]; cf. also Hutchins III, 735.[2] The second el. is OE *hām* 'farm, homestead', or possibly *hamm*. East and West Pulham are on the maps.

Grange Fm is referred to as (*apud*) *grangiam abbatis de Bynendon de Pulham* 1237 Cl, and (*usque ad*) *Grangias monachorum de Binnedune* t. Hy III (14th) Cerne (cf. *supra* 35). This was consequently a grange belonging to Bindon Abbey, cf. *supra* 133 n. 2.

Kingstag is *Kingestake* 1337 DorchesterR. The material is scanty, but the second el. looks like OE *staca* 'stake', cf. NED s. v. *stake* sb. 1. The boundaries of the parishes of Pulham, Lydlinch and Haselbury Bryan meet on the bridge over the Lydden here, and a "King's stake" may have marked that point in ancient times; cf. Stake Ford, some seven miles to the west, marking the spot where the parishes of Lillington, Leigh and Yetminster meet; cf. also Markstakes Fm in PN Sx p. 297. As a matter of fact, the existence of a boundary-stake of some kind at Kingstag is confirmed in a very interesting way by a passage in the 13th cent. perambulation of Blackmoor Forest (Cerne Cartulary) reprinted *supra* 35 f. The perambulation follows the boundary of the adjacent parish of Holwell and then comes *ad truncum qui stat in tribus divisis*. We need not hesitate to identify this 'trunk' with the '(King's) stake' just alluded to.

---

[1] For that word and its connexion with OE *pōl*, cf. Ekwall, ERN p. 329.

[2] "Seems to derive its name from its low and watery situation, *quasi* Pole-ham, a dwelling by a pool or lake that runs on the west side of it, and divides it from Glanville's Wotton and Holwell."

Popular tradition has associated this name with the well-known story of King Henry III and the White Hart of Blackmoor. Coker, the old Dorset historian, calls the bridge King's Stagge Bridge, and a small inn in the vicinity still bears the name 'King's Stag'; see Hutchins III, 737 f.

Town's End Fm should probably be connected with *atte Londdeshende* occurring in 1333 *SR* (p) under Duntish. Since the next name in the Roll is West Pulham, and Town's End Fm lies between Duntish and that place (just within the border of Pulham parish), the connexion between the two names seems very likely. Cf. Woodsend Fm *supra* 30.

Wootton Glanville
Wootton Glanville 130 E 6

Widetone 1086 DB, *Wotton* 1316 FA, 1317 FF, 1333 *SR*

Wottingglayvile (sic) 1291 Tax, *Wotton Gla(u)nvyll* (*-vyle*) 1330, 1341 Cl, 1361 Fine *et passim*

Wolfrenewotton [*Wolvernewotton*] 1303 FA, *Wolver(e)n Wotton* 1310 Inq aqd, 1346 FA

Glamvileswotton 1396 FF, *-vyles-* 1431 FA, *Glanvile Wotton* 1428 FA, *Glanfyld* (*-fild*) *Wotton* 1535 VE

Wotton Glaunvyle al. *Wolverne Wotton* 1428 FA

OE *wudu-tūn* 'wood-farm'; we are here in the heart of Blackmoor Forest, cf. next name. Henry de *Glaunvyle* held land here in 1303 (FA). The other distinctive name *Wolfrene, Wolverne, Wolver(e)n* seems to go back to the OE fem. pers. name *Wulfrūn*; cf. Wolverhampton (St), Duignan p. 174.

Blackmoor (Forest and **Vale)** and **Newland** are referred to as *Blakamore maner' voc. Newelond* (*cum bosco de Blakamore*) in 1396 IpmR and in a similar entry from 10 Hy IV (ib.); cf. also 'the manor of *Blakemore* in the parish of *Wotton Glamvile*' 1445 FF. Newland is self-explanatory and denotes some new enclosure in Blackmoor Forest, cf. Hutchins III, 744 (with some notes on the earlier history of this manor). The name Blackmoor (or Blackmore) is also clear, the numerous 13th cent. forms (from 1205 ClR onwards) which I have seen being practically always spelt *Blakemor(e)*, *-mora*; OE *blæc* 'black' and *mōr*. There is nowadays not much left of the old woods, but many names in this part of the county remind us of them.

Osehill Green is *Oswoldeshulle* 1314 Pat, *Osweldeshulle* 1315 Pat. 'The hill of *Ōsweald*', a common OE pers. name.

XXVI. Sherborne Hundred

sireburne 1086 GeldRoll, *Syreburna*, *-e* c. 1160 Sarum, 1212 Fees (90), 1238 Sarum
Shireburn 1265 Misc, 1275 RH (with later *-born*), *Schireburn* 1303 FA, *-bourne* 1333 *SR*, *Shyreburn* 1275 Cl
Shirburn 1285 FA with later *-born*, *-bourne*
See Sherborne *infra*.

Beer Hackett

Beer Hackett 130 D 3
Bera 1175-6 to 1185-6 P (p), 1194, 1195 P (p), 1203 RC
Bere 1285 FA, 1290 Ch, 1299 Ipm *et passim*
Berehaket 1362 FF, *Bere Haket(t)* 1382 IpmR, 1383 Cl, *Beere Hakett* 1483 IpmR, *Bear juxta Yatemynstre* 1412 FA

See Bere Regis *supra* 68. The person who occurs here from 1175-6 to 1185-6 (P) is called *Haket* de Bera. The only other person bearing this name that I have found in connexion with this place is Wm *Haket* (1203 RC). Beer Hackett is near Yetminster.

Knighton is *Knygth.* 1348 BM I, *Knyghton* 1362 FF, 1412 FA (*juxta Yatmynstre*), 1431 FA, 1438 BM I. OE *cnihta-tūn*, cf. Knighton Ho *supra* 52.

Sputel (lost) is *la Spitell*, *la Spytel* 1244 *Ass* (p), *Spytell* 1431 FA, *Sputtell* 1483 IpmR. The statement in Hutchins (IV, 120) that this anciently belonged to the Knights Hospitallers, is confirmed not only by the name itself but also by an entry in 1203 RC (p. 112); cf. West Stafford *supra* 159.

Trill Fm
  Trelle 1086 DB
  Tryll(e) 1316 FA, 1384 FF, 1426, 1447 IpmR, 1466 FF
  Trill(e) 1412 FA, 1421-2 IpmR, 1466 FF

Trill Fm probably preserves the name of the (now nameless) brook on which it stands. For stream-names of this type cf. Ekwall, ERN pp. 418, 409 f.[1]

Bradford Abbas

Bradford Abbas 130 C 3
  (*apud*) *Bradeford*, (*æt*) *Bradan forda* 933 (12th) BCS 695
  (*in*) *Bradanford* 998 (12th) KCD 701
  Bradeford 1086 DB, 1204 Cur, 1285 FA *et passim*
  Braddeford Abbatis 1386 IpmR

OE (*æt*) *brādan forde* '(at) the broad ford'. It belonged to Sherborne Abbey; hence the additional name.

Coombe is *Comb'* 1333 *SR* (p). Self-explanatory, OE *cumb*.

Long Burton

Long Burton 130 D 5
  Burton 1244 *Ass*, 1333 *SR*, 1428 FA, *Buryton* 1285 FA,
    Bourton 1316 FA, *Borton* 1415 IpmR

OE *burhtūn*, cf. Bourton *supra* 3. *Long* apparently because of the length of the village; Little Burton is on the 6" map.

Castleton

Castleton (130 C 5)[2]
  Castelton 1333 *SR*, *Casteltown* 1535 VE

This place, adjoining Sherborne to the east, takes its name from Sherborne Castle, the ancient residence of the bishops of Sherborne. It was originally a small parish, surrounded on all sides by Sherborne (Hutchins IV, 204), but in 1897 part of

---

[1] To the early forms on p. 418 referring to another lost *Trill* in Dorset (now called Darknoll Brook) near Sturminster Newton should apparently be added (*op of stoure on*) *trildoune vppe tril* 968 (14th) BCS 1214.

[2] On the OS map of 1811, but now only on parish maps.

Castleton was added to Sherborne and a new and larger Castleton parish was formed, encircling the town of Sherborne.

Coombe Fm is *Combe* 1316 FA. OE *cumb* 'valley'. In 1327, 1333 *SR*, there is also mention of an *Ouercomb'* and a *Nithercomb'* (*Nyther-*) here, both probably surviving locally (Kelly).

Pinford is *Pinefort* c. 1160 Sarum, *Pinford* 1264 Ipm, 1303 FA, *Pyneford(e)* 1276 Ipm, 1285 FA, 1299 Ipm, 1316 FA, 1333 *SR*, 1344 Orig, 1431 FA, *Pynefford* 1331 Orig, *Pynford* 1346, 1428 FA. Possibly a compound of OE *pīn-* in *pīntrēow*, *pīnbēam* 'pine-tree', and *ford*. For other possibilities of interpreting names of this type, cf. Ekwall, PN in *-ing* p. 8, Karlström p. 103, Wallenberg p. 304 f.; for the evidence of a pers. name *Pinna* cf. PN Wo p. 334 s. n. *Pinton*.

Prinsley (lost)[1] is *Primeslee* 1204 Cur, *Pruneslegh* 1244 *Ass* (p), *Prummeslegh* 1252 FF, *Prymmeslegh* 1264-72 Buckland, *Prinnesl[e]* 1285 FA, *Promeslegh* 1327 *SR*, *Promesley* 1535 VE. The second el. is of course OE *lēah* 'clearing'. The first is difficult, but one might tentatively suggest a pers. name *Prym*, *Prin* or the like. *Prim* and *Prin* occur as names of moneyers (or of one and the same moneyer), and are supposed by Redin (p. 34) possibly to be of Celtic-Latin origin.

Sherborne Park is mentioned at least as early as 1161-2 P (*in parco de Scireburna*); see Sherborne *infra*.

Wyke Fm[2] is *Wyke* 1290 Ch, 1316 FA, 1319 FF, *Wyke* al. *Wykam* 1415 IpmR. OE *wīc* 'dairy-farm'.

Bishop's Caundle

Bishop's Caundle 130 D 6

> *Candel* 1224 to 1286 Sarum, 1225 ClR, 1228 FF, *Caundele* 1294 Ch, *Caundel Episcopi* 1285 FA *et passim*
> *Caundel Bishops* 1294, 1297 Pat

See Stourton Caundle *supra* 39. This Caundle belonged to the bishops of Salisbury; hence the distinctive name.

---

[1] "About a mile south-east from Sherborne" (Hutchins)

[2] Earlier in Bradford Abbas.

Caundle Wake

Kaundell Boyum 1290 Ch, *Ca(u)ndel Beym'* 1316 FA
Caundel Wake 1333 *SR*, 1360 Cl *et passim*

Cf. the parish name. The editors of FA (II, 40) are apparently justified in correcting *Beym'* to *Bevin*, for a certain Wm
Bevin occurs in connexion with *Candel* in 1235-6 Fees (p. 426).
For the *Wake* family cf. East and West Stour, and Stoke Wake
supra 16, 192; Ralph *Wake* was here in 1290 (Ch).

Caundle Marsh

Caundle Marsh 130 D 6, **Marsh Court**

Candelemers 1245 FF, *Candelmareis* 1284 FF, *Ca(u)ndel Mareys*
    1297 Pat, 1361 AD I, 1383 FF, *Caundelmers(s)h* 1333 Orig,
    1334 FF *et passim*
la Mers(s)h 1349 Ipm, 1431 FA, *Mershe* 1449 BM I

See Stourton Caundle *supra* 39. "It receives its additional
name from its low and marshy situation" (Hutchins); OE *mersc*.

Ashcombe Fm is *Ascumbe* 1205, 1206 Cur, *Esscumbe* 1244 FF,
Estcumbe 1245 FF, *Asshcomb'* 1333 *SR* (p). 'Ash-tree valley' (OE
æsc, cumb), the form *Estcumbe* being apparently wrong.

Poll Bridge Fm (6")[1] is probably to be connected with *Deoulepole*
in the perambulation of Blackmoor Forest reprinted *supra* 35 f.
This looks like 'devil-pool', whatever the exact significance may
have been; another *Dewelepole* occurs in 1285 FA and seems to
refer to some lost place in Beaminster Hundred; cf. *aqua de
Nikerpoll* in Sussex (Ekwall, ERN p. 329; PN Sx p. 562) containing OE *nicor* 'water-demon'.

Purse Caundle

Purse Caundle 130 B 6

Candel 1086 DB, Exon, 1091-1106 *et passim* Montacute, 1100-22
    (1270) Ch, 1203 Athelney (p)
Purscaundel 1241 FF, 1285 FA *et passim*, *Purscandel* 1252
    FF, 1273 (etc.) Athelney, 1291 Ipm, *Purschondel* 1252 FF,
    Pruscandel 1275 RH

[1] The site is just SE of Caundle Marsh, near point 218 on the 1" map.

Caundel Purs 1291 Tax, 1333 *SR*, 1340 NI *et passim*
This is the last of the obscure Caundle names, cf. Stourton
Caundle *supra* 39. The distinctive appellation is probably a
pers. name. I have frequently met with such a name but not
in connexion with this place.[1]
The context in which Robert de *Columbers* is mentioned in
the Register of Athelney Abbey (p. 183) seems to suggest that
Candell Columbers 1259 FF (*Robert de Columbariis*) refers to
Purse Caundle or some part of it, and such may also be the
case with the form *Whetenecandel* 1252 FF.

Up Cerne

Up Cerne 130 G 5
(*æt*) *Upcer* . . 1002-14 (orig.?) KCD 708, *Obcerne* 1086 DB,
Upecerna 1166 RBE, *Uppecerne* 1219 FF, *Upcern(e)* 1285 FA
onwards

See Cerne Abbas and cf. Nether Cerne *supra* 196 f.

Compton, Over and Nether

Over Compton, Nether Compton 130 C 3
(*on, to*) *Cumtun* (*bricgge*) 946-51 (12th) BCS 894
Cumbtun 998 (12th) KCD 701, *Contone* 1086 DB, *Comton(a)* c.
1160 Osmund, *Cumpton(e)* 1236 FF, 1285 FA
Nether(e) (*Nethir, Nyther*) is prefixed from 1297 Pat, *Over* from
1316 FA, *Nythercompton Abbatis* 1396 FF
Cumpton Hauwey 1303 FA, 1318 FF (*Harveye*), *Compton Howey*
1320 Cl, *Compton Hawey(e)* 1342 Misc *et passim*
Compton Hawy al. *Over Compton* 1423 Pap

'Valley farm', OE *cumb, tūn*; cf. Compton Abbas *supra* 21.
Joh. de *Hawey* held half a knight's fee in (Over) Compton in
1285 (FA); cf. also Hutchins IV, 167. Both places belonged to
Sherborne Abbey.

Stallen is *Stawell* 1285 FA, 1333 *SR* (p), 1535 VE, *Stauwell*
1290 Ch, the last form corresponding to *Stanwell* in the older

---

[1] Cf. Derewinus *Purs* 1175-6 P (Bk), Rob. *Purs* 1178-9 P (Gl), Adam *Purs*
1260 FF (So), Richard *Purs* 1274 Cl (Lei), Adam *Purs* 1275 Cl (K), Yewan *Purs*
1291 Pat (He), Walter *Purs* 1299 Pat (So), John and Richard *Purs* 1305 Pat (Sr).

edition of the Charter Rolls (ChR p. 120). Whether the *Stan*-reading is correct or not, the etymology is probably OE *stān-wielle* 'stony spring', Stallen thus affording us a fourth Dorset example of loss of *n* before a labial consonant; cf. Stoborough, Stafford and High Stoy *supra* 130, 159, 200. The modern form of the pl.-n. is noteworthy.

Folke

Folke [fouk] 130 D 5

The early spelling of this name is simply *Folk* (from 1244 *Ass* onwards), interchanging with *Folke* from the beginning of the 14th century. This does not tell us very much, and I am unable to suggest a plausible etymology; an OE *folc* 'folk, people' would, as far as my knowledge goes, be without parallel as a pl.-n. The place belonged to the bishop of Sarum, and Hutchins (IV, 174) states that in 12 Hy II "William de Perci de Fulk" held half a knight's fee of the bishop. This assertion is evidently taken from the *Carta Episcopi Sarrisbiriensis* of 1166 printed in RBE (p. 236)[1], where the text runs: *Willelmus de Percy de Fulc-[inges], dimidium militem.* There can be little doubt that the entry refers to Folke, for members of the de Percy family appear as tenants here in 1285 (etc.) FA. The somewhat mysterious form *Fulc[inges]* may be of some help in settling the origin of Folke, but as the MS is not accessible to me, I cannot say what the form is worth.

Allweston

Alfletheston 1244 *Ass* (201 m. 6)

Alfeeston 1244 *Ass* (200 m. 10), *Alpheston* 1268 FF

Alveston 1316, 1431 FA, *Alueston* 1333 *SR*, 1377 FF

Alfeston 1390, 1436 FF[2]

This would seem to mean '*Æþelflǣd*'s (*Ælflǣd*'s) farm', if the first MS form above can be trusted. For the inorganic gen. *s* cf. Arfleet Mills *supra* 118.

---

[1] Hutchins apparently quotes the parallel document Liber Niger.

[2] As early as 1214 there occurs a pl.-n. *Alfeston* in FF which possibly belongs here.

Bishop's Down is *Doune* 1333 *SR*, *Bysshopysdoune* 1468 FF. Self-explanatory, OE *dūn*; the whole district belonged to the bishops of Salisbury.

Butterwick[1] is *Boterwyk(e)* 1327 FF, 1333 *SR* (p) *et passim* to 1466 FF, *Butterweke* 1535 VE. 'Butter-farm', OE *butere, wīc*.

Densham Fm is *Denesham* 1333 *SR* (p). This may contain the pers. name *Dene* (Redin p. 6), but the material is too late and scanty for a definite suggestion.

Font le Roi [font lə rɔi]. This is named after the *Fauntleroy* family, landowners in this and neighbouring parishes for many generations, cf. e. g. 1393, 1436 FF and 1431 FA. It is indicated in Hutchins (IV, 179 f.) that the family came over to England (Dorset) in the time of Edward III. This cannot be true, for in the two unprinted Assize Rolls of 1244 I have found a certain Rogerus *Le Enfaunt le roy* (*Ass* 201 m. 6)[2] in connexion with Allweston in this parish, which clearly shows that the history of this family in Dorset must be considerably older than has hitherto been supposed.

West Hall is *Westhalle* 1352 FF; in later records (1412 FA, etc.) *Westhall*. Probably a late name containing *hall* 'manor-house'; cf. EPN s. v. *heall*.

Haydon

Haydon 130 C 6

(*æt*) *Hægdune*[3] 1046 (12th) KCD 1334
Heydone, -a c. 1163 Sarum, *-don* 1253 Misc, *Heidon* 1201-2 FF,
  1204 FineR, *Haydon* 1285, 1316 FA *et passim*
Haddon 1303 FA, *Haidon juxta Shirburne* 1412 FA

It is often very difficult to distinguish between the three elements *hēg* 'hay', *hege* 'hedge', and *(ge)hæg* 'hedge, enclosure', cf. EPN. The first of them is considered to enter into most English Haydons (cf. EPN s. v.), and this is probably the case here, too.

---

[1] Butterwick Wood (1″), Butterwick Fm (6″).
[2] Called Rogerus *fauntleray* in *Ass* 200 m. 10.
[3] Identification made by EPNS.

Holnest

Holnest [houlnest] 130 E 5

Holeherst 1184-5 to 1187-8, 1194, 1195 P

Holenhurste t. Hy III (14th) Cerne

Holnest 1316 FA, 1327, 1333 *SR*, 1412 FA *et passim*

Probably 'holly-tree wood', OE *holegn-hyrst*, this being the etymology suggested by Wallenberg (p. 248) for a lost Kentish pl.-n. going back to *holen hyrst* in BCS 753.

Boys Hill is probably to be associated with the family of Adam and William *Boye* 1314 Pat.

Leweston

Leweston 130 D 5

Leweston 1244 *Ass* (p), 1256 FF, t. Hy BM I *et passim*

Leuerston (rectius *Leuston*) 1303 FA

Leuston 1333 *SR* (p), 1340 NI (p), 1346, 1431 FA

The 1303 form *Leuerston*, suggesting a derivation *Lēofhere*'s *tūn*, stands unique, and the correction in FA is therefore perhaps justified. The other forms would seem to point to the pers. name *Lēof*, but no certainty is possible. Cf. IPN p. 131.

Lillington

Lillington 130 D 4

Lilliton' 1179-80 to 1184-5 P (p), *Lillinton* 1179-80 P (p), 1232 Ch, *Lillington* 1200 Cur, 1260 FF *et passim*, *Lillingeton* 1265 BM I; *Uverlillington* 1244 *Ass*, *Overelilengton* 1256 FF, *Over-*, *Nitherlillyngton* 1356 FF

Lullinton 1200 Cur, 1209 Abbr, *-ing-* 1201 Cur[1]

Lyllinton 1285 FA, *-yng-* 1291 Tax, 1333 *SR* (p), 1334 AD I (p), 1340 NI, 1431 FA, *-ing-* 1316 FA, 1333 Ipm (p)

Probably from OE *Lillingtūn* 'farm of *Lilla*'s (or *Lil*'s) people'; an exact parallel seems to be Lillington (Wa): *Lillintone*, *Illintone* 1086 DB, *Lillington* 1316 Ipm, *Lyllyngton* 1428 FA; cf. Duignan PN Wa p. 81; Stenton, PN Berks p. 40.

---

[1] Only one more *u* spelling has been noted (1382).

The Place-Names of Dorset 217

Bailey Ridge Fm is *Baillye juxta Yat(e)minster* 1387, 1419 IpmR, *Le Bailly* 1412 FA[1], the name being due to the fact that John Streche who held the place, also held the bailiwick of the county of Dorset in the time of Richard II, cf. Hutchins IV, 196. Ridge is probably *atte Rygg'* 1333 *SR* (p); OE *hrycg.* The site is about 2 m. from Yetminster.

Stockbridge Fms is *Stokbrige, -brigg* 1244 *Ass* (p), *Stokbrigge* 1327 *SR* (p), *Stokebrygeyate* 1488 Ipm, and must have been named from a 'bridge made of trunks', OE *stocc, brycg*; cf. Stockbridge, PN Sx p. 14.

Whitfield Fm is *Whitefeld juxta Shireburn* 1309 Orig; cf. Whitefield *supra* 76.

Lydlinch
Lydlinch 130 D 8

Lidelinz 1181-2 P, 1206 Cur (p), *Lidelinch* 1285 FA, 1291 Tax, ⁋1303 FA, *-lynch(e)* 1337 BM I, 1428 AD I
Lydelinch 1285 FA, 1291 Tax, 1297 Pat, Cl, 1302 Ipm, 1306 FF, *-linche* 1346 FA, *-lynche* 1297 Misc *et passim*
Ludelynch 1303 Ipm, 1461-2 IpmR, *Ledelynch* 1316 FA
Lyndelinche 1318 FF, *Ludenlynche* 1428 FF

Cf. also Hydes *infra* (this parish).
Lydlinch means 'bank (OE *hlinc*) of the river Lydden', an interpretation which has long been clear to local experts, cf. Hutchins IV, 188. For the river-name itself, cf. Ekwall, ERN p. 242.

The name of the river Lydden also enters into the now lost name of a wood somewhere in the vicinity, to which we have reference in *Lydeneholte in Blakemore* 1313 Ipm, *Lydenholte in Blakemore* 1319 ib., *Lyndeholte in Blakemoure* 1345 ib. OE *holt* 'wood'.

Blackrow Fm is *Blakerewe* 1421 FF, 1425 BM I, 1432 FF, 1433 BM I, *-rew* t. Hy VI AD VI. The elements are OE *blæc* 'black' and *ræw* 'row', but the exact meaning of the compound is not quite clear.

---
[1] The identification in FA (vol. VI) must be wrong.

Haydon is *Haydun'*, *-don'* 13th GlastonC, *Haydon* 1415 FF. Cf. Haydon *supra* 215.

Holebrook Green

(*on*) *Holambrok'* 968 (14th) BCS 1214

Holebrouk 1333 *SR* (p), *-brok* 1412 FA, *-broke* 1415 FF

'Brook in the hollow', OE (*æt*) *holan brōce*.

Hydes

Lidelynche Baret 1375 Cl, *Ludelynchebaret* 1384 Cl, *Lydelynche Baret* 1421 FA, *Lydlynch Baret* t. Hy VI AD VI *Hydes* 1431 FA, *Lydelynch Baret* al. *Hydys maner'* 1450 IpmR

See Lydlinch *supra* 217. Henry *Baret* held land in Lydlinch in 1297 (Misc), Wm *Baret* in 1316 (FA). The latter and Henry de *la Hyde* were parties to a fine concerning land *inter alia* in Lydlinch in 1318 (FF). OE *hīd*.

Plumber Fm[1] is *Plūbere* 1086 DB, *Plumber'* 1242-3 Fees (753), 1333 *SR* (p), *-bere* 1275 Cl (p), 1316, 1346 FA *et passim*, *Plumbare* 1270 Ipm (p), *Plomber* [*Plumbere*] 1303 FA, *Plumbeare* 1412 FA, *Plymber* 1429 IpmR. The first el. is evidently OE *plūme* 'plum, plum-tree', the second probably OE *bearu* 'grove, wood'; cf. Todber *supra* 18.

Ramsbury (lost)[2] is *Remmesberi* t. Hy III BM I, *-by* 1412 FA, *-burry* 1418 AD I, *-bere* 1421 FF *et passim* to 1442 IpmR, *-beare* 1435 IpmR, *-bury* 1455 IpmR; *Rammesbere* 1316 Ipm, 1336 Ch, 1438 IpmR, *Parva Remesbere* 1417 Inq aqd, *Remmesbere, Rammesbere* 1425, 1433, 1439 BM I. For the first el. cf. Renscombe Fm *supra* 128. The second may be either *burh* (*byrig*) or *bearu* (see Todber *supra* 18). Cf. Ramsbury in Wilts (Ekblom p. 138).

Rodmore Fms[3] is *Rodmor* 1318 FF. Probably a compound of OE *hrēod* 'reed' and *mōr*.

---

[1] Plumber, or at least part of it, was earlier in Pimperne (*Hunesberge*) Hundred, cf. Eyton p. 131 n. 3.

[2] On Taylor's map of 1765 the site is just N of Ridge in this parish.

[3] Rodmore Fm (6″), Little Rodmore Fm (1″).

Stock Gaylard Ho[1]
Stoches 1086 DB, *Stoke* 1316 FA, *Stocke* 1333 *SR*, 1431 FA
Stoke Coilard 1304 Ipm, 1305 Cl, *Stocke Kuylard* 1304 Ipm,
Stokke Coilard 1332, 1345 FF, *Stokk Coillard* 1335 BM I,
Stokke Coylard 1379 Cl *et passim*
Stoke Gaillard 1316 Inq aqd, *Stoke Goillard* 1340 NI
Stokkeylore 1412 FA

OE *stoc* 'place'. The distinctive name probably comes from
some family *Coilard*, but I have not been able to track it out.

Stroud Fm was apparently the home of Alan *Stroude* 1340 NI;
cf. Stroud Bridge *supra* 66.

Oborne

Oborne 130 B 5
(apud) *Woburnam*, *(æt)* *Womburnam*[2] c. 975 (12th) BCS 1308
(in) *Wonburna*[3] 998 (12th) KCD 701 (= Thorpe p. 294)
Wocburne 1086 DB
(inter) *Woburnam* c. 1160 Sarum, *Woburn* 1249 FF, 1271 FineR
(p), 1285 FA *et passim*, later *-bo(u)rne*
Wuburn 1227 FF, *-born* 1268 FF (p), *Wouburn* 1316 FA, FF
Wodebourne (sic) 1428 FA, *Woborne*, *Ob(o)urne* 1535 VE

Oborne is a compound of OE *wōh* 'crooked, twisting' (EPN)
and *burna* 'stream', a name which very appropriately describes
the winding brook that flows through the village; cf. also Ekwall, ERN p. 468 f. The two charter forms *Womburnam*, *Wonburna* would seem to point to the OE oblique form *wōnburnan*,
cf. Stoborough *supra* 130.

---

[1] Stock Gaylard was formerly an independent parish (including *Ramsbury*)
in Brownshall Hundred, but is now attached to Lydlinch parish for civil
purposes (Hutchins, Kelly).
[2] Wrongly identified by Birch with Wimborne; cf. Hutchins IV, 200, and
VCH Do II, 62. The form (apud) *Woburnam* occurs only in the rubric.
[3] Wrongly identified by Kemble and Thorpe with Wimborne; cf. VCH
Do II, 63, and Ekwall, ERN p. 469. Two of the pl.-ns in this Sherborne charter
cannot now be identified, viz. *Osanstoke* (possibly Stoke Abbott *infra*) and
Wulfheardigstoke; cf. Karlström p. 124.

Sherborne

Sherborne 130 C 5

More than enough material has already been given (cf. the hundred-name *supra* 209) to illustrate the origin of the name of this old episcopal see. For the sake of completeness, however, it may be added that in BCS (26 onwards) the usual form is (æcclesia, etc.) *Scireburnensis* (*passim*) with the variant spellings *Scira-* (266), *Scir(a)-* (312), *Shcire-* (447), *Schire-* (461, 872, 1179), *Sciri-* (468), *Scir-* (733, 747), *Scyr-* (766); cf. also *Sciraburnanscis* (469), *Schirabornensis* (472), (ad æcclesiam) *Siraburnensem* (614); we also find (æt) *Scireburnan* (510, 533), *Schyrburn* (554), *Schyrborn* (555), (æt) *Scyræburnan* (1174), (æt) *Scirburnan* (1308), and (ad) *Scireburnensem* (615).

The forms in KCD (and Crawford Ch) are of equally little interest except to note that, in KCD, the spelling *Scirburnensis* is somewhat more common than *Scire-*; we also find *Shyre-* (686), *Schira-* (817), *Scyre-* (1289), (æt) *Scireburnan* (1302, 1309, 1334), *Scireburnia* (702); the same Latinized from *Sir(e)burnia, Scireburnia* occurs in RBE; 1154-89 (1326) Ch has *Sirebornia*.

(æt) *Scira burnan* is found in ASC(A) s. a. 860; otherwise the common form there is (æt) *Scireburnan*; DB has *Scireburne* (*passim*).

Shire-, Schire-, Scire- are the usual spellings in P (1158-9 onwards) and in most later records (from about 1200 alternating with *Shyre-, Sc(h)yre-*)[1], whereas the French spellings *Sire-, Syre-* are common in RBE and a great many records from the former half of the 13th cent. (Cur, FineR, Cl(R), Pat(R), Lib, Fees, etc.), the last two *Syre*-spellings having been noted from 1261 (Misc) and 1285 (FA).

The following *e* spellings have been found: *Shereburn* 1288 Pat, Fine, *Sherbourn* 1333 Cl, *-born(e)* 1415, 1422 IpmR.

The place is called *Schirborn Abbatis* in 1291 Tax, and *Schireburn Camel* in 1303 FA, the latter addition apparently recording the memory of a family *Camel*, of which Robert *Camel* was tenant here in 1375, cf. Hutchins IV, 214.

Sherborne means 'clear stream', OE *scīr, burna*[2]; cf. e. g. EPN p. 52; Ekwall, ERN p. 362.

---

[1] A unique from is *Shirneburn* 1333 Fine.

[2] Cf. Leland (I, 296): "John Myer abbate of Shirburne said that he had

Hyle Fm (6″) is *La Hyle by Shirbourne* 1334 Ipm, and *Hile near Shirbourne* 1334 Cl. See Hile Fm *supra* 46.

Thornford

Thornford 130 D 3

   Thornford 946-51 (12th) BCS 894, 1249 FF, 1285 FA, 1290
      Ch *et passim*, *Thorne-* 1249 FF, 1316 FA *et passim*
   Torneford 946-51 (12th) BCS 894 (rubric), 1086 DB
   Dorford 998 (12th) KCD 701

   OE *þorn* 'thorn-bush' and *ford*.

Lake Fm is possibly to be connected with the boundary-mark (*and lang*) *lace* 933 (12th) BCS 695. OE *lacu* 'stream, water-course'.

North Wootton

North Wootton 130 C 5

   Wotton c. 1180 Sarum, 1285 FA, 1294 Ch, 1431 FA, *W(o)ttune,*
      W(o)tton(e) 1228 Sarum, *Wotton Episcopi* 1316 FA, 1383 FF,
      1412 FA, *Wotton Bishops* 1393 FF

   OE *wudu-tūn* 'wood-farm'. This Wootton anciently belonged to the bishops of Sarum. *North* in relation to Wootton Glanville *supra* 208.

XXVII. Yetminster Hundred

   Etheministre 1084 GeldRoll, 1244 *Ass*
   Ettminster (rubric), *Ecceministre* c. 1160 Sarum
   Eteministre 1212 Fees (90), 1244 *Ass*
   Ettemunstr' 1230 P, *Etteministr'* 1244 *Ass*
   Yetemenistre 1265 Misc, *Yadeministre* 1303 FA, *Iatmynstre* 1316
      FA, *Yatemenstr'* 1327, 1333 *SR*, 1340 NI, *Yetminstre* 1431 FA

   See Yetminster *infra*.

---

redde in Latine bookes of his house that Shirburne was caullid Clarus fons."
There is of course the possibility that the first el. may be OE *scir* 'shire', as
in a few other English *scir*-names, but that possibility seems very small in
this case.

Batcombe

Batcombe 130 G 4

Batecumbe 1244 *Ass*, 1274 Ipm *et passim* with variants *-cumb*,
-co(u)mb(e), *Battecumbe* 1244 *Ass*
Badecombe 1336 Ch, 1337 FF *et passim*, later *-coumbe*

Bad(d)a is a well-evidenced OE pers. name (Redin p.
44), but the forms with *d* are late in comparison with those containing *t*.[1]
The pers. name *Bata*, on the other hand, is recorded only as a
by-name in OE (Ælfric *Bata*, Redin p. 131) but seems to enter
into a few pl.-ns, the safest instance being Batcombe (So), referred to as (*æt*) *Batancumbæ* in BCS 1174; cf. PN Wo p. 162
s. n. Battenhall. Hence possibly '*Bata*'s valley', OE *cumb*.

Newland's Fm is *Neulond* 1274 Ipm, *Nywelond* 1333 *SR*. Cf.
Newland *supra* 208.

Chetnole

Chetnole [tʃetnəl] 130 E 3

Chateknolle 1314 Pat, *-knoll* 1316 FA, *Cheteknoll'* 1333 *SR*
Chetnoll 1535 VE

The second el. is OE *knoll* 'knoll, hill'. The first is difficult.
Förster (p. 182) takes it to be the pers. name *Ceatta*, but that
seems rather doubtful.[2]

Clifton Maybank

Clifton Maybank 130 D 3

(*æt*) *Cliftune* 1002-14 (orig.?) KCD 708, *Clistone*[3] 1086 DB

---

[1] I have noted at least ten *Bate-* spellings previous in date to the first
Bade- form (in 1336).

[2] The evidence for this pers. name is very unsatisfactory. Searle's only
instance of an independently recorded name *Ceatta* (p. 126) seems to be of
little value (cf. Redin p. 88), and that *ceattan broc* and *ceattan mære* KCD 636
(Cod. Winton.) really contain a pers. name, remains to be proved; cf. the
discussion in connexion with Lowbrook Fm *supra* 47. Since the second el. of
Chetnole (OE *knoll*) is in itself not likely to be compounded with a pers. name,
the interpretation of the first el. had better be left open.

[3] Other forms showing this mistranscription of *s* for *f* are *Clistune* 1158
France, and *Cliston*, *Clyston* 1291 Tax.

Clifton 1216 ClR *et passim* (alternating with *Clyfton* from 1244
Ass), with *Mabank* added from 1319 FF
Clifton Maubank 1404 IpmR, *Clyfton Maubanke* 1454 FF

OE *clif* 'cliff, steep sloping ground' and *tūn*. The earliest of
the *Maubanks* that I have come across in a ME record in connexion with Clifton is Wm *Maubanc* 1216 (ClR), but, as pointed
out by Eyton (pp. 123 and 113 f. with foot-note 8), even the
William who in DB held this and several other Do manors of
Comes Hugo (of Chester) bore the surname *Malbanc*, this being
made clear by an entry in the GeldRoll of 1084 (Exon p. 21)
where he is called Willelmus *malbeenc*; cf. also Tait p. 121.

Halstock[1]

Halstock [hælstək, hɔːlstək] 130 E 1/2
(in) Halganstoke 998 (12th) KCD 701
Halgestok(e) 1191 Sarum, c. 1192-3 Osmund, 1238 Sarum, 1265
  Misc, 1291 Tax, 1306 BM I, *Haleghestok* 1244 *Ass*, 1279 Cl,
  Halghestok(e) 1244 *Ass*, 1285 FA *et passim*
Hagelestok' 1230 P (*Halewestok* ChancR)
Halwestok(e) 1316 Orig, Inq aqd, 1379 BM I *et passim*
Halghenstoke 1386 BM I, *Halustoke* 1392 IpmR
Halystoke, Halewestocke 1535 VE

'Holy place', OE *(æt) hālgan stoce*; it may have been so called
simply because it belonged to the church of Sherborne.

Halstock Leigh (Higher and Lower) may have been the home of
Jordan de *Legh* 1285 FA (II, 4). OE *lēah*.

Moryate (lost) is *Morgete* early Hy III BM I, *Morzete* 1313 Ipm,
La Mouryate 1319 Ipm, *atte Moreyate* 1333 *SR* (p), *Moryate*
1345 Ipm. OE *mōr* 'moor, barren land' and *geat* 'gate'.

Netherstoke is *Nitherstoke* 1166 RBE, 1244 *Ass*, 1333 *SR* (all p),
Niperstok t. Hy III BM I, *Netherestok* 1236 Pat (p), *Netherstok(e)*
1246-59 BM I, 1285 FA (p) *et passim*. The place apparently
got its name because of its situation in relation to Halstock; cf.
Nether Cerne *supra* 197.

[1] A Liberty; cf. Liberty Fm a mile NE of the village of Halstock.

Wyke Fm is *la Wike* 1244 *Ass* (p), *Wyke* 1401 FF. OE *wīc* 'dairy-farm'.

Leigh

Leigh [lai] 130 E 4
    Lega 1228 FF, *Legh* 1244 *Ass et passim* to 1535 VE
    Leye 1348 Cl, *Leighe* 1359 Inq aqd, *Leygh* 1361 Fine
    Lye or *Leigh* 1765 Taylor
    Cf. Leigh *supra* 79.

Crocker's Knap, cf. foot-note to *Crockern Stoke supra* 55.

Totnell is *Totenhulle* 1327 *SR*, *Todenhull* 1333 *SR* (p). The second el. is OE *hyll* 'hill', but more material is needed to interpret the first.

Withyhook Mill (6″)
    Widihoc 1197-8 FF, 1200 Cur, Abbr
    Wodehoc 1201-2 FF, *La Wytheoc* 1283 Ipm
    Wydihok' 1325 FF, *Wydihouk* 1351 BM I, *Widyhouk* 1385 FF,
      Wydehouk 1399 FF, *Wydyok* 1401 FF, *Widioke* 1412 FA,
      Wydeok 1431 FA (cf. *Widehokesrewe* 1314 Pat)

    Probably a compound of OE *wiðig* 'withy, willow' and *hōc* 'hook', the latter presumably referring to the projecting corner of land formed by the confluence of two brooks here. On intervocalic *d* for OE *ð* cf. Zachrisson in IPN p. 110; the common dial. form *widdy* for *withy* is recorded *inter alia* from Devon (EDD) and occurs in many Devon pl.-ns, cf. PN D (*passim*). Just N of Withyhook Mill is a place called Heniford Withy Bed (6″).

Melbury Bubb

Melbury Bubb 130 F 3
    Meleberie 1086 DB, *-beria* Exon, *Mellebir'* 1202 Cur, *Melebir'* 1212 Fees (94)
    Melebir' Bubbe 1244 *Ass*, *Maleburi Bobbe* 1290 Ch, *Melebury Bubbe* 1291 Tax *et passim*, *Melburybubbe* 1306 Abbr (*et passim* with unimportant variants[1])

---

[1] Note the curious form *Melebulibuckeby* (!) from 1303 FA.

Maleburn' Bulbe (sic) 1244 Abbr, *Melleburn' Bubbe* 1244 *Ass*,
   Meleburne Bubbe 1276 FF
Bub Melebur' 1280 FF, *Bubbe Melebur'* 1284 FF
Melebury Bobeton 1328 Orig, *Bubbeton* 1412, 1431 FA

The three adjoining parishes Melbury Bubb, Melbury Osmond
and Melbury Sampford are, of course, originally one and the
same name, evidently etymologically identical with Melbury
Abbas *supra* 27 (in another part of the county). Melbury Bubb
owes its distinctive name to a family called *Bubbe*[1], William
Bubbe being tenant here in 1212 (Fees p. 94) and his son Ralph
Bubbe in 1244 (*Ass* 200 m. 1; cf. 1244 Abbr p. 120); as pointed
out in Hutchins (IV, 432), Peter and Walter *Bubbe* are mentioned
as holding land in Dorset as early as 1166, see RBE p. 217.
Melebury Bobeton and *Bubbeton* are interesting examples of a
very late formation with *-ton*. In still later sources the place is
sometimes called *Bubtown* or *Bubdown*, the latter of these two
forms being probably a development of the former. Bubb Down
Hill is now the name of the high hill, on the NE slope of which
the village of Melbury Bubb is situated.

Heniford Fm (6″). The only fairly safe reference I have seen is
Hinn'ford 1333 *SR* (p), but *Himerford* 1314 Pat possibly belongs
here, too. In view of this scanty and uncertain material I must
leave the name unexplained.

Woolcombe

Wellecome 1086 DB, *-cumbe* 1200 Cur, 1316 FA, *-combe* 1314
   Pat, 1316 FA, *Welecomb(e)* 1303, 1346, 1428 FA
Wullecumb' 1236 Cl, *Wullecumbe Mautravers* 1281 FF
Wollecumbe 1286 FF, *-coumbe* 1314 Pat, *Wolecumbe* 1303 FA,
   1313 FF, *-combe* 1338 BM I, *Wolcombe* 1318 Ch *et passim*
Owelcombe 1356, 1357 FF, 1380 Cl
Wolcombe Mautravers 1386 Cl, IpmR *et passim*

'Valley with a spring', OE *wielle, cumb*; cf. the same name in
Toller Porcorum *infra*. For the phonetic development cf. Wool
supra 150. The *Mautravers* family held Woolcombe from the
time of DB up to the middle of the 14th cent.; cf. Lytchett
Matravers *supra* 112.

---

[1] Presumably from the OE pers. name *Bubba*; cf. Brictmarus *Bubba* (DB),
see Redin p. 87.

Melbury Osmond

Melbury Osmond 130 F 3

Melesberie 1086 DB, *Melesberia* 1121 AC
Melebire, -bery 1091-1106 Montacute, *-biri* 1107-22 ib., *-beria*
1100-22 (1270) Ch, *-biriam* 1135-54 France
Melebir' Priur 1235 Cl
Melebury Osmund 1243 BM I, 1291 Tax *et passim*

Other forms are without interest except to mention that the
medial *e* begins to disappear about the beginning of the 14th cent.

See Melbury Bubb *supra* 224. *Priur* because the prior of
Montacute had land here. *Osmund* possibly on account of the
dedication of the church to St Osmund[1] (bishop of Salisbury
1078-99).

Ryme Intrinseca

Ryme Intrinseca[2] 130 E 3

Rima c. 1160 Sarum
Ryme 1229 Pat, 1284 FF, 1333 *SR*, 1349 Fine *et passim*
Rym 1280 FF, 1297 Pat, 1298 Ch, 1303 FA *et passim*

This must be OE *rima* 'rim, verge, border', the place being
very near the Somerset border; (*æt*) *Rimtune* BCS 730, *Rimtun(e)*
ib. 931, now Rimpton (So), apparently contains the same element,
cf. Middendorff p. 108. *Intrinseca* "in contradistinction to the
outlying manor of Ryme Extrinseca in Longbridy" (Hutchins
IV, 491; cf. II, 188), a name no longer extant; cf. Dowerfield
infra.

Caswell Fm is *Carswell* 1535 VE, 1625 Do Ipm, and means 'cress-
grown spring', OE *cærse, wielle*; cf. also EPN p. 13.

Frankham Fm is *Frankehā* 1244 *Ass* (p), *Francham* 1332 Ipm,
1340 NI (p), *Frankham* 1383, 1386 FF (*juxta Ryme*). Probably
'*Franca's* farm' (OE *hām*). For the pers. name *Franca* cf. e. g.

---

[1] This is Hutchins' own suggestion (IV, 437) which the later editors of his
Do History are not quite willing to accept, probably because Osmund was not
canonized until 1457; cf. Osmington *supra* 155 (n. 1).
[2] Almost always called simply Ryme.

Redin p. 75 f. (with literature) and PN Wo p. 346 f. s. n. Frankley.

Stockwood

Stockwood 130 F 3

Stocwode 1221-3 Montacute, 1274 Ipm, *Stokewod(e)* 1265 Pat
 et passim, *Stokwode Poyntz* 1331 Ipm
(capella de) *Stokes Sancti Edwoldi* 1228 Pat
Stoke 1248 Pat, 1338 Cl, 1811 OM
Stoke St. Edwald 1274 Ipm, Cl, 1312 Ipm, 1337 Cl, *Stokes St.*
 Edwald 1274 Fine, 1288 FF, *Stoke St. Edwold* 1320 FF
Stokes St. Edward 1274 Pat, *Stoke St. Edward* 1338 Cl
Stokwod de Seint Edwold 1368 FF

This place appears originally to have been called simply *Stoke* (OE *stoc* 'place') and to have taken its early distinctive name from the dedication of its chapel (Hutchins IV, 442), while the name *Stok(e)wode* would seem to refer to the wood (or park) belonging to *Stoke*.[1] *Poyntz* because a member of the liberty of Sutton Poyntz *supra* 156.

Yetminster

Yetminster 130 E 3

Etiminstre 1086 DB, *Eteminster* 1091 Osmund, *Eteministr(e)*
 1226 Osmund, 1229 Pat, *Etteministr(e)* 1244 *Ass*
Etheminster c. 1209 Sarum, *Etheministre* c. 1209 Sarum, 1244
 Ass (p), *Ethemenistre* c. 1226 Sarum[2]
Yateminstre c. 1226 Sarum, 1314 Pat *et passim*, with variant
 spellings *-ministre* 1244 *Ass*, 1315 Pat, *-mynstre* 1324 Cl *et*
 passim, *-menstr'* 1333 *SR*, *-munstre* 1360 Cl, *-mystre* 1447
 AD I, *-mestre* 1473 BM I; from 1361 (FF) onwards also *Yat-*
 Geteministr. 1226 Osmund, *Gateministre* 1243 BM I
Yttreminster 1250 Pap
Jateministre 1291 Tax, *Iatmynstre* 1316 FA
Yeteministre, *-menstre*, *-menystre* 1297 Pat

---

[1] Cf. 1274 Ipm (p. 19): "Stoke St. Edwald. The manor, with the advowson of a certain chapel, including pastures called Priureswode and Moryelese, and a park called Stocwode".

[2] *Ethemenistre Tancredi* and *Ethemenistre W. de Len.* "These were the prebends of Yetminster Secunda and Yetminster Prima, which were held (c. 1226) by Tancred and by Will. de Len respectively" (Sarum p. 208 n. 1).

Yatesministre 1300 Ch, *-minster* 1391-3 ChR
Cf. *Yatemynstre Over Bire* 1324 Cl, *Overbury in Yatemunstre*
1360 Cl, *Yatmenstre Upbury* 1519 AD V
Cf. also the forms for Yetminster Hundred *supra* 221.

The second el. is of course OE *mynster* 'church'. The first
is presumably a pers. name. OE *Eta* (fem.), recorded once (in
the gen. form *Etan* BCS 167; cf. Redin p. 117)[1], would account
for some of the earliest forms but would leave the many *Yat(e)-*
forms unexplained. The well recorded name *Eat(t)a* would
therefore seem to be a more likely base, though the absence of
At(t)e spellings makes one somewhat doubtful. For the initial *y*
cf. Yalding (K), Yapton (Sx) and numerous Devon names; see
Ekwall, PN in *-ing* p. 42, PN Sx p. 144, and PN D *passim*
(e. g. p. xxxiii).

Overbury and *Upbury* are other names for the prebend of
Yetminster Prima (Hutchins).

Winterhays is *Wynterheie* 1333 Ipm, *Wynterheye* 1333 *SR*, 1340
NI (all p), *Winterhayes* 1625 DoIpm. 'Winter-enclosure', i. e.
one used in winter; OE *winter, (ge)hæg*.

XXVIII. Tollerford Hundred

tolreforde 1084 GeldRoll, *Tolreford* 1244 *Ass* (also *Toure-*),
1265 Misc *et passim*, *Tollreford* 1244 Fees (1387)
Thol(l)ereford, *Thelreford* 1275 RH, *Tollerford* 1428 FA

'The ford across the river *Toller*'. The river itself is now called
the Hooke, a back-formation from Hooke *infra* (cf. Ekwall, ERN
p. 410), but its original name is also preserved in Toller Fratrum,
Toller Porcorum and Toller Whelme *infra*. Tollerford (1″) is
according to Hutchins (II, 651) now only the name of a ground
near the original ford.

Chelborough, East and West
East Chelborough, West Chelborough 130 F 2[2]
Celberge 1086 DB, *Celberga* Exon

[1] For the evidence of an OE *Etha* cf. Redin p. 94 (note 4).
[2] For difficulties of identification see *supra* 75 n. 1.

Chalbergh, -berge 1150-1200 Montacute, *Westchalbergh* 1341 Fine,
   Chalburgh 1412 FA
Chauberge 1207 FineR, 1235-6 Fees (424), 1291 Tax, *Chaubergh*
   1279, 1281, 1285 Ipm, 1327, 1333 *SR*[1]
Cheleberg' 1242, 1244 Cl, *Cheleburg'* 1244 Cl
Chelbergh 1316 Ipm *et passim*, with *West* prefixed from 1337
   (Cl, Fine) and *Est* from 1340 (NI)
Chelberwe 1321 Inq aqd, *West Chelberwe* 1381 IpmR
Chelburgh 1351 Cl (*West*), 1355 Fine, 1431 FA, 1434 IpmR
   (*Est*)
Chelborowe 1535 VE

The second el. is OE *beorg* 'barrow, hill', but without OE forms
it seems impossible to make any definite suggestion about the
first. Is Chilbridge *supra* 84 to be compared? Cf. Zachrisson,
StNPh V, 60 n. 1.

For the many *a* spellings (*Chal-, Chau-*) cf. the earliest forms
given for Chelmscott in PN Bk p. 84; cf. also Zachrisson, AN
Infl. p. 147 f.

Lewcombe is *Leucumbe* 1297 Pat, *Lucumbe* 1297 Pat (p), *Lu-
combe* 1535 VE. This may be OE *hlēow-cumb* 'sheltered valley';
cf. Lewell *supra* 154. Luccombe Fm *infra* would seem to have
the same origin.

Chilfrome

Chilfrome [tʃilfru:m] 130 H 3
   Frome 1086 DB (*froma* Exon)
   Childefrome 1206 RC, 1235-6 Fees (424) *et passim*
   Childeresrome, Childesrome (sic) 1275 RH

Chilfrome is named after the river Frome, see *Frome Billet
supra* 159. The first part of the name is OE *cild* 'child' in the
gen. plur. form *cilda*, the first of the two RH forms (to be read
Childerefrome) probably preserving traces of another gen. plur.
form *cildra*. For the meaning of 'child' cf. Child Okeford *supra*
13. It may be worth noting that this *Frome* was held TRE
by 3 *taini in paragio*.

---

[1] Cf. also *Chawberge* [*Schaweberge*], *Westchawberge* [*Westchamberge*] 1303 FA.
On *sch* for *ch* cf. Zachrisson, AN Infl. p. 156 ff.

Compton Valence

Compton Valence 140 E/F 3

Contone 1086 DB, *Cumton'* 1212 Fees (94), 1235-6 ib. (573)
Cumpton 1252 Ch, 1253 FF, 1275 RH, *Compton* 1296 Cl
Cumpton Pundelarche 1265 Misc, 1296 Ipm, *Cumpton Pundel-arge* 1291 Tax, 1428 FA, *Compton Poundelarge* 1297 Pat
Compton Valence 1325 Ipm, Cl *et passim, Compton Valauncez* 1340 NI, *Compton Valans* 1431 FA

'Valley farm', OE *cumb, tūn*; cf. Compton Abbas *supra* 21. The history of the distinctive names may be illustrated by mentioning that William de *Pont del Arch* held *Cumton* of Adam de Port[1] in 1212 (Fees), that Robert de *Pondelarch* held it in 1235-6 (Fees), and, finally, that William de *Puntdelarch* (brother and heir of Robert de *Puntdelarch*) gave to William de *Valencia* (earl of Pembroke) *inter alia* the manor of *Cumpton*, as stated in 1252 Ch (p. 402). Cf. also Hutchins II, 292 f.; as suggested there, the family of *Puntdelarch* apparently derived their name from the town of Pont de l'Arche in Normandy (S of Rouen).

Evershot

Evershot 130 G 3

Teversict 1201-2 FF, *Teuerset, Theu'esete* 1244 *Ass*
Evers(h)et 1286 Ch, *Evershete* 1453 IpmR, *Euershete* 1476 FF
Euershut 1293 FF, *Evershut* 1341 Ipm
Theversshut 1345 Ipm, *Thevershut(e)* 1361 Cl, IpmR
Evershytte 1412 FA, *Evershit* 1431 FA (p), *Evershot* 1487 Ipm

The second el. of this name has been discussed by Zachrisson (ZONF II, 146 f.), who shows that by the side of OE *scēat* 'corner, nook, point' there must have existed an *i*-mutated variant **sciete* with much the same meaning. Zachrisson further points out that compounds with *-scēat, -sciete* often contain the name of a tree or an animal in the first el. and translates Evershot with 'the boar-nook' (OE *eofor*) on the strength of the single form *Everset* (1286 Ch). If this interpretation is correct, the initial *T-* (*Th-*) in some of the early forms (among them the

---

[1] Hugo de Porth was DB tenant-in-chief; cf. also 1166 RBE p. 207.

three earliest) must be due to the preposition *æt* having been prefixed to the forms in question. This may be so, but it seems more likely that *T* originally belonged to the name, and that it was later on lost by the common process of misdivision. What seems to me to strengthen this assumption is the name (*æt*) *Tæafersceat* 1012 (12th) KCD 721.[1] This has never been identified, but a comparison with the early forms of Evershot printed above, shows that identification with that place itself should probably be taken into consideration.[2] At any rate the two names should be compared. *Tæafersceat* would seem to contain OE *tēafor*[3], a word glossing *minium* ('red lead') and preserved in dial. *tiver* ('red ochre for marking sheep'); *Tæafersceat* (and Evershot) would consequently mean 'the nook (etc.) where *tiver* is found'. — Professor Zachrisson prefers to derive the first el. in Evershot from OE *þēofeþorn* 'hawthorn' (?).

Girt Fm (6″) is *atte Grutte* 1327 *SR* (p), *atte Gruite* 1340 NI (p). OE *grēot* 'gravel' with later metathesis.

Loxtree Fm is *Loxtrowe* 1361 Cl. The second el. is OE *trēow* 'tree'; the first is possibly OE *lox* 'lynx', but better material is needed to support this.

Frome St Quintin

Frome St Quintin 130 G 3

Litelfrome 1086 DB, *-a* Exon, *Littlefroma* 1242-3 Fees (750), *Litlefroma* 1264 Ipm, *Lytlefrome* 1268 FF *et passim* with variant spellings *Lit(t)le-*, *Lytel-*
Froma 1107 (1300) Ch, *From(e)* 1205 Cur, 1217 ClR *et passim*
Parva Frome 1235-6 Fees (426)
Frome Quentyn 1291 Tax *et passim*, the additional name being also spelt *Quintin*, *Quyntin*, etc.

---

[1] Cod. Winton.; also in Thorpe p. 552 ff.

[2] Many pl.-ns in this charter are difficult to identify, but at least one is a Dorset name, viz *Gyssic*, now Gussage *supra* 91.

[3] Suggested already by Williams, Anglia XXV, 517. Binz, Anglia Beiblatt XXXVIII, 281, looks upon *Tæafersceat* as an example of a pl.-n. showing the survival of heathen belief. Is that necessary?

Named after the river Frome, cf. *Frome Billet supra* 159. For
the distinctive name see Fifehead St Quintin *supra* 53.

Short Cross is probably to be connected with *atte Cruce* 1333
SR (p), as suggested by Mr Gover. If this is correct, ME
cr(o)uche 'cross' must later on have been displaced by the word
cross itself.

Frome Vauchurch

Frome Vauchurch 130 I 3

Frome 1086 DB, *Fromesfrogge Cherche* (sic) 1259 FF, *Frome
Noghechirch* (sic) 1291 Tax, *Frome Voghechurche* 1297 Pat
et passim, with the second name showing a long list of
variant spellings such as *Foechurch* 1303 FA, *Fouchurche*
1303 FA *et passim*, *Vowechirche* 1305 Ipm, *Foghechirche* 1329,
1337 FF, *Vowechurch(e)* 1333 *SR*, 1412 FA, *Voechurche* 1341
IpmR, *Fowechirche* 1361 Cl, *Voucherch(e)* 1385 IpmR, 1403
FF, 1412 FA, *Vouchurch(e)* 1386 Cl, 1486 Ipm, *Fowchurche*
1428 FA, *Vauchurche* 1535 VE

Fromesfoghechurche 1319 FF, *Fromesvauchurch* 1455 FF

Named after the river Frome, cf. *Frome Billet supra* 159.
Vauchurch means 'the stained church', see EPN s. v. *fāg*.

Maiden Newton

Maiden Newton 130 I 3

Newetone 1086 DB *et passim*, *Niweton* 1275 RH

Mayden Nywton 1303 FA, *Maydene Nyweton* 1311, 1319 Ipm
Maydene Neweton 1316 BM I *et passim*, *Mayndenenyweton*
1346 FA

Nyton Lyles 1405 IpmR, *Neweton Lisles* 1412 IpmR

Newton is self-explanatory. On the problem of *Maiden* in
English pl.-ns cf. e. g. Skeat, PN Berks p. 63 f.; Ekwall, Scandinavians and Celts p. 42; PN BedsHu p. 71 f. The reason
why *Maiden* was prefixed to the name of this place is unknown
to me. The last two forms above refer to the part of Maiden
Newton which during the 14th and 15th cent. belonged to the
family of *Lisle*; see Hutchins II, 683, 19 Edw III Ipm p. 427
(Bartholomew de *Insula*), 18 Edw III Ipm p. 376 (John de *Lyle*).

Crockway Fm [krɔkwei] (6″) is *Crokweye* 1333 *SR* (p), 1350, 1370
FF, 1405, 1412, 1428 IpmR. The second el. is apparently OE
weg 'way, road', but the first is doubtful. It may be, however,
that the name is comparatively late and that the first el. is ME
crok(e) 'crook' (something crooked). Cf. the discussion of similar
names in PN Wo p. 316. It should be noted, also, that Cruxton
(next pl.-n.) is less than a mile distant.

Cruxton [krɔkstən]
   Frome 1086 DB[1], *Fromma Johannis Croc* 1177-8 P
   Crocston' 1195 P, *Crokeston'* 1204 Cur, *Croxton* 1205 FineR,
   1329 FF, *Crokestun* 1223 Pat, *Crokeston* 1227 FF, 1235-6
   Fees (424), 1279 Ipm *et passim*, with variants *Croukeston*
   (1346 FA, etc.), *Croukerston* (1428 FA), *Crokkeston* (1428,
   1431 IpmR)

Cruxton is a clear example of a post-Conquest name in -*ton*,
the place being originally called *Frome* (after the river) up to
about the end of the 12th century. Besides the above *Johannes
Croc*, who must have held the place in or just before 1177-8,
we have mention of William *Croc* here in 1195 (P) and 1205
(FineR)[2]; cf. also the members of the *Croc* family here mentioned
in 1227 FF (p. 42 f.). The pers. name *Croc*, of Scandinavian
origin, was fairly common in medieval England and has been
assumed to enter into several pl.-ns in the Danelaw, cf. e. g.
Björkman, Nord. Personennamen p. 89 and Zur engl. Namenkunde p. 58. The appearance of this pers. name in a 12th
cent. pl.-n. far outside the Scandinavianized part of England is
in itself of little interest[3], but it may be worth noting that
Grimstone (*supra* 186), containing the originally Scandinavian
pers. name *Grim*, is only a couple of miles distant.

Notton is *Natton* 1350 FF, 1405, 1412, 1428 IpmR, *Neton* 1370
FF. Probably 'cattle farm', OE *nēat*, *tūn*; cf. Netton in PN D
p. 258.

---

[1] f. 81 b, cf. Eyton p. 139 f. The DB tenant-in-chief here was Wm de
Moion, and the identification is corroborated by the fact that in 1235-6 (Fees)
Reginald de Moyun held *inter alia* one knight's fee in *Crokeston*.

[2] Cf. also Hutchins II, 685. *Gillebertus Croc et Willelmus filius ejus* are mentioned several times under Do in the Pipe Rolls of Henry II.

[3] In DB we find *Croc* in Wilts and Hants.

Throop Dairy Ho (6″)

atte Thrope 1333 *SR* (p), *Throupe* 1348 FF, *Throp(e)* 1350 FF,
1405 (etc.) IpmR, *Le Throp(e)* 1370 FF, 1386 Cl, *La Thrope
juxta Frompton* 1385 IpmR, *Thorpe* 1811 OM

OE *þrop* (*þorp*) 'out-lying farm', cf. Throop *supra* 168.

Melbury Sampford

Melbury Sampford 130 F 3

Meleberie 1086 DB, *Melebir'* 1227, 1228 FF, *Mellebir'* 1236 Cl,
Melebyr' 1247 FF, *Melebury* 1333 *SR*
Melebir' Turbervill' 1235 Cl, 1242-3 Fees (750), 1257 FF (*Thurbervill*), *Mellbury Turbervyle* 1303 FA, *Melbury Turbervill*
1346, 1428 (*-vile*), 1431 (*-vyll*) FA

The present additional name appears from the beginning of
the 14th cent., first in the form of *Saunford* (*Melebury Saunford* 1313 FF), later as *Sandford* (1361 FF) and *Sampford* (1389 FF).
See Melbury Bubb *supra* 224. The *Turbervilles* here are the
same as those met with in connexion with Winterborne Muston
supra 71, the earliest mention of Walter de *Turbervill* here having
been found in 1227 (FF p. 33). On the *Saunfords* here (end of
13th cent.) see the detailed account in Hutchins (II, 656).

Rampisham

Rampisham [ræmpiʃəm, rænsəm] 130 G 2

Rameshā 1086 DB, *-ham* 1235-6 Fees (425), 1244 *Ass*, 1266
Ipm, 1291 Tax, 1296 Ipm *et passim* (the usual form)
Rammesham 1238 Ch, 1340 NI, 1350 Ch, 1359 BM II *et passim*
Ramesham al. *Rammesham* 1299 Ipm
Rampsham 1401 IpmR, *Ramsham* 1471 IpmR, *Ramsan* 1479
IpmR

The constant *Ram(m)-* spellings may seem to point to derivation from OE *ramm* 'ram', but as *ramm* does not seem to have
been used as a pers. name in OE (cf. Mawer, MLR XIV, 241 n.)
and it is rather unlikely that the animal's name itself (in gen.
sing.) could be compounded with *hām* 'farm', it is perhaps best
to leave the first el. unexplained, in particular as the evidence
for an OE pers. name **Hræfn* is not quite convincing; cf. e. g.
PN BedsHu p. 212 f. OE *hræfn* 'raven' is probably excluded

here for the same reason as *ramm*; cf. Renscombe Fm and *Ramsbury supra* 128, 218.

Yard Dairy is *La Yrde, Yerde, Le Yerde* t. Hy III BM I, *Le
Yerde* 1354 Ipm, *La Yurd* 1360 Ipm, *Yerd(e)* 1386 Cl, IpmR,
1399, 1401 FF, *La Yarde* 1414 IpmR, *Yard* 1471 IpmR. This
name has apparently the same history as several places called
Yard in Devon, assumed in PN D p. 48 to go back to OE *gierd*
'area of land about one-fourth of a hide' (30 acres), reference
being given to NED s. v. *yard* sb. 2, sense 10; cf. Yard Fm
infra (in Marshwood).

Toller Fratrum

Toller Fratrum [tɔlə] 130 I 3
   Tollr' 1250 Cl, *Tolre Fratru'* 1340 NI, *Toller Fratrum* 1428 FA

See Toller Porcorum (next name) and Toller Whelme *infra*.
Fratrum because the place anciently belonged to the Knights
Templars, cf. Hutchins II, 696; VCH Do II, 92. The popular
name is Little Toller.

Toller Porcorum

Toller Porcorum 130 I 2
   Tolre 1086 DB, 1091-1106 (etc.) Montacute, 1100-22 (1270) Ch,
      1195 P, 1236 FF *et passim*, *Tore* 1235-6 Fees (426 f.)
   Suinestholre, Swynestholre 1259 FF, *Swynnestolre* 1337 Cl,
      Swynestolre 1386 Cl, IpmR, 1428 FA
   Swyninge & Tolere (sic) 1275 RH
   Swyne Tolre 1303 FA, *Swynetolre* 1346 FA
   Swenenetolre 1329 FF, *Swynentolre* 1337 FF, 1345 Orig, 1360
      Cl, *Swynenetolre* 1360 FF, Cl, 1361, 1362 Cl
   Tolre Porcorum 1340 NI (onwards), *Swyntoller* 1457 IpmR

See Toller Whelme *infra* and cf. Tollerford *supra* 228. Toller
Porcorum "seems to receive its additional name from great
quantities of swine being anciently fed in the commons and
woody tracts with which this parish abounded" (Hutchins).
Here, as in several other Do names, the Latin addition is seldom
used by the people; they call the place Great Toller.

Frogmore Dairy Ho is *Frogmore* 1340 NI (p), *Froggemore* 1360
Cl, *Frogmere* 1455 FF, *Frogmer* 1486 Ipm. See Frogmore Fm
supra 25. In spite of the two earliest spellings the second el.
may well have been OE *mere* 'pool' in the present name, too.

Kingcombe, Higher and **Lower** [kiŋkəm]
Chimedecome (twice) 1086 DB
Kendecumb 1212 Fees (94), *Kemthecumb* 1226 FF, *Kemtecumbe*
     1244 *Ass* (p), *Kemdecumb(e)* 1275 RH (p)
Kentecumba 1236 Fees (581), *Kenta-* ib. (p), *Kentecumb(e)* 1285
     FF, 1297 Cl *et passim* with variant *-co(u)mbe*
Keindecumbe (prob. for *Kemde-*)[1] 1285 FA
Nether Keinecumb [*Nuther Keincombe*] 1303 FA
Nethere Kentecombe 1315 FF, 1346 FA (*Nither*) *et passim* (with
     small variants), *Overkentcombe* 1385 IpmR

The second el. is of course OE *cumb* 'valley', but the first is
very difficult. Ekwall suggests (ERN p. 228) that it might be
OE *cymed* 'wall-germander'. The almost constant *e* spellings
would seem to speak against this assumption, but I have no
better suggestion to make.

Woolcombe Fm
Wellacome, Wilecome 1086 DB, *Wulecum* 1204 (1313) Ch, *Ule-*
     cumbe 1244 Abbr, *Ullecumbe* 1255 Sarum, *Wllecumba* 1265
     Misc, *Wollecumbe* 1285 FA, *-combe* 1327 *SR*
Wulcome Bingham 1303 Ipm, *Wollecombe* [al. *Wellecombe*] *Bynge-*
     ham 1312 Ipm, *Wolcombe Byngham* 1412 FA
Wollecombe Piterych 1318 Ipm

See the same name *supra* 225. This Woolcombe belonged to
the *Binghams* of West Stafford and Bingham's Melcombe (*supra*
159, 191), Robert de *Bingeham* being mentioned as lord of *Wlle-*
cumba in 1265 (Misc p. 200). The *Piterych* of the 1318 form is
unknown (cf. Petersham Fm *supra* 82).

---

[1] *Kenilecumb* 1251-2 Fees (1268), if really belonging here, is probably corrupt,
as are also *Kemlecumbe* 1305 FF and *Overkenilecumbe* 1311 FF. They may all
stand for *Kemte-*.

Wynford Eagle

Wynford Eagle 130 I 3

Wenfrot 1086 DB, *Winfrod(e)* 1227, 1260 Ch, 1273 Ipm, 1291 Ch, *Wynfrod* 1232, 1243 Cl, *Winifrod'* 1233 Cl *Womfrod'* 1234 Cl, *Wymfred* 1333 *SR* *Wynford Aquile* 1275 RH *Wymfrodegle* 1291 Tax, *Wynfrid Egle* 1303 FA, *Wynfred Egle* 1309, 1310 Cl, 1311 Ipm *et passim, Wyndfred Egle* 1309 Ipm, 1310 Fine, *Winford Egle* 1412 FA, 1431 FA *(Wyn-)*

See Winfrith Newburgh *supra* 148, and Ekwall, ERN p. 462. The manor was a member of the Honour of Eagle (cf. Hutchins II, 701), Gilbert de *Aquila* being mentioned as the owner of *Winfrod* in 1227 (Ch). Cf. also Tait, IPN p. 122.

XXIX. Eggardon Hundred

gⁱo-chresdone (sic) 1084 GeldRoll *Ekeresdon, Egresdon* 1244 *Ass, Ecresdon* 1265 Misc *Ekerdon(e)* 1275 RH, 1285, 1303 FA, 1326 Orig, 1327 *SR*, 1329 *Ipm et passim* to 1431 FA, *Ekerton* 1334 Misc *Egerdon* 1303, 1346, 1428 FA, *Egardon* 1535 VE

Cf. also the early forms for Eggardon Fms *infra*.

The hundred takes its name from Eggardon Hill, the large camp 1 ½ m. NE of Askerswell. The second el. is of course OE *dūn* 'down, hill', but I am unable to suggest any plausible interpretation of the first.

Askerswell

Askerswell 140 F 1

Oscherwille 1086 DB, *Oscheruulla* Exon *Oscareswell'* 1185-6 P, *Oskareswell'* 1185-6 P, 1235-6 Fees (425), *Oskereswell* 1201-2 FF, 1244 *Ass*, 1269 Misc *(-wull)* (p), 1285 FA *(-will)* (p), 1288 FF, 1324 FF *(-wille)*, 1333 *SR*, *Oskerswelle* 1303 FA, *Oxkereswell* 1393 AD I *Oskerwell(e)* 1194 P (p), 1346 FA (p), *Oskervill'* 1200 Cur (p), *Oskerewell* 1262 Pap *Eskereswelle, -will* 1285 FA, *Eskareswolle* 1291 Tax, 1428 FA

Askereswell 1340 NI, 1379 Cl *et passim* (later *Askers-*), *Askerswill* 1346 FA, *Askereswill* 1412 FA

The second el. is of course OE *wielle* 'spring, well'. The first is probably the OE pers. name *Ōsgār*, though the constant *k* (for *g*) is remarkable. It may be noted, however, that the corresponding Scand. name *Asgar* is occasionally recorded in England as *Ascarus* (c. 1060 KCD 806) and *Askerus* (1223 ClR).[1] On the other hand it seems clear that, since all the earliest forms for Askerswell show the type *Os-*, we cannot believe that it is the Scand. name itself that lies behind the first el. of this pl.-n. But it may be suspected that some sort of confusion took place between the English and Scand. pers. names, otherwise it seems difficult to account for the later *Es-* and *As-* spellings; cf. the discussion of the *As-* names in Björkman, Nord. Personennamen p. 10 ff. It may further be mentioned that, according to Fabricius (p. 38) and Jakobsen (in Danske Studier 1911 p. 66), the name of the viking chieftain (*Ásgeirr*), who in 841 sailed up the Seine, appears in Norman Chronicles as *Oscher*.

The name of the river Asker, which flows past Askerswell, is a clear back-formation from the village-name.

Eggardon Fms is *Jekeresdon'* 1204 Cur, *Ekerdun* 1285 FA, *Ekerdon(e)* 1310 Inq aqd, 1348 FF (*North-*), 1356 FF *et passim*, *Egerdon* 1357 FF, 1364 FF, IpmR, *Egreton* 1364 Cl, *Ekerton* 1375 IpmR. Named from Eggardon Hill, see Eggardon Hundred *supra* 237.

Long Bredy

Long Bredy 140 F/G 2

(*in*) *Bridian* (twice)[2] 987 (copy) KCD 656

Langebride 1086 DB, 1325 Inq aqd, *Langebridia* 1086 Exon, 1244 *Ass*, *Langebrid'* 1212 Fees (92), *Langebridie* 1275 RH (p), 1285 FA, *-bridye* 1303 FA, *-brydy* 1431 FA

Longa Brydye 1291 Tax, *Long Brydie* 1297 Pat, Cl (*Brydy*) *Langbredy* 1443 IpmR, *Langebrede* 1441-5 Inq aqd

---

[1] See Björkman, Nord. Personennamen p. 13 and Zur engl. Namenkunde p. 15.

[2] *in Bridian sex, in ulteriore Bridian duodecim* (*mansas*), referring to Little and Long Bredy respectively. (*to*) *Brydian* c. 910 (c. 1100) Burghal Hidage probably belongs here, too; see Maitland p. 503, and Ekwall, ERN p. 52.

Long Bredy as well as Little Bredy, Bredy Fm and Burton Bradstock (all *infra*) derive their names from the river Bride, discussed by Ekwall, ERN p. 52 f. (suggested meaning: 'gushing, surging, torrential stream'). *Long* because of its greater length in comparison with Little Bredy.

Ashley

Asseleghe 1246 FF, *Asshele* 1333 *SR*, *Ashle* 1340 NI (p)
Ayhsleg(h) 1251 Ch, AD II, *Ayshleg'* 1382 Cl
Hassel 1275 RH, *Hesele* 1278 QW, *Eslee* 1285 FA

'Ash-tree clearing', OE *æsc*, *lēah*.

Baglake Fm (6″)

Bagelag' 1244 *Ass* (p), *Baglage West* 1325 Inq aqd
Bagelake 1275 RH (p), *Baggelake* 1281 FF (p), 1329 AD II, 1372, 1392 FF, *Estbagelake* 1300 FF, 1443 IpmR
Babelake 1389 Cl, 1403 FF, -*bb*- 1408 FF

The second el. must be OE *lacu* 'stream, watercourse'; for the first el. cf. *Baggeridge supra* 93.

Dowerfield Fm (and Dairy Ho) [dauəfi:ld]

The only early reference that I have seen is *Dowerlond* 1431 FA. The material is scanty, but it may be suggested that the first el. is the word *dower* in one or other of the senses 'the portion of a deceased husband's estate which the law allows to his widow for her life', 'the property which the wife brings to the husband' (NED). I suppose the first sense is the one here. As pointed out in EPN (p. 44), *land* is often compounded with a first el. denoting tenure (*bōcland*, *folcland*, *sundorland*), and *dowerland* would consequently be another example of that kind.[1] A similar type of names, containing OE *morgen-giefu* 'morning-gift', is discussed in PN Sx p. 519 s. n. Morgay Fm.

According to Hutchins (II, 188) another name for Dowerfield was Halling's Manor, called *Hallynges maner'* (*in Langbredy*) t. Hy VI IpmR, Inq aqd. I have not been able to trace the person

---

[1] The compound *dowerland* is not recorded in NED until 1862, but cf. the phrase given there from 1528: "To Margarete, my wif, hir hoole dore of all mv landes."

after whom the manor was named. It was a member of *Ryme Extrinseca* (cf. *supra* 226).

Gorwell Fm is *Gorewull* 1285 FA, *Gorwell(e)* 1290 Ch, 1381 Cl, *Gorewell(e)* 1337 FF, 1348 IpmR *et passim*, *Gorwill(e)* 1380, 1471 IpmR, *Gorewill(e)* 1382, 1386 Cl, 1386 IpmR, *Gorwyll* 1471 IpmR. 'Dirty spring', OE *gor, wielle* (EPN).

Hooke

Hooke 130 H 1
   Lahoc 1086 DB, *Hoc* 1091-1106 Montacute, *Hoch* c. 1155 ib.
   (Rob.) *del Hoc* 1200 Cur, (Walt.) *del Hoke* 1244 *Ass*
   Hoke 1235-6 Fees (424) *et passim* with variant *Houk(e)* from
      1346 (FA), *La Hoke* 1244 *Ass et passim* to 1369 Cl

OE *hōc* 'projecting corner, sharp bend in a stream' (cf. EPN s. v.), both meanings suiting the topography very well. The stream in question is now called the Hooke, a clear back-formation from the village-name; cf. Tollerford *supra* 228.

Stapleford (lost) is *Stapelford* 1244 *Ass* (p), 1285 FA *et passim*, *Stapulford* 1360, 1385 IpmR, 1447 FF, *Stapylford* 1471 IpmR. 'Ford marked by a staple or post', OE *stapol, ford* (EPN).

Powerstock[1]

Powerstock [pauəstɔk], earlier [pɔ:stɔk] 130 I 1
   Povrestoch 1086 DB, *Pourestocha* Exon
   Porstok(e) 1157, c. 1160 Sarum (also *-stocha*)[2], 1205 (etc.) ClR,
      1207, 1213 PatR, 1213 Osmund, 1224 (etc.) Pat, 1230 (etc.)
      Cl, 1237 Lib, 1273 Ipm *et passim* to 1333 *SR*
   Porestok(e) 1157, c. 1160 Sarum, 1205 (etc.) ClR, 1201-12 RBE,
      1217 Pat (*-stoc*), 1230 (etc.) Lib, 1231 (*et passim* to 1386)
      Cl, 1236 FineR, and occasionally up to 1480
   Poursteda (sic) 1194 P, *Pourstok(e)* 1195 P, 1205 RC, 1205
      (etc.) ClR, 1207 PatR, 1212 Fees (93) *et passim*

---

[1] In 1275 RH (p. 97) there is mention of a hamlet in Eggardon Hundred called *Walletmull*, which answered at the court of Powerstock for the fifth part of a tithing; cf. also Hutchins II, 315 f. I can find no trace of this *Walletmull* in any other record.
[2] Once *Powe(r)stok*.

Poerstoke 1194-5, 1196-7 RBE, 1150-1200 Montacute
Purstock 1206 ChR, *Purstok* 1219 Fees (263), 1287 Cl, 1340
  NI, 1363 Cl, *Purestok* (in rubric) 1255 Sarum
Poverstoke 1201-12 RBE, *Pouerstok* 1236 Cl, *Pourestoke* 1364
  Cl, 1375 BM I, 1412 FA, *Pouerestok* 1380 BM II, *Power-*
  stok(e) 1355 IpmR, 1535 VE
Portstok 1226 FF, 1228 Lib, *Postak'* 1251 Cl

The second el. is of course OE *stoc* 'place', but I can offer no
satisfactory explanation of the difficult first element. It seems
clear, however, that Poorton (North and South) *infra*, about a
mile to the north, must contain the same first element; cf. also
Porton (W), left unexplained by Ekblom (p. 136). The district
here is very hilly and must once have been well wooded.
Whatever may have been the origin of the first part of Powerstock and Poorton, it seems fairly certain that it was at an
early date associated with the word *poor* (OFr *povre, poure* >
ME *pouere, poer, powere* etc.).[1] It can hardly, however, be the
word *poor* itself, since that word is not recorded in English until
about 1200 (NED).

In the Introd. to Osmund (vol. II, foot-note to p. LXXXVI f.) it
is stated that the DB under-tenant of Powerstock, Hugo, bore
the surname *le Poer* (in a Sarum charter of 1152), and the conclusion is drawn that Powerstock took its name from him (cf.
Pierston Fm *supra* 8). The statement is interesting, but it seems
to me far from certain that the conclusion is correct.

Gray's Fm should probably be associated with the family of
Robert *Grey*, who in 1401 (FF) was granted three acres of
meadow in Lower Kingcombe (a mile NE) and one-third part of
the manor of Chilfrome.

Mappercombe
Mepercumb(e) 1285 FA, *Mep'combe* 1291 Tax
Sopcūbe (sic) 1291 Tax, *Mopercumbe* 1303 FA, *Mopercome* 1318

---

[1] Cf. the following passage in Hutchins (II, 318): "Here still (i. e. in 1865)
remains a tradition, that there was a wood of several hundred acres, given to
the poor of the parish for fuel, now called the Common of Poorwood — —.
Here was also a park of about forty acres, now divided into several grounds
still retaining that name."

Ch, *Mop'combe* 1333 *SR,* 1535 VE, *Mapercombe* 1636 SoDo
NQ VIII

The second el. is self-evident, but I am unable to interpret
the first. The modern form may have been influenced by
Mapperton *infra* (3 m. NW).

West Milton is *Mideltone* 1086 DB (*-tona* Exon), *-ton* 1212 Fees
(92), 1285 FA, *Middletone* 1255 Sarum, *Mylton* 1303 FA, *Milton*
1318 Ch. 'Middle farm', OE *middel, tūn. West* probably to
distinguish it from Milton Abbas *supra* 191.

Nettlecombe
Netelcome 1086 DB (*-coma* Exon), *-cum'* 1205 RC, *-cumb(e)*
1212 Fees (92), 1285 FA, 1291 Tax, 1303 FA
Netlecumb(e) 1205 ClR, 1219 FF, *Nettlecumb* 1206 PatR, FineR
ChR, *Nettlecome* 1318 Ch

'Nettle valley', OE *netele, cumb.*

South Poorton is *Pourtone* 1086 DB, *Supereporthon* 1229 BM II,
South Pourton 1386 Cl. See North Poorton *infra.*

Wytherstone Fm
Wytheston 1269 Ch. Misc, *Witheston* 1311 Pap, 1336 Ch
Wydeston 1269 Ch, 1291 Tax
Wytherstone, Witherston 1285 FA

The second el. may be 'stone' (OE *stān*), and if so, the first
is possibly OE *wīðig* 'withy, willow' (cf. Withyhook Mill *supra*
224), provided we take the *Wyther-* type to have developed from
the *Wythe-* type. If on the other hand the second el. is *tūn*,
the first must be left unexplained.

Winterborne Abbas
Winterborne Abbas 140 F 4
(*in*) *Winceburnan* (sic) 987 (copy) KCD 656
Wintreburne 1086 DB, 1212 Fees (92), *Winterburn* 1285 FA

With additional name it appears as *Wynterburn Abbatisse* (sic)
de Cerne 1244 *Ass, Wynterbor Abbots* 1257 Pap, *Winterburn (Wyn-)*

Abbots 1297 Cl, Pat, *W. Abbatis* 1340 NI. See Winterborne
Came *supra* 162. It is also called *Watreleswyntreburn* 1291 Fine,
1292 Orig (and the like in 1292 Abbr, 1306 Pat, 1365 FF) and
Wynterborn Waterlyse 1303 FA, 'waterless' (OE *wæterlēas*) being
a good description of what the stream is like in dry seasons.

Wraxall

Wraxall [ræksəl] 130 H 2/3
  Brocheshale 1086 DB, *Brochessala* Exon
  Wrokeshal' 1196 Cur, 1206 RC, 1212 Fees (94), 1219 FF, -*hale*
    1242-3 Fees (751) 1269 Misc, 1285 FF
  Wrochehall 1204 (1313) Ch
  Wrockesh̃ 1206 RC, -*hal* 1219 FF, 1285 FA (p), -*hall* 1244 *Ass*,
    -*hale* 1291 Tax, 1323 FF, 1428 FA, *Wrokkeshal* 1316 Ipm
  Wroxhale 1253 Ch, 1275 RH (p), 1285, 1303 FA *et passim*,
    Wroxale 1310 Inq aqd, *Wroxalle* 1321 Inq aqd
  Wrokeshale Deneys 1285 FF, *Wroxhale Deneys* 1369 BM II
  Wraxhale 1483 IpmR

The second el. is OE *healh* (dat. *heale*) 'corner, angle, (inner)
slope of a hill'. The first should be compared with names like
Wraxall, North and South (W), two Wraxalls in So[1], Wroxall
(Wa and Wt), Roxhill (Beds), Wroxton (O), and Wroxham (Nf).[2]
Those of the enumerated pl.-ns which have been discussed earlier
have all been taken to contain an OE pers. name **Wroc(c)*, not
recorded in independent use but postulated from the pl.-ns
themselves, above all from (*æt*) *Wroccesheale* KCD 768, now
Wroxall (Wt).[3] My own doubts about the correctness of this
explanation have now been confirmed, for Zachrisson has recently
(StNPh V, 60 n. 1) suggested another etymology, **wroc* being
according to him a descriptive word from *wrocen*, past participle
of *wrecan*, with the original sense of 'something driven up or

---

[1] 1. Wraxall (parish, 6 m. W of Bristol): *Werocosale* 1086 DB, *Wroxale* 1390
FF So, *Wroxhale* 1406 FF So. 2. Wraxall (hamlet, 1 m. W of Ditcheat), of
which I can find no certain early forms.
[2] *Wrokesham* 1283 Ipm, *Wroxham* 1302 Ch, FA.
[3] Cf. Skeat, PN Beds p. 29; Alexander, PN O p. 229; Duignan, PN Wa p.
130; Ekblom, PN W p. 180; Zachrisson, StMSpv IX, 124, 141; PN Beds
Hu p. 80.

together', 'a wrinkle or fold'. There seem to be good reasons
for believing that this new interpretation should be preferred to
the earlier one.[1]

The temporary addition *Deneys* is from the 13th and early
14th cent. owners; cf. Osbertus *Dacus* (i. e. *Danicus*) 1204 (1313)
Ch, 1206 RC, 1212 Fees (94), in a later entry (1269 Misc) called
Osbert *le Deneys* ('the Danish'), and Adam *Dacus* 1206 RC, Adam
le Daneys 1253 Ch, etc.; cf. also Hutchins II, 201.

XXX. Uggescombe Hundred

oglescome 1084 Geld Roll

Vggescumbe 1195 P, *Ugescumb'* 1212 Fees (93), *Uggescumbe* 1244
   Ass, 1269 Misc *et passim* (variant *-combe*)

Huggescumb(e) 1244 *Ass*, 1275 RH, 1278 QW, 1329 Ipm (*-combe*),
   Hugescumb' 1251-2 Fees (1268), *Hoggescumbe* 1265 Misc

Uggecombe 1278 QW, *Ogescombe* 1425 IpmR

The Geld Roll form is probably corrupt. A weak pers. name
*Ucga has been inferred from *ucganford* BCS 1030, now Ugford
(W), and has been assumed to enter inter several other pl.-ns.[2]
A corresponding strong name **Ucg* may lie behind the first el.
of Uggescombe. Hence possibly *'Ucg's* valley', OE *cumb*.

Uggescombe is nowadays lost as a pl.-n., but it is stated in
Hutchins (II, 714, 763) that the hundred courts were formerly
held in a valley "now called Mystecomb"[3], a little north of
Portisham, and this valley is supposed to be the ancient *Uggescombe*.

Abbotsbury

Abbotsbury 140 H 3

Abbodesbyrig n. d.[4] KCD 841, 942, *-birie* 1066-78 (1269) Ch

---

[1] After this was written my attention has been drawn to a similar interpretation made by Grundy in Arch. Journal LXXXIV. 320.

[2] Cf. e. g. Ekblom p. 164; Ekwall, PN La p. 65 s. n. Ogden; Blomé p. 97
s. n. Uggaton; PN D p. 284 s. n. Ugborough.

[3] There is no such name on any modern map, but it is found on the OS
map of 1811 and on Greenwood's map of 1826.

[4] Thorpe (p. 576) assigns KCD 841 to the year 1045.

Abedesberie, Abodesber' 1086 DB, *Abbatesberia* Exon
Abbotesbiria 1178-87 (1269) Ch, *-burie* 1154-65 (1269) Ch

Later forms are of little interest. *Abbodesberia* (*Abbedesberia*)
is the common form in RBE and the early Pipe Rolls, the
former document showing occasional spellings *-bery, -biry, -buria,
-byria*. Montacute (c. 1170) has *Abotesbire, Abbotisbire*. A few
s-less forms have been noted: *Abbodebi* 1201 FineR, *-bire* 1242-3
Fees (1135), *Abbedebyria* 1210-2 RBE, *Abotebir'* 1212 PatR, *Abbote-
bir'* 1213 PatR. Two 13th cent. forms *Abbesbury* (1258 Pat)
and *Abbesbiry* (1288 Cl) may indicate the local pronunciation of
the time.

'The abbot's *burh*' (dat. *byrig*). If *burh* here has its primary
sense of 'fortified place', it may refer to the old camp called
Abbotsbury Castle, about 1 ¹/₂ m. NW of the village.

A monastery was built here by *Orc*, steward of King Canute
(see under Tolpuddle *supra* 179); it should, however, also be
noted that land here belonged at a very early date to Glastonbury Abbey; cf. Hutchins II, 714 f.

Elworth
Aleurde 1086 DB, *Ellewrd'* 1212 Fees (93)
Elleworth 1281 Ipm, 1285 FA (*-wurth*), 1305 Ipm, 1327 *SR* (p),
    1340 Cl *et passim, Elworthe* 1361 Cl, 1535 VE
Elleworth(e) Payn 1346, 1428, 1431 FA[1]
Est Elleworth 1371 FF (*juxta Portesham*), 1391 IpmR
Ellesworth(e) 1398 IpmR (*juxta Abbottesbury*), 1425 IpmR

Probably 'elder-tree enclosure', OE *ellen, weorþ. Payn* from
the 13th and 14th cent. tenants, the *Fitz Payns* (cf. Okeford
Fitzpaine *supra* 45), *Robertus filius Pagani* being mentioned here
in 1212 (Fees p. 93); cf. Hutchins II, 726.

Rodden is *Raddon* 1244 *Ass* (p), 1285 FA (*-dun*), 1333 *SR et
passim*. 'Red hill', OE *rēad, dūn*. "From the colour of the soil,
a rich red clay" (Hutchins). The transition of *a* to *o* is probably
very late.

Little Bredy
Little Bredy 140 G 3
Litelbride 1086 DB (*-brida* Exon), 1346, 1428 FA (*-tt-*)

---

[1] 1303 FA has an evidently corrupt form *Ebbeworth [Eglesworth] Payn*.

Litlebridie 1204 Cur, 1205, 1219 FF *et passim* with variants
  Littl(e)-, *Litel-*, and *-bridye* 1285, 1303 FA
Litlebrid' 1212 Fees (92), *Litlebrid* 1275 RH
Parva Brudye 1291 Tax, *Lytelbrydye* 1333 *SR*

See Long Bredy *supra* 238.

Chilcombe

Chilcombe 140 F 1
  Ciltecome 1086 DB
  Chiltecumbe 1285 FA, 1331 Pap, *-combe* 1297 Pat, 1326 Cl
  Childecombe 1333 *SR* (p), 1346 Orig, 1428 FA
  Childcomb 1340 NI, *Chilcomb* 1662 Hutchins

After the discovery of a place called *le Chilte* (1357) in West
Chiltington (Sx)[1] it seems very doubtful if we are right in
assuming the existence of an unrecorded pers. name **Cilta*, as
has earlier been done (cf. Ekwall, PN in *-ing* p. 56, and PN Sx
p. 174 f.), and Zachrisson has recently (StNPh V, 60 n. 1) assumed
that there was an OE hill-name **celte*, **cilte*. The district round
Chilcombe is very hilly. Chilcombe in Hants (*Ciltancumb* BCS
620, 621) seems to be an exact parallel to the present name.

Fleet

Fleet 140 K 5
  Flete, *Fleta* 1086 DB, Exon, 1212 Fees (93), c. 1215 (etc.)
    Sarum, 1219 FineR, 1235-6 Fees (426) *et passim*
  Flote 1086 DB, Exon, *Fleota* 1213 Osmund
  Flicta 1157 Sarum, *Flute* 1227 FF

Fleet derives its name from the narrow arm of the sea (East
Fleet, West Fleet) which separates Chesil Bank from the mainland; OE *flēot* 'water, inlet, estuary'.

Kingston Russel

Kingston Russel 140 F 3
  Kingeston 1212 Fees (92), 1278 Fine, *Kynkeston'* 1251-2 Fees
    (1268), *Kyngeston* 1279 FF *et passim*

---

[1] See PN Sx p. 4, and Ekwall, ERN p. 78.

Kingeston Radulfi Russel 1240 Sarum
Kyngeston Russel from 1284 Ch onward

That Kingston Russel was originally a royal manor is shown by the entry from 1212 Fees (92) which tells us that Johannes *Russel* held it of the king *ex tempore Willelmi Bastard'* (— — *per serianciam essendi marescallus buteilerie domini regis*). The Ralph Russel of the 1240 form above was his son; see also Hutchins II, 189.

Whatcombe Down is *Whatecome* 1340 Cl. Cf. Whatcombe *supra* 68.

Langton Herring

Langton Herring 140 I 4

Langetone 1086 DB (*languetona*, *Langat'*. Exon) *et passim*, the medial *e* being very persistent
Langedon 1212 Fees (93), 1428 FA
Langeton Sarnevil' 1278 QW, *Langton Heryng* 1372 IpmR

Cf. Langton Long Blandford *supra* 55. *Sarnevil'* in the 1278 QW form is a reminiscence of the family of *Salmonville* or *Sarmunvile* here, see Hutchins II, 745[1]; cf. Walditch *infra*. For the present distinctive name cf. Chaldon Herring *supra* 138; Philip *Harang* (mentioned under Winterborne Herringstone and Herrison *supra* 163, 182) was here in 1268 (FF).

Litton Cheney

Litton Cheney 140 F 2

Lideton 1204 Cur (p), 1212 Fees (93), *Lid(d)e-* 1244 *Ass*, *Lidi-* 1304 Ch
Ludeton 1204 Cur (p), 1236 FF, 1244 *Ass* (p), 1248 Ch, 1275 RH, 1285 FA, 1297 Pat, Cl, 1303 FA, *Ludi-* t. Hy III Ipm, *Ludy-* 1301 FF
Ludinton' 1205 Cur (p), 1235-6 Fees (425), *-yn-* 1287 FF, *-yng-* 1291 Tax
Lyditune 1272 Ipm, *Lydinton* 1304 Pat
Litytone 1278 QW
Lutton(e) 1324 Ipm, 1333 *SR*, 1337 FF *et passim* to 1428 FA

---

[1] The eighth part of a fee in Do which Philip de *Salmonville* held of Alfred de Lincoln in 1166 (RBE p. 216) is identified in Hutchins with this place.

248   Anton Fägersten

Luiton(e) 1324 Cl, 1346 FA
Lytton 1380 BM II, 1431 FA, 1431, 1477 IpmR, 1535 VE
Litton 1384 BM I, 1412 FA

I take the first el. of this name to be OE *hlȳde* (obl. case *hlȳdan*) 'torrent, swift stream'[1], Litton Cheney being thus an addition to the group of names discussed by Ekwall in ERN p. 272 f.[2] The *Cheyne* or *Cheyny* family were here from about 1400 (Ralph *Cheyny* 1400-1 IpmR).

Coombe, Higher and **Lower,** is *Cumbe* 1301 FF, *Combe* 1324 Ipm. OE *cumb* 'valley'.

Stancombe Barn is *Stancombe* 1337 FF, *Stankombe* 1412 FA. 'Stony valley', OE *stān, cumb*.

Portisham

Portisham[3] 140 H 3/4

(*æt*) *Porteshamme* 1024 (orig.) KCD 741
Porteshā 1086 DB, *portesã* Exon
Portesham 1212 Fees (92), 1285 FA *et passim*

If the above charter form can be trusted, the second el. would seem to be OE *hamm*, here probably in the sense of 'enclosed possession, fold'. The first el. is difficult. A pers. name **Port* is inferred from place-name material by the editors of PN Sx (p. 289 s. n. Portslade), but the evidence for such a name seems

---

[1] No stream is visible here on the 1″ map, but we are told in Hutchins that "a little west of the parsonage house, a beautiful spring breaks out in the grounds of the rectory, which runs through the village in a plentiful stream of the clearest water. A new grist-mill has lately been erected on this stream." Both spring, stream (an affluent of the river Bride) and mill are marked on the 6″ map (the mill also on the 1″ map). The district is very hilly, and it is clear that the current must be strong enough for the stream to be termed a torrent.

[2] Among the charter forms enumerated by Ekwall (p. 273) two refer to a Do stream, viz. (*on*) *hlydan pol* KCD 1309, and (*on*) *hlyda pol* ib. 1322. The stream in question must be one of the now nameless brooks near Corscombe. That district also is very hilly.

[3] I am unable to say if older pronunciations like "Posham, Possum" (Hutchins) can still be heard.

to me far from conclusive. On the other hand there can hardly be any question of OE *port* (Latin *portus*) 'town' or 'harbour' in connexion with Portisham (as for instance in the case of Portsmouth), but OE *port* (Latin *porta*) 'gate, entrance' was evidently used as a second el. in pl.-ns (cf. Westport *supra* 131), and I can see no reason why it should not have been used in the first (even in its genitive form). Cf. also Wallenberg p. 312.

Corton Fm

Corfetone 1086 DB, *Corftona* t. Hy I BM I, *Corfton* c. 1165, c. 1170 Montacute, 1217 ClR, 1244 *Ass*, 1264 Ipm, FineR, 1285 FA *et passim* to 1414 BM I, *Corvfton* 1303 FA
Corston (sic) 1218 ClR, 1291 Tax, 1333 *SR*, 1428 FA
Crofton 1346, 1412, 1428 FA, *Corton* 1430 IpmR

Less than half a mile W of Corton is a place called

Coryates [kɔrieits, kɔriəts]

(*on*) *corf getes westran cotan* 1024 (orig.) KCD 741
Corryatts 1698 SoDoNQ VIII

Both these names contain *corf* 'a cutting, a pass', see Corfe Castle *supra* 116. The second el. of Coryates is OE *geat* 'gate', preserved in its genitive form after the dropping of the word *cote* 'cot, cottage'; cf. further Corscombe *infra*.

Shilvinghampton [ʃilviŋtən]

Sevemetone[1], *Scilfemetune, Silfemetone* 1086 DB
Sifhātun' 1194 CurR, *Sifhaintun* 1194-5 Abbr
Selfameton' 1212 Fees (92), *Selfhamptun'* 1235-6 Fees (426), *Shelfhamton* 1253 FF
Schilfhamton 1244 *Ass*, 1303 FA, *Schilfamtun* 1285 FA
Shulfhampton 1292 Pat, 1333 *SR*, 1340 NI[2], 1346 FA, 1402 IpmR, 1428 FA, 1456 IpmR, *Estshylshampton* (sic) 1330 FF, *Westshulhampton* 1385 FF
Shilvyngton 1431 FA, *Shelvington* 1765 Taylor

The suggestion in Hutchins (II, 762) that this place "perhaps derives its name from the shelving ground or declivity on which

---

[1] Corresponding to *Sefemetona* in Exon.
[2] Mistranscribed as *Shuls-*.

it stands", is evidently correct, the first el. being OE *scylf*.[1] It is difficult to be sure whether the latter part of the name is OE *hāmtūn* 'farmstead', or whether it should be interpreted as *-hǣmatūn*; cf. Witchampton *supra* 108.

Waddon (1″), Little Waddon (6″)

Wadone 1086 DB, *Waddon* 1201 Cur (p), 1212 Fees (93), 1244
   Ass, 1285 FA *et passim*, *Westwaddon* 1275 RH *et passim*
Wadun Cray 1235-6 Fees (426), *Waddon Krey* 1303 FA
Little Waddone 1305 Ipm, *Waddon Parva* 1398 IpmR
Picheheres Waddon 1321 Orig

'Woad hill', OE *wād*, *dūn*. According to Hutchins, (West) Waddon is popularly called *Pitcher's Waddon*, which must be a continuation of *Picheheres Waddon* above. The pers. name which apparently lies behind this can however not be traced. Nor have I been able to find the source of *Cray* (*Krey*), the earlier distinctive name of Little (or East) Waddon. Cf. also next name.

Friar Waddon

Wadone 1086 DB, *Waddon* 1206 PatR, 1206, 1207 ClR, 1242
   Pat, 1251 Ch, AD II, *Bradewadon'* 1175-6 P, *Bradewaddon*
   1235 Cl, 1244 *Ass*, *Brodewaddon* 1212 Fees (93) *et passim*
Whaddon Monks 1299 Pat, *Freren(e) Waddon* 1384 Cl

See preceding name. *Broad* probably because it was the bigger place in relation to the other two Waddons. *Friar* (*Frerene*) must refer to the brethren of the Hospital (Knights Templars), there being mention of land in (West) Waddon restored to the order on its re-establishment under Philip and Mary, see Hutchins II, 764, and VCH Do II, 91 n. 16; cf. Fryer Mayne *supra* 154. *Monks*, on the other hand, seems to be due to the fact that, in the 13th cent., (Broad) Waddon belonged to Netley Abbey in Hants, which had got it from the abbess of Monti-villiers (France), the DB owner; see references above, in particular 1242 Pat (p. 333).

---

[1] This is also the etymology given by Zachrisson, AN Infl. p. 148, in connexion with the treatment of the AN dropping of *l* before a consonant, cf. the above spellings *Sev-*, *Sef-*, *Sif-*.

Puncknowle

Puncknowle [pʌnəl] 140 G 1

Pomacanole, -a 1086 DB, Exon
Pumernolle (sic) 1201-2 FF, *Pinneknoll* 1268 Abbr
Pomeknoll(e) 1271 FineR (p), 1285 FA, 1291 Tax (*-cnolle*),
    1333 *SR*, 1362, 1379 IpmR, 1380 Cl, 1431 FA
Poineknoll 1280 Ch, *Poin Knoll* 1437 IpmR
Pomcnolle 1303 FA, *Pomknoll(e)* 1331 AD II, 1340 NI *et passim*
    to 1445 FF, *Pompknoll* 1363 FF, *Pomknowle* 1412 FA
Poncknoll(e) 1332, 1334, 1363 FF, *Pounknoll* 1380 FF, AD VI,
    Ponknolle 1457 IpmR, *Punckenoll, Ponckenoll* 1535 VE

The second el. is clearly OE *cnoll*, here not in its modern sense of hillock but referring to the large hill of 594 ft., still called The Knoll, which rises just S of the village. The first el. offers great difficulties. We should probably start from a form *Pume-*, (*Pome-*)[1], but I can find nothing to connect that with, except possibly the mysterious *pume lond* in BCS 502 (K).

Bexington Fm (East and West)[2]

Bessintone 1086 DB, *-tona* Exon
Buxinton' 1212 Fees (94)
Bixinton 1234 (copy) BM I, *Estbixinton* 1269 Ch
Bexinton 1234 (1279) Ch, 1242-3 Fees (751), 1269 Misc, Ch
    (*Est-*), 1275 RH, 1279 Ch, 1296 Pat, 1344 Inq aqd
Bexingtun 1285 FA, *-tone* 1291 Tax, *-yng-* 1340 NI
Bexyngeton 1291 Tax, 1428 FA
Betsyngton 1296 Pat (p), *Bexton* 1297 Pat (p)

With some hesitation I take this to go back to an OE *Beorhtsigingtūn* 'farm of the people of *Beorhtsige*'. If this is correct, the development may have taken place along the line *Berhsing-*, *Be(r)csing-*, *Bexing-*, with early loss of *t*[3] and later

---

[1] *Pinne-*, *Poin(e)-* are apparently mistranscriptions for *Pume-*, *Pom(e)-*.

[2] East Bexington is partly in Abbotsbury parish.

[3] The pers. name *Beorhtsige* appears in BCS and KCD *inter alia* as *Berhsige* (BCS 632), *Biorhsige* (BCS 675), *Birhsie* (BCS 1248), *Byrhsige* (BCS 1063, 1064), *Bryhsige* (KCD 1290), *Bryxsige* (KCD 763), *Bryxie* (BCS 1065), *Byrcsige* (BCS 1130). BCS 1063 and 1064 are original charters from about 961.

dropping of *r* before the consonant group *hs* (*cs*), though one
would have liked to come across one or two spellings with -*r*-
to feel sure. For the DB form cf. Zachrisson, IPN p. 114.

Look Fm is *Luk'* 1212 Fees (94), 1291 Tax, *Luca* 1234 BM I,
1234 (1279) Ch, *Louke* 1336 Ch, *Lowke* 1535 VE. Look may
preserve the name of the brook which runs past the farm; no
etymological suggestion can be offered. Less than a mile SE of
Look Fm are the remains of St Luke's Chapel (6″) in Ashley.
The resemblance between the two names may be due to mere
chance, but the fact seems worthy of note.

Swyre

Swyre 140 G 1
  Suere 1086 DB, 1227 FF, 1244 *Ass*, *Swer(e)* 1199 FineR, 1205,
    1206 Cur, 1207 FineR, 1212 Fees (88) *et passim*
  Suure 1275 RH, *Swre* 1275 Ipm, *Swure* 1285 FA, *Sw'r*
    1291 Tax
  Swyre 1275 Ipm, 1303 FA, 1328, 1344 FF *et passim*

  OE *swēora* 'neck, col', cf. Swyre Head *supra* 121.

Berwick is *Berewich* 1194, 1195 P, *Berewyk* 1250 FF *et passim*
with variant spelling -*wik(e)*. OE *bere-wīc* 'barley-farm' (cf. EPN),
the only Dorset example of this common pl.-n.

Chaldecote (lost) is *Cheldecote* 1275 Ipm, *Chaldecote* 1280 Ipm.
See *Chaldecots supra* 134.

Modbury (6″) (site of)
  Modberg(e) 1236 FF, 1244 *Ass*, -*bergh(e)* 1275, 1280 Ipm, 1316,
    1328 FF, 1340 Ipm, 1344 FF, -*burgh* 1412 FA
  Motberge 1275 Ipm, -*bergh* 1341 Ipm, -*borughe* 1344 Ipm, Cl

  Probably from OE *(ge)mōtbeorg* 'barrow or hill of meeting', cf.
Modbury *supra* 193.

Winterborne Steepleton

Winterborne Steepleton 140 G 4
  Wintreburne 1086 DB *et passim* with variant *Winter-*

It appears as *Stipelwinterburn'* in 1199 CurR and as *Stepelton* alone in 1219 FF, 1326 Ipm, but the common type is *Wynterburn* (etc.) *Stepelton* (with variants *Stepil-*, *Steple-*) from 1244 *Ass* onwards, interchanging with *Wynterburn* (etc.) *Stupilton* (with variants *Stupel-*, *Stupul-*, *Stuple-*) from 1260 FF. We have further noted *W. Stipulton* 1333 *SR*, *W. Stipelton* 1420 FF; *W. Stypulton* 1382 IpmR, *W. Stypelton* 1471 IpmR; *W. Stapelton* 1420 IpmR.[1] See Winterborne Came *supra* 162. There are not more than two or three medieval church steeples in the whole of Dorset, and since one of them is here, we need not be in doubt about what 'steeple' (OE *stīepel*) refers to in this case; cf. Steepleton Iwerne *supra* 57.

XXXI. Godderthorn Hundred

goderonestona 1084 Geld Roll, *Godrunesthorn* 1194, 1195 P
Goderisthon' 1212 Fees (93)
Guthredethorn, *Gudredethorn*, *Guyerenethorn* 1244 *Ass*
Guthern (sic) 1265 Misc[2]
Gothernethorne 1285 FA, *Godernethorn(e)* 1303 FA[3], 1334 Misc, *God(e)renethorne* 1327, 1333 *SR*
Gondrenesthorn 1326 Orig, *Goudernettethorn* 1329 Ipm, *Goudernethorn* 1340 NI, *Geudernethorn* 1346 FA
Gonderthorne 1354 IpmR, *Gouderthorn* 1428 FA
Gouderedethorn 1431 FA

The second el. is OE *þorn* 'thorn-bush'. The first is difficult, but the majority of forms would seem to suggest the pers. name

---

[1] The place was also called *W. Belet* (1285, 1412, 1431 FA, 1405, 1416 IpmR) or *W. Bylett* (1502-4 BM I), the addition being due to the *Belet* family. Robert *Belet* was here at the beginning of the 13th cent. (1210-2 RBE p. 545, 1212 Fees p. 88), but already one of the places called *Wintreburne* in DB (f. 84 b) was held by Wm *Belet*; cf. *Frome Billet supra* 159.

[2] The text (p. 199) has "Hundreds of Ecresdon, Guthern and Thirne", the last two names being identified by the indexer with Godderthorn and Cerne. If that were right, it would involve not only a curiously abbreviated form of Godderthorn but also a unique spelling of Cerne. I suppose the word 'and' (between Guthern and Thirne) is a translation of what was erroneously believed to be the Latin *et*, and that the three words should be read *Guthernetthirne* (i. e. Godderthorn); cf. OE *þyrne* 'thorn-bush'.

[3] The bracket form is *Gutternesthorne*.

Guðrun. Guthrun in the Durham Liber Vitæ and *Goderun* in
DB are looked upon by Björkman (Nord. Personennamen p.
54) as being of Scandinavian origin and probably feminine; it should
also be mentioned that the originally Scandinavian masculine
name *Guðrum (Gyðrum* in BCS 856) is sometimes written *Guðrun*
(BCS 857, 675), cf. op. cit. p. 48 f. If there was a genuine OE
Gūðrūn, which would have been quite a regular formation, that
name must have been feminine.

Godderthorn is now lost as a place-name, and the site of the
hundred meeting-place is unknown, but the interesting mention
of a *Godrenelonde* (1321) near the present Matravers (*infra*) in
the parish of Loders[1] makes one believe that *Godderthorn* was
situated in that part of the hundred, too.

Allington
Allington 139 F 13

   Adelingtone 1086 DB, *-ton* 13th AD I, *Addelyngton* 1472 IpmR
   Halington 1199 FineR
   Alingetun 1205-6 FF, *Alingeton* 1235-6 Fees (425), 1262 FF
   Athelington(e) 1227 FF, 1285 FA, 1329 Ipm *et passim* with
      variant *-yng-, Athelinton* 1236 FF
   Athelyngeton 1308 FF, *Hathelyngton* 1340 Cl

This may be an *-ing* name (containing *Æðel* or *Æðelwine*,
pers. names), but it seems safer to take the first el. to be OE
æðeling 'nobleman', as suggested by Zachrisson[2]; for similar
pl.-ns cf. also PN BedsHu p. 183 f. s. n. Elton, and Karlström
pp. 79, 83, 102, 113.

Bilshay Fm

   Bilesheye 1244 *Ass* (p), *Billeshage* 1285 FA (p), *Bilshegh* 1330,
      1337 FF, *-heygh* 1348 IpmR, *Billesheye* 1396 IpmR
   Byleseye 1333 *SR* (p), *Bylshey* 1415 AD III

'*Bil*'s farm or enclosure', OE *(ge)hæg*, ME *hay*.

Note. Names ending in *-hay* are rare in Dorset except in this
part (Marshwood Vale and its surroundings) where they abound. In

[1] See SoDoNQ VII, 229.
[2] See AN Infl. p. 112, where *d* for *ð* in the DB form is also accounted for.

PN D p. 129 (s. n. High Hayne) it is suggested that the Devon names of this type, which are especially common in the parts that border upon Dorset, probably all derive from ME *hay*, OE *(ge)hæg* 'enclosure', and that they are as a rule compounded with the name of a medieval owner, *hay* (being here of ME origin) meaning probably little more than 'farm' or 'holding'. This appears to be true of the Dorset names, too.

Pymore[1] [paimə]

Pimore 1235-6 Fees (425) (p), 1244 *Ass* (p)

Pymor(e) 1244 *Ass* (p), 1275 Cl (p), 1285 FA, 1311, 1318 FF *et passim*, *-mowre* 1457 AD I, *-mour* 1487 Ipm

Pumore 1327 *SR* (p), *Pyemore* 1431 FA

The second el. is of course OE *mōr*, and the first may be OE *pīe* 'insect'. The meaning would thus be 'swampy ground infested by insects'; cf. Pyworthy (D) in Blomé p. 153 and PN D p. 162. Pymore lies low on the river Brit.

Bothenhampton

Bothenhampton [bouþənhæmtən][2] 139 F 13

Bolem'tona (sic) 1107 (1330) Ch

Bothenamtone 1285 FA, *Bothnamton* n. d. AD I, *Bouthenhamtun* n. d. AD VI, *Bothehampton* 1535 VE

Bawmpton 1535 VE, *Baunton* 1610 Speed

The material is scanty, but the meaning may be 'homestead (OE *hāmtūn*) in the valley', the first el. being presumably ME *bothem* (cf. OE *botm* 'bottom') found in names like Ramsbottom and Shillingbottom (PN La p. 64). There is a Bottom Wood just N of Bothenhampton, and Kelly mentions a Bothewood here. Cf. Bothenwood *supra* 82.

Hyde is *la Hyde* 1244 *Ass*, *la Hide* n. d. AD VI, *atte Hude* 1324 AD I, *atte Hide* 1327 *SR*, *atte Hyde* 1340 NI (all p), *Hyde* 1459 AD I. OE *hīd* 'hide'.

Walditch

Waldic 1086 DB, *Waldice* 1212 Fees (93), *Waldich* 1263 Pap,

---

[1] Partly in Bradpole.

[2] I have not heard the older pronunciation *Baunton*.

256 Anton Fägersten

1285 FA *et passim* with variant *-dych(e)*, *Waldik* 1264 Ipm,
Waledich 1329 Ipm

Waudich 1236 FF, n. d. AD VI (p), *Waledych Sermevill* 1307 FF

The second el. is OE *dīc* 'ditch, dyke'. The first is presumably OE *weall* 'wall'; cf. the boundary-mark (*and lang þære*)
weal dic BCS 969 (Cod. Winton.), tentatively suggested in B. T.
to mean 'a walled ditch'; cf. also (*on þar Elde*) *Waldich* BCS
768 (Do).

Jordan de *Sermunvill* was here before 1236 (FF p. 63, and
Hutchins II, 208). An earlier entry (1227 FF p. 41) shows that
he belonged to the family met with in connexion with Langton
Herring *supra* 247.

Wych is *Wyche* 1539 AD VI, *Wyke* 1811 OM. Probably OE *wīc*
'dairy-farm'.

Burton Bradstock[1]

Burton Bradstock 139 G 13

Brideton(e) 1086 DB, Exon, 1156-7, 1174-82 France, 1190
(1332) Ch (*-tona*), c. 1207 BM I (*-tuna*) *et passim*
Britidon 1142-54 France
Briditonia 1156-7 France, *-tuna* c. 1207 BM I, *-ton* n. d. Os-
mund, *Briditone Sancte Wandrigesili* 1285 FA
Breddintun 1252 Ch
Brudeton 1291 Tax, 1428 FA, *Brytton* 1327 SR, *Bruton* 1333
SR, *Brutton* 1340 NI, 1346, 1428 FA, *Britton* 1436 IpmR
Burton 1535 VE

Burton means the 'farm (*tūn*) on the river Bride', cf. Long
Bredy *supra* 238, and Ekwall, ERN p. 52. In DB part of this
place was held by the abbey of St Wandrille, Normandy (*ecclesia
Sancti Wandregisili*); afterwards it came to the abbey of Braden-
stoke in Wilts; hence the present addition *Bradstock*; cf. e. g.
1285 (1286) Ch p. 329, and Hutchins II, 280.

Bredy Fm is *Bridie* 1086 DB, 1285 FA *et passim*, *Bridye* [*Pridie*]
1303 FA, *Bonevilesbridge* (sic) 1412 FA, *Bonevylesbryde* 1431 FA,
Bonevilesbride 1455 FF, *Bonvyles-Bridy* 1486 Ipm. Named from

---

[1] In Frampton Liberty.

the river Bride, see the preceding name. Stephen de *Bonevil*
held half a knight's fee here in 1285 (FA), and members of
that family are mentioned here as late as 1455 (FF). Cf. Bhompston Fm *supra* 184.

Graston Ho

Gravstan 1086 DB, *Graustan* Exon
Grauestone 1269 Ch, 1285 FA, 1291 Tax[1], *Grau(e)ston* 1269
    Ch, *Graveston* 1269 Misc, 1280, 1336 Ch

The second el. is apparently OE *stān* 'stone'. The first might
be either OE *grāf* 'grove, copse' or *græf* 'pit, trench, grave', but
neither of these words seems very likely as the first el. of a
compound in which 'stone' is the second el. Another possibility
should therefore perhaps be taken into consideration. In the
original charter BCS 451 (Devon) from the year 847 there is a
boundary-mark (*to*) *græwan stane*[2] meaning the 'grey stone'
(Earle, Middendorff, B. T. Suppl.).[3] If OE *græwan stāne* was
shortened at an early date, *æ* would become *a*, and the whole
name might consequently appear as *Grau(e)stone* in ME. 'Grey
stone' occurs several times as a boundary-mark in OE charters,
see Middendorff s. v. *grǣg*, and cf. also Redhone *infra*.

Loders

Loders 139 E 14

Lodre 1084 GeldRoll, 1086 DB, 1091-1106 (etc.) Montacute,
    1100-22 (1270) Ch, (ad) *Lodrā* 1086 DB, Exon
Lodres 1086 DB, Exon, 1107-20, 1142-55, 1201 France, 1201-2
    FF, 1205 FineR, 1212 Fees (92) *et passim*
Lodris 1107 (1330) Ch, *Loddres* 1244 *Ass*, 1327, 1332 Cl,
    Londres (sic) 1260 Pap, *Loderes* 1291 Tax
Lodere 1327 *SR*, 1339 Cl, *Loder* 1412 FA, 1539 AD VI
Lodre Prioris 1337 FF, *Lodres Priour* 1397 FF
Loders 1364 Cl, *Lother* 1557 AD VI, *Lothers* 1765 Taylor

---

[1] Mistranscribed as *Granestone*.

[2] Repeated (with the same spelling) in the Thorndon Hall charter mentioned
in PN D p. 264.

[3] On the form *grǣw-* as a variant of *grǣg*, see Sievers in PBr Beiträge IX,
203 f., and Jellinek ib. XIV, 584.

I suppose Loders is an old river name.[1] We have probably
to start from a form *lod(d)re*. If the name is English, one feels
inclined to connect it with OE *loddere* 'beggar', cf. OHG *lotar*
(adj.) 'vain, idle, empty'. Does the meaning 'beggar' (of OE
loddere) go back to an earlier meaning 'the idle one, the sluggish
one, the empty one'? A river might apparently be called by one
or other of these appellations, but I am not in a position to
judge if any of them would suit this stream. If *Lodre*, rather
than *Lodres*, is the original form of Loders, the final *-s* should
probably be looked upon as the plural ending (cf. *Sture : Stures*,
Ekwall, ERN p. 380), there being in reality several places called
Loders; cf. Matravers and Uploders *infra* (this parish).

The priory here was a cell to the Abbey of Montebourg (Normandy). Cf. VCH Do II, 116.

Colhay (lost) is *Coleheygh* 1415 AD III, *Colehay in Lodrez* 1442
IpmR. The second el. is apparently *(ge)hæg* (cf. Bilshay *supra*
254); the first may be OE *cōl* 'cool'.

Innsacre Fm is *Hynesacre* 1327 SR (p), *Insacr'* 1333 SR (p),
and was probably the home of Johannes *Jusacre* (sic) 1285 FA,
one of the jurors of Godderthorn Hundred. The material is late
and scanty, but the interpretation may be '*Ine*'s land' (OE *æcer*),
as suggested in Hutchins (II, 283).

Matravers [mətrǽvəz]. According to Eyton (p. 127 f.) one or
two of the *Lodre* forms in DB belong here; cf. the parish name.
Later on the place is called *Lodres Lutton(e)* 1285, 1303 FA,
Lodere Lucton (sic) 1318 FF, *Loderlucton* (sic) 1452 FF, or
simply *Lutton* (1326 Ipm, 1346, 1428, 1431 FA) from its vicinity
to or associations with Litton Cheney (*supra* 247) three miles
away. It appears once as *Lodres Byngham* (1314 FF), Richard
de *Bingeham* being mentioned as tenant in 1285 (FA), and from
1356 (FF) onwards as *Lodres Mautravers*, the place being one
of the many Dorset possessions of the family of *Mautravers*; cf.
Lytchett Matravers *supra* 112. John *Mautravers* was tenant here
in 1303 (FA).

---

[1] The river in question is now called the Asker (6″), a back-formation from
Askerswell *supra* 237.

Uploders is *Uploders* 1535 VE, and is called so in relation to Loders (*supra* 257) which in late documents is often referred to as Lower Loders. Some of the early forms given under Loders may in reality belong here (cf. Eyton p. 127 f.).

Yondover is *Yandover* 1535 VE. This must go back to OE *begeondan ōfre* 'beyond (on the farther side of) the river-bank', a name which aptly describes the situation of Yondover in relation to Loders. There is another Yondover (6″) in Netherbury, divided from that place by the river Brit. These two places are consequently in the West of the county, not far from the border of Devon where there are numerous cases of this type of name, cf. PN D p. xxxvii.

Shipton Gorge

Shipton Gorge 139 F 14

Sepetone, -a 1086 DB, Exon, *Spepton* (sic) 1206 RC, *Septun* 1265 Misc, *Sceptone* 1285 FA, *Shep-* 1333 *SR*

Shipton 1232 Cl, 1313 FF, 1346 FA, 1383 FF, 1428, 1431 FA

Sipton 1235-6 Fees (425), 1245 Cl, *Schipton* 1303 FA

Sypton n. d. (13th?) France, *Shypton* 1247 FF, 1269 Misc, 1382 FF, 1515 BM I, *Shupton* 1327 Cl

Shupton Maur(e)ward 1305 Cl, Ipm (*Sch-*), *Shipton Maureward* 1396 IpmR, 1412 FA, 1436 FF (*Mauleward*)

Shipton George (sic) 1765 Taylor

'Sheep-farm' OE *scēap* (*scīp*), *tūn*; cf. Shapwick *supra* 86. The first of the *Maurewards* that I have come across here is Thomas *Maureward* in 1206 (RC); cf. the earlier distinctive names of Winterborne Zelstone *supra* 73 and Kingston (in Stinsford) *supra* 185. Shipton Gorge owes it present additional name to the family of *de Gorges*, of whom Thomas *de Gorges* was here as early as 1285 (FA); cf. a still earlier Ralph *de Gorges* mentioned in connexion with Bradpole (2 miles away) in 1244 and 1250 (Fees pp. 1387, 1182 f., 1239).

Bennett's Hill Fm is possibly to be associated with a certain Edward *Benet* mentioned under the adjacent parish of Loders in 1244 *Ass* (201 m. 12).

Hawcombe (lost) is (boscus de) *Havocŭbe* 1086 DB, *hauocŭba*
Exon. 'Hawk-valley', OE *h(e)afoc, cumb*. Not on maps, but
stated in Hutchins (II, 284) to be the name of a ground near
Shipton Hill.

Sturthill, Higher and **Lower**[1]
   Sterte 1086 DB, *Sterta* Exon, *Stertes* 1227 FF
   Stertel 1212 Fees (93), 1274 Ipm, 1285 FA, 1341 Ipm
   Sturtel 1250 FF, 1280, 1299 Ipm, 1303 FA, 1333 *SR*, 1340 NI
   Sturtul 1275 Ipm, *Sturtyl* 1291 Tax, *Scurtil* (sic) 1316 FF
   Sturale 1368 BM II
   Stertill 1383 IpmR, *Sterthill* 1428 FA, *Stertull* 1515 BM I
   Stirtell 1431 FA (only form with *i* in first syll.)

With prefixed epithet it appears as *Nithersturtel* 1329, 1337,
1347 FF, *Netheresturtel(e)* 1334 FF, and as *Upsturtel* 1333 *SR*,
Uppesturtehill 1436 FF; we also find *Nither-, Upstertyl* 1346 Ipm,
Nytherstertell 1397 FF, *Netherstertill* 1483 IpmR.

As suggested in Hutchins, the first el. is OE *steort* 'tail, cape
of land' and the second OE *hyll* 'hill', the whole name apparently
describing a hill, shaped like a tail; cf. Woodstreet Fm *supra*
151. For the *u* spellings cf. Durweston *supra* 52.

XXXII. Beaminster Forum and Redhone[2]

beieministre 1084 GeldRoll
Beministr(e) 1212 Fees (90), 1244 *Ass et passim*
Bemenistr(e) 1227 Fees (378), 1235 FineR, 1238 Sarum, 1265
   Misc, 1285 FA, *-minstr(e)* 1236 Orig, 1275 RH
Bemynistre 1244 *Ass*, 1324 Cl, *-mynstre* 1324 Ipm *et passim*
Beministre Gorges 1244 *Ass* (201 m. 12)
(hd de) *Reministr'* (sic) *forinseco* 1251-2 Fees (1268)
Beministre Foreign 1265 Misc, *Bemynstr' For'* 1340 NI
Bymenistre 1280 Ch

---

[1] Lower Sturthill is in the parish of Burton Bradstock.
[2] These two hundreds have been placed together partly for practical and
partly for historical reasons, cf. Hutchins II, 81, 153. I here also include
Broadwindsor Liberty (= Broadwindsor parish).

Bed(e)ministre 1303 FA, *Bedmynstreforum* 1432 IpmR [1]
Beymistre 1316 FA, *Beymunstr'* 1333 *SR*, *Beymenstr'* 1340 NI,
    Beymynstre Forum 1412 FA
Bemestre 1330 FF, 1396, 1457 IpmR, *-mystre* 1428 FA

See Beaminster *infra*. *Forum*, as pointed out in Hutchins, is
due to a misunderstanding of the abbreviation of the Latin
forinsecum (*forin'*, *for'um*), originally denoting the 'out-hundred'.
Gorges in one of the *Ass* references is from the lords, the *de
Gorges* of Bradpole; cf. Shipton Gorge *supra* 259.

redehane 1084 GeldRoll, *La Redehan'* (twice) 1235 FineR
la Radehan' 1236 Orig
Redehone 1244 *Ass*, 1324 Cl, 1457, 1475 IpmR, 1486 Ipm
la Rydehawe [2] 1251-2 Fees (1268), *Ridehowe* 1275 RH
la Ridehone 1265 Misc, *La Ridehoue* 1292 Ipm, *La Rydehone*
    1333 *SR*, 1340 NI, *Rydehove* 1346, 1431 FA, *Ridehove* 1428 FA
La Redehone 1280 Cl, 1301 FF
Redehoue 1324 Ipm, 1396 IpmR, *La Redehoue* 1330, 1456 FF
Rodhoue [2] 1383 IpmR, *Rodehove* 1412 FA
Redhone 1432 IpmR

I take this to be OE (*æt*) *rēadan hāne* '(at the) red boundary-
stone'; cf. Middendorff p. 65 s. v. *hān*, and NED s. v. *hone* sb. 1.
The OE examples quoted by Middendorff show that the word
hān is always compounded with an adjective denoting colour,
usually 'red', once 'grey'. [3] The above *i* and *y* spellings, however,
are curious and might seem to point to OE *hrēod* (*hrīod*) 'reed'
rather than *rēad* 'red', but both the constant medial *-e-* and,
above all, the documentary evidence that *hān* is as a rule compounded with *rēad* are decidedly in favour of the *rēad* explanation; moreover, from the point of view of meaning, OE *hrēod*
'reed' seems in itself unlikely as part of a compound with *hān*
'stone'. If the etymology suggested is correct, we must look
upon the *Ride-*, *Ryde-* spellings as the result of the ME raising
of *ĕ* to *ĭ* before dentals, especially common when the vowel is

---

[1] The *Bed(e)-* forms may have been influenced by Bedminster (So).

[2] The entry in which this form occurs shows several clear mistranscriptions.

[3] One of Middendorff's examples, *to þare rede hane*, is from an East-Dorset
charter (BCS 708).

preceded by *r*; see Luick § 379, Jordan § 34. Cf. Redlane (Hundred) *supra* 3.

I cannot find Redhone on any modern map, but on Taylor's map (1765) there is a Redhone just NW of Beaminster, and the OS map of 1811 has a Redhove about two miles S of Beaminster. According to Hutchins (II, 153) the meeting-place of the hundred-courts was at a place (which he erroneously calls Redhove[1]) three miles SE of Beaminster, in North Poorton.

Beaminster

Beaminster [beminstə[2], bemistə] 139 C 13

> *Beiminstre* 1086 DB
>
> *Begminister* 1091 Osmund
>
> *Beministre* 1226 Osmund, 1244 *Ass*, 1284 Ch, *-menistre* 1228 FF, 1285 FA, 1298 Ipm, *-mynstre* 1360 Cl *et passim*
>
> *Beymenistre* (*Valentin*[3], *Rogeri*), *Beymin(i)stre* c. 1226 Sarum, *Beyminister*, *-munster* 1291 Tax, *-minstr'* 1306 FF, *-mynstre* 1316 FA, *-menstr'* 1340 NI
>
> *Bymynstre* 1337 Cl
>
> *Beymystre* 1351 AD I, *Bemystre* 1390 Cl, 1428 FA

Cf. also the early forms of the hundred-name *supra* 260.

The second el. is OE *mynster*, here probably in its general sense of 'church'. The first is difficult, but I am inclined to suggest that it is OE *bēag* 'ring'. If so, that word may have been used here in some topographical sense, cf. Middendorff's assumption (p. 12) that *bēag* could mean "Krümmung, Bogen (eines Baches, Landrückens etc.)". Beaminster is at a well-marked bend of the river Brit. A similar suggestion has been made by Wallenberg for a group of Kentish and other English pl.-ns, see StNPh II, 97 f. and Kentish PN p. 342 f. — Forms like *Beymistre*, *Bemystre* (cf. the modern pronunciation) have parallels among other *-minster* names, cf. PN Sx p. 170.

---

[1] The above list of early forms shows that *-hone* has often been mis-transcribed or misread as *-houe*; cf. Hutchins (loc. cit.): "Redhone Hundred, commonly so called, but more properly (!) Redhove Hundred."

[2] The pronunciation given in BBC.

[3] "Valentine, who went with bishop R(ichard) Poore to Durham, held the prebend of Beaminster Secunda in 1226" (Sarum p. 207, n. 5).

Axnoller Fms

Axnolre 1285 FA, *Estaxenabre* (sic) 1339 FF, *Axinaller* 1431
FA, *Est Axnollar* 1553 Hutchins, *Est Axnolle(r)* 1571 ib.
Ax Knolle c. 1540 Leland, *Axknoll(er)* 1864 Hutchins

Ax Knolle (in Leland) is considered by Dorset historians to
be the "correct" form and would indeed suit the topography
excellently, for the spring of the river Axe breaks out in a moor
on the slope of a hill here (Hutchins II, 126). But it is impossible
to reconcile *Ax Knolle* with the earlier forms. I take Axnoller
to be a compound of the river-name Axe[1] in its oblique form
Axan, and OE *alor* 'alder-tree'. For the change of *a* to *o* in
alor cf. Ekwall, PN La p. 21, and EPN s. v.

Buckham

Bochenhā 1086 DB, *Bukenhā* 1244 *Ass* (p)
Bukeham 1244 *Ass* (p), 1285 FA, *Bukkeham* 1285 FA (p)
Bucham 1297 Abbr, 1298 Ipm, 1413 FF, *Bukham* 1387 IpmR
Bokham 1303 FA, *Bocham* 1303, 1431 FA, *Boucham* 1346,
1428 FA

Probably 'goat-farm', OE *bucca* 'he-goat' and *hām*; cf. Bockhampton *supra* 184. For different possibilities of interpreting
names of this type cf. e. g. PN Nth p. 133 s. n. Boughton.

Chapel Marsh is *Capella* 1244 *Ass* (p), *La Chapele* 1256 FF (p),
1285 FA. The site of an ancient chapel here is marked on the
6″ map; cf. Hutchins II, 127.

Hewstock Fm (local)[2]

The only early forms which certainly refer to this place are
Westhenedstok 1268 FF, *Hethstoke* 1412 FA, *Estheuedstok* (twice)
1413 FF, *Hewstoke* 1431 FA, and *Heuedstok* 1442 SoDoNQ X,
267, but there are good reasons for believing that here also
belongs *Henestok'* 1251-2 Fees (1267), held by Walter de *Hande-
stok'*, who is referred to as Walter de *Hadestok(e)* in 1250 Fees
(1182, 1240).

---

[1] The Axe in question is the one which gives name to Axminster and
Axmouth; see Ekwall, ERN p. 152. Cf. also Axe Fm *infra* in Broadwindsor.
[2] The site of East Hewstock is marked on the 6″ map.

Hewstock is apparently identical in origin with the common boundary-mark *hēafod-stocc* (see BCS 229, 473, 689, 705, 817, 967[1], 970[2], 1121, and KCD 641), for which Toller (see B. T. Suppl. s. v.) gives the meaning 'a stock or post on which the head of a criminal was fixed after beheading', in support of which he adduces an interesting passage in Ælfric's Lives of Saints (I, 492): *and ða heafod-leasan man hengc on ða port-weallas. and man sette heora heafda swilce oþra ðeofa buton ðam port-weallon on ðam heafod-stoccum.* The lost *Hewstock* in Hinton St Mary (*supra* 41) is a second example of this sinister place-name.

Langdon Fm is *Langedon* 1244 *Ass*, 1285 FA, 1294 Ch, 1316 FA, *Langgedon* 1333 *SR*. 'Long hill', OE *lang, dūn*.

Parnham

 Perham 1228 FF, *Perhā, Perham* 1244 *Ass* (p)
 Perhamme (twice) 1413 FF, *Parnham* 1431 FA

The 1413 FF form suggests that the second el. is OE *hamm*, which here may well mean '(low-lying) land near a river' (the Brit). The first el. is OE *peru* 'pear'; cf. West Parley *supra* 103, and PN Sx p. 152 s. n. Parham. The *n* in the later forms is excrescent.

Shatcombe Fm is *Shotecumbe* 1306 FF, *-combe* 1412 FA, *Shatecombe* 1412 FA, *Shotcombe* 1486 Ipm. The second el. is OE *cumb* 'valley', and the first would seem to be OE *scēat* 'corner, angle, promontory, bosom' (or perhaps OE *scēata* with much the same meaning); it may be noted that there is a White Sheet Hill close by. Another Shatcombe Fm in Wynford Eagle may have the same history, but I have found no early forms for that name.

Wellwood is called *Well* in 1483 IpmR and 1487 Ipm, and was probably the home of Geoffrey de *Welles* 1244 *Ass*, Wm de *Welle* 1285 FA and John de *Well* 1340 NI. Self-explanatory, OE *wielle*; several springs are marked here on the 6″ map.

---

[1] *on ða heaford stoccas* in BCS 967 corresponds to *on ða heafodstoccas* in KCD 442 (vol. III p. 439).

[2] The boundaries start with *on heaued lakes* (sic) and end with *on heued stockes*.

Bradpole

Bradpole 139 E 13

Bratepolle 1086 DB, *bratepolla* Exon
Bradepol(e) n. d. France, 1212, 1219 Fees (92, 261), 1238 Cl,
    1244 Fees (1387) *et passim*, -*poll* 1408 (etc.) AD II
Bredepole c. 1213 Osmund, *Bradipole* c. 1215 Sarum
Bradeford (sic) 1227 Fees (378), *Bridepol'* 1250 Fees (1239)
Bradpole 1486 Ipm, *Brappoll(e)* 1535 VE

'(At the) broad pool', OE (*æt*) *brādan pōle*. The form *Bride-pol'* is probably due to the adjacent Bridport.

Broadwindsor

Broadwindsor 139 C 12

Windesore 1086 DB, 1212 Fees (94), 1268 Pat
Windesores 1167-8 RBE (p), 1293 Misc, *Wyndesores* 1210-2
    RBE (p), *Brodewyndesores*, *Brodewindesores* 1293 Misc
Windleshor' 1219 Fees (260), 1244 *Ass*, 1251-2 Fees (1266)
Windelesover 1244 Fees (1387), *Wyndelesover* ib. (p)
Windessovers 1244 Fees (1387), *Windesouer* 1244 *Ass*
Windelesor' 1244 *Ass*, *Windlesor'* 1250 Fees (1182)
Wyndlesor' 1244 *Ass*, *Wyndelsore* 1265 Misc, 1291 Tax
Windes' 1247 Cl, 1250 Fees (1239), 1275 RH
Magna Wyndesor 1249 FF, *Wyndesore* 1264 Ch *et passim*
Windesl' 1250 Fees (1239), *Wineshor'* 1251-2 Fees (1267)

After 1291 only one *l* spelling has been noted, viz. *Brode Wyndelsore* 1431 FA; cf. also the early forms for Littlewindsor *infra*.

This name is identical in origin not only with the famous Berkshire Windsor but, as pointed out in PN D p. 262, also with one Winsor in Devon and one in Hants, two further Windsors in Devon, two in Cornwall and one in Pembroke, the first el. being found also in Windlesham (Sr) and in *wyndelescumb* BCS 721 (D).[1] "All these", say the editors of PN D (loc. cit.), "point to a pers. name *Windel*, a diminutive of *Wind(a)*." I do not believe in that assertion. It would in itself be remarkable if no less than six or seven Win(d)sors should be compounds of

---

[1] To these should be added Wyndlam Fm *supra* 9.

this unrecorded pers. name and OE *ōra* 'bank' (or OE *ōfer* with much the same meaning). The editors seem themselves inclined to admit that this is somewhat curious but try to explain away the coincidence by assuming that some of these names may contain the pers. name *Winel* rather than **Windel,* and that at least one of the Windsors (the Pembrokeshire one) may have been named after the Berkshire place. The latter suggestion might possibly be true, but there is practically no evidence for the *Winel* theory.

In my opinion all the names enumerated above contain an OE noun *windel,* the meaning of which must have been 'something winding', cf. OE *windel* 'basket', *windelstān* 'tower with a winding staircase', *windelstrēaw* 'windle-straw', *windeltrēow* 'oleaster'; cf. also *gewind* 'winding path' (*supra* 200 s. n. High Stoy). In the case of the Berkshire Windsor there can be little doubt that *windel* refers to the very conspicuous bend of the river Thames at that place — a suggestion made thirty years ago by Middendorff (p. 151). Unfortunately I am not familiar with the topography of the other places.

Attisham

> *Adesham* 1251-2 Fees (1267), 1279 Ipm, 1293 Misc *et passim*
> to 1427 IpmR, *Adysham* 1333 FF, 1343 Ipm
> *Atesham* 1322 Ipm, 1412 FA, *Athesham* 1406 IpmR

Probably '*Æd(d)i*'s homestead', OE *hām.* For that pers. name see Redin p. 131.

Axe Fm is *Axe* 1251-2 Fees (1267), 1355, 1469 FF. Named after the river Axe, cf. Axnoller Fms *supra* 263.

Blackdown (Hill) and **Blagdon Hill,** some two miles apart, are identical in origin. *Blakedon* 1275 RH[1] may refer to the former, whereas *Blakedon* 1324 Ipm probably refers to the latter. Cf. Blagdon *supra* 100.

---

[1] The same entry in RH (p. 98) contains three other pl.-ns in Broadwindsor, viz. *Fursgore, Northdon* and *Weleslond.* All three seem to be lost, but the first two are repeated in 1293 Misc (*Fursgore, Nerthdon*). *Fursgore* means 'triangular piece of land (OE *gāra*) overgrown with furze' (OE *fyrs*), *Northdon* is self-explanatory, and *Weleslond* may contain the word *wielle* 'well', cf. Wellwood *supra* 264.

Childhay is *Childheya* 1234 Pat (p), *Childehey(e)* 1244 *Ass* (p), 1250 Fees (1240) (p) *et passim* with variant spellings *-hegh, -heigh, Chyldheye* 1244 *Ass* (p), 1254 FF, *Childheye* 1250 Fees (1182)[1], *Chyldehegh* 1333 *SR*. — OE *cild* and *(ge)hæg* 'enclosure'; for the meaning of *cild* see Child Okeford and cf. Chilfrome *supra* 13, 229.

Dibberford

(*æt*) *Dibberwurðe* 1002-14 (orig.?) KCD 708
Diberwurth 1244 *Ass* (p), *Diberwrth'* 1251-2 Fees (1267)
Dybrewurth 1255 FF, *Wyberwurth* (sic) 1268 FF
Dibberwood 1688 SoDoNQ XII

The second el. is of course OE *weorþ* 'enclosure, homestead', the present terminal *ford* being a later corruption. I can find nothing to connect the first el. with. To judge from the map the place lies very high and there is no watercourse in the immediate neighbourhood.

Drimpton

Dremeton 1244 *Ass* (p) (*passim*), 1251-2 Fees (1267)
Dremintun', Driminton' 1250 Fees (1240, 1182) (p)
Drempton 1316, 1321, 1325 FF, 1327 *SR* (p), 1469 FF

Drimpton should probably be compared with (*to*) *dreaman uuyrðe* 824 (orig.) BCS 378, now Trimworth (K). Wallenberg (p. 149) takes this to contain either a pers. name **Drēama* (cf. OE *Drēamwulf, Dremca*) or a river-name **Drēame*, formed from the stem of OE *drēam* 'song, music' (OE *drȳman* 'sing aloud'). These considerations may be applicable to the Dorset name, too. Drimpton is near a nameless stream (a tributary of the Axe) which runs through a very hilly district, and the current of which may consequently be rapid enough for the stream to be called 'the singing one'. Hence '**Drēama*'s farm' or 'the farm near (a river called) **Drēame*'.

Langley (lost) is *Langelegh'* 1251-2 Fees (1267). Self-explanatory, OE *lang, lēah*.

---

[1] We also find *Chisdeye* and *Chisdeheye* in 1251-2 Fees (1267), clear errors of transcription for *Childeye* and *Childeheye*.

Littlewindsor is *Windresorie* 1086 DB, *-oria* Exon, *Parva Wyndes(s)ora* 1204 (1313) Ch, *Parva Win(d)lesor* 1210 FF, *Parva Windelessor'* 1235-6 Fees (426), *Parva Windesouer* 1244 *Ass* (p), *Parva Windeshor'* 1251-2 Fees (1268), *Little Windesore* 1279 Ipm, *Little Wyndelsore* 1285 Ipm, *Windesore Parva* 1325 Inq aqd. See Broadwindsor *supra* 265.

Netherhay is *Netherhey, -hagh* 1244 *Ass* (p), *Nethereheye* 1251-2 Fees (1267), *Nitherhegh* 1355 FF. Second el. OE *(ge)hæg* 'enclosure'. 'Nether' in contrast to the lost *Uphay infra*.

Newnham Fms is *Newenham* 1227 FF, *Niweham* 1244 *Ass* (p), *Neweham* 1251-2 Fees (1266), *Nywenham juxta Brodewyndesore* 1316 FF. Cf. *Newnham supra* 38.

Park Fms, so called after Broadwindsor Park, mentioned *inter alia* in 1324 Ipm.

Sandpit

Saunput 1244 *Ass* (p), *Sanputte* 1293 Misc (p), 1316, 1324 FF
Stenipette, Stanputte 1250 Fees (1182, 1240) (p)
Sampite 1251-2 Fees (1267), *-putte* 1297 Fine
Sandputte 1256 FF (p), 1325 Inq aqd, 1469 FF

This evidently means exactly what it appears to mean, the elements being OE *sand* and *pytt*, but the two forms from 1250 Fees would seem to indicate interchange with *stǣnig* 'stony' and *stān* 'stone' in the first element. Cf. Sandford Orcas *infra*.

Uphay (lost) is *Uppeheye* 1244 *Ass*, 1323 FF, 1333 *SR*, *Huppeheye* 1250 Fees (1182), *-hee* ib. (1240) (all p), *-leg'* (sic) 1251-2 Fees (1267), *Uppehay* 1298 Ipm (p). Cf. Netherhay *supra* 268.

Wantsley Fm (6") [wɔnsli]
Wanteslegh(e) 1244 *Ass* (p), 1251-2 Fees (1267)
Wantesleye 1326 Ch

This is apparently identical in origin with Wansley Barton (D), for which Blomé (p. 53) and the editors of PN D (p. 119) give the meaning 'Want's clearing, the pers. name *Want* being on record in LVD; cf. also PN Sx p. 219 s. n. Wantley Fm.

Whetley Fm is *Whethill* 1209-10 FF, *Whatley* 1811 OM. 'Wheat-hill', OE *hwǣte, hyll*. It is however not absolutely certain that the earliest form belongs here. Cf. Sandley *supra* 8, earlier *Sandhull*.

Cheddington
Cheddington 139 B 13
> *Cedindon* 1244 *Ass* (p), 1285 FA, *Chedyndon* 1280 FF, 1304 Orig, 1363 FF, *-in-* 1302 Orig, *-yng-* 1340 NI, 1386 Cl, 1397 FF
> *Cedynton* 1298 Fine, *-yng-* 1333 *SR* (p), *Chedyngton* 1337 FF *et passim*, *Chiddyngton* 1431 FA
> *Codyngton* 1316 FA, *Codyngdon* ib. (p)

The second el. is apparently OE *dūn* 'down, hill' (which later became *-ton* through dissimilation); if so, the first is probably not a pers. name. Chidham (Sx) is supposed by Ekwall (Studies on PN p. 70) to contain OE *cēod(e)* 'a bag', used as a topographical term. Such may be the case with Cheddington, too. To judge from the map Chedington (Court) lies in a hollow surrounded by high hills. Cf. Chudleigh in PN D p. 489.

Corscombe
Corscombe 130 F 1
> *Corigescumb* 1014 (12th) KCD 1309, 1035 (12th) KCD 1322
> *Coriescumbe* 1086 DB
> *Coriscumbe* 1086 DB, 1169-70, 1170-1 P (*-cumba*), 1204-5 FF, 1244 *Ass* (p), 1285 FA
> *Corscumbe* 1086 DB, 1191 Sarum, 1291 Tax *et passim*
> *Croscumb'* (sic) 1202 Cur
> *Coruscumb(e)* 1244 *Ass*, *West Coruscumbe* 1265 Misc
> *Corescumbe* 1244 *Ass*, 1281 Ipm (*West-*), 1289 Orig (*Est-*, *West-*), 1291 Tax, *Westkorescumb* 1256 FF
> *Corscombe Abbots* 1290 Ch, *Corsecombe* 1316 FA, 1339 FF

Corscombe has been dealt with by Ekwall in his Studies on PN p. 70 ff. (cf. also ERN p. 96 f.). He takes Corscombe, as well as Croscombe (So), to go back to an OE **Corfwegescumb*, the first part of this being the genitive of a postulated compound **Corfweg* 'road in the pass', cf. Corfe Castle *supra* 116. Ekwall is evidently on the track of the correct solution, and it may

well be that he is right in the case of Croscombe (So), which is
Correges cumb in 705 BCS 113, but I do not think Corscombe
(Do) can have exactly the history suggested. In my opinion[1]
Corscombe goes back to an OE **Corfge(a)tescumb*, the first part
of which is the genitive of the well recorded compound *Corfgeat*
'gate in the pass', cf. Corfe Castle (*supra* 116) which in ASC
appears as (*æt*) *Corfes geate* and (*at*) *Corf geate* (Latin *Porta
Corf*), and Coryates (*supra* 249) which is (*on*) *corf getes* (*westran
cotan*) in 1024 (orig.) KCD 741. Above all, however, it should
be noted that the word occurs among the boundaries of Corscombe itself, viz. in KCD 1322, where we find *on leas ende on
Corfget, of ðam gete on cruc middeweardne*, corresponding to *on
leas ende, ðanone on miclan corf, on miclan cruc middeweardne* in
KCD 1309. A valley named after this *Corfget* would have been
called **Corfgetescumb*, and the phonetic development may easily
be explained as having taken place along the line *corfgetescumb
> cor(f)yetscumb > coryescumb*, cf. the earliest spellings *Coriges-,
Cories-, Coris-*.[2]

Abbots because of the holding of Sherborne Abbey here.

Benville (Manor, Lane, Knap, Bridge) should probably be associated
with the family of John de *Benefeld*, mentioned under the parish
of Corscombe in 1340 (NI), for in an early 18th century deed
quoted in Hutchins (II, 91) there is mention of land "in Benvill
alias Benfield in Corscombe". The meaning must be 'land where
beans grow', OE *bēan, feld*; cf. Binnegar *supra* 144. On the
corruption of *feld* to *ville* see EPN s. v.

Catsley Fm
  Catesclive 1086 DB, 1200 Cur (also *Kates*-), 1200-1 FF, 1209
    Abbr, 1291 Tax, *-cliue* 1199 CurR, 1244 *Ass* (p)

---

[1] I may be allowed to mention that I had written down my suggestion a
couple of years before Ekwall's Studies on PN appeared and before his treatment of the *corf*-names in general (in ERN p. 96 f.) came under my notice.

[2] Cf. also Coryates (*supra* 249) where *t* has been preserved; in Corscombe
t was apparently dropped at a very early date owing to its position before *sc*.
The 13th century form *Coruscumbe*, in which *u* is taken by Ekwall (p. 72)
probably to be a relic of original *w* (*Corwes-* > *Corus-*), should, I suppose, be
interpreted as a spelling for **Coryscumbe*, cf. the many *Coris*-forms.

Cattesclive 1227 FF, 1275 RH (p), 1285 FA (p), *-cliue, -clyue* 1244 *Ass* (p), *-clyve* 1299 Ipm (p)
Catclyf 1535 VE

The second el. is OE *clif* 'cliff'; the slope here is very steep. The first el. offers the same difficulties as that of Cattistock *supra* 194, but in the present case I believe we have the animal name; cf. Catstor Down in PN D p. 230. Hence 'the (wild) cat's cliff'.

Coringdon (lost)
Curndun 1145 Hutchins[1], *Corundon* 1163 Hutchins[1]
Curendon 1244 *Ass* (p), *Querendun* ib. (p), 1285 FA (p)
Querendon, Queryndon, Coryngdon 1306 to 1385 BM I
Coryngdon 1385 FF, 1415 IpmR, 1441 FF, *-yn-* 1392 IpmR

This is a compound of OE *cweorn* 'quern, hand-mill' and *dūn*, a common pl.-n. probably denoting a hill where mill-stones were quarried, cf. Cornford Hill Fm *supra* 35. For the development of the svarabhakti vowel between *r* and *n*, cf. Farrington *supra* 11.

Pipsford Fm
Pippes 1196-7 FF, *Pipesie* 1203 Cur, *Pipeseie* 1204 (1313) Ch
Pepesia 1202 Cur
Pipsford 1802 Hutchins, 1811 OM

The spellings of the older forms would seem to point to OE *īeg, ēg* 'island' in the second el.; if so, the first must be left unexplained.[2] But there is apparently no 'island' here, and the district is so hilly that even the meaning 'land in the midst of marshes' seems to be excluded. I therefore venture the suggestion that the second el. is, instead, OE *sēað* 'hollow, pit, fountain', etc., a word which is well evidenced as a place-name element; cf. e. g. Middendorff s. v. If so, the first el. is OE *pīpe* 'pipe, tube', and the whole name may be an interesting illustration of the use of *sēað*, pointed out by Crawford in IPN p. 144. There are, however, certain phonological difficulties concerning the second el., but I think these might be overcome if we ex-

---

[1] Cf. Dugdale I, 339.
[2] The pers. name *Pipe* (DB) is ambiguous (cf. Redin p. 130), and nobody knows what lies behind the first el. in *pippes leage* BCS 743.

plain the earliest spellings above as being due partly to AN influence, partly to analogy with names in *ēg*, cf. Zachrisson, AN Infl. p. 85 and IPN p. 111. Moreover, if we assume a base *pīpesēað*, we may be able to account for the modern form Pipsford. A name **Pipseth* would in Do probably have been pronounced *Pipsed*, and from that pronunciation may have arisen a false reconstructive spelling *Pipsford*; cf. e. g. Dibberford *supra* 267, which must have developed from *Dibberwurth* through the intermediate stage of *Dibber(w)ood*.

Toller Whelme [tɔlə welm]

> (*on*) *Tollor æwylman* 1035 (12th) KCD 1322
> *Tolre* 1086 DB, *Toure* 1201 Cur, *Tor(e)* 1202 Cur, *Torne* 1203 Cur, *Tolye* 1251-2 Fees (1268)
> *Tolreewelme* 1334 FF, *Tollarwylme* 1550 BM II
> *Pinnys Toller* 1811 OM

This means 'the source (OE *æwielm* 'river-spring') of the river *Toller*', see Hutchins II, 92, Ekwall, Namn och Bygd XIV, 132 and ERN p. 410; cf. Tollerford, Toller Fratrum and Toller Porcorum *supra* 228, 235. For the river-name see Ekwall, ERN loc. cit., and cf. Zachrisson in ZONF VI, 248 f. — Spellings like *Toure*, *Tore* illustrate the AN tendency of vocalizing or dropping *l* before a consonant. *Pinnys* (1811 OM) is due to the name of the 17th cent. owners, the *Pennes* of East Coker (So), cf. Hutchins loc. cit.

Urless Fm is probably to be identified with *Hurdleye*, *Hurdlegh* 1333 *SR* (p), *Urdleye* 1340 NI (p), the modern form showing pseudo-manorial *-s* (1811 OM: *Urles*). The second el. is OE *lēah* 'enclosure'. The first is possibly OE *heord* 'herd, flock', but more and earlier material is necessary to substantiate this.

Mapperton

Mapperton 139 D 14

> *Ma(l)peretone* 1086 DB, *malperretona* Exon[1]
> *Mapeldoreton'* 1235-6 Fees (426), *Mapelderton* 1279 Ipm
> *Mapelarton* 1275 Abbr, 1285 Ipm

---

[1] *Mapertune* DB f. 75 a (*mapertona* Exon p. 26) has not been identified, cf. Eyton p. 103.

Mapelerton 1291 Tax, 1297 Pat, 1340 NI, 1368 BM II
Maperton 1297 Cl *et passim* (later *North-*, *S(o)uth-*)
Mapelarton Bret 1312 Ipm, *Brittes Maperton* 1412 FA

'Maple-tree farm', OE *mapuldor*, *tūn*; cf. the same name *supra*
74. *Bret*, *Brittes* because once held by a family called *le Brett*
or *Bryte* (Wm *le Bret* 1279 Ipm), for which see Hutchins II,
158 and 857.

Coltleigh Fm

Cottelegh 1244 *Ass* (p), Abbr (p), 1274 Fine (p) *et passim* to
1440 IpmR, with variant spelling *-ley(e)*
Cotele 1246 Pat (p), *Cotley* 1431 FA, *Cotlegh* 1465 IpmR

This name is probably identical with one Cotleigh and two
Cotleys in Devon (PN D pp. 435, 625, 655). These are taken
(op. cit. p. 625) to mean '*Cotta*'s clearing', the word *cote* 'cottage'
being rejected on account of the many *-tt-* spellings. The present
name also shows a great number of *-tt-* spellings[1], but I am
not convinced that this forbids us to take *cote* as the first element. — The modern form Coltleigh is curious and may partly
be due to popular etymology.

Mosterton

Mosterton 139 B 12

Mortestorn(e) 1086 DB, 1256 FF, 1276 Ipm, 1398 IpmR[2]
Mortesthorn(e) 1209-10 FF, 1244 *Ass* (p), 1276 Ipm *et passim*
to 1431 FA, *Morttes-* 1333 *SR*, *Morthes-* 1362 Cl
Morteshorn 1298 Ipm (p), *Mostreston* 1354 AD II
Mortherstorne 1412 FA, *Mottesthorn* 1428 FA, 1486 Ipm
Mosterne al. *Mosterton* 1654 SoDoNQ IX

Mosterton belongs to a group of English pl.-ns containing the
difficult first el. *mort(a)-*.[3] The whole group has recently been

---

[1] I have noted about twenty *Cotte-* forms for Coltleigh. It should further
be mentioned that among the boundaries in KCD 1322 (12th) there is a *Cotte*
(*Cotta*) *dene*, the first el. of which might possibly be identical with that of
Coltleigh.

[2] Spelt *Mortesterne* 1218 Sarum.

[3] The second el. of Mosterton is OE *þorn* 'thorn-bush', the *-torn(e)* forms
showing the common AN feature of substituting *t* for *th*. The modern form
of the name has probably been influenced by the neighbouring Misterton (So).

discussed in PN D p. 53 (s. n. Morthoe), where it is made clear that, at least in the majority of the names (including Mosterton), the element in question cannot be a stream-name, as was suggested by Blomé (p. 24) for Morthoe (D), but that it may rather denote a height of some kind.[1] To judge by the topography, this may very well be true of Mosterton, too. It should be added that in 1281 Ipm there is mention of an unidentified *Mortescombe*, tentatively assumed to have been in Dorset, cf. *Mortescumbe* 1240 Sarum (p. 265); is *murtes wyll* KCD 1322 (Do) also to be compared?[2]

Bluntsmoor Fm is *Blountescourte* 1486 Ipm, and apparently takes its name from a family called *le Bl(o)unt* or *Blount*, tenants in Mosterton in the 13th and 14th centuries (Thomas *le Blunt* 1285 FA, Thomas and Wm *le Blount* 1340 NI, Thomas *Blount* 1346 FA), cf. Hutchins II, 165; a diminutive of this pers. name enters into Bluntshay *infra*. The original terminal *court*, which was at a late date replaced by *moor*, seems, instead, to have been transferred to a farm close by called

Chapel Court. This is *Chapell* 1486 Ipm; there is a chapel near by.

Netherbury

Netherbury 139 D 13

Niderberie 1086 DB, *Niderbiri* 1091 Osmund
Nutherbir. 1226 Osmund, *Nytherbyre, Nyth[er]bire Roberti*[3] c.
    1226 Sarum, *Nytherbury* 1291 Tax *et passim*
Netherbire in Terra c. 1226 Sarum, *Netherburi* 1295 Pap, *-bury*
    1306 FF *et passim*
Nitherbury 1285, 1428 FA, *Nithirbiry* 1329 FF

---

[1] From the assumption that *mort(a)* is allied to the Germanic stem found *inter alia* in Icel. *murtr* 'short', MHG *murz* 'a cut off piece', Engl. dial. *murt* 'small person, small fish', the conclusion is drawn that some of the *Mort*-names must contain "a pers. name *Mort* or *Morta* derived from this stem and ultimately of nickname origin". The relation to this stem may well be correct, but I cannot see that this must necessarily involve the assumption of a pers. name.

[2] *murtes wyll* perhaps rather contains an OE **murt* 'small fish', cf. the preceding note and Hellquist s. v. *mört*.

[3] "The prebend of Netherbury in Terra was held c. 1226 by Robert the Scot" (Sarum p. 207 n. 6).

Self-explanatory, OE *neoðera* (*-i-*, *-y-*) 'nether, lower' and *burh* (*byrig*).

Ash is *Esse* 1207 ClR, 1231 FF, 1285 FA, *Assh(e)* 1306 FF *et passim* (with variant spellings *Ashe, Assch'*), *Aysshe* 1430 IpmR. OE *æsc* 'ashtree'.

Bidlake Fm (6″) is *Bitelak* 1225 FF, *Bitelake* 1376 FF, *Bydelake* 1430 IpmR, 1431 FA, *Bitlake* 1765 Taylor, *Bittlelake* 1811 OM. The second el. is OE *lacu* 'stream, watercourse', Bidlake being near the confluence of two brooks. If the first el. contains an original *d*, the name may be compared with Bibbern *supra* 37, but the earliest forms would seem to point to an original *t* rather than *d*. If so, the name should perhaps be compared with Bittadon (D), which has been assumed to contain a pers. name **Bytta* (Blomé p. 13) or **Bitta* (PN D p. 29). This seems extremely uncertain, in particular as neither of these names is on record, and the first el. of Bidlake had therefore better remain unexplained.

Bingham's Fm
> *Woth* 1207 ClR, 1333 *SR* (p), *Woz* 1231 FF
> *Worth* 1236 FF, *Wo[r]th* 1285 FA
> *Woth' Chamiel juxta Brideport* 1326 FF
> *Bynghamnesworth* 1428 FA, *Bynghamyshoth* (sic) 1431 FA,
> *Bynghams Wothe* 1448 IpmR, *Bingham Worth* 1811 OM

Ekwall has pointed out (ERN p. 469) that the river which is now called *Brit* (see Bridport *infra*) must have had an earlier name *Wooth* (aqua de *Woth* 1288 *Ass*), preserved in the pl.-n. Wooth Grange *infra*. The list of early forms for Bingham's Fm shows that this was also originally called *Woth*, and Ekwall's assertion is further borne out by the names of the neighbouring places Camesworth and Watford (both *infra*), cf also Watton *infra*.[1] Ekwall takes *Wōth* to be an English name and compares it with OE *wōþ* 'sound, clamour, melody, song', and assumes

---

[1] Cf. also Roger de *Woth* 1237 FF, Joh. de *Woht* 1382 SoDoNQ VII, Thomas de *Wouth* 1402 ib., Joh. de *Wotht* 1417 ib., Thomas and Robert *Wooth* 1406 AD I.

that there may have been an adjective *wōþ* meaning 'vocal, sounding'; alternatively he suggests derivation from a side-form without *i*-mutation of OE *wēþe* 'pleasant, mild'.

The *Binghams* were here as early as 1231 FF (Wm de *Bingham*), cf. Bingham's Melcombe *supra* 191. *Chamiel* (in *Woth' Chamiel*) may simply be a mistranscription for *Channel*, cf. the form *Woch chanel* (1288 *Ass*) given by Ekwall (loc. cit.). As was to be expected, *Woth* has often been mixed up with the common pl.-n. *Worth*.

Bowood, North and **South** [bouwud]

Bovewode 1086 DB, *Suthbouewode* 1310 FF, *Bouewode* 1316 FA
Bowodo 1166 RBE (*Bowoda* LN)
Buwod' 1207 Cur, 1208-9 FF, *Buwude* 1260 FF
Bouwode 1244 *Ass* (p), 1251 FF, 1303, 1346 FA, 1376 FF
Bowode 1244 *Ass* (p), 1285 FA, 1298 Ipm (p) *et passim*

This probably goes back to OE (*on*) *bufan wuda* 'above the wood', both North and South Bowood being on high ground. Cf. Boveridge *supra* 100, Bovingdon Green (Bk), Boveney (Bk)[1], Bowcombe (Wt): *Bovecome* 1086 DB, *Bouecome* 1263 Ipm, *Bouecumbe* 1316 FA; Bowood in Abbotsham (D) would seem to be an exact parallel, see PN D p. 84. Cf. also Richard de *Bouethemelne* ('above the mill') in 1244 *Ass* (201 m. 9), mentioned in connexion with Broadwindsor.

Brinsham Fm (6″) is *Brynsham* 1340 SoDoNQ VII (p), 1377 Cl, 1406 AD I, 1417 SoDoNQ VII, 1431 FA, *Brynshaump* 1412 FA, *Brynysham* 1430 IpmR. Probably '*Bryni*'s *ham(m)*'. For this pers. name see Redin p. 121.

Broadenham Fm is *Bradenham* 1327, 1333 *SR* (p). OE (*æt*) *brādan ham(m)* '(at the) broad homestead or enclosure'.

Camesworth is *Kaymesworth* 1333 *SR* (p), *Caymeswouth* 1340, 1372, 1402, 1424 SoDoNQ VII, *Caymeswooth* 1431 ib., *Kaymesowith* (sic) 1493 Ipm, *Caymyswothe*, *Kaymyswoth*, *Keymeswoth*, *Kaymysworth* 1518 SoDoNQ VII. See Bingham's Fm *supra* 275. The first part of the name is obscure.

[1] See PN Bk pp. 187 and 215.

Cullington (6″) is *Colyngdon* 1333 *SR*, 1402 SoDoNQ VII, *Colyndon(e)* 1340, 1372 SoDoNQ VII, *Colundon* 1382 ib., *Colyngton* 1431 FA (all p). The second el. is OE *dūn* 'hill', but the forms are too late to allow of any certainty concerning the first el. If *-yn(g)-* is the result of a late development, the OE base may be (*æt*) *cōlan dūne* '(at) the cool hill'.

Elwell (**Fm** and **Lodge**) is *Ellewell* 1333 *SR*, *Elle-Wille* 1372 So DoNQ VII, *El(l)wyll*, *Elwill* 1417 ib. (all p). Probably 'elder-tree spring', OE *ellen, wielle*; cf. Elwell (2) and Elwill Dairy in PN D pp. 36, 291, 599, and Elworth *supra* 245.

Filford

Filleford(e) 1327 *SR* (p), 1406 AD I, 1430 IpmR
Fulleford 1333 *SR* (p), *Fulford* 1412 FA
Feleford 1382 SoDoNQ VII
le Fylleford 1417, 1456 SoDoNQ VII
le Filleford 1441 SoDoNQ VII

This may be from OE **filiðford*, a compound of *filiðe* 'hay' and *ford*; cf. PN D pp. 42, 145, 285, 345 s. nn. Filleigh, Great Velliford (*Filleford* 1292), Fillham and Fyldon; cf. also Middendorff p. 51 and (*on*) *filithleighe* BCS 1214 (Do). There is perhaps even the possibility that Filford may go back to an OE (*æt*) *filiðlēage forda* 'the ford by the meadow', cf. (*to*) *fileþ leage forda* BCS 1027. Cf. Feltham Fm *supra* 15.

Ford Fms is *atte Forde* 1333 *SR* (p). Self-explanatory.

Furleigh is *Farleghe* 1427 IpmR, *Firley* 1489 Ipm. No suggestion is possible until we get earlier and better material.

Hincknoll Hill is *Henknoll* 1441 SoDoNQ VII (p), 1486 Ipm. Apparently from OE (*æt*) *hēan cnolle* '(at) the high knoll', as suggested in Hutchins (II, 114).

Kershay Fms is *Kyrseheye* 1306 FF (p), *Curseheygh'* 1333 *SR* (p), *Curseyah* 1340 SoDoNQ VII (p), *Kyrsey* 1583 ib., *Cirshay* 1811 OM. The second el. is OE (*ge*)*hæg* 'enclosure' (ME *hay* 'farm, holding'), but no explanation of the first el. can be offered.

Kingsland is *Kyngeslond* 1333 *SR* (p), 1489 Ipm, *Kingesland* 1427 IpmR. Self-explanatory.

Lambrook is *Lambrouk* 1333 *SR* (p). The first el. may be either OE *lām* 'loam' or *lamb* 'lamb'.

Limbury Fm is *Lymbury* 1406 AD I, and was probably the home of Wm de *Limbur[i]* 1285 FA. As in the case of Lymburgh's Fm *supra* 43, the elements are presumably OE *lin* 'flax' and *beorg* 'hill'.[1]

Loscombe is *Loscumbe* 1268 FF, 1291 Tax, 1319 FF *et passim* (with later *-combe*). Probably 'pigsty-valley', OE *hlōse, cumb*; cf. *hloscumbes heafud* BCS 695 (Do).

Luccombe Fm is *Leucom* 1251 FF, *Leucumbe* 1260 FF (p). Probably identical in origin with Lewcombe *supra* 229.

Mangerton [mæŋɡətən]
Mangerton(e) 1207 Cur, 1285, 1303, 1316 FA *et passim*
Maugerton (sic)[2] 1208-9 FF, 1306 FF (*juxta Beyminstr'*)
Mangereston 1274 Cl, *Mangerston* 1303 FA
Manggerton 1333 BM I, *Mangreton* 1376 FF

The first el. is apparently OE *mangere* 'dealer, monger', cf. *Mangersford* (1442) in PN D p. 9. For names of this type cf. (*on, of*) *cypmanna delle* BCS 179, 628, 905 (Ha) and (*on*) *chypmanna ford* BCS 879 (W), containing OE *cīepmann* 'merchant' (Middendorff p. 25).

Melplash
Melpleys c. 1155 Sarum (p), *Melepleis* 1160-1 Sarum (p)
Mellepeis 1166 RBE (p), *Melepeis* 1209 FF, *Melepes* 1285 FA
Melepleys [*Melipas*], *Melepleychs* [*Meliplech*] 1303 FA

---

[1] Cf. VCH Do II, 344: "One of the oldest industries in Dorset is that connected with the manufacture of hemp and flax — —. The centre of the trade — — has been, from time immemorial, the town and neighbourhood of Bridport." Limbury Fm is less than two miles from that town.

[2] *u* here is clearly a mistranscription for *n*, cf. *Mangerton* vel *Maugerton* 1479·IpmR.

Meleplesh(e) 1306 FF (*West*), 1333 FF (*Est*) et passim with variant spelling *-pless(c)h*, *Melplessh* 1346, 1428 FA *Meleplayssh* 1333 SR, *Meleplaisch* 1350 BM I (*Eyst*), *Melplayssh* 1412 FA, 1447 BM I (*Est-*), *West Melpalysh* 1486 Ipm

Melplassh 1391 FF (*Est-*), 1392 BM I (*Est*) et passim *Milplassh, Est Milplaysh* 1449 BM I

The second el. is apparently OE *plæsc* 'shallow pool, (dïal.) plash'. The first may be identical with the first el. of Melbury Abbas *supra* 27 (cf. Zachrisson, Romans p. 52).[1]

Silkhay Fm is *Selkeheye* 1333 SR (p) with mention of Andrew *Selk* in the same parish, see PN D p. 89 s. n. Silkland. It is clear that the place was named after that man or his family, cf. the note to Bilshay Fm *supra* 254. *Selke* occurs as a sur-name in Dorset from the 12th century, cf. Edward *Selke* 1169-70 P, and William *Selke* 1201-2 FF (in Askerswell). *Selk(e)*, I suppose, goes back to the OE pers. name *Seolca* (Redin p. 158); cf. also the lost *Silkden* in PN Sx p. 166.

Slape Ho [sli:p]
Slepa 1226 Osmund, *Slepe* c. 1226 Sarum, 1263 Pat, 1360 Cl *Slape* 1291 Tax, 1535 VE

OE *slæp* 'slippery place, (dial.).slape' (EPN); cf. Slepe *supra* 113, 130.

Strode [stroud]
Strod(e) 1225 FF, 1244 *Ass*, 1268 Pat (all p), 1280 FF, *et passim*
le Strode 1265 Pat (p), *la Strode* 1267 Pat (p)
Stroude 1333 SR (p), 1369 Cl (p), 1412 FA

OE *strōd* 'marshy land owergrown with brushwood' (EPN); cf. Stroud (Bridge, Fm) *supra* 66, 219.

Watford[2] (6″) was the home of Philip de *Wothford* mentioned in (n. d., prob. 13th cent.) AD VI (C 4834), this single form being

---

[1] Ekwall (Namn och Bygd XVII, 168) suggests that Melplash may contain OE *mylen* 'mill'. But the *Mil-* spellings of 1449 (BM I), on which Ekwall bases this suggestion, are unique, and the persistent *Mel(e)-* forms are decidedly against derivation from *mylen*; cf. Milborne St Andrew *supra* 173.

[2] Bridge and Fm (just S of Wooth Grange), the latter in the parish of Bradpole.

enough to show that Watford means 'the ford over the river *Wooth*; see Bingham's Fm *supra* 275.

Waytown is *atte Wey(e)* 1327 *SR* (p), 1417 SoDoNQ VII (p). Self-explanatory (OE *weg*); *town*, here in its Devon sense of 'farm', was apparently added at a fairly late date, cf. PN D p. 676.

Wooth Grange is *Woth Fraunceys* 1276 FF, *Woch Fraunceys* 1294 FF, *Wrothfraunceys* 1306 FF, *Wothfrances* 1382 SoDoNQ VII, *Wooth Frances* 1406 AD I, *Othe* 1431 FA, 1472 IpmR, *Nethir Worth* (sic) 1487, 1488 Ipm. See Bingham's Fm *supra* 275. The earlier addition *Fraunceys* (*Frances*) is evidently due to some tenant bearing that name, cf. John *Fren(s)che* and Robert *Fren(s)che* (also called *le Frense*) occurring as land-holders in the adjacent parish of Loders in 1321, 1326 SoDoNQ VII, 229 ff.

South Perrott

South Perrott 139 A 13

  Pedret, Sudperet 1086 DB, *Sutpetret, Sutpedret, Sutperret* Exon,
    Paret, Superet(e) 1218 Sarum
  Suthperette 1275 Cl (p), *Suthperret* 1308 Orig, 1337 FF
  Suthpeured 1298 Ipm, *Suthperred* 1333 *SR*
  South Perret 1340 NI *et passim, Southperrot* 1431 FA

South Perrott takes its name from the river Parrett, on which see Ekwall, ERN p. 320 ff. *South* in relation to North Perrott (So).

Picket Fm is *Pikyate* 1236 FF, 1412 FA, *Pikiete* 1285 FA, *Pykeyate* 1398 IpmR, *Pikat* 1425 IpmR, *Pykyate* 1431 FA, *Pykyet* 1433 IpmR, *Pikeyate* 1486 Ipm. The second el. is OE *geat* 'gate' (EPN). According to EPN, OE *pīc*, 'sharp pointed instrument', is not found in the charter material in a topographic sense, and ME *pike*, 'pointed hill', is confined to the North of England. It seems almost certain, however, that the first el. of Picket must be *pīc* (or *pike*) in the sense of 'hill-top', for the farm is just below the summit of a very steep hill. For a similar compound cf. (*to*) *cnollgete* BCS 596 (Ha).

North Poorton

North Poorton 130 H/I 1

Powrtone, Povertone 1086 DB, *PoWrtona, pouertona* Exon
Poertona 1167-8 P (p), *Poerton* 1244 *Ass*
Purton' 1235-6 Fees (425)[1], 1244 *Ass* (p)
Poorton 1244 *Ass, Poreton'* 1244 Abbr (p)
Pordon 1269 Misc, *Porton(e)* 1280 FF *et passim*
Pourton 1333 BM I, 1346 FA, 1386 Cl (*North*) *et passim*

See Powerstock *supra* 240. *North* in relation to South Poorton
supra 242.

Burcombe Fm[2] is *Burcūbe* 1244 *Ass* (p), *Burcome* 1346 FA,
Burcombe 1386 Cl, IpmR *et passim, Bourcome* 1428 FA, *Bor-
combe* 1431 FA. I suppose this is a compound of OE *burh* and
cumb, cf. (*in summitate vallis quæ*) *byrigcumb* (*dicitur*) BCS 476 (So).

Stoke Abbott

Stoke Abbott 139 C 12

Stoche 1086 DB, *Stokes* 1191, 1238 Sarum, 1247 Cl, *Stoke* 1238
 Sarum, 1285 FA *et passim*
Stoke Abbots 1275 FF *et passim, Stoke Abbatis* 1285 FA, 1291
 Tax, *Abbodestok* 1312, 1334 FF, *Abbot(e)stoke* 1335 Inq aqd,
 1396 BM I *et passim, Stoke Abbas* 1358 AD I

OE *stoc* 'place'. It anciently belonged to Sherborne Abbey.

Blackney Fm is *Blakēheye* 1333 *SR* (p). Probably a compound
of OE *blæc* 'black' and (*ge)hæg* 'enclosure'.

Brimbley Fm

Bromleye 1295 Ipm, 1303 Cl *et passim* with variant spellings
 -legh, -le, Bromele 1392 IpmR, *Bromeleygh* 1428 FA
Brumlegh 1325 FF
Bremeleygh 1412 FA, *Bremleygh* 1431 FA, *Bremley* 1441 AD I

---

[1] We should probably also compare Galfridus de *Pourton'*, mentioned in
1212 Fees (88) as tenant in eastern Dorset; cf. 1210-2 RBE p. 547. His name
is spelt *Portun'* in 1219 Fees (260).
[2] The DB form *Bovrtone* (Exon *bourtona*), assumed by Eyton (p. 137 f.) to
belong here, may refer to Poorton instead.

'Broom clearing', OE *brōm, lēah* (dat. *lēage*); cf. Brimley (D) in Blomé p. 131 and in PN D pp. 411, 467, 619, 626; cf. also Broomhill *supra* 148.

Brimbley Coombe Fm is *Cume* 1236 FF (p), *Combe* 1327 *SR* (p), 1441 AD I. OE *cumb* 'valley'.

Chart Knolle Fm. I have found three early references to a place in this parish called *Charteray* (1240 Sarum (p), 1415 IpmR) or *Charterey* (1431 FA), which cannot now be found on the maps. There are, however, good reasons for believing that the name actually survives in the name of the present Chart Knolle Fm. What *Charteray* means is difficult to say, but the second el. is probably OE *(ge)hæg* 'enclosure'.

Laverstock Fm is *Lauerestok, Larkestok* 1244 *Ass* (p), *Laverk(e)-stok(e)* 1285 FA (p), *Lau'kestoke* 1333 *SR* (p), *Lanerkestok* (sic) 1340 NI (p), *Larkestoke* 1431 FA, *Larstock* 1811 OM. A compound of OE *lāwerce* 'lark' and *stoc* 'place'; cf. Laverstock (W), Ekblom p. 112.

Lewesdon Hill may be identical with *Leweston* 1324 Ipm, but the material is too scanty to allow of any suggestion.

Venn Fm is *atte Venne* 1333 *SR* (p), *atte Wenne* 1340 NI (p). OE *fenn* 'fen, marsh', cf. Black Venn *supra* 17.

Wall Fm is *atte Wall(e)* 1333 *SR* (p), 1340 NI (p). Self-explanatory, OE *weall*.

XXXIII. Whitchurch Canonicorum Hundred

Witchirce 1084 GeldRoll, *Whitechirche* 1159-60 P
Witcherch(e) 1167-8 (etc.) P, 1212 Fees (94), *Whytcherch* 1244
    Ass, Whitecherch 1295 Misc
Witchurch 1229 FF, *Wite-* 1244 FF, *Whit-* 1269 Ch *et passim*
Wytchirche, Wite- 1244 *Ass, Whit-* 1269 Ch *et passim*

See Whitchurch Canonicorum *infra.*

Bettiscombe[1]

Bettiscombe 139 C 11

Abbetescomba 1174-82 France
Bethescomme 1190 (1332) Ch, *Betescumbe* 1244 *Ass* (p)
Bertescumbe 1252 Ch
Bettescum 1276 Cl (p), *-cumbe* 1291 Tax, 1428 FA, *-comb(e)*
     1327, 1333 *SR*, 1340 NI, 1436 IpmR
Beddescombe 1428 FA, *Battiscombe* 1441 AD I (p)

The place belonged to the Abbey of St Stephen, Caen (Normandy), and this probably accounts for *Abbetes-* in the oldest
form above. In all probability, however, the name does not
contain 'abbot' but some OE pers. name, presumably *Betti* (cf.
Redin p. 126). *Bertescumbe* (1252) would seem to point to the
well-recorded name *Berht* (Redin p. 10), but the form may be
a corruption. Hence probably '*Betti*'s valley', OE *cumb*.

Bridport

Bridport 139 F 13

Brideport 1086 DB (*-porta, -porti* Exon), 1156-7 France, 1158-9
     (etc.) P, 1190 (1332) Ch, 1201 RC *et passim*
Bridiport 1142-54 France, 1157 Sarum, 1172-3 (etc.) P, 1189
     (1313) Ch, 1205 ClR, 1230 Cl, 1232 Pat *et passim*
Brudiport 1154-5 (etc.) RBE, 1207 PatR, *Brudeport* 1252 Pat,
     1278 QW, 1291 Tax, Ch *et passim* to 1382 Cl
Bridepord 1164-5 P, 1212 Fees (95), *Brideporth* 1275 Cl
Briddeport 1225, 1249 FF, 1270 (etc.) Pat, 1278 QW
Bridport 1243 Sarum (p) *et passim*, *Bredeport* 1266 Pat
Briteport 1276 Pat, *Britport* 1426 AD VI, 1428, 1431 FA
Bryd(d)eport 1278 QW, 1299 Pat, *Brypport* 1418 AD II
Byr(d)porte 1526 AD II, *Byr(t)port* 1535 VE

Bridport stands on the river Brit, but Ekwall (ERN p. 52 f.)
is apparently right in assuming that the present name of that
river must be a back-formation from the form *Britport* (see
above)[2], and that Bridport itself took its name from the village
(earlier borough) of Bredy (*supra* 238); Bridport would thus
originally mean 'the port belonging to Bredy'. This interesting

---

[1] In Frampton Liberty.
[2] For an earlier name of the river Brit cf. *supra* 275 s. n. Bingham's Fm.

transference of the name of Bredy — originally the name of
the present river Bride — thus ultimately resulted in the formation of a new river-name Brit.[1]

Burstock

Burstock 139 C 11

   Burewinestoch 1086 DB

   Burgestoche 1178-9 (etc.) P, *Burgestok(e)* 1199 CurR, 1200 Cur,
     1200-1 FF, 1204 (1313) Ch, 1244 Sarum

   Burghestokes, -stok(a) 1227 FF, *Burghstoke* 1318 Inq aqd

   Burhestok, Burestoke (Borestoke) 1245 Sarum

   Burstok 1291 Tax *et passim, Brigstoke* 1316 FA

The DB form looks as if it contained the pers. name *Burg-
wine* (*Burewine*), for which see Searle p. 122, but the later forms
do not tell in favour of that, since *-wine-* could hardly have
disappeared without leaving any trace. I suppose Burstock is
a compound of OE *burh* and *stoc*; cf. the similar compounds
burhsteall, burhstede, and *burhtūn* (EPN p. 11).

Hursey[2] is *Herstanesheia* 1201-2 FF, *Herstonesleg'* 1203 RC, *Her-
stenehot* (sic) 1251-2 Fees (1267), *Hurstenesheye* 1311 FF, *Herstenes-
hegh* 1386 FF, *Hurstensey, Hurstenseleghe* 1413 IpmR, *Hurstenes-
heys* 1450 IpmR, (*Burstock et*) *Hurstonshay* 1535 VE. The second
el. is apparently OE *(ge)hæg* 'enclosure', and the first must be
the OE pers. name *Heorstān* (Searle p. 291), occurring *inter alia*
in the original charter BCS 648.

Catherston Leweston

Catherston Leweston 139 E 10

   Cardeston 1293 Pat

   Cattereston [*Chatereston*] 1303 FA

---

[1] The two rivers Bride and Brit, which rise far from each other, happen
to fall into the Channel only a mile from one another, and it is not to be
wondered at that their names are often mixed up even by Dorset people.

[2] Hutchins mentions, besides this Hursey in Burstock, a place in the parish
of Whitchurch Canonicorum called *Hurstoneshay* (or *Hurstenhay*). Since no
such place is to be found on the maps, I have no doubt that his article on
Hurstoneshay (II, 260), which contains several of the above references, refers
in reality to this Hursey in Burstock.

Cardeston et Lesterton (rectius *Cardeston Leuston*) 1316 FA
Cartereston(e) 1325 Inq aqd, 1346 FA, *Carterston* 1431 FA
Carteston 1428 FA
Catereston 1428 FA, 1488 Ipm, *Catherston* 1535 VE

The material for this name is so late and conflicting that I
must refrain from making any suggestion.

Charmouth

Charmouth[1] 139 E/F 10
Cernemude 1086 DB, *Cernem'* 1204 (1313) Ch
Cernemue 1212 Fees (94), 1227 FF, 1236 Fees (1468), 1240
  Sarum, 1244 FF, 1278 Ch, 1291 Pat, Tax
Cernemuwe 1242-3 Fees (751), *Gernemuwe* (sic) 1286 Ipm
Chernemewe 1316 FA, *-muthe* 1325 Inq aqd, *-mothe* 1398 IpmR
Charnemouth 1428 FA, 1488 Ipm, *Charmouth* 1535 VE

'Mouth (OE *mūþa*) of the river *Cerne*', now called the Char,
that name being in its present form a back-formation from
Charmouth; see Ekwall, ERN p. 73.[2] Cf. Charminster and Cerne
Abbas *supra* 181, 196. For the AN spellings cf. also Weymouth
supra 161.

Lily Fm is *Lidleghe* 1240 Sarum, *Lydlege* 1327 *SR* (p), *Lydeley*
1398 IpmR, *Lydlegh(e)* 1425 IpmR, 1475 FF (p). The second el.
is OE *lēah* 'clearing', and since the farm is on a steep slope,
the first may be OE *hliþ* 'slope, cliff, hill-side'.

Chideock

Chideock [tʃidik] 139 F 11
Cidihoc 1086 DB, *cidiohoc* Exon
Cidioc 1240 Sarum, *Cydiok* 1240 Sarum, 1276 Ipm

---

[1] The place called (*æt*) *Carrum* in ASC, where the Danes were fought by
King Ecgbryht in 833 and by King Æþelwulf in 840, has constantly been
identified with Charmouth. Some years ago, however, Mr Bruce Dickins showed
that (*æt*) *Carrum* should, instead, be identified with Carhampton in Somerset;
see Mawer, PN and History p. 10.

[2] An earlier reference than *aqua de Cerne* 1288 *Ass* (noted by Ekwall) is
cern hlinces herpaδ (see Ritter p. 155), found among the boundaries which
belong to KCD 772 (Tengstrand).

Chidiok 1276 Ipm, 1316 FA, 1334 FF, *Chidioc* 1313 Cl
Chydyoc 1281 Ipm, *Chydiok* 1316 FA (p), *Chydyok* 1359 IpmR
Chidihouk 1344 Cl (p), *Chedioke* 1416 IpmR, *Chidyok* 1431 FA
Chideok 1462 IpmR, *Chidwik* c. 1540 Leland

Ekwall (ERN p. 77) compares this with the latter part of the
name Dunchideock (D), for which he suggests derivation from
an adjective corresponding to W *coediog* 'wooded, woody' (from
coed 'wood'); see also PN D p. 495.[1]

Frogmore Hill (1″) and **Fm** (6″) is *Frogghemore* 1324 AD I (p).
See Frogmore Fm *supra* 25.

Lyme Regis

Lyme Regis 139 F 9
  Lim 774 (12th) BCS 224, 998 (12th) KCD 701, 1174-91 BM I,
    1212 Fees (88, 94) *et passim*, *Lime* 1086 DB *et passim*
  Lym 938 (14th) BCS 728, 1086 DB, 1191 Sarum *et passim*
    (variant *Lyme*), *Netherlym* 1252 FF
  Lyme Regis 1285 (1321) Ch, *South Lym'* 1297 Cl

Lyme Regis takes its name from the river Lyme (called *Lim*
on the OS maps), for which see Ekwall, ERN p. 274. *Nether*
and *South* in relation to Uplyme (D). The place became a royal
borough in the time of Edward I.

Cobb, referred to as (*in*) *la Cobbe* 1295 Misc, is a semicircular
stone pier probably dating from the time of Edward I.[2] The
word *cob(b)* has various senses in English, all probably going
back to a common meaning of 'something rounded or forming
a roundish lump', cf. NED s. v. *cob* sb. 1.[3] The above form

---

[1] The name of the small stream which runs through Chideock is **Winniford**,
spelt *Wynreford* in a 13th cent. charter printed in Hutchins (II, 255 note a).
An alternative name seems to be *Chid* (not on maps), which — as pointed out
by Ekwall (loc. cit.) — is a back-formation from Chideock.

[2] To judge from the maps the pier itself is called The Cobb, while Cobb
is the name of the part of Lyme Regis which is nearest to the pier.

[3] Cf. also NED s. v. *cob, cobb* sb. 7: "The mole or pier of Lyme Regis was
originally constructed of cobble-stones heaped together; thence perhaps *cob* =
cobble in sense 1." (*i. e.* "a water-worn rounded stone, *esp.* of the size suitable
for paving"). I feel more inclined to believe that, in the present case, *cobb* may
have had a sense similar to that of Swedish *kobbe* 'a small rounded rocky islet'.

from 1295 carries the history of the word *cob* in English more than a hundred years back in time and tends to strengthen Wallenberg's assumption (StNPh II, 90 and Kentish PN p. 244 s. n. Cobham) that a nature word of the meaning suggested may have existed in OE; cf. Middendorff p. 28 s. v. *cobbe*. If so, some at least of the many *Cob-* names in Devon, all of which are taken by Blomé and the editors of PN D to contain an unrecorded OE pers. name **Cobba*, will probably have to be reconsidered.[1]

Colway

  Coleweye 1242-3 Fees (751), 1308 FF, 1386 Cl, IpmR, 1396
      BM I
  Coleheoh' juxta Lim 13th GlastonC
  Calwehagh 1333 *SR, Calwehegh* 1346, 1428 FA, *-hey* 1398 IpmR
  Coleweheys 1335 Ch, *-heye* 1340 NI (p), *Colowhey* 1425 IpmR
  Coleheygh' inter Uplym in Devonia et Netherelym in Dorset 14th
      GlastonF
  Colbe(y)gh, Colebegh' juxta (Nether)lym 14th GlastonF
  Calewey 1431 FA, *Coleweyishome* 1437 IpmR

The run of early forms is bewildering, and without still earlier spellings it is impossible to be sure about the etymology. The *Coleweye* forms would seem to suggest a meaning 'cool way' (OE *cōl, weg*), whereas the *Calwehegh* forms, as pointed out by Ekwall (Contrib. to the Hist. of OE Dial. p. 13), rather indicate that the first el. is OE *calu* 'bald, bare, callow', the second being OE *(ge)hæg* 'enclosure'; the third "type" *Coleheygh* looks as if it contained *cōl* and *(ge)hæg*. Is *Coleweye* perhaps the original name to which was later on added a *hay*, and was **Coleweyhay* understood as containing *calu* 'callow'?

Haye Fm (6″) is (*in Lim' et*) *Hegh* 1227 ClR, *Heigh*1395 AD I. OE *(ge)hæg* 'enclosure'.

---

[1] The pl.-n. *Cobheye*, occurring in the same entry as the above *la Cobbe* (1295 Misc p. 473), may have been named after *la Cobbe* itself, but is more probably a mistranscription for *Coleheye*, in which case it may belong to Colway (next name).

Marshwood

Marshwood 139 D 10

Mersoda ante 1174 France, *Merswude* 1187-8 P (p), 1205 ClR
et passim with variant spellings *-wod(e)*, *-uuode*
Mereswud' 1200 FineR, *Mersewd'* 1212 Fees (94)
Mershewode 1291 Fine *et passim* with variant spellings *Merssh(e)-*,
Mersc(h)-, *Marshwode* 1462 IpmR

Self-explanatory, OE *mersc, wudu*. The rich and fertile Marshwood Vale[1], which comprises large parts of this hundred, extends
on both sides of the river Char and its tributaries. It was
formerly more deserving of its name, being then "hardly passable
by travellers but in dry summers" (Hutchins). The abundance
of *hay*-names here would seem to point to a comparatively late
colonization; cf the note to Bilshay Fm *supra* 254.

Baber's Fm (6″) is *Babireshey* 1398 IpmR, *Baberesheys* 1410, 1438
BM I, *-heighe* 1425 IpmR, *Babersheyes* 1437 FF, *-heye* 1440
IpmR. Probably a late name in *-hay* containing the family name
Baber (Bardsley p. 71).

Colmer Fm is *Colemor'* 1333 *SR* (p), *Colemere* 1398 IpmR. 'Cold
swampy ground', OE *cōl, mōr*. Alternatively the second el. may
be *mere* 'pool'.

Little Dunster Fm is *Donstrowe* al. *Dunstrowe* 1338, 1379, 1405,
1409, 1410 BM I, *Donstrowe* 1376 FF, 1398 IpmR, *Dunstrowe*
1396, 1409 FF, 1440 IpmR, *Donestrowe* 1425 IpmR. The elements would seem to be OE *dūn* 'down, hill' (in gen.) and OE
trog 'trough' (often spelt *trow* in ME), the whole name thus
probably denoting some trough-like depression or conduit in
the down; cf. EPN s. v. *trog*, NED s. v. *trough* sb. (5 and 6).

Forstershay (lost) is *Forestarehege* 1240 Sarum, *Forstereshegh*
1320 FF, *-hey(e)* 1333 *SR* (p), 1391 FF, *-heigh* 1398 FF, *Forsters-
hey(e)* 1325 AD VI (p), 1425 IpmR. The second el. is OE *(ge)hæg*
'enclosure' or rather ME *hay* (cf. Bilshay Fm *supra* 254), for the

---

[1] *Mershoudewalle* 1331 BM I, *Mersshewode Vale* 1335 Ch (*et passim*), *Vallis de
Merchewod* 1338 BM I.

first el. can hardly be anything else than the word *forester* (*forestarius*), frequently met with as a pers. name in ME.[1]

Hackeridge Fm (6″) is *Hakerigg(e)* 1334 FF, 1387, 1402 IpmR, -*rigghe* 1425 IpmR, -*rygge* 1425 FF. The second el. is OE *hrycg* 'ridge', and the first may be OE *haca* 'bolt' (originally meaning 'hook') used in some topographical sense; cf. Blomé p. 9 s. n. Hakeford (D). The exact topography of the place is unknown to me.

Harmshay Fm (6″) is *Heremaunseya* 1261 FF, *Hermenneshegh* 1320 FF, -*hey* 1391 FF, *Hermenesheigh* 1398 FF, *Hermerseye* 1398 IpmR, *Harmeshey* 1437 FF, 1438 BM I, 1440 IpmR. '*Hereman*'s enclosure', OE *(ge)hæg*.

Harper's Fm (6″) is *Harporeshegh* 1398 IpmR, -*heighe* 1425 IpmR, *Harpereshayes* 1475 FF. This probably contains the common family name *Harper* (OE *hearpere*, Anglo-Fr *harpour*). The second el. *(ge)hæg* was later dropped (and replaced by "farm"), as in Baber's Fm *supra* 288.

Hogboro' Cottages (6″) is *Hokbere* t. Hy III or Edw I BM I, 1383 IpmR, *Hokebere* 1333 SR (p), 1384 Cl, 1425 FF, 1430, 1437 IpmR, *Hocbere* al. *Hogbere* 1333 BM I. The second el. is probably OE *bearu* 'grove' (cf. Todber *supra* 18), and the first may be OE *hōc* 'hook'; cf. Hooke *supra* 240.

Marshalsea is *Marshalshay* 1636-7 DorchesterR. Probably a *hay*, named after some family called *Marshal*. Hutchins (II, 263) has a form *Maskylsay* from 1448, for which cf. Bardsley s. n. *Mascall*.

Monkwood is *Munkewode* 1244 Abbr, 1396 FF, 1409 BM I, *Monekwode* 1317 FF, *Monk(e)wode* 1379 BM I, 1398 IpmR, 1409 FF *et passim*. Self-explanatory, OE *munuc, wudu*; cf Monkwood Hill Fm *supra* 205.

---

[1] Cf. the following early examples from Dorset: William *Forestarius* 1201-2 (FF), William *le Forester* 1249 (FF), Robert *Forrester* 1269 (Ch); cf. also PN Sx pp. 188, 229 f., 470 f.

Nash Fm is *Nayssh* 1351 Cl; cf. also Roger *Attenasshe* who was party to a fine concerning land *in A . . . enasshe* (etc.) in *Merswodenaal* (sic) 1319 FF. See Nash Court *supra* 43.

Oakford Fm is *Okford* (*in valle de Mershewood*) 1387 IpmR. Self-explanatory, OE *āc, ford*.

Park Fm is *atte Parroke* 1327 *SR* (p), (by the bridge) *Atteparrok* 1344 AD II, *Parrok* 1412 FA, *La Parrok* 1414 BM I, *Littilparrot* 1437 FF, *Lytil Parrok* 1438 BM I, *Littil Parrok in Mershwodevale* 1440 IpmR. OE *pearroc* 'small enclosure, paddock'.

Shave Cross is *la Schaghe* 1325 AD VI (p), *atte Shawe* 1333 *SR* (p), *Schaue* 1398 IpmR. OE *sceaga* 'small wood, copse, (dial.) shaw'. For the development of *w* to *v* cf. PN D p. xxxv; the earliest *v* spellings in NED (s. v. *shaw* sb. 1) are from the 18th century.

Woodmill (lost) is *Wodemulle* (*in Merswde*) 13th AD I, *la Wodemulle* 1325 AD VI, *la Wodemill* 1344 AD II, *Wodemille in Merswodevale* 1438 AD I, *Wodemylle* 1441 ib. (*et passim* in AD). Self-explanatory, OE *wudu, mylen*.

Yard Fm (6″) is *la Yrde* 1303 FA (p), *la Yrdde* 1305 AD II (p), *atte Yerde* 1333 *SR* (p), *la yherde* 1337 SoDoNQ XIII, *la Yerde* 1346 FA (p), *Yerd(e)* 1396, 1409 FF, 1440 IpmR, *Attezard* 1398 IpmR, *Attzurd* 1425 IpmR. Identical in origin with Yard Dairy *supra* 235.

Pilsdon

Pilsdon 139 D 11

Pilsdon(e) 1086 DB, 1201-2 FF, 1240 Sarum, 1244 *Ass*, 1346 FA

Pillesdun' 1167-8 P, -*don'* 1168-9 (etc.) P, 1209 Abbr (all p), 1244 *Ass*, 1250 Fees (1182) (p) *et passim*

Pillesden' 1169-70 P (p), *Pilesden'* 1199 CurR (p)

Pulesdon' 1200 Cur (p), 1406 AD I, 1431 FA, *Pulles-* 1412 FA

Pillisdon(e) 1235-6 Fees (427), 1325 AD VI (both p)

Pylesdon 1244 *Ass*, 1305 AD II, *Pylesdun'* 1250 Fees (1240) (p), *Pylisdon* 1332 FF

An unrecorded pers. name *Pīl has been supposed to enter
into a number of pl.-ns[1], but I do not think we need reckon
with that doubtful possibility here. As pointed out in PN D
p. 420, such a name as Pilemoor (D) may contain OE pīl 'stake',
in particular as we have frequent mention of the surname atte
Pyle from the Subsidy Rolls, attention being also drawn to Pile
Hill (Sr), atte Pile 1332 SR; cf. Pile Lane supra 39. I am convinced that Pilsdon, too, contains OE pīl 'a pointed object, spike,
nail, stake', here apparently referring to the form of the hill,
OE dūn.[2] The village of Pilsdon is at the foot of Pilsdon Pen,
the highest eminence in Dorset (909 ft.); cf. Hutchins II, 235:
"This hill (i. e. Pilsdon Pen) is conspicuous and remarkable
on account of the peaked form its southern extremity presents,
as seen from many parts of the adjacent country, a peculiarity
from which its name perhaps arose."

Stanton St Gabriel

Stanton St Gabriel[3], **St Gabriel's Ho** 139 F 11
Stantone 1086 DB, 1240 Sarum, *Staunton* 1316, 1431 FA
Staunton Gabriell 1434 FF, *Staunton Gabriel* 1465 IpmR

'Enclosure made of stone', OE stān, tūn. On aun for an cf.
Stourton Caundle supra 39. St Gabriel's House is near the
ruins of the old church dedicated to St Gabriel.

Pitland Coppice (6") is *Putlond* 1310 AD I, VI, *Pytlond* 1397
BM I, *Pittelond* 1410 BM I, *Pyttelond* 1440 IpmR. OE pytt 'pit,
grave' and land. There is a gravel pit marked on the 6" map
a few hundred yards NE of the coppice.

Symondsbury

Symondsbury [simənzbəri] 139 E 12
Simondesberge 1086 DB (-b'ga Exon), 1253 Pap, -bergh 1300 FF,
1309 Ipm et passim, -berwe 1318 Ch, -borg 1304 Cl

[1] Cf. e. g. Ekwall, PN La p. 54 s. n. Pilsworth; PN NRY p. 23 s. n. Pil-
moor; PN Nth p. 231 s. n. Pilsgate.
[2] For the meaning of this type of genitive compounds (pilesdūn) cf. e. g.
Hatchwell (D), earlier *Hatteshull* (1352), 'hill shaped like a hat' (PN D p. 527).
[3] Stanton St Gabriel is the parish name and occurs only on parish maps·

Simunisberge 1212 Fees (92), *Simonisbergh* 1291 Tax
Symundesberg 1237 FF, *-berwe* 1300 FF, *Symondesbergh* 1316
   FA, 1329 Ipm *et passim*
Simondberew 1281-2 Abb
Symundesburgh 1302 FF *et passim* with variant spellings
   Simondes-, *Symondes-*; *Simonsburgh* 1325 Inq aqd
Symondesbaurgh 1421 AD I, *-bargh* 1431 FA
'*Sigemund*'s hill or barrow' (OE *beorg*), cf. PN Bk p. 24 s. n.
Simpson. Simons Burrow (D) is an exact parallel, see PN D
p. 617.

Atram is *Atrem* 1086 DB, *Atrum* 1086 Exon, 1166 RBE, 1189
(1313) Ch, *Atrom* 1200 Cur, 1225 FF, *Atron* 1200-1 Abbr, *Athram*
[*Accham*] 1303 FA, *Atreham* 1333 *SR* (p), 1340 FF, BM I, *Attram*
1346 FA, *Atram* 1347 FF, 1375 IpmR *et passim*, *Ateram* 1431 FA.
The different farms called Atram are all situated on or very near
different branches of the little river Simene[1], so Atram may
possibly preserve the old name of that river. But I can make
no etymological suggestion.

Coppet Hill may be identical with *La Coppedehall* n. d. (Hy III)
Hutchins (II, 255 n. a) and, if so, probably also with *Choppudehulle* 1281 Ipm, for these two forms would seem to refer to the
same place. The first form contains OE *coppede* 'having the
copp or summit cut off' (or possibly 'rising to a *copp*'), cf. EPN
s. v.; the second el. is probably a misreading for *hull* (OE *hyll*
'hill'). If the form *Choppudehulle* is reliable, it must mean 'the
chopped or cut off hill', thus affording a remarkably old example
of the verb *chop* 'cut off'; cf. NED s. v. *chop* vb. 1, where the
earliest references are from the latter part of the 14th century.

Great Ebb[2] is *Hebbe* 1329 Ipm. In modern standard English
ebb usually means 'the reflux of the tide' (NED s. v. *ebb* sb.),
but dialectally it may sometimes also mean 'the foreshore, the
part between high and low water' (EDD s. v. *ebb* sb. sense 3).
This must be the meaning here, Great Ebb being the name of

---

[1] "Better known as the river Atram" (Hutchins). The name Simene is a
back-formation from Symondsbury, cf. Ekwall, ERN p. 366.

[2] Just to the west (in Chideock) is East Ebb Cove.

the part of the beach which is visible only at low water. Since
the dictionaries give no early examples of *ebb* in this particular
sense, the above form from 1329 may be of some interest. Cf.
Hellquist s. v. *ävja*.

Eype [i:p] is *Estyep* 1300 FF (*juxta Symundesberwe*) *et passim*
(with variant *Estyepe*), *Yep(e)* 1365, 1389 Cl *et passim, Est Epe*
al. *Yepe* 1612 SoDoNQ VII. Eype is on the slope of a valley
which opens towards the sea (Eype Mouth) and in the bottom
of which flows a small brook. I take the name to go back to
OE *gēap* 'open, wide, steep, deep', here used as a noun in the
way assumed for OE *stēap* 'steep' in the pl.-n. Steep (Ha), see
PN BedsHu p. 85 s. n. Steppingley; cf. also PN Sx p. 469 s. n.
Bucksteep.

Moorbath
  Mordaat 1086 DB (prob. identical)
  Morba 1200, 1201 Cur (p), 1244 *Ass* (p), 1269 Misc (p)
  Morpad'e 1201 Cur (p), *Morban* 1235-6 Fees (427)
  Morbath(e) 1244 *Ass*, Abbr, 1269 Misc *et passim* with later
    variant spellings *Mour(e)-* (1376), *More-*

This is apparently identical in origin with Morebath (D), containing OE *mōr* 'marshy land' and *bæð* 'bath', cf. Blomé p. 82
and PN D p. 536. If there are any medicinal springs here
that can account for the use of the term *bath*, I cannot say.
Loss of *th* in some of the early forms must be due to AN influence, cf. Weymouth *supra* 161.

Vearse Fm and **Watton**[1]
  Wotton Ver 1304 Cl
  Watton(e) 1329 Ipm, 1412, 1431 FA, *Vereswatton juxta Symondes-*
    bergh 1371 FF, *Verres Watton* 1421 AD I

Watton is on a height near the river Brit, earlier called *Wooth*
(see Bingham's Fm *supra* 275), and it is very tempting to suggest
that both this and another Watton (Hill) 1 ½ m. NE (on the
other side of Bridport) go back to an earlier **wōþ-dūn* 'hill by
the river *Wooth*'; Watford, earlier *Wothford* (*supra* 279), is just
N of Watton Hill.

[1] Less than half a mile from one another.

Vearse Fm *(Wotton Ver, Vereswatton)* takes its name from a family called *Veer*, which lived here from the time of Henry III (Hutchins); Robert *le Veer* occurs under this hundred in 1244 *Ass* (201 m. 12).

Thorncombe

The parish of Thorncombe (139 B 10) belonged to Devon up to 1842 and has therefore been included in PN D (p. 648). I have nothing of interest to add to the discussion there except to mention that in 1200 Cur there is a form *Sottesberges*, identified by the indexer of Cur with **Sadborow** in this parish.

Whitchurch Canonicorum

Whitchurch Canonicorum 139 E 11

Witcerce 1086 DB *(Witcercie* Exon), *Witcherch(a)* 1142-54 France,
    c. 1200 Osmund, *Wittecheriche* c. 1228 Sarum
Witchureche c. 1207 BM I, *Wite-, Wit(t)churche* 1240 Sarum
Whitchurch Canonicorum (Album Monasterium) 1262 Pap
Whitchirch by Lime 1264 Pat, *Wychirch* 1265 Misc

'White church', OE *hwīt, cirice*; cf. Winterborne Whitchurch *supra* 67. Whitchurch Canonicorum anciently belonged to the abbey of St Wandrille in Normandy and afterwards to the church of Sarum; hence the distinctive name.

Baker's Cross may be identical with *Bakeresheyes* 1440 IpmR, apparently a comparatively young *hay*-name containing the surname *Baker*. ME *hay* or OE *(ge)hæg* forms the second el. in many of the following names; cf. Bilshay Fm *supra* 254.

Beaushens (lost) is *Bessynishegh* 1325 AD VI (Robert de *Bessyn*), *Bouchenesheye* 1333 *SR* (p), *Besschin(n)eshegh* 1344 AD II (Robert *Besschin*), *Besschyneshegh* 1398 IpmR, *Beawshenysheyis (in Mershwodevale)* 1463 AD I (Wm *Beawshen*), *Beawshene* 1463 AD I, *Beaushens* 1482 AD I (Wm *Beaushen*), *Beawshinhaies* 1616 SoDo NQ VII. The family which gave name to this place held land in Wiltshire, too; cf. Wm *Beaushin* (1329) of Bradford (Hutchins), and Thomas *B(e)aushyne (Beaushene)* of Atworth (1402, 1428 FA).

Berne (Fm, Manor Ho) is *La Berne* 1281 Ipm, 1376 FF, *atte Berne* 1333 *SR* (p), 1346 FA (p), 1348 FF (p), *Le Bernes* 1431 FA, *Berne* 1462, 1473 IpmR, 1475 FF, *Barne* 1488 Ipm. OE *bern* 'barn' (EPN).

Bluntshay is *Blondelesheye* 1312 SoDoNQ XIII, 1340 FF, 1398 IpmR, *-hegh* 1376 FF, *Blundleshay* 1329 BM I, 1408 BM II, *Blondelsheye* 1383 FF, *Blundeleshay* 1396 FF *et passim* (*Bloundeleshey* 1425 IpmR), *Bloundeshay* 1412 FA, *-heys* 1422-3 BM I, *Blontyshay* 1431 FA, *Blounteseys* 1446 BM I.[1] This contains the common family name *Blundel, Blondel* 'the blonde, the yellow-haired' (see Bardsley s. n. *Blundell*, and Weekley, Romance of Names p. 214). I have not met with it in Do, but it is not rare in other counties from the beginning of the 13th cent. onwards, cf. e. g. Jordan *Blundel* (So) 1205 FineR. Cf. Bluntsmoor Fm *supra* 274.

Cards Mill Fm is *Casemyll* 1462 IpmR, 1475 FF, *Casimill* 1811 OM. First el. obscure.

Great Coombe is *atte Comb'* 1333 *SR* (p). OE *cumb* 'valley'.

Cothays Fm (6"), **Cuthay Fm** (6"), **Cutty Stubbs**
  Cuttehegh 1269 SoDoNQ VIII (p), *Cutehaghe* 1316 FF (p)
  Cutehay 1317 FF
  Cotehegh 1398, *-heygh* 1416, *-heighe* 1425 IpmR, *-hay* 1412 FA

The above forms all refer to places (or persons) in Marshwood Vale, but it is almost impossible to be sure about their identification. The three *Cut(t)e*-forms probably refer to Cuthay Fm or Cutty Stubbs[2], and may have another origin than the *Cote*-forms, which presumably refer to Cothays Fm; cf. Coltleigh Fm *supra* 273. It should be noted that *Cute* is found as a surname in ME, cf. Ricardus *Cute* 1193 P (Beds).

Gerneshill (lost) is *Jerynshulle* 1379 BM I, *Grynsattehille* 1396 BM I, *Gerynsattehull* 1396 FF, 1409 BM I *et passim* (with small

---

[1] BM I also includes the forms *Blundreshey, Blondeleshegh, Blondelsheie, Blundeleshay*, taken from various manuscripts dating from 1338 to 1524.

[2] Situated very near one another and probably the same name originally.

variants in spelling), *Jeryneshull* 1398 IpmR, *Gerneshull* 1425
IpmR, *Geronys* 1431 FA, *Gerens atte Hill(e)* 1448 BM I, 1465
IpmR, *Gerens* 1524 BM I. The first part of the name looks
like *Gerin*, a pers. name of Continental-Germanic origin (cf.
Forssner p. 108). That this assumption is correct is proved by
an entry in 1236 FF (p. 62), telling us that Matilda de *Lahull*
and *Gerinus de Merswude* were parties to a fine concerning land
in Marshwood.[1]

Griddleshay Fm (local)
  Greleshegh 1280 FF
  Greyleshegh 1398 IpmR, *-heyghe* 1416 IpmR, *Greylesshey* 1425
  IpmR, *Greylesley* or *Greyleshay* 1488 Ipm

The clue to the solution of the first el. should apparently be
sought in a 13th century charter of Robert de Mandeville[2] to
the church of Whitchurch Canonicorum (printed in Hutchins II,
270), where there is mention of a certain Walter *Grael* ("a domo
que fuit Walteri Grael") in such a connexion as to make us
sure that he must have lived near the parish church. This
Grael, I believe, is the ME form of the pers. name **Grǣgel*,
supposed to enter into the two Sussex names Graylingwell and
Grainingfold; cf. Ritter p. 103, PN Sx p. 11 f., Mawer, Problems
of PN Study p. 88 f.

Gummershay Fm is *Gomboldesheye* 1333 *SR* (p), *Gombeldesheye*
1340 NI (p), *Gumblesey* 1765 Taylor. '*Gumbeald*'s enclosure', OE
(ge)hæg. Gummershay Fm in Stalbridge (*supra* 38) contains a
different pers. name.

Hincombe (lost) is *Hyndecomb(e)* 1312 SoDoNQ XIII, 1316 FF,
1325 AD VI, 1327 *SR* (all p), 1416 IpmR, 1488 Ipm, *Hende-
comb'* 1333 *SR* (p), *Hyncombe* 1412 FA. Probably OE *hinda-
cumb* 'valley of the hinds'. The place is mentioned as late as
1710 in Mayo's Bibliography of Dorset (p. 134).

Mandeville Stoke Fm is *Maundevile Heis (in Mershwode)* 1350
IpmR, *Maundevilleshey* 1398 IpmR, *Mandevileshey* 1425 IpmR,

---

[1] Cf. also the mention of one Johannes *Geryn* (1312, 1337) in three 14th
cent. Marshwood charters printed in SoDoNQ XIII, 318 ff.

[2] See further under Mandeville Stoke Fm *infra* (this parish).

The Place-Names of Dorset

297

Manvelsheyes 1612 SoDoNQ VII, and evidently preserves the memory of Robert de *Mandeville*[1] (or his family), who at the beginning of the 13th century held the honour of Marshwood; cf. e. g. 1205 ClR p. 51, and 1212 Fees p. 94.

Morecombelake has not been found in ME records, but is spelt *Morecomblake* in 1577 (Hutchins II, 253 n. c.). The name is probably self-explanatory, the elements being OE *mōr* 'barren land, swampy ground', *cumb* 'valley', and *lacu* 'stream'.

Pitt Fm is (*la*) *Putte* 1240 Sarum, *la Pitte* 1244 *Ass* (p), *Pitte*, *Pytte* 1318, 1438 BM I, *atte Putte* 1333 *SR* (p), *Pitte* 1437 FF, *Pytt* 1440 IpmR. OE *pytt* 'pit, grave'.

Purcombe Fm[2]

Perecumb, *Purecumbe* 1244 *Ass* (p)
Piricume t. Hy III BM I, *Pirycumbe* 1275 Cl
Pirecome 1310 AD VI (p), 1333 *SR* (p), *Pircombe* 1379 BM I
Pyrcombe 1332 FF (p), 1396 FF *et passim*, *Pyre-* 1376 FF

'Pear-tree valley', OE *pirige*, *cumb*.

Ramesham (lost). In 1358 BM I there is mention of a *Rammeshameslond* together with Purcombe. This is probably identical with *Ramesham* 1396, 1409 FF and 1440 IpmR, but nothing more is known about it. Cf. Rampisham *supra* 234.

Ryall is *Rihull* 1240 Sarum, *Rihull*, *Rohull* ib. (p), *Ryle* 1811 OM. Apparently 'rye-hill', OE *ryge*, *hyll*.

Stoke Wallis (lost) is *Stoches* (twice) 1086 DB, *Stoke Walays* (*Waleis*, *Waleys*) t. Edw I BM I, 1316 FA *et passim*, *Wylyshstoke* 1376 FF, *Stokeways* 1411 BM I. OE *stoc* 'place'. The distinctive name is obviously due to some ancient owner called (*le*) *Waleys* (cf. Langton Matravers *supra* 122), but I have not been able to track him down.

---

[1] Cf. under Griddleshay Fm *supra* 296.
[2] I have included all the early forms for Purcombe here, though some of them may perhaps refer to another Purcombe about 2 m. N (in Marshwood).

Studley (lost) is *Stodlege*[1] 1086 DB, *Stodlegh* 1377 Cl, *Stodley* 1524 Hutchins, *Studley* 1534 Hutchins. 'Stud clearing', OE *stōd, lēah*.

Thurstanshay (lost) is *Turstanesheygh* 1396 IpmR, *Thurstaynesheghes* 1424 IpmR. Nothing further is known about this place, but according to Hutchins (II, 266) it was in this parish. The first el. must be the pers. name *Thurstan*, and it is perhaps more than a mere coincidence that the DB tenant-in-chief of the two *Stoches* recorded under the lost *Stoke Wallis* (*supra* 297) bore that name.[2]

Abbott's Wootton Fms
(*æt*) *wudetune* 1044 (orig.) KCD 772
Widetone, -tona 1086 DB, Exon, *Wdeton'* 1212 Fees (92), *Wudeton* 1269 Misc, *Wodeton* 1269 Ch, *Wotton* 1318 Ch
Parva Widitone [*Wyditone, Woditone*] 1240 Sarum
Wodeton Abbatis 1240 Sarum, 1316 FA, 1336 Ch

OE *wudu-tūn* 'wood-farm'. This Wootton belonged to Abbotsbury Abbey. *Parva* probably in relation to the neighbouring Wootton Fitzpaine (next name).

Wootton Fitzpaine

Wootton Fitzpaine 139 E 10
Wodetone, Odetun 1086 DB, *Wudeton* 1244 *Ass*, *Wodeton* 1244 *Ass*, 1291 Tax, 1302 FF *et passim*, *Wotton* 1346 FA
Wodeton Roberti (*filii Pagani*) 1316 FA, *Wotton Fitzpayn* 1405 IpmR *et passim* (variant *Fytz Payn*)
Wodeton Matravers 1375 IpmR[3]

---

[1] *Slitlege*, mentioned in DB (f. 84 b) a few lines before *Stodlege*, may be a corrupt form referring to this place, too.

[2] *Turstinus filius Rolf*. "This was Turstin fitz Rou le Blanc; he who having borne Duke William's Gonfanon at Hastings, was rewarded for his prowess with estates in Dorset and other counties" (Eyton p. 76). On the name *Thurstan* see Björkman, Nord. Personennamen p. 161 f.

[3] In 1280 FF there is mention of a *Wotton Flemeng* (called *Wotton Flemyng* in 1290 Cl). This should apparently be considered together with the *Wutton* of 1228 FF and the *Wottune* of 1256 FF, the tenants of which were Roger *le Flameng* and Walter *le Flameng* respectively. The site of this lost **Wootton Fleming** was evidently somewhere in Marshwood Vale. In 1303 (FA) Amicia,

See the preceding name. The *Fitz Payns* here were the same
as those of Okeford Fitzpaine *supra* 45. In the time of Edward
III Robert Fitz Payn sold this manor to John *Mautravers* of
Lytchett Matravers (*supra* 112), cf. Hutchins II, 274.

Champernhayes Fm and **Marsh.** The only old form noted is
Champrenheghe 1482 IpmR; this does not enable me to say what
the first el. may be; is perhaps Chambercombe (PN D p. 46)
to be compared? Hutchins calls the place *Womeslegh*, alias *Cham-
prenlegh*, or *Champernhays*. The first of these names appears
as *Womeshegh* 1440 IpmR and *Womeshaghe* 1482 IpmR. Here
again the first el. is obscure.

Guppy[1] is *Gopeheye* 1333 *SR* (p) and should be compared with
Guphill (D), which Blomé (p. 68) takes to contain a pers. name
*Guppa, a pet-form of such names as *Gūpbeald*, *Gūpbeorht*; cf.
Wallenberg (StNPh II, 91) who suggests possible connexion
with OE *gupe* 'buttock'; see also PN D p. 336 s. n. Guphill,
where attention is drawn to the name Gupworthy (So), *Guppe-
wurpe* 1155-8 (1334) Ch, *Gopeworthy* 1327 *SR*. The situation of
Guppy on the slope of a considerable round hill would seem
to tell in favour of Wallenberg's suggestion, but no certainty
is possible until we get more comparative material.

Hogchester
Hoggeshurst(e) 1236 FF, 1244 *Ass* (p), 1398 IpmR
Hoggehurste 1425 IpmR
Hoggecestr' 1436 IpmR, *Hogcestre* 1488 Ipm, *Hogsester* 1654
SoDoNQ IX, *Ogchester* 1765 Taylor

This is apparently a compound of OE *hogg* 'hog' and *hyrst*
'wooded height', the nature of the second el. favouring the
supposition that the first el. is the name of the animal itself
and not a pers. name[2]; cf. such names as Hogford, earlier

wife of Walter *le Fleming*, was one of the tenants of Atram (*supra* 292); cf.
the mention in 1312 (SoDoNQ XIII, 318) of a wood in Marshwood Vale belonging to Thomas *le Flemyng*.

[1] There is also a Guppy's Fm (6") about a mile to the north.

[2] A pers. name **Hogg* is not recorded in OE but has been supposed to enter
into several pl.-ns, cf. e. g. PN Bk p. 67 f. s. n. Hoggeston. In ME it was
a common surname, cf. Joh' *Hogh*, Joh' *Hog*, Joh' *Hogges*, noted under different
Do parishes in 1340 NI.

Hoggesford (*supra* 86), *Hoggeslond* (1347) in PN Sx p. 560, Hogs-
land (D), earlier *Hoggeslond* (Blomé p. 140, Wallenberg, StNPh II,
98, PN D p. 137), Hogsbrook (D), earlier *Hoggesbrok* (PN D
p. 602).
For the curious change of *Hoggeshurst* into Hogchester, cf.
Bedchester *supra* 23.

Monkton Wyld, Wyld Fms
Wila 1204 (1313) Ch, *la Wile, la Wylle* 1244 *Ass* (p)
Wyle 1316 FA *et passim* to 1496 Ipm, *la Wyle juxta Lym*
   1323 FF
Monkynwyll 1535 VE, *Weald* 1811 OM

OE *wielle* 'spring, well' would have given either *well* or the
typical Dorset form *wool* (cf. Wool, Woolbridge and the two
Woolcombes *supra* 150, 145, 225, 236), and it is therefore impossible to believe that we have that word here. I cannot
suggest any plausible etymology, but OE *welig, wylig* 'willow'
should perhaps be taken into consideration.
Monkyn- and *Monkton* because the place anciently belonged
to Forde Abbey.

Penn is *la Penne* 1244 *Ass* (p). OE *penn* 'enclosure, pen'.

Ridge is *Rugge* (in the parish of Whitechurch[1]) 1431 AD II.
Self-explanatory, OE *hrycg*.

Spence Fm is *atte Spence* 1333 *SR* (p). The word *spence* (OFr
despence), now dial. or archaic, means a place where provisions
are kept, a buttery or pantry; see NED and EDD s. v.

Westover Fm is *Westouer* 1333 *SR* and should possibly be associated
with the Johannes *Westour'* or *Westovere* who in 1250 and 1251-2
(Fees pp. 1182, 1240, 1267) held one virgate of land in Netherhay in Broadwindsor. The meaning is probably 'west river-
bank', OE *west, ōfer*. Cf. Southover Ho *supra* 179.

---
[1] The parish of Whitchurch Canonicorum was formerly much larger than
it is to-day.

Formerly in Somerset[1]

Goathill

Goathill 130 C 6

Gatelme 1086 DB, *Ingatelma* (= *In Gatelma*) Exon
Gothull(e) 1290 Ch, 1316 FA, 1320 Ipm *et passim*
Gotehull 1487 Ipm, *Gotehill* 1495 Ipm, 1535 VE

Self-explanatory, OE *gāt, hyll.*

Poyntington

Poyntington 130 B 5

Ponditone 1086 DB, *-tona* Exon
Pondintun(e), *-tone* 1091-1106, 1107-22, 1152-8 Montacute
Pundinton(e) 1100-18 Montacute, 1198-9 FF
Puntintuna 1100-22 (1270) Ch, *-tun* 1135-7 Montacute, *-ton*
1249 FF, *Puntington* 1258 FF, 1316 FA, *-yn-* 1281 Ipm
Puthintone 1152-8 Montacute
Poncintone (sic) 1166 RBE (p): *Puncintone* (sic) LN
Pudynton 1258 Ch, *Pudington* 1284-5 FA
Pontynton [al. *Potington, Putington*] 1285 Ipm
Poyntington 1326 Ipm *et passim* with variant *-yn-*
Pontindon 1331 Ipm

The list of early forms seems to point to a base *punt-*, the early *d* spellings being probably due to AN influence. If so, the whole name may mean (1) 'the farm of the descendants of *Punt*', the pers. name *Punt* being evidenced from about 1106, see PN Sx p. 393 s. n. Pounsley[2]; (2) 'the farm of the *punt* dwellers', as suggested by Karlström (p. 63) for Pointon (Sr), OE *punt* having probably the wide sense of 'raft, river ferryboat, floating bridge' and the like. The situation of the village of Poyntington on both sides of a stream seems to me to tell strongly in favour of the latter alternative.

---

[1] Seaborough in Crewkerne Hundred, the others in Horethorne Hundred. They were transferred to Dorset in 1896. I am indebted to Mr J. E. B. Gover for some of the early forms.
[2] Cf. also Mawer, Problems of PN Study p. 102.

Sandford Orcas

Sandford Orcas 130 A/B 4

Sanford(a) 1086 DB, Exon, 1278 Misc, *Sandford* 1242-3 Fees
(753), 1303 FA, *Saun(d)-* 1276 RH, 1284-5 FA
Saumford 1316 FA, *Sampford* 1431 FA
Saunford Crescoys (sic) 1353 Cl
Sandford Orskoys 1428 IpmR, *Sampford Orkas* 1535 VE

Self-explanatory, OE *sand, ford*. *Orcas* from its 12th century
lords, the *Orescuils*, see Eyton, DB Studies: So I, 66 f.

Weathergrove

(on) wederangrafe scagan 938 (12th) BCS 730
(oþ) wederan grafes suð ende 956 (12th) BCS 931
Weregrave 1086 DB, *Weregraua, Werregraue* Exon
Wedegrave 1278 Misc
Wedergrove 1276 RH, 1310 Cl, *Wedergrave* 1303 (etc.) FA[1]
Wethergrave 1470-1 IpmR

For different suggestions concerning the first el. of this difficult name see PN Wo p. 336 (s. n. Weatheroak Hill) and Middendorff p. 144. I can offer no plausible interpretation. Second
el. OE *grāf(a)* 'grove'.

Trent

Trent 130 B 3

Trente 1086 DB (*Trenta* Exon), 1249 FF, 1265 Misc, 1276
Ipm, 1284-5 FA *et passim*, later *Trent*

Trent Brook, a tributary of the river Yeo, runs just S of the
village, and there can be little doubt that the village was named
after that brook; cf. Ekwall, ERN p. 416 (bottom).

Adber

Ateberie 1086 DB, *Ateberia* Exon (p. 334)
Ettebere 1086 DB, *Eattebera* Exon (p. 457)[2]

---

[1] *Wedergrave* 1284-5 FA (IV, 273) is identified by the indexer with Wydergrave in Hardington (near Frome), and that is also Eyton's identification of
Weregrave in DB; cf. VCH So I, 455 and foot-note 2. It would indeed be interesting to find this name repeated in (another part of) Somerset, but I
cannot find "Wydergrave" on the 1″ map.

[2] *(In)etesberia* Exon (p. 259) seems also to belong here.

Attebare 1091-1106 Montacute, 1303 FA (p)
Athebare 1100-18, 1152-8 Montacute, *Atebare* n. d. Montacute,
   Over Attebar 1303 FA, *Parva Atebar(e)* 1303, 1346 FA
   Atebere 1221-3 Montacute (p), 1303 FA, *Over Ateber* 1346 FA
   Overateberg 1274 Ipm
   Ateber', *Ateleber'* 1276 RH
   Attebere 1280 Montacute *et passim* (*Nether-, Ouer-*)
   Atebear 1321 Ipm, *Attebeare* 1325 Ipm, *Atbare* 1428 FA
   Adebere 1429 IpmR, *Adbere* (*Nethir, Over*) 1496 Ipm

The second el. is apparently OE *bearu* 'grove, wood'. The
first may be either the pers. name *Eat(t)a* (*Aetta*)[1], or the whole
name may be interpreted as *æt þǣm* (> *atte*) *bearwe* 'at the grove'.
The latter alternative is in itself very attractive, but Adber is
by no means so clear a case as Eccliffe *supra* 6.

Hummer is *Humbre* 1091-1106 (*et passim*) Montacute, *Homere*
1311 (*et passim*) FF, 1346 FA (p). Hummer is near a small
stream, a tributary of the Yeo, and Ekwall (ERN p. 203) is
probably right in suggesting that the stream was once called
Humber. On this common English river-name see Ekwall loc. cit.

Plot (6") was the home of Henry *atte Splotte* 1333 *SR*, 1340 NI.
This is evidently OE *splott* 'spot, patch of ground, plot of land',
still surviving in the SW of England, see EDD s. v. *splot* and
PN D p. 137 s. n. Splatt. OE *plot* had the same meaning, so
the transition to this latter word is easy to understand.

Seaborough

Seaborough 139 B 12
   Seveberge 1086 DB, *Seueberga, Seuuebeorga, Seuuoberga* Exon
    (pp. 142, 143, 477)
   Seveberugh 1256 FF, *Seuebergh* 1303 FA, 1316 FF, FA
   Seweberge 1285 FA, *Soueberge* 1297 Pat
   Seuenbergh 1306 FF
   Seueburgh 1346 FA, 1355 FF, 1428 FA

The second el. is OE *beorg* 'barrow, hill'. I do not think the
first is an unrecorded pers. name *Seofa*, as suggested in PN

---

[1] Cf. (*to*) *ættandene*, (*to*) *ættan wylle* BCS 695 (Do) among the boundaries of
Bradford Abbas, c. 3 m. away.

Sx p. 68 s. n. Seabeach. From a formal point of view it may equally well be OE *seofon* 'seven', and this assumption is strongly supported by the numerous pl.-ns and boundary-marks containing that word; cf. e. g. PN Sx loc. cit., Wallenberg p. 13, PN D p. 50 s. n. Seven Ash ('seven ashes'), ib. p. 287 s. n. Zeaston ('seven stones'), ib. p. 482 s. n. Soussons ('seven stones', (*oð*) *sufon stanas* BCS 1323), ib. p. 565 s. n. Sowell ('seven springs', cf. also Blomé p. 96), PN Nth pp. 40, 139 s. nn. Seawell and Sywell where many parallels of the type 'seven springs' are adduced; cf. further Middendorff p. 116[1], and (*at*) *seuen diche* (*suð ende*) BCS 970 (Do).

---

[1] Note in particular (*on, of*) *sevenburges* BCS 1127. Another important parallel to the present name is *Seueberghe* 1293 FF (Ess), see PN Sx loc. cit.

ELEMENTS, APART FROM PERSONAL NAMES, FOUND IN DORSET PLACE-NAMES

This list also includes elements used in the first part of place names. Under each element the examples are arranged in the following order: uncompounded names; second elements; first elements. It should be understood that in some cases the names do not go back to the OE period, although the elements are as a rule given in their OE form. Words which only appear as a very late addition have as a rule not been included. Some very doubtful cases have also been excluded.

abbud 'abbot'. Abbotsbury. Cf. also names like Abbott Street, Bradford Abbas, etc.

āc 'oak'. Oakford, Okeford, Oakley (2).

æcer 'field, cultivated land'. Innsacre.

ǣl 'eel'. Almer.

ærn 'house, shed'. *Crockern Stoke*, Minterne (?), Potterne.

æsc 'ash-tree'. Ash (2), Nash (2); Ashcombe, Ashington, Ashley, Ashmore, Ashton. Cf. also Anderson.

æt 'at' (prep.). Eccliffe, Adber (?).

æðeling 'nobleman'. Allington.

ǣwiell 'river-spring'. Alton Pancras.

ǣwielm 'river-spring'. Toller Whelme.

alor 'alder'. Aller; Axnoller; Alderholt.

ānstīg 'path for one, narrow path'. Ansty.

bæð 'bath' (possibly 'spring'). Moorbath.

bār 'boar'. Bowerswain.

bēag 'ring', probably 'bend' (of a river, etc.). Beaminster.

bēan 'bean'. Benville, Binnegar.

bearu 'grove, wood' (or in some cases possibly **bǣre** 'pasture'). Barford (earlier *Bere*), Beer Hackett, Bere (Marsh, Regis); Adber, Bagber (2), Colber, Haselbury, Hogboro', Middlebere, Plumber, *Ramsbury* (?), Todber.

begeondan 'beyond' (prep.). Yondover.

*bell(e), see Belchalwell.

beorg 'hill, barrow'. Barrow Hundred (earlier *Hundredesberg*), Charborough, Chebbard, Chelborough, Dogbury, Limbury, Longbarrow, Loosebarrow Hundred, Lymburgh's Fm, Modbury (2), Rowbarrow Hundred, Seaborough, Stoborough, Symondsbury, Woodbury.

bere 'barley'. Barcombe.

bere-tūn literally 'barley-farm'. Barton.

bere-wīc literally 'barley-wick'. Berwick.

bern 'barn'. Berne.

bī 'by' (prep.). See Bestwall.

binnan 'within, inside of' (prep.). Bindon.

blæc 'black'. Blackdown, *Blackland*, Blackmoor, Blackney, Blackrow, Black Venn, Blagdon (2).

*blæcen, see Blashenwell.

blǣge (gen. plur. **blǣgna**) 'gudgeon'. Blandford.

bōcland 'land granted by book or charter'. Buckland (2).

bothem (ME) 'valley', cf. OE **botm** 'bottom'. Bothenhampton, Bothenwood.

brād 'broad'. Bradford (3), Bradle, Bradpole, Broadenham, Broadley. In Broadmayne, Broadway, Broadwindsor, and a few other names, the epithet 'broad' is comparatively late.

brōc 'brook'. Fernbrook, Holebrook, Honeybrook, Key Brook, Lambrook, Lowbrook, Southbrook, Stanbrook, Westbrook; Brockhampton, Brockington.

brōm 'broom'. Brimbley, Broomhill.

brūn 'brown'. Burngate.

*brunc, see Branksea Island.

brycg 'bridge'. *Bridge*; Chilbridge, Stalbridge, Stanbridge, Stockbridge, Woodbridge (2), Woolbridge.

bucc(a) 'buck, goat'. Bockhampton, Buckham.

bufan 'above' (prep.). Boveridge, Bowood.

burh (dat. sing. **byrig**) 'earthwork', etc., cf. EPN s. v. Abbotsbury, Badbury Hundred, Bulbury, Chalbury, Dudsbury, Henbury, Melbury (Abbas; Bubb, Osmond, Sampford), Netherbury, *Ramsbury* (?), Shaftesbury, Spettisbury; Burcombe, Burstock.

burhtūn 'farm near a **burh**'. Bourton, Burton (4). *Not* present in Burton Bradstock.

burna 'stream, *burn*'. Bibbern, Cheselbourne, Cranborne, Milborne, Oborne, Sherborne, Wimborne, Winterborne (two streams).

butere 'butter'. Butterwick.

byden 'bushel, tub', prob. 'valley'. Bibbern.

cǣg 'key'. Key Brook.

cærse 'cress'. Caswell.

canne 'can, vessel', prob. 'valley-basin'. Cann; Canford (?).

castel 'castle'. Castle Hill, Castleton.

catt '(wild) cat'. Catsley.

ceald 'cold'. Belchalwell, *Chaldcot(e)s* (2).

cealf 'calf'. Chaldon.

ceaster (Latin *castra* 'camp') 'city, town'. Dorchester. *Not* present in Bedchester and Hogchester. Alcester is a transferred name.

cēode 'bag, pouch'. Cheddington, Chitcombe (?).

ceole 'throat, gorge, chasm'. Chilbridge.

ceorl 'peasant, rustic'. Charlton (3).

ceosol 'gravel, shingle'. Cheselbourne, Chesil Bank.

cēt (from Celtic) 'wood'. Lytchett, Orchard (parish); Chetterwood, Chettle.

chapel(e) (ME) 'chapel'. Chapel Court, Chapel Marsh.

cīeping 'market'. Blandford Forum, earlier *Chepingblandford*.

cild 'child (young nobleman)'. Childhay, Child Okeford, Chilfrome.

*cilte, see Chilcombe.

cirice 'church'. Frome Vauchurch, Whitchurch (2); Chescombe. Cf. also Church Knowle and Milborne St Andrew.

clǣg 'clay'. Claywell, Clinger.

clif 'cliff, steep slope'. Clyffe; Catsley, Duncliffe, Eccliffe, Whitecliff; Clifton.

cnave (ME) 'child, servant'. Knaveswell (?).

cniht 'youth, servant' (cf. EPN s. v.). Knighton (4), *Knightstreet*.

cnoll 'knoll, hill, hillock'. Knoll (2), Knowle (2); Bucknowle, Chetnole, Hincknoll, Puncknowle; Knowlton.

*cob, see Cobb.

cocc 'cock'. Cockhill, Cogdean Hundred.

cōl 'cool'. Colber, *Colhay*, Colmer, Colway (?), Cullington.

coppede 'having the *copp* or summit cut off, pollarded'. Coppet Hill.

*corf 'a cutting, a pass, a gap'. Corfe Castle, Corfe Mullen; Corfe Hill, Corscombe, Corton, Coryates.

cot(e) 'cot, cottage'. *Chaldecot(e)s* (2), Woodcutts; Coltleigh (?), Cothays (?).

courte (ME) 'court, farm-yard', etc. Abbot's Court, Bluntsmoor (earlier *Blountescourte*), Moorcourt.

cran 'crane'. Cranborne.

crāwe 'crow'. Tarrant Crawford.

crocc 'pot, crock'. *Crockern Stoke.*

crocker (ME) 'potter'. Crocker's Knap.

crouche (ME) 'cross'. Short Cross.

cryc (Celtic **cruc**) 'hill, barrow'. Creech; Pentridge; Crichel.

cū 'cow'. Cowgrove, Cowridge.

cumb 'coomb, valley'. Combe (2), Coombe (7); Ashcombe, Barcombe, Batcombe, Bettiscombe, Bincombe, Brenscombe, Burcombe, Chescombe, Chilcombe, Chitcombe, Corscombe, Encombe, *Foulcombe, Hawcombe, Hincombe*, Holcombe, Kingcombe, Lewcombe, Longcombe, Loscombe, Luccombe, Lyscombe, Mappercombe, Melcombe (2), Motcombe, Nettlecombe, Purcombe, Renscombe, *Rocombe*, Shatcombe, *Southcombe*, Stancombe, Thorncombe (3), Totcombe Hundred, Uggescombe Hundred, Watcombe, Watercombe, Whatcombe (2), Whitcombe, Woolcombe (2); Compton (4). It forms the middle el. of Morecombelake, but is *not* present in Combs Ditch.

*****cunuc**, see Combs Ditch.

cweorn '(hand-)mill'. *Coringdon*, Cornford.

cymed 'wall-germander'. Kingcombe (?).

cyne- 'royal'. Kington.

cyning 'king'. Kingsettle, Kingsland, King's Mill, Kingstag, Kingston (4). Cf. also names like Bere Regis (earlier *Kingesbere*), Winterborne Kingston, etc.

denu 'valley'. Dean (3), Den Wood; Cogdean, Tincleton.

dīc 'ditch, dike'. Combs Ditch, Walditch.

docga 'dog'. Dogbury.

dower (ME), see Dowerfield.

dūn 'down, hill'. Bishop's Down (earlier *Doune*); *Bestedon*, Bindon, Blackdown, Blagdon (2), Chaldon, Cheddington, *Coringdon*, Cullington, Eggardon, Farrington, Hambledon, Haydon (2), *Hewdon*, Langdon, Morden, Pilsdon, Rodden, South Down, Sutton Holms, Waddon, Watton; Duncliffe, Dunster, Duntish.

ēast 'east'. *Bestedon*, Bestwall, Eastington.
ebbe (ME), see (Great) Ebb.
edisc 'enclosed pasture, (deer-)park'. Duntish.
ellen 'elder-tree'. Elwell (in Netherbury), Elworth.
ende 'end'. Town's End, Woodsend.
ened 'duck'. Enmore.

fæger 'fair, beautiful'. Verwood.
fāg 'stained, variegated'. Frome Vauchurch.
fearn 'fern, bracken'. Farnham, Farrington, Fernbrook.
feld 'field, open land'. Benville, Blynfield, Bowerswain, Hillfield, Merryfield, Whit(e)field (2). It forms the middle el. of Hethfelton, but is *not* present in Whitfield (in Bradford Peverell); Dowerfield is earlier *Dowerlond*.
fenn 'mud, fen'. Venn; Black Venn.
fīf 'five'. Fifehead (4). Cf. also Anderson.
filiðe 'hay'. Feltham, Filford.
***fitel**, see Fiddleford.
flēot 'inlet, estuary'. Fleet; Longfleet.
ford 'ford'. Ford; Barford, Blandford, Bradford (3), Canford, Cornford, (Tarrant) Crawford, Fiddleford, Filford, Hanford, Hayward, Heniford, Hogford, *Horyford*, Huntingford, Langford, *Leftisford*, *Lovard*, Muckleford, Nutford, Oakford, Okeford, Pinford, Romford, Sandford, Sherford, Stafford, *Stapleford*, Stinsford, Stokeford, Thornford, Tollerford, Walford, Watford, Woodsford; Fordington. *Not* present in Culliford Tree, Dibberford, Pipsford, and Wynford. Durnford is a transferred name.
forst 'frost'. Fossil.
frogga 'frog'. Frog Lane, Frogmore (3).
fūl 'foul, dirty'. *Foulcombe*.
funta 'spring'. Fontmell.
fyrhð(e) 'wood, wooded country'. Frith.

gærs-tūn 'grassy enclosure'. *Southgarston*.
gafol 'tribute, tax'. Galton.
gāra 'triangular piece of land'. Gore; Gorewood.
gāt 'goat'. Gatemerston, Goathill, Goathorn.
gēap 'wide, deep' (used as a noun). Eype.

geat 'gate'. Park Gate, Verne Yeates (earlier *ghate, Yate*); Biddlesgate, Burngate, Coryates, *Moryate*, Picket, Woodyates. It forms the middle el. of Corscombe.

gierd 'area of land, usually 30 acres'. Yard (2).

gor 'dirt, filth'. Gorwell.

grǣw- (*grǣg*) 'grey'. Graston (?).

grāf(a) 'grove, copse'. Cowgrove, Hargrove, Hartgrove, Thorngrove, Weathergrove, Yardgrove. See also Graston.

grēot 'gravel'. Girt.

gyr 'mud, marsh'. Gussage.

***gyll, *gill** 'pool'. Gillingham.

haca 'bolt, hook'. Hackeridge.

(ge)hæg 'enclosure, farm'. Haye; Bilshay, Blackney, Bluntshay, Champernhayes, Childhay, *Colhay*, Cothays, Cuthay, Cutty Stubbs, *Dudley, Forstershay*, Griddleshay, Gummershay (2), Guppy, Harmshay, Hursey, Kershay, Marshalsea, Netherhay, Silkhay, *Thurstanshay, Uphay*, Winterhays; earlier it formed the second el. also of Baber's Fm, Baker's Cross, *Beaushens*, Chart Knolle Fm, Harper's Fm, and Mandeville Stoke Fm; cf. also Colway. The majority of Dorset names containing this el. are apparently of ME origin, cf. the *note* to Bilshay.

hǣlu 'health'. Elwell (in Upway) (?).

hǣme, see Bockhampton and Witchampton.

hæsel 'hazel'. Haselbury, Hasler Hundred.

hǣð 'heath'. Hethfelton.

***hǣðra** 'heather'. Hatherly.

hālig 'holy'. Halstock, Holwell (in Radipole).

hām 'farm', etc. Attisham, Brinsham, Broadenham, Buckham, Densham, Edmondsham, Farnham, Feltham, Frankham, Gillingham, Langham, Moulham, Newnham (2), Parnham, Petersham, Portisham, Pulham, Rampisham, Tyneham, Wareham, Witcham, Wyndlam. Some of these names, in particular Feltham, Parnham, Portisham, and Wyndlam, may however rather contain **hamm** 'enclosed possession, fold, land near a river', and this latter word, in the sense of 'low-lying land in the bend of a river', is evidently present in Ham Common, Hammoon, Hampreston, and Hamworthy.

hāmstede 'homestead'. *Hampstead.*

hāmtūn 'home farm'. Bothenhampton, Brockhampton, Brockington,

Shilvinghampton, Stubhampton, Witchampton; cf. also **hǣme**. *Not* present in Athelhampton.

*hamel, see Hambledon Hill.

hān '(boundary-)stone'. Redhone Hundred.

hangra '(wooded) slope'. Binnegar, Clinger.

hār 'grey, hoar; boundary'. Hargrove, Hartgrove. These names may alternatively contain **hara** 'hare'.

*har, see Arne.

*harad, see Chetterwood.

h(e)afoc 'hawk'. *Hawcombe*.

hēafod-stocc 'a stock or post on which the head of a criminal was fixed after beheading'. Hewstock (2).

hēah (dat. sing. **hēan**) 'high'. Handley, Hanford, Henbury, Henley, Hinckoll, Hinton St Mary.

healf 'half'. *Halfhide*.

healh 'corner, angle, (inner) slope of a hill'. Wraxall; Hilton (?).

heall 'hall, manor-house'. West Hall.

hēg, hīeg 'hay'. Haydon (2), Hayward Bridge.

henn 'hen'. Encombe.

heord 'herd, flock', Urless (?).

heorot 'hart, stag'. Hartley.

hīd 'a hide of land'. Hyde (6), Hydes; Fifehead (4), *Halfhide*, Piddletrenthide, Woodyhyde.

hīgna (gen. plur. of **hīwan**) 'members of a family' (esp. of a monastic community). Hinton Martell and Parva, Piddlehinton, Tarrant Hinton.

hind 'hind, female of the hart'. *Hincombe*.

hīwisc 'land for one household'. Hewish, Huish (2); Belhuish.

hlēow 'shelter; warm sunny'. Lewcombe, Lewell (?), Luccombe.

hlinc 'bank, hill-ridge, (dial.) *linch*'. Lynch; Lydlinch, Sydling.

hlið 'slope, cliff, hill-side'. Lily.

hlōse 'pigsty'. Loscombe.

hlȳde 'torrent'. Litton Cheney.

hnot 'bare'. Nottington (?).

hnutu 'nut'. Nutford.

hōc 'hook, projecting corner, sharp bend in a stream'. Hooke; Withyhook; Hogboro'.

hōd 'hood'. Hod Hill.

hogg 'hog'. Hogchester, Hogford.

holegn 'holly-tree, (dial.) *holm*'.   Holme; Holnest.

hol(h) 'hollow' (noun and adj.).   Holcombe, Holebrook, Holway, Holwell (2), Holworth.

holt 'wood'.   Holt; Alderholt; Holton.

horh 'dirt, mud'.   Horton.

horig 'foul, dirty'.   *Horyford*.

hors 'horse'.   *Horsith*.

hræfn 'raven'.   *Ramsbury*, Renscombe.   Cf. also Rampisham.

hrēod 'reed'.   Radipole (?), Redlands (?), Rodmore.

hring 'ring'.   Ringstead.

hrōc 'rook'.   Roke Fm.

hrycg 'ridge'.   Ridge (2), Bailey Ridge; *Baggeridge*, Boveridge, Cowridge, Hackeridge.

hundred 'hundred(-court)'.   Barrow Hundred, earlier *Hundredes-berg*.

hungor 'hunger'.   *Hungerhill*.

hunig 'honey'.   Honeybrook.

hunta 'huntsman'.   Huntingford.

hwǣte 'wheat'.   Watcombe, Whatcombe (2), Whetley.

hwīt 'white'.   Whitchurch (2), Whitecliff, Whitefield, Whiteway (2), Whitfield (2).

*hygel 'hill'.   Hile, Hyle.

hyll 'hill'.   Hill (2); Broomhill, Brownshall Hundred (and Brunsell's Fm), Chettle, Cockhill, (Colehill), Coppet Hill, Corfe Hill, Crichel, Fossil, *Gerneshill*, Goathill, *Hungerhill*, Marnhull, Osehill, Pamphill, Ram's Hill, Roger's Hill, Ryall, Sandhills, Sandley, Sturthill, Thornhill, Thorn Hill, Totnell, *Uphill*, Whetley; Hillfield.   Cf. also names like Bennett's Hill, Boys Hill, etc.

hyrst 'copse, wood'.   Hurst; Bedchester, Hogchester, Holnest.

hȳð 'landing-place on a river'.   *Horsith* (?).

īeg, ēg 'island'.   Branksea Island.   Cf. also Green Island.

īegland 'land amidst marshes'.   Nyland.

-ing. The only uncompounded Dorset pl.-n. in *-ing* is Uddens Ho.   Cf. also Dodding's Fm, and Snelling.

-ingaham. Gillingham.

-ingtūn. Allington (?), Baltington, Bexington, Bovington, Chalmington, Didlington, Fordington, Ibberton, Ilsington, Lillington,

Mannington, Nottington, Osmington, Pallington, Povington, Poyntington, Putton, Rollington.

īw 'yew'. Iwerne (?).

lacu 'stream, watercourse'. Lake (2); Baglake, Bidlake, Morecombelake.

lām 'loam', or **lamb** 'lamb'. Lambrook.

land 'land'. *Blackland*, Dowerfield (earlier *Dowerlond*), Kingsland, Newland, Newland's Fm, Pitland, Portland, Redlands, Studland, Woodlands, Woolland; Town's End is earlier *Londdeshende*. Cf. **bōcland**.

lane, lanu 'lane'. Redlane Hundred, Winterborne Stickland.

lang 'long, tall'. Langdon, Langford, Langham, *Langley*, Langton (3), Longbarrow, Longcombe, Longfleet. Cf. also names like Long Bredy, Long Crichel, etc.

lāwerce 'lark', Laverstock.

lēah (dat. sing. **lēage**) 'wood, clearing'. La Lee, Leigh (2), (Halstock) Leigh; Ashley, Barnsley, Bradle, Brimbley, Broadley, Bugley, Coltleigh, Furleigh, Handley, Hartley, Hatherly, Henley, *Langley*, Lily, Loverley, Oakley (2), Parley, *Prinsley*, Stickley (?), Stockley, *Studley*, Tiley, Urless, Wantsley, Westley, *Wishley*. *Not* present in Catsley, *Dudley*, Sandley, Whetley.

līn 'flax'. Limbury, Lymburgh's Fm.

lox 'lynx'. Loxtree (?).

lūs 'louse'. Loosebarrow Hundred.

lytel 'little'. Littleton. Cf. also names like Little Bredy, Little Puddle, Littlewindsor, etc.

mǣd 'mead, meadow'. Roke Fm, earlier *Rokemede*.

mægden 'maiden'. Maiden Newton (ME addition).

***mǣl(e)** 'variegated'. Melbury (Abbas; Bubb, Osmond, Sampford), Melplash. Very uncertain, cf. p. 27.

(ge)mǣre '(strip of land forming a) boundary'. Gatemerston (?).

mangere 'trader, monger'. Mangerton.

mapuldor 'maple-tree'. Mappowder; Mapperton (2).

meoluc 'milk'. Melcombe (2).

mere 'mere, pool'. Often difficult to distinguish from **mōr** and **(ge)mǣre**. Almer, Ashmore, Colmer (?), Enmore, Frog Lane (earlier *Froggemere*), Frogmore (3), Rushmore Hundred.

mersc 'marsh'. Marsh (5); Middlemarsh; Marshwood. Cf. also names like Caundle Marsh, Margaret Marsh, etc.

middel 'middle'. Middlebere, Middlemarsh, *Middlestreet*, Milton (3).

minte 'mint', or **mynet** 'coin, money'. Minterne (?).

mōr 'swampy ground, barren land, moor'. (West) Moors, Moorside (earlier *More*); Blackmoor, Colmer (?), Lodmoor, Pymore, Rodmore, Smedmore; Moorbath, Moorcourt, Morden, Morecombelake, Moreton, *Moryate*. Cf. also More Crichel. Bittles Green is earlier *bytelesmor*, whereas Bluntsmoor is earlier *Blountescourte*.

*mort, see Mosterton.

(ge)mōt 'meeting-place'. Modbury (2), Motcombe.

mūl, see Moulham.

munuc 'monk'. Monkwood (2). "Monkton" occurs as a late addition in several names.

mūða 'mouth, estuary'. Charmouth, Small Mouth, Weymouth.

myl(e)n 'mill'. Arfleet Mills, Cards Mill, King's Mill, *Woodmill*; Milborne.

mynecen 'nun'. Minchington.

mynster 'monastery, church'. Beaminster, Charminster, Iwerne Minster, Lytchett Minster, Sturminster (2), Wimborne Minster, Yetminster.

myrig 'pleasant, merry'. Merryfield.

nēat 'cattle, (dial.) *neat*'. Notton.

neoðera 'nether, lower'. Netherbury, Nether Cerne, Netherhay, Netherstoke. Bingham's Melcombe is earlier *Nethermelcombe*.

netele 'nettle'. Nettlecombe.

nīwe 'new'. Newland, Newland's Fm, Newnham (2), Newton (6).

norð 'north'. Northwood.

ōfer 'shore, bank' (in one or two cases perhaps rather **ōra** 'border, margin, bank'). Ower; Goathorn, Hasler Hundred, Southover, Westover, Windsor (Broad-, Little-), Yondover.

orceard 'orchard'. Orchard (in Church Knowle). *Not* present in East and Orchard (parishes).

ord 'point, spit of land'. Red Horn.

pāl 'pole, stake'. Pallington.

parke (ME) 'park'. Park (2); Parkstone.

pearroc 'small enclosure, paddock'. Park (in Marshwood).

pen (Celtic) 'head, top'. Sixpenny (and Pen Hill); Pentridge (and Penbury Knowle).

penn 'enclosure, pen'. Penn.

peru 'pear'. Parley, Parnham.

pīc 'pointed instrument; hill-top'. Picket.

pīe 'insect'. Pymore.

pīl 'a pointed object, spike, nail, stake'. Pile Lane; Pilsdon.

pīn(-trēow) 'pine-tree'. Pinford (?).

pīpe 'pipe, tube, channel'. Pipsford.

pirige, pyrige 'pear-tree'. Perry; Purcombe.

plæsc 'shallow pool, (dial.) *plash*'. Melplash.

plūme 'plum, plum-tree'. Plumber.

*plysc, see Plush.

pōl 'pool'. Poole; Bradpoole, Chapman's Pool, Poll Bridge (earlier *Deoulepole*), Radipole.

port I. 'port, harbour'. Bridport; Portland; II. 'portal, gate, entrance'. Westport; Portisham.

pott 'pot'. Potterne.

prēost 'priest'. Preston (3), (Ham)preston, Priest's Way.

pull 'pool, stream'. Pulham.

punt 'punt, raft, floating bridge'. Poyntington.

pur 'bittern'. Purbeck (?).

pytt 'pit, grave'. Pitt; Sandpit; Pitland.

quarere (ME) 'quarry'. Quarr.

rā 'roe-buck'. *Rocombe.*

rǣw, rāw 'row'. Rew; Blackrow, Woodrow (2).

rēad 'red'. *Radesloe*, Radipole (?), Redhone Hundred, Red Horn, Redlands (?), Redlane Hundred, Rodden.

rima 'rim, verge, border'. Ryme Intrinseca.

rīð 'small stream, brooklet'. Chetterwood (?).

rūh 'rough'. Romford (?), Rowbarrow Hundred.

rūm 'roomy, spacious'. Ram's Hill (?).

ryge 'rye'. Ryall.

rysc 'rush'. Rushmore Hundred, Rushton (in East Stoke). *Not* present in Tarrant Rushton.

sǣte 'dwellers, inhabitants'. Dorset.

sand 'sand'. Sandford Orcas, Sandhills, Sandley, Sandpit, Sandway.

sceaft 'pole, shaft; crag (?)'. Shaftesbury (?).

sceaga 'copse, thicket, (dial.) *shaw*'. Shave Cross; Buckshaw (?).

scēap, scīp 'sheep'. Shapwick, Shipton Gorge.

scēat 'corner, angle, promontory'. Shatcombe. In Evershot we
have rather the word *scīete with much the same meaning.

scīr 'clear, shining'. Sherborne, Sherford.

scīr-gerēfa 'sheriff'. Shroton.

*scitere, see Shitterton.

scylf 'rock, shelving terrain, shelf'. Shilvinghampton.

sealh 'willow'. Silton.

sēað 'hollow, pit, fountain'. Pipsford.

seax 'knife, dagger; (probably) cliff'. Sixpenny.

seofon 'seven'. Seaborough.

setl 'seat'. Kingsettle.

sīc 'small stream, (dial.) sitch'. Gussage.

sīd 'broad, wide'. Sydling.

slæd 'low flat valley'. Slait Barn.

slǣp 'slippery place, (dial.) slape'. Slape, Slepe (2).

sleyte (ME) '(sheep-)pasture'. Sleight.

slōh 'slough, mire'. Radesloe.

smæl 'small, narrow'. Small Mouth.

smēðe 'smooth'. Smedmore.

spence (ME) 'buttery, pantry'. Spence.

*spe(o)ht, see Spettisbury.

spitel (ME) 'hospital'. Sputel.

splott 'patch of land, plot of ground'. Plot.

staca 'stake'. Kingstag.

stān 'stone'. Graston, Parkstone, Wytherstone (?), (cf. also Hurpston); Stafford, Stallen, Stanbridge, Stanbrook, Stancombe,
Stanton, Stoborough, (High) Stoy.

stapol 'post, staple'. Stalbridge, Stapleford.

stede 'place, site'. Ringstead. Cf. hāmstede.

steort 'tail, tail-shaped piece of land'. Woodstreet; Sturthill.

sticol 'steep'. Stickley, Winterborne Stickland.

stīepel 'steeple'. Steeple; Steepleton (2).

stint (OE *stynt), see Stinsford.

stoc 'place'. Stock Gaylard, Stoke (4); Burstock, Cattistock,
Crockern Stoke, Halstock, Laverstock, Netherstoke, Powerstock,
Turberville Stoke; Stokeford, Stockwood.

stocc 'stump, trunk, stock'. Stockbridge, Stockley. Cf. also
hēafod-stocc.

stōd 'stud, herd of horses'. Studland, Studley.

strǣt 'street, road'. Abbott Street, *Knightstreet, Middlestreet* (cf. also Week Street); Stratton. *Not* present in Woodstreet.

strōd 'marshy land overgrown with brushwood'. Strode, Stroud (2).

stybb 'stump of a tree, stub'. Stubhampton.

sūð 'south'. Southbrook, *Southcombe*, South Down, *Southgarston*, Southover, South Perrott, *Southway*, Sutton (3).

swān '(swine-)herd'. Swanage.

swēora 'neck, col'. Swyre (2).

swīn 'pig, swine'. Toller Porcorum, earlier *Swyne(s)tolre*.

tēafor 'red lead, (dial.) *tiver*'. Evershot (?).

tigel 'tile'. Tiley.

trēow 'tree'. Culliford Tree, Loxtree.

trog 'trough, conduit'. (Little) Dunster.

tūn 'enclosure, farm, manor'. See also **-ingtūn**. Many of the names enumerated below are of ME origin. Acton, Admiston, Afflington, Allington, Allweston, Alton Pancras, Anderson, Ashington, Ashton, Athelhampton, *Bardolfeston*, Barnston, Bhompston, Blackmanston, Bryanston, Burleston, Burton (Bradstock), Caplestone (?), Castleton, Catherston Leweston, Charlton (3), Chaston, Clifton, Compton (4), Corton, Cruxton, Drimpton, Durweston, Eastington, Egliston, Ellston, Forston, Frampton, Galton, Gatemerston, Godlingston, Godmanstone, Grimstone, Herrison, Herston, Hethfelton, Hilton, Hinton (2), Holton, Horton, Kingston (4), Kington, Kinson, Knighton (4), Knitson, Knowlton, Langton (3), Lazerton, Leeson, Leweston, Littleton, Litton, Luton, Madjeston, Mangerton, Manston, Mapperton (2), (*Milborne*) *Michelston*, Milton (3), Minchington, Monkton (2), Moreton, Muston, Newton (6), Notton, *Philipston*, Piddlehinton, Pierston, Poorton, Preston (4), Puddletown, Pulston, Quarleston, Ranston, Rushton, Shillingstone, Shipton, Shitterton, Shroton, Silton, Stanton, Steepleton Iwerne, Stratton, Sutton (2), T[arrant] Hinton, T. Keynston, T. Launceston, T. Monkton, T. Rawston, T. Rushton, Tatton, Thorton, Upton, Walton, Waterston, Weston (3), W[interborne] Clenston, W. Herringstone, W. Houghton, W. Kingston, W. Monkton, W. Muston, W. Steepleton, W. Tomson, W. Zelstone[1], Wolfeton, Woolgarston,

---

[1] *-ton* is the second element in a number of other post-Conquest names, which are now lost.

Wootton (5), Wytherstone (?). Cf. also **bere-tūn, burhtūn**, and **hāmtūn**.

tūnincel 'small farm'. Tincleton (?).

tȳning 'closing, fencing'. Tyneham (?).

þēofeþorn 'hawthorn' (?). Evershot (?).

þorn 'thorn-bush'. Godderthorn Hundred, Mosterton; Thorncombe (3), Thornford, Thorngrove, Thornhill, Thorn Hill, Thorton.

þrop (þorp) 'out-lying farm'. Throop (2).

þyrne 'thorn-bush'. Turnworth.

ūle 'owl'. Ulwell.

upp(e) 'up, above'. Up Cerne, Uphay, Uphill, Uploders, Up Sydling, Upton, Upway, Upwimborne.

wād 'woad'. Waddon.

wæter 'water'. Watercombe.

walu 'ridge'. Holwell (parish) (?).

weall 'wall'. Wall; Bestwall, Holwell (parish) (?); Walditch, Walton.

weargrōd 'scaffold, gallows'. Worgret.

wearm 'warm'. Warmwell.

weg 'way, road'. Waytown (earlier Weye); Colway (?), Crockway, Holway, Priest's Way, Sandway, (High) Stoy, Whiteway (2).

welig, wylig 'willow'. (Monkton) Wyld (?).

wer 'weir, dam, fish-trap'. Wareham.

west 'west'. Westbrook, West Hall, Westley, Weston (3), Westover, Westport, West Wood, Westwood.

wīc 'dairy-farm'. Week (Street), Wych, Wyke (4), Butterwick, Shapwick, Swanage; Witcham, Witchampton. Cf. **bere-wīc**.

wīd 'wide, broad, long'. Whitcombe.

wielle 'spring, well'. Well (Bottom), Wellwood (earlier Well), Wool; Armswell, Askerswell, Belchalwell, Blashenwell, Caswell, Claywell, Elwell (2), Gorwell, Holwell (2), Knaveswell, Lewell, Poxwell, Stallen, Ulwell, Warmwell, Whitfield (in Bradford Peverell); Woolbridge, Woolcombe (2). Not present in Holwell (parish). Whitwell is a manorial name.

wind 'wind' (or **windig** 'windy'). Woodbury. Woodstreet may contain either this or the next word.

windel 'something winding'. Windsor (Broad-, Little-), Wyndlam.

*winn 'meadow'. Wimborne.

winter 'winter'. Winterborne (two streams), Winterhays.

wisc 'damp meadow, marsh'. *Wishley.*

wīðig 'withy, willow'. Withyhook, Wytherstone (?).

wōh 'crooked, twisting'. Oborne.

worþ, weorþ 'enclosure, farm'. Worth Matravers; Bloxworth, Charisworth, Dibberford, Elworth, Hemsworth, Holworth, *Kentleworth,* Keysworth, Lulworth, Piddles Wood, Turnworth, Wilksworth. *Not* present in Camesworth.

worðig, the expanded form of **worþ,** is almost unknown in Dorset. Its appearance in Hamworthy is late; cf. also some of the early forms of Wilksworth.

*wroc, see Wraxall.

wudig 'woody'. Woodyhyde (?). Cf. also the *note* to Woodyates.

wudu 'wood'. Ailwood, Bothenwood, Bowood, Gorewood, Marshwood, Monkwood (2), Northwood, Oakers Wood, Stockwood, Verwood, West Wood, Westwood, Wilkswood; Woodbridge (2), Woodcutts, Woodlands, *Woodmill,* Woodrow (2), Woodsend, Woodyates, Wootton (5). *Not* present in Chetterwood, Piddles Wood, Woodbury, Woodsford, and Woodstreet.

*wuduc, see Wilksworth.

PERSONAL NAMES COMPOUNDED IN DORSET PLACE-NAMES[1]

I. In place-names of presumably OE origin. Places called after the holder TRE are also included, in which case (DB) is printed after the pers. name. The date after the place-name denotes the year of the earliest form recorded. Names such as Affpuddle and Tolpuddle have been excluded.

Æd(d)i	Attisham (1251-2)
Ælfrūn (DB), fem.	Afflington (1086)
Æþelflǣd, fem.	Arfleet Mills (1318), Allweston (?) (1244)
Æþelgȳþ, fem.	Ailwood (?) (1084)
Badda	Badbury Hundred (901)
Bata	Batcombe (?) (1244)

---

[1] Names not found in independent use are marked with an asterisk. In the case of *Bēaghild* and *Mæðelgār* the asterisk has been considered unnecessary.

Bēaghild, fem.	Belhuish (1303)
Beorhtsige	Bexington (1086)
Beorn (DB)	Barnston (1333)
Beornheard	Barnsley (1177-8)
Betti	Bettiscombe (1174-82)
Blæcman	Blackmanston (1086)
*Bloc(c)	Bloxworth (?) (987)
Bofa	Bovington (1086)
Brūn	Brownshall Hundred (?) (1084), Brenscombe (?) (1086)
Bryni	Brinsham (1340)
Bucge, fem.	Bugley (1275)
*Cæntel	*Kentleworth* (?) (1236)
*Ceatwa	Chebbard (?) (869)
Cēol	Chalbury (?) (946)
Cēolhelm, Cēolmund	Chalmington (c. 939)
Cidda	Chitcombe (?) (1327)
Cnihtwine	Knitson (1318)
Cotta	Coltleigh (?) (1244)
Cynestān	Kinson (1086)
Dene	Densham (?) (1333)
Dēorwine	Durweston (1086)
*Drēama	Drimpton (?) (1244)
Dud(d)	Dudsbury (?) (1086)
Dyddel	Didlington (?) (946)
Ēadbeorht	Ibberton (1086)
Ēadmund	Edmondsham (1086)
Ealdwine	Allen, River (1278)
Eat(t)a	Adber (?) (1086), Yetminster (?) (1086)
Elesa	Ilsington (1086)
Eli	Ellston (?) (1227)
Eormengȳþ	Armswell (1225)
Fitela	Fiddleford (?) (1244)
Franca	Frankham (1244)
Godman	Godmanstone[1] (1166)
Grim (Scand.)	Grimstone[1] (1212)
Guðrun (Scand.?)	Godderthorn Hundred (1084)
Her (DB)	Herston (1086)

---

[1] Possibly of post-Conquest origin.

*Hnott	Nottington (?) (1212)
Ine	Innsacre (?) (1327)
Lēof	Leweston (?) (1244)
Lēofgēat	Leftisford (?) (1086)
Lēofsige	Leeson (?) (1242-3)
Lēofwaru, fem.	Loverley (1091-1104)
Lilla	Lillington (1179-80)
Lulla	Lowbrook (?) (1264), Lulworth (1086)
Mæðelgār	Madjeston (1205)
Man(n)	Manston (1086)
Mann(a)	Mannington (1086)
Ōsgār	Askerswell (1086)
Ōshelm, Ōsmund	Osmington (c. 939)
Ōsweald	Osehill (1314)
*Peohtric	Petersham (?) (1086)
*Poc	Poxwell (987)
Podda	Putton (1237)
*Prym (Prim)	Prinsley (?) (1204)
Rǣdel	Rollington (?) (1086)
Sigemund	Symondsbury (1086)
*Tēcca, *Tacca	Acton (?) (1086)
Tata	Tatton (1086)
Tot(t)a	Totcombe Hundred (1130)
*Ucg	Uggescombe Hundred (?) (1084)
Udda (?)	Uddens (?) (956)
Want	Wantsley (1244)
Wulf-	Wolfeton (1235-6)
Wulfgār	Oakers Wood (1465), Woolgarston (1086)

II. In place-names ending in -hay, OE (ge)hæg.[1]

Baber, Baker, Beaushin, Bil, Blundel, Cotta (?), Cute (?), Dud(d)el, Forester, Grael, Gumbeald, Gummǣr, *Guppa (?), Harper, Hereman, Heorstān, Mandeville, Marshal, Selk, Thurstan.

[1] Place-names containing this terminal are enumerated supra 310. The pers. names are of various origin.

INDEX

OF PLACE-NAMES IN DORSET

Lost names are printed in italics.

Canford, Little, 102
Canford Magna, 109
Cann, 20
Caplestone, 128
Cards Mill Fm, 295
Carey, 147
Castle Hill, 100
Castleton, 210
Caswell Fm, 226
Catherston Leweston, 284
Catsley Fm, 270
Cattistock, 194
Caundle, Bishop's, 211
Caundle Marsh, 212
Caundle, Purse, 212
Caundle, Stourton, 39
Caundle Wake, 212
Causeway Fm, 158
Cerne Abbas, 196
Cerne Hundred, 193
Cerne, Nether, 197
Cerne, Up, 213
Chalbury, 78
Chaldecote (in Swyre), 252
Chaldecots (in Kimmeridge), 134
Chaldon Herring (or East), 138
Chaldon, West, 139
Chalmington, 195
Chamberlayne's Fm, 68
Champernhayes Fm, 299
Chantmarle, 195
Chapel Court (in Mosterton), 274
Chapel Marsh (in Beaminster), 263
Chapman's Pool, 119
Charborough Ho, 75
Charisworth, 111
Charlton Dairy Fm (in Woodlands), 94
Charlton Fm (in Charminster), 182
Charlton Marshall, 110
Charminster, 181
Charmouth, 285
Chart Knolle Fm, 282
Chaston Fm, 203
Chebbard Fm, 173
Cheddington, 269
Chelborough, East and West, 228

Chescombe Fm, 191
Cheselbourne, 188
Cheselbourne Ford (or Little), 177
Chesil Bank, 165
Chetnole, 222
Chetterwood, 80
Chettle, 95
Chickerell, 153
Chideock, 285
Chilbridge Fm, 84
Chilcombe, 246
Childhay, 267
Child Okeford, see Okeford, Child
Chilfrome, 229
Chitcombe Fm, 192
Church Knowle, 132
Claywell, 125
Clifton Maybank, 222
Clinger Fm, 203
Clyffe, 179
Cobb, 286
Cockhill Fm, 40
Cogdean Elms, 109
Cogdean Hundred, 109
Colber Crib Ho, 48
Colehill, 79
Colhay, 258
Colmer Fm, 288
Coltleigh Fm, 273
Colway, 287
Combe Almer, 114
Combe Deverel, see Puddle, Little
Combs Ditch Hundred, 63
Compton Abbas (East), 21
Compton Abbas (West), 197
Compton, Over and Nether, 213
Compton Valence, 230
Coombe (in Bradford Abbas), 210
Coombe (in Langton Matravers), 123
Coombe Fm (in Castleton), 211
Coombe, Great (in Whitchurch Can.), 295
Coombe, Higher and Lower (in Litton Cheney), 248
Coombe Keynes, 140
Coppet Hill, 292
Corfe Castle, 116

Plot, 303
Plumber Fm, 218
Plush, 205
Poll Bridge Fm, 212
Poole, 113
Poorton, North, 281
Poorton, South, 242
Portisham, 248
Portland, 165
Potterne Fm, 108
Povington, 137
Powerstock, 240
Poxwell, 143
Poyntington, 301
Preston (parish), 156
Preston Fm (in Tarrant Rushton), 107
Preston Ho (in Iwerne Minster), 27
Priest's Way, 124
Prinsley, 211
Puddle, Bryants, 167
Puddle, Little, 175
Puddletown, 175
Puddletown Hundred, 170
Puddle, Turners, 168
Pulham, 207
Pulston, 183
Puncknowle, 251
Purbeck, Isle of, 115
Purcombe Fm, 297
Purse Caundle, see Caundle, Purse
Putton, 153
Pymore, 255

Quarleston Fm, 63
Quarr, 128

Radesloe, 155
Radipole, 157
Ramesham, 297
Rampisham, 234
Ramsbury, 218
Ram's Hill Fm, 43
Ranston, 11
Redhone Hundred, 260
Red Horn, 126 n. 2
Redlands, 153

Redlane Hundred, 3
Rempstone Hall, 120
Renscombe Fm, 128
Revels Inn Fm, 205
Rew, 187
Ridge (in Arne), 130
Ridge (in Wootton Fitzpaine), 300
Ringstead, 156
Rocombe, 198
Rodden, 245
Rodmore Fms, 218
Roger's Hill Fm, 168
Roke Fm, 69
Rollington Fm, 120
Romford, 102
Rowaldsway, 152
Rowbarrow Hundred, 116
Rushmore Hundred, 72
Rushton (in East Stoke), 145
Rushton Fm, see Tarrant Rushton
Ryall, 297
Ryme Intrinseca, 226

Sadborow, 294
St Aldhelm's Chapel, 129
St Andrew's Fm, 142
St Gabriel's Ho, see Stanton St Gabriel
St George Hundred, 180
Sandford Orcas, 302
Sandhills, 36
Sandley, 8
Sandpit, 268
Sandway, 4
Scoles Fm and Gate, 121
Seaborough, 303
Shaftesbury, 31
Shapwick, 86
Shatcombe Fm, 264
Shave Cross, 290
Sherborne, 220
Sherborne Causeway, 29
Sherborne Hundred, 209
Sherborne Park, 211
Sherford, 76
Shillingstone, 104
Shilvinghampton, 249